UNDERWATER WARRIORS

Also by Paul Kemp

Bismarck and Hood
Convoy!
Convoy Protection
Pictorial History of the Sea War 1939-1945
Sea Warfare
U-boats Destroyed

UNDERWATER WARRIORS

THE FIGHTING HISTORY OF MIDGET SUBMARINES

PAUL KEMP

CASSELL&co

Cassell Military Paperbacks

Cassell & Co
Wellington House, 125 Strand
London WC2R OBB

First published by Arms and Armour 1996
This Cassell Military Paperbacks edition 2000

British Library Cataloguing-in-Publication Data
.A catalogue record for this book is available from the British
Library

ISBN 0-304-35454-6

Edited and designed by Roger Chesneau/DAG Publications Ltd

Printed and bound in Great Britain
by Cox & Wyman, Reading, Berks

Contents

Preface   7

1   Machines for the Annoyance of Shipping   11
2   Shock After Shock   22
3   The Pillars of Hercules   35
4   From the Black Sea to the Hudson River   49
5   In the Land of the Rising Sun   66
6   Birth of a Legend   78
7   From Madagascar to Sydney   86
8   Midget Mortality   99
9   Jeeps and Chariots   115
10 A Potent Weapon of War   128
11 Cool Courage and Determination   144
12 Improbable and Unworkable Designs   158
13 From Bergen to Normandy and Back Again   165
14 Cruisers and Telephone Cables   176
15 The K-Verband   183
16 Desperate Measures   194
17 Götterdämmerung   207
18 The Future   215

Appendix: Warships and Merchant Ships Sunk or Damaged
   by Midget Submarines or Human Torpedoes   233
Notes   235
Bibliography   247
Index   251

Preface

The midget submarine is one of the most potent weapons of war developed in the twentieth century, yet it is an extremely old form of naval warfare, with the first, although unsuccessful, attack being launched in 1776. In the early days of submarine warfare this century, all submarines were midget craft. But, as the submarine grew, there arose a requirement for small craft which could penetrate a defended harbour and attack shipping. This single requirement has since been expanded to include a host of other roles. Experience with the midget submarine showed that these craft could accomplish operations of considerable strategic importance with effects out of all proportion to their small size.

During the Second World War the major navies, with the exception of the United States, France and the USSR, employed midget submarines or specially trained assault frogmen. The absence of France from this field is easily explained: the country's capitulation in June 1940 effectively removed it from the war. The United States possessed conventional forces in abundance and thus did not need to resort to this form of warfare. The absence of the Soviet Union from this area of operations is puzzling, given the pioneering work done by Russian engineers in submarine development. However, the highly individualistic nature of midget submarine operations did not sit easily alongside the centralised Soviet command structure.

Three kinds of midget submarine made their appearance during the Second World War: human torpedoes (the Italian *Maiale* and British Chariot); small submersibles (the German *Neger* and associated craft and the Japanese *Kaiten*); and true midget submarines (the Japanese *Ko-Hyoteki*, the Italian CA/CB types, the British X-Craft and the German *Seehund*). These craft can be further divided into the practical and therefore successful (British X-Craft, Italian *Maiale*); those that were enthusiastically designed but impractical (British Chariot, Japanese *Ko-Hyoteki*, German *Biber*); and the suicidal, either by accident or design (British Welman, German *Neger* and Japanese *Kaiten* and its various derivatives).

It was the Italians who led the way with the development of the two-man human torpedo, the *Maiale*, which was used to such deadly effect at Alexandria and Gibraltar. The activities of the Italian CA/CB midget submarines are less well known but worthy of attention, particularly the operation to attack shipping in New York—which would have had the most serious effects in America but which was cancelled on the Italian armistice.

Japan was another of the early pioneers in this field. Before the war the Japanese developed the excellent two-man *Ko-Hyoteki*, an extremely advanced midget submarine. Japanese war plans concentrated on the great battleship engagement between the American and Japanese fleets which would, it was hoped, decide the course of the war. To whittle down the American superiority in capital ships, *Ko-Hyoteki* were to launch mass torpedo attacks. It was an ingenious idea and one that may well have worked, but the Japanese decision to destroy the US fleet by a carrier strike removed the *raison d'être* for these attacks. Instead the craft were employed in harbour penetration—a task for which they were not suited and at which they were less than successful. As the tide of the war went against Japan, the Japanese resorted to suicide weapons such as the *Kaiten* and *Kairyu*. These were intended to overwhelm the Americans by sheer weight of numbers, but, once deployed, they proved no match for the range of anti-submarine measures employed by the Americans.

It was Italian activities in the Mediterranean which spurred the British into the field. Britain had traditionally made no attempt to develop this sort of weapon: since the Royal Navy was the pre-eminent naval force in the world, there was no requirement. It was only the need to attack the German battleship *Tirpitz* which pushed a reluctant Admiralty in this direction. The British initially copied the Italian two-man human torpedo and produced the Chariot, but these craft proved unsuccessful and never justified the time and resources devoted to them. Far more successful was the X-Craft, a potent four-man midget submarine which could be put to a variety of uses. At the other end of the scale was the Welman, a useless craft whose design shows the effects of allowing enthusiasm to triumph over practicality. British midgets saw action in all three theatres of war and their most significant success was the crippling of the German battleship *Tirpitz* in September 1943.

The Germans were the last into this field. While the U-boats were scoring significant successes in the Atlantic, the *Kriegsmarine* showed no interest in these craft. It was only when the Germans were staring at the prospect of an Allied invasion of Europe that their attitude changed. In many ways the Germans' attitude mirrored that of the Japanese and was a tacit admission that their naval strategy had failed. German midgets were weapons of desperation, founded in the hope that if used in sufficient numbers they would interrupt the Allied cross-Channel supply lines. With the exception of the excellent *Seehund* two-man submarine, German midgets were poorly constructed and most were as lethal to their crews as they were intended to be to the opposition.

The operations of the various midget submarines during the Second World War remain some of the most supreme examples of cold-blooded courage in history. In a war which became dominated by technology and weapons of mass destruction, the achievements of the midget submariners of all countries stand out and hark back to an earlier and more honourable age, where individual bravery and skill-at-arms were the attributes which won wars. Following the failure of the Japanese attack on Sydney, Rear-Admiral Stuart Muirhead-Gould, in charge of the harbour defences at that city, paid the following tribute to the Japanese officers and men who had perished in the attack:

> Theirs was a courage which is not the property, or the tradition, or the heritage of any one nation. It is the courage shared by the brave men of our own countries as well of the enemy and, however horrible war and its results may be, it is courage which is recognised and universally admired. These men were patriots of the highest order. How many of us are really prepared to make one-thousandth of the sacrifice these men have made?

These words are a fitting epitaph for all such men.

ACKNOWLEDGEMENTS

I am deeply grateful to the following for their help in the preparation of this book: Marija Batica for producing the line drawings in the data sections; Harvey Bennette; Admiral Gino Birindelli; Dick Boyle, officer-in-charge of the United States Navy's only midget submarine, the ill-fated *X1*; Gus Britton of the Royal Navy Submarine Museum, for his comments (both profane and constructive) on the manuscript; Colin Bruce and Allison Duffield of the Department of Printed Books at the Imperial War Museum; Dr John Bullen; Mrs Eve Compton-Hall, for permission to quote from the diary of her late husband; Commander Donald Cameron VC RN; Ed Finney of the US Navy Historical Service; Lieutenant-Commander Ian Fraser VC DSC RNR; *Oberfähnrich zur See (ad)* Klaus Goetsch; Frank Goldsworthy; Eric Grove; Peter Hart of the Sound Archive at the Imperial War Museum; David Hill, for producing the line drawing of HMS *Trooper*; Lieutenant-Commander George Honour DSC RNVR; Peter Jung of the *Kriegsarchiv* in Vienna; Klaus Matthes; Jane Middleton, *Dott.* Achille Rastelli; Simon Robbins of the Department of Documents at the Imperial War Museum; Captain Richard Sharpe OBE RN, Editor of *Jane's Fighting Ships*; Marco Spertini; Commander J. J. Tall MBE RN, Director of the Royal Navy Submarine Museum; Captain A. V. Walker DSC RN; and the late Commander H. P. Westmacott DSO DSC RN. The authorities of the Democratic People's Republic of Korea and of the Islamic Republic of Iran felt unable to answer any of my requests for information on the midget submarines in their service.

I am especially grateful to Commander Richard Compton-Hall MBE RN, former Director of the Royal Navy Submarine Museum, for his encouragement and advice—despite our working on similar projects; to David Gibbons and Tony Evans of DAG Publications; and to Roger Chesneau, my long-suffering editor. Finally, my thanks are due to my wife, Kitty, for her endurance of her husband's preoccupation with little else but this book over the past three years.

Paul Kemp

Chapter 1

Machines for the Annoyance of Shipping

What will become of maritime wars, and where will sailors be found to man ships of war, when it is a physical certainty that they may every moment be blown into the air by means of a diving boat, against which no human foresight can guard them?—The *Naval Chronicle*, 1802

In July 1802 the *Naval Chronicle* published a report from Paris concerning a new invention, the Bateau Plongeur, by an American designer, Mr Robert Fulton. After describing the craft's capabilities, the *Naval Chronicle* looked ahead:

> Mr Fulton has already added to his boat a machine by means of which he blew up a large boat in the port of Brest; and if, by future experiments, the same effect could be produced on frigates or ships of the line, what will become of maritime wars, and where will sailors be found to man ships of war, when it is a physical certainty that they may every moment be blown into the air by means of a diving boat, against which no human foresight can guard them?[1]

The *Naval Chronicle*'s correspondent was not aware that he had accurately predicted the shape and form of midget submarine warfare in the First and Second World Wars. It was all to do with attacking ships in defended anchorages and harbours. Hence midget submarine operations pre-date submarine warfare on the high seas.

Fulton's 'invention' was, however, preceded by another craft some thirty years earlier. The American designer David Bushnell has the best claim to be called the 'father' of midget submarine warfare for his attack on HMS *Eagle* in New York during the American War of Independence. Bushnell had a lively and enquiring mind but was physically unprepossessing and suffered from poor health. He had already made improvements to agricultural machinery but while at Yale University expanded his studies into other fields. Bushnell carried out a number of experiments to establish the destructive effects of underwater explosions, and these experiments with mines (or torpedoes, as they were known in early days) led him inexorably towards the development of a craft to deliver the weapons. A small boat was out of the question, as were the clumsy divers' suits of the day. The answer lay in a submersible—a craft that could approach its target unseen. Bushnell's experiments took place at a time of rising tension in North America between those colonists who wished for self-government and the British authorities who wished to maintain the link with Britain. These developments lent a sense of urgency and purpose to Bushnell's work, so while the political situation deteriorated into open warfare, Bushnell and his brother Ezra worked on the craft at their farm at Saybrook.

We know very little about the *Turtle*, as Bushnell's craft was named, largely because Bushnell himself destroyed the plans to prevent their falling into the hands of the British. Bushnell's own account remains the most comprehensive. In a letter dated 13 October 1787 to Thomas Jefferson, Bushnell described his submarine thus:

The external shape of the submarine vessel bore some resemblance to two upper tortoise shells of equal size joined together ... the inside was capable of containing the operator and air sufficient to supply him thirty minutes.[2]

Turtle was a one-man, hand-operated craft. David Bushnell was not strong enough to operate the craft, so his brother Ezra was the first to take it into the water. The 'weapon' was a 150lb charge of gunpowder, packed in a watertight package and fitted with a clockwork fuse. The charge was attached by a lanyard to an auger, a large pointed screw that could be worked from within the *Turtle* so as to pierce the wooden hull of the target and secure the charge. When the charge was safely secured to the target's hull, *Turtle* would retire. The only instrumentation was a compass, lit by fox-fire (rotten stumpwood), and a primitive depth gauge, eighteen inches high and one inch in diameter. The gauge was open to the sea at the bottom, and depth was indicated by a floating cork.

Propulsion was by a two-blade propeller worked by the operator's feet. If the operator was pedalling at full speed, a speed of 3kt might have been possible but it would have been exhausting work and would have left him too tired to do much else. Some reports speak of a hand-cranked propeller, but there is no doubt that it would have been much easier to use feet rather than hands. The *Turtle* was kept stable by means of a 200lb mass of lead ballast suspended beneath her by means of a 50ft rope. The weight of this ballast combined with that of the operator also sufficed to trim the *Turtle* so low in the water that only the top of the hatch and the glass viewing ports were visible from the surface. The craft could be further submerged by means of a vertical screw oar and by admitting water to a small tank in the bottom of the craft which could be pumped out by hand if necessary. In theory it was possible to submerge the craft to a depth of several feet with reasonable accuracy of control. The operator was supplied with air by means of tubes passing through the upper hatch and fitted with shut-off valves. An interesting feature of the design was that all inlets and outlets were covered by perforated plates to prevent their becoming blocked by debris.

By the summer of 1775, when the first armed clash between colonists and British troops took place at Lexington, the *Turtle* was nearly ready. However, sudden heavy frosts in the autumn extinguished the supplies of fox-fire, and no more would be available until the spring of 1776 at the earliest. Other than a candle (which was unacceptable on the grounds that it used up precious air) there was no other means of illumination. *Turtle*'s operational début had to be postponed.

By the time fox-fire reappeared in the spring of 1776, *Turtle* has suffered badly and needed substantial repairs. Moreover, Ezra Bushnell's fitness had fallen off during the winter and he needed a good deal of practice. Repairs to the craft and training for the operator were swiftly put in hand, and *Turtle* was shipped down to New York where British ships were known to be anchored and where the insurgent forces possessed a secure base on the Battery (the southern tip of Manhatten Island). On 13 July 1776 the British 64-gun ship-of-the-line HMS *Eagle*, flying the flag of Admiral Lord Howe, arrived from England and moored off Staten Island. The flagship was near enough to the insurgent forces encamped on the Brooklyn Heights across the Narrows for them to claim that they could smell the English! A more obvious or suitable target could not have presented itself. Just as the *Turtle* was ready, misfortune struck again when Ezra Bushnell fell ill and it was clear that he would not be fit for the planned operation. In the face of pressure from Generals Putnam and Washington to proceed with the operation, a volunteer was sought to carry it out in Ezra Bushnell's place.

It was a serious undertaking: it was necessary to find a man who could learn in a matter of weeks what Ezra Bushnell had spent five years of his life perfecting. Nevertheless, one Sergeant Ezra Lee, a soldier of good character from Old Lyme, Connecticut, stepped forward and was accepted. Even though Lee underwent arduous training in Long Island Sound, it was inconceivable that he could equal the skill of his predecessor. However, on the night of 5/6 September 1776 Lee stepped down into the *Turtle*. A rowing boat came alongside and, with a full moon and an ebb tide, made off with the *Turtle* in tow downstream to where the *Eagle* lay, some five miles distant.

It is at this point that apocryphal accounts of Lee's voyage and what we can deduce from known facts and experience of midget submarine operations part company. The accepted version is that Lee navigated his way downstream until reaching the *Eagle*. The current was so strong that he was swept past the flagship and he had to pedal furiously in order to regain position. Once under the *Eagle*'s stern, he attempted to secure the charge to her hull but was defeated by the copper sheathing which covered the hull (to protect the ship against the depredations of the teredo worm); an alternative version is that it was iron bands strengthening the quarter section which frustrated his efforts. Whatever the truth, the day was now breaking and the tide was flooding, so Lee gave up and made his way upstream. En route he was spotted and chased by a British guard boat. In an effort to distract his pursuers, Lee jettisoned the explosive charge, which is supposed to have drifted northward and exploded at the entrance to the East River. Meanwhile the *Turtle* had been spotted by friendly forces and a boat was dispatched to bring the exhausted Lee back to the Battery and safety. Subsequently at least two attacks were made on shipping above New York in the Hudson River, but to no effect.

That is the version of the attack which every schoolboy knows and which has entered the literature of the American War of Independence. However, using our knowledge of midget submarine operations gained during the Second World War, certain facts can be established. First, it is inconceivable that Lee could have made his way down to the *Eagle* and positioned the *Turtle* directly under her hull: it is hard enough for modern midget submariners to position their craft correctly with the aid of reliable motors, controls and an accurate compass. Lee would have had to be his own commanding officer, navigator, helmsman, look-out, propulsion engineer and, eventually, weapons engineer. He simply had too much to do: this was a failing common to all such one-man operated craft. It is possible that Lee managed a form of controlled collision with the *Eagle*. However, the latter was well guarded by Royal Marine sentries whose standing orders were that the 'All's Well' was to be given every ten minutes. Moreover, in order to keep the men awake, they were to be relieved regularly and at short intervals. It is unthinkable that the *Turtle* could have made her approach and a very noisy submergence under the noses of guards who were alert. Furthermore, there is no reference in the *Eagle*'s log to any attack by an underwater craft or, indeed, to anything out of the ordinary—including the explosion of the charge at the entrance to the East River.[3] Finally, the story that the attack forced Lord Howe to lift his close blockade of New York is not true: the fleet remained off New York until January 1777.

So what did happen? There is no doubt that the *Turtle* existed and that attacks were mounted on British ships. However, the exaggerated accounts of Lee's operations were probably due to the insurgent forces' making the most out of a useful propaganda opportunity. Lee was probably overcome by carbon dioxide during the operation. The physical effort required to operate the *Turtle*, coupled with his increased rate of respiration as the result of his apprehension at undertaking the mission, would have seen off the thirty minutes' air supply in no time at all. CO_2 poisoning would account for Lee's symptoms of confusion, anxiety and generally weakened condition which historians can infer from the various accounts of the operation. In the words of one commentator, Lee would not have known 'whether it was Christmas or Marble Arch'.[4] What most probably happened is that Lee set off, then, as CO_2 poisoning set in, he merely bumbled around the Narrows getting weaker and weaker until he decided to give up and try to return. On the return journey, his compass was not working and he had to open the hatch to see where he was going. The fresh air saved his life. None of this detracts from the fact that Lee was a very brave man and that the whole operation was a daring effort. It was the legend of what happened in the Narrows on the night of 5/6 September 1776 which inspired the early pioneers of the modern submarine. Today it is doubtful that one in a thousand of the workers who crowd into Manhatten realise the significance of what took place beneath their office skyscrapers two hundred years ago.

Thereafter midget submarine development languished until the end of the nineteenth century. Certainly in the Royal Navy Bushnell's initiative was not highly regarded at all. In 1812 a boatswain who proposed disposing of a French frigate by attaching an explosive charge to the ship's hull was dismissed for 'a suggestion not in keeping with the highest traditions of His Majesty's Service.'[5]

Then, in the 1870s and after, there was a resurgence in submarine development with the activities of J. P. Holland in the United States, the Reverend Garrett in Britain and the various Russian designs. However, as submarine technology progressed and improved (relative terms, given the nature of early submarine technology), the emphasis of development moved towards ocean-going boats and away from harbour penetration. Nevertheless, there were some interesting designs in the field, among them a Russian boat built in St Petersburg in 1879. This craft was armed with two 110lb mines carried in recesses in the upper part of the hull and fitted with spikes. The mines would be released beneath a target and would rise up and become embedded in the hull. Subsequently the charges would be fired electrically via a cable attached to the submarine. Not surprisingly, such a design implied a high mortality rate among the operators, and most (fifty were ordered) were used as buoys or pontoons. The Russians did maintain an interest in small submarines for harbour defence. Three four-man craft loosely based on the *Holland* type submarine were ordered by the Russian Army in 1913 for local defence duties in the Black Sea. The craft were turned over to the Navy in 1914. Two were transported to the Arctic, where both were lost in accidents. The third was dispatched to the Danube, where the Russians intended to use her against the ships of the *Donauflottille*. Unfortunately she was captured at Reni on 12 March 1918 by the Austrians. Plans were laid to send the submarine to Budapest and Vienna to drum up support for war loans, but these came to nothing and the craft's eventual fate is unknown.

Russian *Holland* Type Midget Submarines

Displacement: 33/44 tons
Length: 20.5m
Beam: 2.3m
Propulsion: 1 x 50bhp diesel engine; 1 x 35hp electric motor
Speed (surfaced): 8kt
Speed (submerged): 6kt
Armament: Two 45cm bow torpedoes
Crew: 4
Number delivered: 3
Production: All boats built in 1913 by the Nevski Yard at St Petersburg for the Army Ministry, to be used in local defence on the Black Sea, but handed over to the Navy in 1914.

Fates: *No 1* transferred to the Arctic in 1916 and lost in collision with submarine *Delfin* off Murmansk 16.04.17. *No 2* transferred to Arctic in 1915 and abandoned after going aground at Svjatoi 15.10.15. *No 3* went to Danube and was captured at Reni on 12.03.18 by Austro-Hungarian forces; subsequent fate unknown.

By 1914 submarine development had reached a point where the boats entering service with the various belligerent navies were sufficiently large to undertake a lengthy ocean voyage and operate on the high seas. There was little or no thought devoted to the development of craft for the covert penetration of harbour defences. However, the French had not completely abandoned the idea of using submarines for such a purpose. In the early months of the First World War French submariners in the Adriatic showed great courage in entering the heavily defended Austrian ports of Cattaro and Pola. In what the Austrian Commander-in-Chief, Admiral Anton Haus, described as an act of 'pure madness',[6] the French submarine *Cugnot* (*Lieutenant de Vaisseau* Dubois) entered the harbour at Cattaro in late November 1914, while on 8 December the French submarine *Curie* (*Lieutenant de Vaisseau* Gabriel O'Byrne) was caught and sunk while attempting to enter the harbour at Pola. The loss of the *Curie* brought these gallant but hazardous operations to an end.

It took the stalemate in the Adriatic to produce a revival of interest in this particular form of warfare. In 1915 Italy had abandoned her commitments to her Austrian and German partners and had joined the Anglo-French Entente, largely on the grounds that an Anglo-French victory would satisfy Italian territorial claims against Austria. The Italian Navy was slightly larger (and was considerably larger when bolstered by Anglo-French forces) than the *KuK Kriegsmarine* across the Adriatic, but both sides adopted a passive strategy, glaring at each other from the behind the heavily fortified ports of Taranto and Pola.

The idea of attacking the Austrian Fleet behind its defences at Pola at the northern end of the Adriatic was first considered by two Italian naval officers, Engineer Lieutenant-Commander Raffaele Rossetti and Surgeon-Lieutenant Raffaele Paolucci.[7] Rossetti first considered the idea in early June 1915—not long after Italy had declared war—when Chief Petty Officer Luigi Martignoni, a senior engineering rating on board the cruiser *Poerio*, asked him if it could be possible to adapt a torpedo to 'human guidance' for an attack against an enemy base. Rossetti was intrigued by the idea, but it was not until September 1915 that he committed it to paper. His superior, *Colonello del Genio Navale* Giovanni Scialpi, was less than impressed and rejected the idea but indicated that he would not be offended if Rossetti took the proposal to the Fleet Command.

Thus on 24 September 1915 Rossetti reported to Vice-Admiral Alberto de Bono, commanding the naval district of La Spezia. De Bono was equally sceptical but advised Rossetti to discuss the matter with the commanding officer of the Torpedo Trials Establishment at La Spezia, *Capitano di Corvetta* Guido Cavalazzi. Cavalazzi merely considered the idea and did nothing, so on 3 November 1915 Rossetti returned to see de Bono, this time with a detailed memorandum about his project. The memorandum stressed the low cost of the project and indicated that two men, wearing diving suits and using a modified Italian B57 torpedo, would have an effective range of 30 nautical miles. This estimate was a little overoptimistic—as Rossetti realised after the war—and led to the project being turned down by de Bono. When the latter was relieved by Vice-Admiral Leone Viale in early 1916, Rossetti tried again but to no avail.

For the next two years Rossetti carried on with work on his project, mostly without the knowledge of his superiors, purloining materials and manpower from other, more legitimate projects to do so. In May 1916, while serving as the Marine Superintendent of the shipyard at Sestri Levante, Rossetti managed to 'obtain' two B57 torpedoes and send them to Genoa. The latter place was not suitable for his purposes, so Rossetti managed to have himself transferred to the Materials Trials Commission at La Spezia in May 1917. It was at La Spezia that the real development work began: two torpedoes, whose disappearance from Sestri Levante had doubtless been covered by some dubious paperwork, were hidden in the changing room belonging to workers at the submarine base. Some of the workers eagerly joined in the project, but before long the resources available in their changing room proved inadequate and Rossetti approached the commander of the naval air station, let him in on the secret, and succeeded in acquiring the use of a hangar. The web of deceit surrounding the project widened, but higher authority remained blissfully ignorant. The first trials of the machine were held on 18 January 1918; further trials were held on 24 January and 27 February. The consumption of pressurized air was measured and different types of propellers and diving suits were tested. The last trial, held on 9 March 1918, convinced Rossetti that the device was ready for operations.

The machine, known as *Mignatta* (Leech), was built around a standard B57 14in torpedo but which was fitted with enlarged, 450mm propellers. *Mignatta* would be taken to a point near to Pola by a torpedo boat. After being lowered into the water it would be towed by an MTB to a point as close as possible to the breakwater without the boat's being detected. The two man crew sat astride the machine, wearing diving suits but no helmets as their heads would be above water. The range of the craft was 10 miles in five hours. The armament was two 170kg warheads which were attached

---

Mignatta Two-Man Human Torpedo

Description: 14ft B57 (the designation 'B' indicates that the body of the torpedo was built of bronze) torpedo with handholds for the two operators
Length: 4.5m
Range: 8–10 miles at a speed of 3–4kt
Propulsion: Torpedo cool-air engine fed by compressed air at 205 atmospheres

Warhead: Two 170kg TNT charges (attached to target by magnets)
Crew: 2
Number delivered: Two (*S1* and *S2*), both constructed by the Arsenale at Venice. *S1* expended on the raid on Pola, 31 October/1 November 1918; *S2* preserved at the Naval Museum at La Spezia

to the target ship by a magnetic clamp. After fixing the warheads the two men would clear the area on the remains of the *Mignatta*.

Now that the work was finished, Rossetti, in order to get approval for the project, had to admit to his clandestine activities over the past two years. His memorandum went as far as Admiral Paolo Thaon di Reval, Commander-in-Chief of the Fleet, who summoned the young engineer to Rome on 1 April 1918. The circumstances of Rossetti's second attempt were much more favourable. To begin with, he had a machine which worked and could be 'shown off' to the sceptics. Moreover, by the spring of 1918 Italy had been at war for three years with little to show for it other than lengthening casualty lists. To di Revel and the Italian Naval Staff *Mignatta* seemed to be the means to strike a blow against the Austrians right in the heart of their most protected anchorage. Thaon di Revel gave a positive response and transferred Rossetti to Venice, where he arrived on 5 April. On reporting to the port commander, *Capitano di Vascello* Constanzo Ciano, Rossetti learned that a group of young officers in Venice were working on similar lines; furthermore, the Italians were developing the tracked, torpedo-armed assault craft, the *Grillo*, as a means of surmounting the harbour defences of Pola. The first operation using the *Grillo* took place on 13/14 May 1918 and was a failure: the craft was disabled and the crew were taken prisoner.

Rossetti feared that there were too many loose tongues in Venice and that the city was unhealthily near the front line. Accordingly, he and the *Mignatta* returned to La Spezia. Development and refinement were continuous: a lighter diving suit was designed and tested and on 31 May 1918 Rossetti took the craft on an 8km trip without exhausting the air supply. Rossetti also chose his 'Number 2', a young naval surgeon called Raffaele Paolucci. Paolucci's first ride on *Mignatta* nearly ended in disaster when he became trapped under it: he was only saved when a nearby salvage vessel was able to pass a strop round *Mignatta* and haul the whole thing out of the water. However, there were problems concerning personnel: Rossetti's relations with Captain Ciano in Venice got worse. Ciano wanted the attack on Pola to be brought forward while Rossetti wanted to wait until *Mignatta* was perfect.

Events now threatened to overtake Rossetti. On 6 October 1918 the Central Powers approached the United States for a negotiated peace settlement. Di Revel realised that it was now or never and ordered that the attack be launched on the next dark moon period at the beginning of November, regardless of the state of development. Rossetti and *Mignatta* (of which there were now two, formally designated *S1* and *S2*) returned to Venice and on 25 October 1918 carried out a successful trial in which she set off from the Arsenale and attacked a ship moored off the church of Santa Maria della Salute without being observed. Everything was now ready.

On the evening of 31 October 1918 the torpedo boat *PN65*, with *S2* on deck and accompanied by the motor torpedo boat *MAS95*, left Venice. Off Brioni island on the

Dalmatian coast, *S2* was lowered into the water and taken in tow by *MAS95* until the pair were 66m from the main breakwater outside the harbour at Pola. At 2213 *S2* slipped away from *MAS95* and just after 0200 on 1 November the crew were inside the harbour, having passed the breakwater and clambered over three rows of nets pulling *Mignatta* behind them. Had the defences been in any way alert, the two Italians were bound to have been spotted. However, events inside the harbour at Pola were anything but normal.

The previous day, 30 October, had seen the end of the *KuK Kriegsmarine* as the Emperor Charles handed over command and control of the Fleet to representatives of the South Slav National Council. The actual handover was on 31 October, with Admiral Nicholas Horthy leaving the flagship *Viribus Unitis* at 1645 after the Austrian colours had been hauled down for the last time. Horthy had been followed by most of the German, Czech and Hungarian nationals (who provided most of the officers and all of the skilled senior rates in the multi-national Austro-Hungarian Navy), leaving the ships in control of the jubilant Slav remains of their crews. British signals intelligence personnel at the Italian port of Brindisi who were monitoring Austrian traffic heard the port commander at Cattaro ask who was in charge at Pola, only to receive the reply, broadcast *en clair* and at full power, 'We are!'[8] *Linienschiffskapitän* Janko Vukovic de Podkapelski took over as Commander-in-Chief but failed to restore any sort of order. The ships were fully illuminated while their crews celebrated, no sentries were deployed and none of the vessels was maintaining any kind of watertight integrity.

Rossetti and Paolucci were unaware of the political developments taking place around them as they steered *Mignatta* between two rows of brightly illuminated battleships. Unfortunately *Mignatta* now began to malfunction. A flooding valve at the stern opened, causing the craft to sink, and buoyancy could only be restored by using some of the precious air required to drive the craft. Moreover, they had used more air than they thought in entering the harbour and Rossetti knew that there was not enough left for them to clear the harbour after the attack: both men would have to abandon *Mignatta* and escape on shore, trusting to the local population, many of whom were ethnic Italians and sympathetic to the Allied cause.

At 0430 Rossetti brought *Mignatta* to the port side of the *Viribus Unitis*. However, on noticing a launch secured to the boom, he resolved to let the current take them round the battleship's bows to the starboard side before fixing the warhead. Rossetti separated one warhead from *Mignatta* and secured it to the battleship's side before the fourth and fifth 15cm guns. He set a two-hour delay on the fuse, swam away to the *Mignatta* and headed off at full speed, leaving a bright fluorescent stern wave. The time was now 0515 and a bugle call roused the *Viribus Unitis*' crew from their slumbers. It was at this stage that the two Italians were spotted and illuminated with a searchlight. The men were wearing rudimentary camouflage intended to disguise themselves as foliage, but it was not successful. As a motor boat came towards them, they set the fuse on the other warhead, set the engine to slow speed and gave *Mignatta* a push.

The Italians were picked out of the water and taken on board *Viribus Unitis*, where their reception was curious but not hostile. Rossetti told de Podkapelski that they had been dropped in the harbour by an aircraft and told him what was about to happen to his ship without being specific. De Podkapelski immediately ordered *'Schiff Verlassen!'* ('Abandon Ship!') and, unusually for a commanding officer, led his crew and the two Italians over the side. Rossetti and Paolucci were picked up by a boat from the *Tegetthoff*, a sister-ship to the *Viribus Unitis*. When no explosion was observed they were sent back to *Viribus Unitis*, where their reception was very hostile. Both men were stripped of their uniforms and their distinguishing badges of rank. At the stroke of 0620 the charge exploded, causing the ship to assume an immediate 20-degree list to starboard. In their anger some of the crew proposed locking Rossetti and Paolucci below decks and letting them drown. De Podkapelski

Alfa, A and B Class Midget Submarines

	Alfa	*A class*	*B class*
Displacement	–	31.25/36.7 tons	40/46 tons
Length	6.03m	13.5m	15.12m
Beam	–	2.2m	2.32m
Propulsion	1 x electric motor	1 x 40/60hp electric motor	1 x 85bhp petrol engine; 1 x 40–60hp electric motor
Speed (surfaced)	8kt	6.8kt	6.9kt
Speed (submerged)	–	5.08kt	5kt
Range (surfaced)	–	12nm at 7kt	128nm at 6kt
Range (submerged)	–	8.5nm at 4.6kt	9nm at 5kt
Torpedoes	–	Two 17in carried externally	Two 17.7in tubes
Crew	1	4	5
Number delivered	Two[1]	Six[2]	Six[3]

Notes

1. *Alfa* and *Beta* discarded 1915–16 without being formally commissioned.
2. *A1* to *A6* all built between December 1915 and March 1916 by the Arsenale at La Spezia. All discarded on 26 September 1918.
3. *B1* to *B3* built between July and November 1916 by the Arsenale at La Spezia. All three discarded on 23 January 1919. *B4* to *B6* laid down at the same yard in July 1916, suspended in 1917, discarded on 23 January 1919 and scrapped from 1920 onwards.

intervened on their behalf and the two Italians abandoned the *Viribus Unitis* for the second time that morning. Fifteen minutes later the 21,000-ton battleship rolled over and sank.

Meanwhile *Mignatta* had been circling round in the current and came to rest under the hull of the liner *Wien*, which was serving as a depot ship for German submarine crews. There it exploded, two hours later, causing the *Wien* to sink on an even keel. The exact number who lost their lives on the *Viribus Unitis* is not known. Some estimates are as high as 400 but this is doubtful in view of the reduced ship's company and the fact that most were on the upper deck when the explosion took place. One certain casualty was de Podkapelski, who stayed on the bridge of his ship until she sank beneath him.

Rossetti and Paolucci were held captive on board the *Habsburg* and later the *Radetzky* before being freed when the Italians occupied Pola on 5 November 1918 after the armistice. Both were subsequently awarded the Cross of the Military Order of Savoy, as was Captain Ciano. A subsequent decree awarded the sum of 1,300,000 lira in gold, to be shared among Ciano, Rossetti and Paolucci. Rossetti was outraged that he and Paolucci should have to share their award with Ciano and after a lengthy battle succeeded in having the sum split between him and Paolucci. It would be nice to think that Chief Petty Officer Luigi Martignoni received something, but there is no record of any recognition of his role in the affair. The two men subsequently arranged for some of the money to be distributed to the widows of those men killed in the *Viribus Unitis*. It was a gesture typical of the honourable, almost chivalrous spirit which underlay Italian activity in this field of naval operations.

There were other Italian developments in this field. The *Regia Marina* possessed eleven midget submarines, *Alfa*, *Beta* and the nine boats of the A and B classes. These boats were employed on coastal defence patrols around harbours on Italy's Adriatic coastline.[9] However, a photograph of the one of the B class boats, sadly unidentified, shows the craft fitted with what can only be described as caterpillar tracks, presumably to allow it to surmount nets and boom defences. Presumably the craft was assigned for an ambitious assault on Pola harbour which also involved the modification of the submarine *Argo* to carry assault frogmen and the conversion of the old battleship *Re Umberto* for use as an attack transport. The operation was cancelled when Austria sued for peace. However, the concept confirms the Italians' interest in this form of warfare—an interest they were to exploit to the full in the next world war.

Chapter 2

Shock after Shock

You are the fighting spearhead of our Navy.—Admiral de Courten, Minister of the Marine, in an address to officers and men of the *Decima Mas*, September 1943.

On the morning of 19 December 1941 everything appeared as normal on the quarterdeck of the battleship HMS *Queen Elizabeth*, flagship of the Mediterranean Fleet. The 'Preparatory' pennant was flying from the yardarm, indicating that the morning ceremony of 'Colours', which heralded the start of the working day, was about to begin. The signalman and his assistant stood by the ensign staff ready to hoist the Ensign, while the officer of the watch and other ratings of the duty watch were in their positions. The Royal Marine band fidgeted in the brisk morning air while the Royal Marine guard stood rigidly at ease under the eagle eye of the Colour Sergeant. A similar bustle on the quarterdeck of HMS *Valiant* moored ahead of the *Queen Elizabeth* indicated that the same preparations were under way. Just before 0830 Admiral Sir Andrew Cunningham, Commander-in-Chief of the Mediterranean Fleet, came up the quarterdeck ladder; the band and guard were brought to attention and, to the strains of the 'God Save the King', the White Ensign was hoisted. To any observer it seemed that it was just another ordinary day for the Mediterranean Fleet.

Yet Cunningham and every officer and man on board those two battleships knew that the ceremonies were but a farce, a farce intended to deceive the all-seeing eyes of Axis air reconnaissance and agents ashore. The truth was that, overnight, Italian human torpedoes had penetrated the harbour defences and laid explosive charges beneath the two battleships and a tanker. The subsequent explosions rendered the two ships unfit for further service without substantial repair . Overnight the balance of naval power in the Mediterranean had been altered.

The Italians responsible for this audacious operation were from the 10th Light Flotilla, the *Decima Mas*, an élite unit specialising in operations involving the use of human torpedoes and assault frogmen.[1] Armchair naval historians who delight in writing off the wartime operations of the *Regia Marina* would do well to remember that, in under three years of warfare, the *Decima Mas* was responsible for sinking or damaging four warships and twenty-seven merchant ships totalling 265,352 tons in operations ranging from Alexandria to Gibraltar. At the end of the war the *Decima Mas* was poised to strike as far afield as New York. No better proof of how the unit was regarded by the Allies can be found than the story of a young *Decima Mas* officer who had been captured by the British at Gibraltar. He subsequently developed tuberculosis and was selected by the Red Cross for repatriation to Italy on compassionate grounds. The officer was one step away from the repatriation ship when he was whisked away and packed off to a prisoner-of-war camp in the United States. The Admiralty had belatedly discovered his name on the list and were not prepared to let him go on account of his potential usefulness to the Italian cause in training human torpedo operators or in directing operations himself.[2]

Before recounting the remarkable story of *Decima Mas* operations, it may be useful to discuss some general points as to why the unit was so efficient when, it must be admitted, the Italian forces declined in effectiveness as the war progressed and turned against them. First—and this is not easy to quantify—their remarkable efficiency came from something in the Latin temperament. The Italians lacked nothing when it came to displaying individual courage and were glad and willing to volunteer for hazardous duty where a man's individual prowess could stand out. They were not, on the other hand, so happy about playing a small part in a large organisation. Secondly, the *Decima Mas* was remarkably free from the class distinctions which bedevilled the Italian armed forces, throughout which officers enjoyed exceptional privileges (even in submarines the wardroom had a separate galley). However, things were very different in the *Decima Mas*, where officers and men enjoyed a close relationship. Paradoxically, many of the officers in the *Decima Mas* came from the nobility while many of their men were from comparatively humble backgrounds. Loyalty both upwards and downwards was absolute. Thirdly, the *Decima Mas* was not prey to the logistic problems which were endemic in the Italian military establishment. This was in no small measure due to royal patronage. The unit was commanded by the Duke of Aosta, a cousin of the King, who used his royal influence ruthlessly and shamelessly to procure the otherwise unprocurable. However, the reverse of this particular coin was that the *Decima Mas* was run very much as a private fiefdom within the *Regia Marina* and the possibility of using its talents to deliver a decisive blow in concert with more conventional forces was not exploited as effectively as it might have been.[3]

The seeds had already been sown with the exploits of Rossetti and Paolucci in Pola harbour, but it was Italy's military adventure in Abyssinia in 1935 that led to the establishment of a unit dedicated to these operations. The war in Abyssinia brought down a good deal of international opprobrium on the Italian government and the situation was very tense. From an Italian perspective, their Navy was sandwiched between the British Mediterranean Fleet at Alexandria and the French Fleet at Toulon together with such British forces as could be deployed from the Atlantic Fleet. To reduce the odds against the *Regia Marina* a weapon was required which could be cheaply and quickly brought to attack naval targets in harbour and thus reduce the number of units ranged against them..

In October 1935 two engineer officers, Sub-Lieutenants Teseo Tesei and Elios Toschi, submitted plans for an improved version of the *Mignatta* to Admiral Cavagnari, Chief of the *Supermarina*, the Italian Naval Staff. Cavagnari approved the idea and work began at La Spezia. Three months later the prototypes were ready. Toschi described the craft as

> ... in reality a miniature submarine with entirely novel features, electrical propulsion similar to an aeroplane ... The crew (pilot and assistant), instead of remaining closed and more or less helpless in the interior, keep outside the structure. The two men, true fliers of the sea-depths astride their little underwater aeroplane, are protected by a curved screen of plastic glass ... At night, under cover of darkness and steering by luminous instruments, they will be able to attack the objective while remaining invisible to the enemy ... They will be able to cuts nets and remove any obstacle with compressed air tools and reach any target ... with long range breathing sets they can operate at depths down to 30 metres and can carry a powerful explosive charge into an enemy harbour. Invisible and undetectable by the most sensitive acoustic detectors, the operator will be able to penetrate inside the harbour and ... find the keel of a large ship, attach the charge to it and ensure an explosion will sink the vessel.[4]

There was, however, no requirement for such a craft in Italy's Abyssinian adventure, so the weapons were stored and their crews drafted to other appointments. But by the summer of 1939 it was clear that war was imminent, so the First Light Flotilla was formed in June under the command of *Capitano di Fregatta* Paolo Aloisi with instructions to

> ... train a nucleus of personnel for employment with given special weapons [to carry out], under the supervision of Admiral Goiran, experiments and tests concerned with the perfecting of the said weapons.[5]

Aloisi was succeeded in command by *Capitano di Fregatta* Mario Giorgini on the outbreak of war, who in turn was succeeded by *Capitano di Fregatta* Vittirio Moccagatta in March 1941. Under Moccagatta's leadership the organisation ceased to be part of the First Light Flotilla but became the Tenth Light Flotilla, *Decima Mas*, in its own right. This is the name by the which the unit will be referred to in these pages. Moccagatta further split *Decima Mas* into two parts, a surface group and a sub-surface weapons group. The former dealt with the operation of the fast explosive motor boats and the latter with human torpedoes and assault frogmen.

A base was established on a secluded stretch of land on the Boca di Serchio and the officers and men involved in the initial tests were recalled from their units. These included Tesei and Toschi as well as Luigi de la Penne, Gino Birindelli, Enrico Manisco and Licio Visintini, all of whom will play a central role in this story. Cavagnari had taken the decision to order twelve prototypes and at the beginning of 1940 the first exercises were held, with the old cruiser *Quarto* as the target, in the Gulf of La Spezia. These were successful, for although two of the craft broke down, the third attached a dummy charge to *Quarto* which would certainly have resulted in her destruction. The concept had become a reality. However, the loss of two years' research and development meant that when Italy declared war on 10 June 1940 the weapon was still at an experimental stage and not many were available for operations.

What was the craft with which *Decima Mas* was to operate so successfully? It was officially known by the designation SLC (*Siluro a Lenta Corsa*),[6] but the name by which it will be forever be known is *Maiale* (Pig). During early trials Tesei had to abandon a sinking SLC and came to the surface with the words, 'That swine got away!' The name stuck. The craft was 7.3m long overall, which included the 300kg warhead at the front which was 1.8m long. The diameter of the craft was 0.53m. The two operators sat astride the craft, the driver in front with the Number 2 behind. Beneath the driver's seat was the forward trimming tank. Between and beneath the two seats was the battery consisting of thirty 60V cells. At a speed of 4.5 knots the *Maiale* had a range of four miles and at 2.3 knots a range of 15 miles. Inside the after portion of the craft was the 1.1hp (later increased to 1.6hp) electric motor and the stern trimming tank. At the stern was the propeller, surrounded by a protective shroud, with hydroplanes and a vertical rudder.[7]

The two operators sat behind shields to lessen the water resistance. The driver controlled the craft by means of a joystick which worked both rudder and hydro-

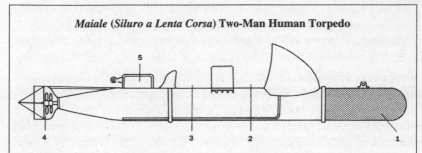

Maiale (*Siluro a Lenta Corsa*) **Two-Man Human Torpedo**

Length: 6.7m (7.3m with warhead)
Beam: 0.53m
Propulsion: 1 x 1.6hp electric motor
Speed (surfaced): 4.5kt
Range (surfaced): 15nm at 2.3kt, 4nm at 4.5kt
Armament: Explosive charge of 220kg (later increased to 250kg and finally 300kg).
Crew: 2

Schematic drawing of an early *Maiale* shows:
1. 220kg warhead attached to nose of the craft.
2. Driver's position (astride the craft).
3. Driver's assistant's position.
4. Single propeller with rudder and control surfaces.
5. Ballast pump.

planes. Speed was regulated by a flywheel connected to a rheostat. Between the two operators was the quick diving tank which was flooded by lever action from the Number 2's position and blown by air from a compressed air cylinder. Behind the Number 2's seat was a locker containing net cutters, a set of working tools, plenty of rope and clamps used to attach the warhead to the hull of the target. The operators wore a one-piece 'Belloni' suit and breathed oxygen through a closed-cycle breathing apparatus (*Austorespiratore ad ossigeno*) which left no tell-tale trail of bubbles on the surface. The apparatus consisted of two high-pressure oxygen cylinders which gave about six hours' breathing time. The oxygen was fed, via a reducing valve and a flexible tube, into the operator's mouthpiece. The operator exhaled through the same tube and the 'exhaust' air was cleaned in a cylinder containing soda lime crystals.

The 300kg warhead (some later *Maiale* could carry two 150kg charges) at the front of the craft was held in position by a metal clutch. The procedure for attaching the warhead to the target was for the driver to position the *Maiale* directly under one of the target's bilge keels. The Number 2 would then dismount and secure a clamp to the keel to which was attached a length of rope. The driver would move the *Maiale* forward under the hull while the diver swam round and attached another clamp to the bilge keel on the other side of the hull. He would then return and attach both cables firmly to the warhead and set the fuse; two and a half hours' delay was possible. When all was secure, he would give the appropriate signal and the driver would release the warhead so that it hung under the target's hull, suspended from the bilge keels. The operators would then get clear.

Initially the Italians thought of delivering the *Maiale* to the operational area by air using a Cant Z.511 flying boat. This idea was swiftly abandoned, although it is interesting to note that in turn the British and Germans discussed the possibility of delivering underwater assault craft by air. Instead, Aloisi turned to the submarine as the most likely means of delivery. The old boat *Ametista* was fitted with pressure-tight containers on her casing, in which the *Maiale* would be kept during the passage. When the submarine was near the target area, the *Maiale* would be removed from the containers and released to proceed on their own. Following the success of trials with *Ametista*, three such containers were fitted to the submarines *Iride*, *Gondar*, *Scire* and *Ambra*. Initially the submarine would surface to launch the SLCs, but the Italians quickly developed exit/re-entry techniques so that the operators would leave the parent through the fore hatch while the boat was dived. This, of course, reduced the risk of the boat being caught on the surface with the containers open and the *Maiale* and their crews on the casing. An important feature of the *Maiale* containers was that they were built to the same constructional standards as the submarine's hull so that the parent boat's commanding officer should not have his freedom of operation constrained.

Closely allied to the story of the *Maiale* is that of the *Gamma* assault frogmen since they used the same equipment and participated in many operations together. The Italians possessed a seemingly inexhaustible supply of superb swimmers and there was no shortage of volunteers for this arduous duty. *Gamma* men wore the Belloni suit and used the same breathing apparatus as the *Maiale* men. The suits worn by *Gamma* men were often camouflaged with foliage to disguise their appearance. They carried limpet mines which they attached to the target's hull. There were two types of mine. First there was the 2kg *Mignatta*, which was secured to the hull by suction. A *Gamma* swimmer could carry four or five of these in a bag around his waist. Then there was the 4.5kg mine which was secured to the bilge keel by a clamp. This mine was actuated by a small propeller which slowly armed the charge as the ship proceeded through the sea. This particularly ingenious device was intended to ensure that the mine blew up at sea and not in harbour, and thereby create confusion as to how the explosion occurred. When the British started regular hull searches of warships and merchant ships in response to *Maiale* and *Gamma* activities, these mines were fitted with booby traps as well as shrouds to prevent the weapons' being dislodged by cables run along the hull.

Alexandria was the first target of the *Maiale*. It was the main base of the British Mediterranean Fleet since, under pre-war agreements, the French Navy was responsible for covering the western Mediterranean. In August 1940 four *Maiale* and their crews under the command of *Tenente di Vascello*[8] Gino Birindelli, were taken in the destroyer *Calipso* to the Gulf of Bomba on the North African coast where the depot ship *Monte Gargano* was waiting. On 16 August the submarine *Iride* (*Tenente di Vascello* Francesco Brunetti) arrived, having sailed from La Spezia on the 12th. The attack was scheduled for the night of 25/26 August when there would be a full moon. Until then the crews practised and prepared their craft. However, just after noon on 21 August, as *Iride* had got under way to carry out a trim dive with the *Maiale* embarked, four Swordfish aircraft from 824 Squadron appeared over the anchorage and began a lightning torpedo attack. Brunetti tried to point *Iride*'s bows at her assailants in order to minimise the target profile but the torpedoes were fitted with CCR magnetic pistols. The explosion threw all those on the bridge into the sea, and the *Iride* quickly sank. The SLC operators subsequently showed great gallantry in rescuing survivors from the *Iride*. The SLCs which had been embarked in *Iride* were recovered and returned to Italy, but '*missione annullata*' was the only verdict for Operation 'GA.1'.

A month later the Italians tried again. This time the submarine *Gondar* (*Tenente di Vascello* Francesco Brunetti) was used to carry three SLCs. *Gondar* sailed from La Spezia on 21 September and had a stand-off at Messina on the 23rd where the six *Maiale* men (plus two reserves), commanded by *Tenente di Vascello* Alberto Franzini, were embarked. At 2215 on 29 September, when only 100 miles from her objective, she was sighted and attacked by the Australian destroyer HMAS *Stuart* which had detached from the main battle fleet owing to a fractured main steam pipe. *Gondar* dived but was subjected to repeated depth-charge attacks by the two destroyers which remained in contact. Early on the morning of the 30th she surfaced, to be attacked by an RAF Sunderland of No 230 Squadron which had joined in the hunt. Brunetti realised that he could not proceed with the operation and scuttled his submarine. Forty-eight of the forty-nine crew members and *Maiale* men—including Elios Toschi, one of the *Maiale*'s founders—were rescued by *Stuart* and became prisoners of war. It was a doubly heartbreaking experience for the Italians because, before *Gondar*'s sinking, they had received a message to abandon the operation on the grounds that the British Fleet was at sea. Subsequently Toschi was anything but a model prisoner. He made numerous attempts at escape and eventually succeeded in reaching the Portuguese colony of Goa, from where he was repatriated.

The *Decima Mas* had hardly enjoyed an auspicious start—two operations written off, two of the valuable transport submarines sunk and four SLC teams taken prisoner. For over a year the *Decima Mas* command left the Eastern Mediterranean alone while they concentrated their operations on Gibraltar, and it was not until the winter of 1941 that they once again turned east to Alexandria. The prize awaiting them there were the battleships HMS *Queen Elizabeth* (the flagship of Admiral Sir Andrew Cunningham) and HMS *Valiant*.

The planning for Operation 'GA.3' was meticulous. Information on net defences was painstakingly gathered by air reconnaissance and from Italian agents ashore. Equipped with the latest intelligence information, the submarine *Scire* (*Capitano di Fregatta*[9] Junio Valerio Borghese), carrying three *Maiale* on her casing, quietly slipped out of La Spezia on 3 December. On 9 December she arrived at Leros, where the rumour was put about that she had been damaged at sea and had arrived for repairs. A few days after her arrival at Leros, an Italian flying boat delivered ten naval officers and ratings equally discreetly. These were the *Maiale* operators, flown in direct from Italy so that they would be fully rested and fresh for the operation. For the record, the names of the six were: *Tenente di Vascello* Luigi Durand de la Penne and *Capo Palombaro 1*[10] Emilio Bianchi (*SLC221*); *Capitano Genio Navale*[11] Antonio Marceglia and *Sottocapo Palombaro*[12] Spartaco Schergat (*SLC222*); and *Capitano Armi Navali*[13] Vincenzo Martellotta and *Sottocapo Palombaro* Mario Marino (*SLC223*).

At 2047 *Scire* came to the surface outside the harbour. The SLCs were hauled out of their containers and given a last check before being mounted by their riders. After a last exchange of good wishes, Borghese and the casing crew went below and *Scire* slowly submerged, allowing the SLCs to float free. They headed along the break-water towards the boom and prepared to cut their way through the net. However, as luck would have it, a number of shipping movements throughout the night of 18/19

December meant that the boom was opened on three occasions for non-essential traffic: between 2017 and 2031 to allow the entry of the tug *Roysterer* towing the sloop *Flamingo*; from 0040 to 0150 to allow the ships of the 7th Cruiser Squadron and 4th Destroyer Flotilla to enter; and from 0242 to 0315 to allow the 14th Destroyer Flotilla to enter harbour. As de la Penne and the others approached the boom they could hear men talking on the breakwater and watched while picket boats dropped 5lb scuttling charges. However, just after 0030 the navigation lights in the harbour were switched on to facilitate the entry of the cruiser squadron. The *Maiale* simply swept through the open boom: the British could not have made things easier.

De la Penne and Bianchi had selected the battleship *Valiant* as their target. They hauled their SLC over the anti-torpedo net surrounding the battleship and in so doing made a good deal of noise, but they were not discovered. During the run-in Bianchi, who was having trouble with his breathing set, was swept off the SLC and swam to a buoy, on to which he clambered to await events. Meanwhile de la Penne continued on alone and slowly came alongside the *Valiant*'s hull. But the SLC now sank beneath him in seventeen metres of water. He dived and located the SLC, but all attempts to restart the motor failed. In what can only be described as a feat of cold-blooded courage and endurance, de la Penne, working alone, in a suit that was leaking and amidst clouds of mud thrown up by his exertions, slowly hauled the SLC along the bottom. He had no idea of the direction in which he was going but he was guided by the noise of some of *Valiant*'s machinery which was running. He finally abandoned the SLC directly under the hull, where the noise was coming from. He lacked the strength to secure the warhead to the hull as he had been trained to do but simply left the device on the bottom with five feet of water between it and the *Valiant*'s hull. He set the fuse and then came to the surface, where he found himself on a level with the ship's 'B' turret. He then swam over and joined Bianchi on *Valiant*'s bow buoy. De la Penne could have made his escape, but, showing the spirit which underpinned *Decima Mas* operations, he was unwilling to abandon Bianchi and so joined him to await capture.

Meanwhile Marceglia and Schergat had laid their warhead under the *Queen Elizabeth*, making a textbook approach and attack. Martellotta and Marino had selected the tanker *Sagona*, which had the destroyer *Jervis* alongside. An apocryphal story holds that Martellotta brought his SLC alongside the quarterdeck ladder of the French battleship *Lorraine*[14] to ask for directions: the quartermaster obligingly pointed out both *Valiant* and *Queen Elizabeth*. Martellotta had other cargo in addition to his 600lb warhead: his SLC carried a number of incendiary bombs which it was intended to use to ignite any fuel spilled from the tanker in the explosion of the main charge. Both Marceglia/Schergat and Martellotta/Marino made their way ashore but were subsequently arrested. Martellotta and Marino were picked up fairly quickly, but the other pair managed to reach Rosetta before being captured. En route they were temporarily embarrassed by the lack of any local currency: the *Decima Mas* planners had given them nothing but Sterling. A British army officer kindly offered to help them change their money, not knowing that the two men he was assisting had just put paid to his chances of receiving bombardment support when he returned to the Western Desert!

But to return to de la Penne and Bianchi clinging to *Valiant*'s bow buoy. De la Penne had been spotted by a sentry on the ship, who raised the alarm. Harbour patrols were intensified and all ships were ordered to pass bottom lines along their hulls to dislodge any explosive devices. Unsurprisingly in *Valiant*'s case, the line failed to find anything since the charge was lying on the sea bed. By 0325 both men had been taken off by a launch and brought on board the battleship. Engineer-Lieutenant Louis le Bailly was Senior Engineer of the cruiser HMS *Naiad*:

> There would be no further sleep that night. As dawn broke our weary sailors rowed round the ship (the motor boat had been riddled with splinters) while our gunner dropped charges rather too close for the nerves of my dynamo watchkeepers.[15]

The two prisoners were briefly interrogated on *Valiant*'s quarterdeck and, after refusing to give any information away, were landed and transferred to military custody at Ras el Tin. During the boat trip to the shore, de la Penne warned the young midshipman in command of the picket boat that if he could find an excuse not to return to *Valiant* he should do so—a curious and rather honourable thing to do. After a brief and wholly ineffectual interrogation by Army officers both de la Penne and Bianchi were brought back to *Valiant* on the direct orders of Admiral Sir Andrew Cunningham, who had been made aware of events and who ordered that the two men be returned to the ship and confined below the waterline.[16]

Arriving back on *Valiant*'s quarterdeck, the two men were asked again about where they had left the charge by Captain Charles Morgan, *Valiant*'s commanding officer. On refusing to give any information, they were taken forward and separated. De la Penne was confined in the cable locker—as it happened, perilously close to where his warhead was lying. The fuse had been set for 0600 and when de la Penne calculated that there were ten minutes left, he asked to see Captain Morgan. He was taken up to the quarterdeck, where he told Morgan that there were but a few minutes left and that he should try to save his ship's company. Morgan was having none of it. When de la Penne once again refused to say where the charge had been laid, he was taken back down to the cable locker.

Morgan had so far refrained from alerting *Valiant*'s ship's company, the majority of whom were still sound asleep in their bunks and hammocks. Now, with minutes to go before the charge went off, the alarm was sounded. Midshipman Adrian Holloway was one of those asleep when the alarm went:

> I was suddenly shaken awake by John Cardew, who said urgently: 'Come on, hurry up and go on deck. The Italian underwater cyclists have arrived.' This was the somewhat

theatrical term which we used for enemy frogmen, and because he had used it I did not at first believe him. I did however believe the loudspeakers which were relaying the order, 'Close all X and Y doors', followed by the most unusual order in any ship, 'All hands on deck'. This means what it says: you leave whatever you are doing, wherever you are and you beat it hell for leather to the upper deck. Things must be serious. The time was 0555 . . . I had only just placed a foot on the ladder when there was a violent explosion from somewhere up forward. I was nearly thrown off the ladder. I arrived on the quarterdeck shaken, bewildered, but strangely not frightened.[17]

In the bleak surroundings of the cable locker, de la Penne remembered that

After a few minutes an explosion occurred. The ship was violently shaken. All the lights went out and the compartment was filled with smoke.[18]

De la Penne now found that his compartment was unguarded, so made his way up to the forecastle where *Valiant*'s Executive Officer, Commander Reid, was attempting to make some order out of chaos. It had been a difficult night and the sudden appearance of de la Penne, unannounced and unescorted, was the last straw for Reid. He curtly ordered de la Penne to be taken aft to the quarterdeck. Midshipman Holloway remembered that

I looked with fascinated interest at the enemy standing only feet away from me. He had discarded his submersible suit and was clad, like our own submariners, in dark blue naval uniform and roll neck pullover. He seemed to be very wet. A good looking man, I thought—now here before me, a prisoner, stands the man who has tried to kill me and everyone else on board *Valiant*. I did not feel, though, any animosity towards him, just curiosity and a hope that he had nothing else up his sleeve.[19]

In fact the charge under the *Sagona* had gone off first at 0558, indicating that Martellotta had done his work well, and this explosion was followed by the appearance of the calcium carbide incendiary devices, none of which ignited. *Sagona* was badly damaged, as was the destroyer *Jervis* lying alongside her. Lieutenant le Bailly, in *Naiad*, observed the course of events:

Soon after *Valiant* had settled, there was a horrendous thud and a vast pall of smoke billowed out from *Queen Elizabeth*'s funnel as the Fleet flagship took a heavy list to starboard.[20]

Admiral Cunningham remembered that

I felt a dull thud and was tossed about five feet into the air by the whip of the ship and was lucky not to come down sprawling. I saw a great cloud of black smoke shoot up the funnel and from immediately in front of it, and knew at once that the ship was badly damaged.[21]

The damage done to both ships was severe. In *Valiant* the charge exploded under the port bulge near 'A' turret. The explosion tore a hole 60ft by 30ft in the bulge. Internal damage was considerable. 'A' turret shell room and magazines were flooded and the revolving trunk for the turret was buckled. The ship was down by the bow and all ammunition and inessential stores had to be offloaded to ease the strain on the ship's structure. Nevertheless, in an emergency, *Valiant* could have sailed. Temporary repairs were effected in Alexandria, after which the ship sailed for Durban. Permanent repairs were completed in July 1942.

Queen Elizabeth was more seriously damaged. Marceglia suspended his charge beneath 'B' boiler room. The explosion blew in the double bottom structure in this area and damage extended under 'A', 'B' and 'X' boiler rooms and both bulges. The total area damaged covered nearly 11,000 square feet. 'A', 'B' and 'Y' boiler rooms flooded to main deck level and the ship settled on the harbour bottom. There was extensive damage to machinery and all hydraulic power was lost. After temporary repairs in the floating dock at Alexandria, *Queen Elizabeth* went to Norfolk, Virginia, for repairs. The battleship was out of action for nearly eighteen months.

As an interesting sideline to the attack, the British held an inquiry to determine just how the Italians had penetrated the harbour so easily. Rear-Admiral R. C. Creswell, in charge of port defences at Alexandria, had nobly offered himself as the scapegoat for the affair. Cunningham, however, remembered that he had repeatedly turned down Creswell's demands for more men and *matériel* for boom defence at Alexandria, describing the base and its staff as 'velvet-arsed'—a favourite phrase of 'ABC''s when referring to the non-seagoing elements of his command. Cunningham was a commander with a fighting reputation second to none. However, he exhibited a curious disinterest when it came to mundane matters such as boom defence. Now that the horse had bolted, Cunningham ensured that the stable door was well and truly shut. Creswell kept his job and the boom defences were considerably strengthened.

Physical damage aside, the strategic consequences were immense. Following so close on the torpedoing of HMS *Barham* by *U331* on 25 November, the immobilising of the two remaining British capital ships altered the balance of power overnight. There were now no British capital ships in the Eastern Mediterranean against an Italian force of five. Admiral Cunningham wrote to Admiral Sir Dudley Pound:[22] 'We are having shock after shock out here. The damage to the battleships at this time is a disaster.'[23] All this was the handiwork of six brave men. The crippling of the two battleships placed the Italians in a position of considerable advantage in the Mediterranean. It would not be untrue to say that the *Regia Marina* was in a state of undisputed command of the sea. The Malta Striking Force, Force K, which had been such a menace to Axis troop convoys, had been reduced to one cruiser after severe losses suffered in December 1941[24] and was subsequently disbanded. Although submarines and aircraft based in Malta continued to harry Axis convoys, they were not nearly as effective as Force K had been. At Alexandria the only sea-going forces were the four cruisers of Rear-Admiral Vian's 7th Cruiser Squadron, while at the other end of the Mediterranean all that remained of Force H was the elderly battleship

Malaya,[25] the ancient aircraft carrier *Argus* and the cruiser *Hermione*. The Royal Navy in Mediterranean had effectively been neutralised. The Axis had the sea to themselves and could have taken the opportunity to pour troops and supplies into North Africa.

The attack could not have come at a worse time for Britain. On every front the news was bad. In the Western Mediterranean, *Ark Royal* had been torpedoed on 13 November. The Japanese were advancing through Malaya, near where the battleships *Prince of Wales* and *Repulse* had been sunk by aircraft on 10 December. In the Atlantic shipping losses were mounting. The First Lord of the Admiralty, the Hon. A. V. Alexander, never spoke a truer word when he referred to the months of November and December 1941 as 'the crisis in our naval fortunes'.

Why, then, did the Italians not make more of the opportunity given them by *Decima Mas*? It is not correct to say that the Italians were unaware of the damage suffered and thus could not act upon it. The evidence was clear to their photographic interpreters who reviewed the results of a sortie flown on 20 December, results which were sent to *Scire* while still at sea. The photographs told their own story. One of the battleships was seen lying on the bottom surrounded by a large oil slick and with submarines alongside (the only reason for their presence was to supply electric power) while the other battleship was surrounded by an armada of harbour craft and stores of all kinds were being unloaded in an effort to lighten the ship.

One reason advanced by Admiral Gino Birindelli, a distinguished *Maiale* operator who was captured in an operation against Gibraltar, was that the operation had been kept too secret,[26] that knowledge of the operation was confined to a select few at *Supermarina* and the *Decima Mas* command. The attack was planned as a drastic blow against the Royal Navy without any thought as to how this fitted into the wider Axis plan of campaign. However, a more likely reason is that the Italian Navy lacked the muscle to make the most of the situation. Before the war the Italian government had made no effort to establish stocks of strategic materials such as oil, and thus when hostilities commenced the Italian economy and war effort was effectively hamstrung.

Nevertheless, Borghese was immensely heartened by the success of this attack and set out to repeat the performance. In May 1942, once new SLC crews had been trained, he sent the submarine *Ambra* (*Tenente di Vascello* Mario Arillo) back to Alexandria with three SLCs to repeat the operation and attack the *Queen Elizabeth* in dry dock and the submarine depot ship HMS *Medway*, the latter being one of the most valuable British naval units left in the Mediterranean in terms of the support she was able to offer to British submarines of the First Flotilla. Two of the SLCs, those piloted by *Guardiamarine*[27] Giovanni Magello and *Sotto Tenente Medicale*[28] Giorgio Spaccarelli, were to attack the floating dock containing the *Queen Elizabeth*; the third, piloted by *Tenente Genio Navale*[29] Luigi Feltrinelli, was to attack the *Medway*.

As in the earlier attack, all three SLCs carried calcium carbide bombs to ignite any fuel spilled in the harbour.

The attack took place on 14 May and, fortunately for the British, was a failure. Before *Ambra* surfaced to launch her SLCs, Arillo sent out three divers to carry out a reconnaissance. The divers left through the fore hatch and returned at 2025 with the 'All clear'. Seven minutes later *Ambra* came to the surface and in less than five minutes the SLCs were away. All three teams failed to find the harbour entrance, scuttled their craft and made their way ashore. Magello and Spaccarelli, with their divers, were captured. Feltrinelli and his Number 2, *Sottocapo Palombaro*[30] Luciano Favale, also had to ditch their SLC, having failed to find the harbour entrance. However, they managed to make their way into Alexandria and contacted Italian sympathisers who were able to shelter them. Their luck ran out on 29 June 1942 when they were finally picked up by the British police.

In his post-operational report, Arillo admitted that the SLCs had been released two miles to the west of the prearranged position owing to a pronounced westerly current. He also commented on the greatly increased defence measures in force, which, he considered, must have caused the SLC crews to waste time in avoiding patrol boats and searchlights—time which could not be made up in view of the hours of darkness available, the distance to be covered and the relatively slow speed of the craft. It was just as well from the Royal Navy's point of view: had Magello and Spaccarelli succeeded in leaving their two 300kg warheads under the floating dock, both battleship and dock would have been written off.

In August 1942 Borghese attempted one more operation in the Eastern Mediterranean. The *Scire* (*Capitano di Corvetta* Bruno Zelich) was ordered to carry eight assault frogmen to attack shipping in the port of Haifa in Palestine. With the deteriorating military situation in the Western Desert, this port had suddenly become extremely important to the British. *Scire* left La Spezia on 2 August and, after collecting the *Gamma* frogmen at Leros, headed for Haifa. The last signal received from her was on 9 August when Zelich reported that a periscope reconnaissance of the harbour revealed a surfeit of targets—transports, tankers, submarines and destroyers. This was the last heard from *Scire*. It was not until the end of hostilities that the Italians learned that she had been sunk on 10 August by depth charges and gunfire from the trawler *Islay* with the loss of the 48 officers and men of her crew together with the eight *Gamma* men and their three support crew. The loss of the *Scire* effectively meant the end of *Decima Mas* operations in the Eastern Mediterranean. With the collapse of Axis forces in the Western Desert following the British victory at El Alamein, the theatre lost much of its importance and attention shifts to Gibraltar at the western end of the Mediterranean, where *Decima Mas* had been waging a relentless campaign since the opening of hostilities.

Chapter 3

The Pillars of Hercules

A gentleman always shaves before going out in the morning. If we are to sink a British battleship today, let us make sure we are properly shaved.—Tenente di Vascello Gino Birindelli, on commencing Operation 'BG.2', October 1940.

At the other end of the Mediterranean lay the naval base and fortress of Gibraltar, the home for a significant portion of Britain's Mediterranean Fleet and for the famous Force H[1] which worked under the direct command of the Admiralty in the Western Mediterranean and Eastern Atlantic. Gibraltar was also an important convoy port, and the starting point for many convoys running eastwards to Malta and Alexandria. With such a range of targets within easy reach of the Boca di Serchio, it was inevitable that *Decima Mas* planners would turn their eyes westwards. For three years the *Decima Mas* waged an unremitting campaign against British shipping at Gibraltar. Lieutenant Frank Goldsworthy, a British diver and counter-intelligence officer at Gibraltar, later wrote:

> Such was the commencement of a three years' war fought out silently below the surface of the Bay of Gibraltar. At the cost of three men killed and three captured, Italian naval assault units sank or damaged fourteen Allied ships of a total tonnage of 73,000 ... Each one of its seven operations demanded of the attackers physical daring and endurance which would have won respect in any navy of the world.[2]

Initially the operations against Gibraltar enjoyed the same lack of success as those against Alexandria. The first, 'BG.1', mounted in September 1940 and involving three *Maiale* carried in the submarine *Scire*, was called off when air reconnaissance of Gibraltar revealed that the harbour was empty: the British Fleet had sailed and was engaged in Operation 'Menace', the rather fruitless attempt to persuade the French at Dakar to come over to the Allied cause. The failure of 'BG.1', coming so soon after the loss of the *Iride* and *Gondar*, caused a certain amount of discussion at the Boca di Serchio concerning the viability of this form of attack. *Tenente di Vascello* Gino Birindelli had been in charge of the *Maiale* aboard *Iride* and on *Scire*'s first trip to Gibraltar. He recalled that

> There was a sort of war council in our base at the Boca di Serchio, and our commander and ourselves, we got to the decision that we must make another try to see whether this concept of attacking enemy shipping in harbours could be carried out. The decision was taken that we would try one more attack against Gibraltar to have objective proof of the possibility of the *Maiale* to have a successful action or not.[3]

Accordingly, the submarine *Scire*, under the command of *Capitano di Fregata* J. V. Borghese, took three *Maiale* and their crews aboard. The *Maiale* crews were the most experienced available in *Decima Mas* and comprised *Tenente di Vascello* Gino Birindelli and *2o Capo Palombaro* Damos Paccagnini; *Capitano Genio Navale* Teseo Tesei and *Sergente Palombaro* Alcide Pedretti; and *Sottotenente di Vascello* Luigi de la Penne and *2o Capo Palombaro* Emilio Bianchi.

On 21 October the *Scire* left La Spezia and passed through the Straits of Gibraltar during the night of the 28th/29th. Borghese had decided to launch the *Maiale* from a position well inside the Bay of Algeciras and made the very difficult submerged passage up the Bay on the 29th, his voyage made relatively easy by the fact that navigational marks on the Spanish side had not been removed. Finally, at 0130 on 30 October *Scire* was in the right position at the mouth of the Guardarranque river. It was at this point that the final reconnaissance information was received from *Supermarina*. This contained the news that the battleship *Barham* and the battlecruiser *Renown*, together with other units, were in the harbour. Accordingly, *Barham* was assigned to Birindelli and *Renown* to Tesei, and de la Penne was given a roving brief to attack any target of opportunity. After the operation, the *Maiale* men would not return to *Scire*: instead they would make their way ashore, where Italian agents would be waiting for them. As Birindelli described it,

> We had an organisation by which if we were able to make an attack and reach the Spanish coast, two Italian agents would meet us and take us to Seville by car and then to Rome by air, so that the next morning at 1 o'clock we would be in the officers' club at La Spezia.[4]

Shortly after 0200 on 30 October *Scire* came briefly to the surface, the *Maiale* crews went out on to the casing and then the submarine dived. Tesei and de la Penne both abandoned the operation because of mechanical problems with their machines and their respirators. They ditched their *Maiale* and made their way ashore. The self-destruction charge on de la Penne's *Maiale* worked as designed, but Tesei's machine ended up on the beach at La Linea.

Meanwhile Birindelli and Paccagnini had started later than the others owing to it having been extremely difficult to remove their *Maiale* from the container on *Scire*'s casing:

> I had many, many troubles getting my *Maiale* out of the cylinder but when I got to the surface I found that de la Penne and Tesei were not there, for the simple reason that they had been waiting for me for the fifteen minutes they had said they would wait. So I was alone—Gibraltar in the distance. The trouble was that not only did I have difficulty in getting the *Maiale* out of the cylinder but the *Maiale* was not working properly because water had seeped into the battery compartment. The trim was difficult to realise and speed and endurance were very much reduced.[5]

Nevertheless, Birindelli went ahead with the operation:

I went over the booms and made the attack. Unhappily the *Maiale* either would stay on the surface or when I made the ballast full would head for the bottom. So until I got to the booms I was on the surface and I never was able to understand how it was that the sentries on the pier could not see us. I could see them [and] hear their voices. We went over the booms, the first set and then the second.

At this stage Paccagnini began having problems with his breathing set. He had no more oxygen left, having been 'submerged' even when the craft was on the surface, owing to the poor state of the trim. Birindelli was not giving up and ordered Paccagnini to abandon the craft and swim to the surface while he carried on alone:

I went to the bottom and started moving towards my target. At a certain moment I discovered that the *Maiale* was not moving. When I was about 60 metres away from the *Barham* I had lost any capacity of thinking clearly, my breathing was very quick and I was very tired. When I realised I was going to collapse, I set the timer and came to the surface. My big target was there but for me it was lost. So the only thing I could do was get out of the harbour.

I went over the pier at 7 o'clock and started walking towards the merchant harbour. There were soldiers and sailors looking at this strange human being but nobody told me anything. I could appreciate the sense of privacy that the British people show![6]

Birindelli managed to get aboard a small Spanish steamer but was seen doing so. The guard was summoned and he was taken off for interrogation. Birindelli attempted to tell his interrogator that he had spent the night in Gibraltar harbour having been dropped from a destroyer. His craft had become entangled with an uncharted wreck and he had had to abandon the operation. However, the British officer asked, 'You want me to believe that a man who has been going all night with a ship and shipwreck would be as fully shaved as you are at 7 in the morning?'[7]

His last shave on board the *Scire* was his undoing. Birindelli was destined for a PoW hospital, as was Paccagnini, who had also been picked up. Birindelli contracted tuberculosis as a result of his underwater activities and would not be fit for some time. However, he managed, by means of a coded phrase inserted into a letter, to let those at the Boca di Serchio know that the had penetrated the harbour and that the *Maiale* concept was viable.

Apart from proving that the *Maiale* concept worked, the operation was the first which involved the use of Spanish territory by the Italians, and over the next three years the Italians would operate regularly from bases in Spain with a complete disregard for Spanish neutrality. How much the Spanish authorities knew of these operations is difficult to fathom. It is clear that there was complicity on two levels. At the highest level of government it is apparent that the Spanish knew what was going on but were prepared to turn a blind eye so long as they were not openly embarrassed. After all, the Franco government had every reason to be grateful to the Italians, who had provided much in the way of assistance during the Spanish Civil War. On a local level, Spanish complicity was much greater. The Italian Consul in

Algeciras, G. Pistono, was extremely energetic in bribing local officials, with the result that he had virtually a free hand to operate. It was Pistono who organised the 'reception' for Tesei and de la Penne and who negotiated with the local *Guardia Civilia* (the paramilitary police force responsible for coastal defence) for that particular section of the beach to be left well alone on the night in question.

In May 1941 the operation was repeated with a new and subtle twist. The *Decima Mas* planners were always keen to ensure that the *Maiale* men were at the peak of their fitness when setting out on an operation. They viewed the long submarine passages from Gibraltar with disfavour on the grounds that the fetid atmosphere and cramped conditions in the submarine were not good preparation for underwater assault operations. Hence, as in the operations at Alexandria, the Italians always tried to send the *Maiale* men to the submarine at the last moment—usually by air or by surface ship. Neither of these means were possible in the case of Gibraltar, but a third way, which was almost ideal, presented itself. In the harbour at Cadiz lay the Italian tanker *Fulgor*, which had been interned on Italy's declaration of war. The *Maiale* men would travel overland to Cadiz and join the *Fulgor* disguised as members of her crew or representatives of the owner. The *Scire* would collect them at night from the *Fulgor* and proceed with the operation as before.

Fulgor was first used in Operation 'BG.3' in May 1941. *Scire* left La Spezia on 15 May with the *Maiale* embarked but not the operators, and after passing through the Straits of Gibraltar on the night of 22/23 May arrived at Cadiz on the 23rd when the six *Maiale* operators were embarked and their craft given one last check. On the 25th Borghese brought the *Scire* back into the Bay of Algeciras but this time the last-minute intelligence briefing from *Supermarina* revealed that there were no warships in the harbour. Instead the *Maiale* men were directed to attack merchant shipping lying in the roadstead.

Almost immediately the operation went awry. Despite a successful launching of the three *Maiale* at 2320 on the 25th, that ridden by *Tenente di Vascello* Amadeo Vesco and *Tenente Genio Navale* Antonio Marceglia broke down almost immediately. Accordingly, *Tenente di Vascello* Decio Catalano, who was the senior *Maiale* officer, directed that the *Maiale* be abandoned and the warhead transferred to that ridden by *Tenente di Vascello* Licio Visintini. Vesco would stay with Visintini as a

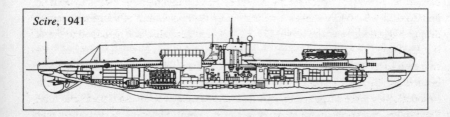

Scire, 1941

third helper, while Marceglia would stay with Catalano. Further disaster struck when Marceglia suddenly collapsed. Catalano and his Number 2, *Sottocapo Palombaro* Giovanni Giannoni, attempted to revive him (and eventually succeeded, despite being spotted by watchers on a merchant ship), but, in doing so, their *Maiale* slipped away and was lost. Giannoni attempted to dive after it but the water was too deep. Meanwhile Visintini, his Number 2 *Sottocapo Palombaro* Giovanni Magro and Vesco and found a target and were busily attaching both warheads to the hull. Misfortune struck for a third time that night when the cables securing the two warheads to the hull suddenly snapped and the *Maiale*, with both warheads still attached, sank to the bottom. The mission was a failure, although all six crewmen reached Spanish territory, where Pistono's excellent arrangements swiftly transported them back to Boca di Serchio. Yet the mission was not without benefit: the British had not been alerted to what had happened, so another attack could still take place, while using the *Fulgor* as an advanced base had proved extremely successful.

Licio Visintini was an officer destined to be intimately connected with operations at Gibraltar. He was one of the later entrants to the *Decima Mas*, and Borghese wrote of him that

> He was a young officer, highly trained professionally. Born and bred at Parenzo, near Trieste, he was brought up in the patriotic spirit typical of the Italian frontiers, where the inhabitants have had to struggle for centuries to preserve their independence and nationality. He spoke little but was always cheerful, loyal, courageous and cool in danger. A first-rate and experienced seamen, he displayed in his behaviour, during the course of this operation, exceptional gifts.[8]

On 19 September *Scire* was back in Algeciras Bay for Operation 'BG.4', having collected the *Maiale* men from the *Fulgor* at Cadiz. This time the last-minute reconnaissance indicated that there was a battleship, an aircraft carrier, two cruisers and a number of other warships in the inner harbour and a convoy of seventeen merchant ships in the roadstead. At 0100 on 20 September *Scire*'s crew went through the now familiar routine of launching the *Maiale*. The *Maiale* men were the same as those in the May operation.

The *Maiale* ridden by *Tenente di Vascello* Amadeo Vesco (with *Sc Palombaro* Antonio Zozzoli as Number 2, replacing Marceglia) had been ordered to attack the battleship. However, Vesco found the defences very much on the alert and both he and Zozzoli were badly shaken and bruised by the concussion of scuttling charges dropped at random into the water. By 0400, when Vesco had not managed to break into the inner harbour, he decided to attack one of the merchant ships instead. The two men successfully attached their warhead to the 2,444grt *Fiona Shell* and then headed for Spanish territory. As they climbed up the beach looking for their 'minder', they were surprised by two *Guardia Civilia*, who arrested them and took them to the detention centre at Algeciras at gunpoint. Pistono's organisation was equal to the occasion: a quiet word with a few officials and the passing of a substantial amount of pesetas ensured that Vesco and Zozzoli were quickly released.

Meanwhile Catalano and Giannoni had also found a target. They too had found it impossible to enter the inner harbour so went for a merchant ship lying outside. But by the light of the moon they could read the ship's name and see that she was Italian, though pressed into Allied service. In a curious and sentimental gesture, they removed their warhead, since they did not wish to sink an Italian ship, and found the 10,900grt *Durham* instead. Both men reached Spain and were spirited away by Pistono's organisation.

Lastly, what of Visintini and Magro? Visintini, a consummate professional, went straight through the harbour defences. But he had lost so much time in doing so that he would not be able to reach the southern end, where the capital ships were berthed, before day broke. Instead he selected a tanker, the 8,145grt *Denbydale*, and secured his warhead underneath her hull in a flawless attack. He and Magro then made their way out of the harbour, ditched their *Maiale* and swam ashore, where one of Pistono's men was waiting for them. 'BG.4' was an outstanding success: three ships were sunk and all six *Maiale* men were safely recovered.

The Italians now wished to intensify their operations against Gibraltar and wanted to make more use of the *Gamma* assault frogmen. The lax attitude of the local authorities, and Pistono's efforts in promoting this attitude, suggested that a base could be established on Spanish soil from which regular attacks could be made. In view of the fact that the passage of the Straits of Gibraltar was becoming increasingly hazardous, the establishment of a base in Spain would have many advantages, not the least of which was that operators and equipment could be smuggled in and out with relative impunity.

But how should such a base be established? Ingenuity was not something lacking at the Boca di Serchio and an answer was very quickly found. Antonio Ramognino, a *Decima Mas* officer, had a Spanish wife, Conchita. On the grounds that his wife was ill and had been recommended to live by the sea for the fresh air, Ramognino rented a small house, the Villa Carmela, at Punta Mayorga near La Linea. The villa enjoyed an unparalleled view over Gibraltar and the merchant ship anchorage. Moreover, it was but a short walk from the beach. A more perfect location could not be imagined.

Once the legal formalities had been completed and Ramognino and his wife had moved in, the first guests, in the shape of twelve *Gamma* swimmers, arrived. They had come to Spain via the Pyrenees or direct from Italy aboard the merchant ship *Mauro Croce*. All were sent to Cadiz under the guise of merchant seamen from the *Fulgor*. From Cadiz they made their way in ones and twos, so as not to attract suspicion, to the derelict tanker *Olterra*, which was lying at Algeciras, and from there to the Villa Carmela. On the night of 13/14 June 1942 the twelve swimmers, led by

Sottotenente di Vascello Agostino Straulino, made their way unobserved into the water and struck out towards the merchant ships anchored in the roadstead. Each man carried three of the suction-type limpet mines. It is extremely difficult to ascertain which *Gamma* man mined which ship as some of the devices failed to explode. However, four ships totalling 9,465grt were badly damaged: *Meta*, *Shuma*, *Empire Snipe* and *Baron Douglas*. All twelve men returned safely, but seven of them were intercepted by the *Guardia Civilia* while making their way up the beach. Once again Pistono got to work and the men were soon released, on condition that they made themselves 'available' to the Spanish authorities for questioning if necessary. We shall soon see just how hollow this restriction was.

Experience gained in Operations 'BG.3' and 'BG.4' had shown the usefulness of having an advanced base close to Gibraltar. *Tenente di Vascello* Licio Visintini wanted to take this idea one stage further and develop a fully operational *Maiale* and *Gamma* base overlooking Gibraltar harbour. For this purpose neither the *Fulgor* nor the Villa Carmela were suitable. The *Fulgor* lay too far away at Cadiz and, in any case, any attempt to move her nearer to Gibraltar would arouse the suspicion of the British. The Villa Carmela was suitable as a temporary holding point for *Gamma* men but could not be used regularly for operations and it would be out of the question to employ *Maiale* from there. Such a course of action would stretch the patience of the Spanish authorities too far.

Instead, Visintini focused on the Italian tanker *Olterra* lying at Algeciras. *Olterra* had been scuttled by her Italian crew on the outbreak of war but had been refloated by the Spanish and secured inside the breakwater at Algeciras. A guard consisting of a corporal and four privates of the *Guardia Civilia* was placed on the ship to prevent any unauthorised personnel from boarding her. In March 1941 members of the *Olterra*'s original crew, including Paolo Dénegri, the Chief Engineer, re-boarded the ship to act as a care and maintenance party. The Italians were provided with special passes allowing them to do so.[9]

Visintini arrived on board *Olterra* on 27 June 1942 with civilian papers identifying him as Lino Valeri, the prospective First Officer of the ship. He brought three technicians with him and also a medical technician. These four men were to become the core of the *Olterra*'s *Decima Mas* detachment and would remain on the ship until operations ceased in September 1943. Visintini lost no time in getting to work. Four members of the *Olterra*'s mercantile crew were transferred to another ship on the grounds that they were indiscreet. At the same time Visintini banned the Spanish guards from visiting the forward part of the ship on the grounds that he suspected them of stealing food. The four 'technicians' fulfilled a number of roles. Preparing the *Maiale* was their most important function, together with acting as 'dressers' for the *Gamma* men, but they also undertook a number of other duties, including daytime reconnaissance of shipping in Gibraltar (they were often spotted by British agents doing this) and acting as enforcers to keep away any curious Spaniards. On one occasion a local fisherman appeared on the beach just as the three *Gamma* men were entering the water for operation 'GG.2' on 14 September 1943. The technicians first tried to bribe the man with 1,000 pesetas, but when he refused to take the money he was given a severe beating.[10]

With the unreliable elements of the crew dismissed and the Spanish guard confined to the stern, Visintini briefed those remaining on *Olterra*'s new role. She would be a base for *Maiale* operations against Gibraltar. In order to facilitate the operation of the *Maiale* a forward bulkhead was cut and hinged to give access to the forepeak. Torpedo racks were manufactured ashore in Algeciras and assembled in the forepeak. Finally the tanker was trimmed down by the stern to allow the cutting of a hinged trapdoor measuring 5ft by 8ft in the hull. The cutting took about two hours, after which the trim was returned to normal so that opening was concealed below the waterline. The cutting party was hidden by pontoons moored alongside for painting and minor repairs to the ship's hull. Cables for charging batteries were brought from the dynamos at the stern concealed inside water pipes.

The *Maiale* arrived in Algeciras by road direct from Italy. They were broken down into their component parts and packed into wooden crates, together with mines, Belloni suits, clamps, oxygen cylinders and all the other equipment needed for *Maiale* operations. Some of the crates were labelled as engineering spares and at least one box was filled with boiler tubes and left with one end opened for the benefit of the curious. Other material was collected by Denegri from the Italian Embassy in Madrid, where it had been sent by diplomatic courier. On another occasion a member of *Olterra*'s crew was granted compassionate leave to return to Italy. On his return he brought a crate of limpet mines with him. The arrival of such a large amount of equipment officially destined for a derelict tanker did not arouse the slightest suspicion or concern among the Spanish authorities.

While all these preparations were in hand the *Gamma* attacks were continuing from the Villa Carmela. Two *Gamma* frogmen arrived in Barcelona disguised as merchant seamen in the ship *Mario Croce*. At Barcelona the three 'deserted' but were picked up by Italian agents and taken on board *Olterra*. On the evening of 14 September, carrying their suits and mines, they went ashore to the Villa Carmela where they were joined by three of the seven *Gamma* men who had participated in Operation 'GG.1'. These gentlemen were, in theory, still 'helping the Spanish authorities with their enquiries' but the Spanish had no objection to their place being taken by three seamen from the *Fulgor*. However, once the Italians were installed in the Villa Carmela it was decided that only three men should go, that being the number of ships in the Bay. The three, who, again, had all taken part in 'GG.1', were: *Tenente di Vascello* Augostino Straulino, *Palombaro Sommozzattore* Bruno di Lorenzo and *Sottocapo* Vago Giari.

The men entered the water shortly after 2330 on the 14th but found that the ships were moored further away from the Spanish coast than on the earlier operation. The British were taking few chances: all merchant shipping was now concentrated at the eastern end of the bay in front of the military harbour. For this reason, and because of a stronger than usual current, Straulino returned without having planted a mine. Giari and Lorenzo returned, having, as it turned out, mined the same ship. Unfortunately, whereas Giari managed to regain the Villa Carmela undetected, Lorenzo came up the beach into the arms of a waiting *Guardia Civilia* and was detained. His detention was short, for the authorities took him back to the Villa Carmela by car. A British agent for the SIS[11] heard from a fisherman, who watched Lorenzo come ashore. According to his report,

> . . . a fisherman called Gangoso . . . happened to see one of the shallow divers emerge from the sea on the morning of the previous day [15 September] and get into a military car, no. ET.3829, and was overheard talking of his experience by carabinieres at Puente Mayorga. They caught him (Gangoso) and gave him a good hiding so that he would learn to keep his mouth shut. Yet another reliable source reports that a shallow diver come out of the sea . . . near Puente Mayorga on the morning of 15 September and approach a carabiniere with whom he had a short conversation. The carabiniere seemed to be directing him. The shallow diver set off at a run towards the Puente Mayorga crossroads.[12]

Next morning revealed that the 1,787grt *Ravenspoint* was down by the stern, and, in front of the gleeful *Gamma* men, she eventually sank at her moorings.

By December 1942 all was ready on board *Olterra* for the first *Maiale* attack. The craft had been assembled and tested exhaustively. Visintini was keeping a tight watch on Gibraltar using, according to Borghese, a pair of high-magnification binoculars stolen from the British Consulate in Algeciras. The operation was planned for 6 December but that afternoon Visintini was encouraged when he saw a powerful British squadron consisting of the battleship *Nelson* and the aircraft carriers *Formidable* and *Furious* enter the harbour. With such prizes within his reach, Visintini took the decision to postpone the operation for twenty-four hours in order to give the *Maiale* one last check-over.

At 2330 on 7 December the three *Maiale* nosed their way out of the underwater trap door in *Olterra*'s bow and headed towards Gibraltar. They were crewed by *Tenente di Vascello* Licio Visintini and *Sergente Palombaro* Giovanni Magro (who would attack the *Nelson*), *Tenente* Girolamo Manisco and *Sottocapo Palombaro* Dino Varini (who would attack *Formidable*) and *Sottotenente* Vittorio Cella and *Sergente* Salvatore Leone, who would attack *Furious*. Visintini kept a detailed diary of his activities aboard *Olterra* during this period. The last entry reads:

> I believe I have made provision for every eventuality. At any rate my conscience is perfectly clear because I know that I have dedicated the whole of my being to the

success of this operation. Before I leave I shall pray to God that He may crown our labours with the award of victory and that He may protect with His gracious favour Italy and my bereaved family. Viva l'Italia.[13]

From the three *Maiale* only Cella returned. He and Leone found the defences to be strong and very alert. The two men spent most of the night dodging patrol boats which were dropping a considerable number of scuttling charges into the harbour. Eventually Cella decided to give up: day was breaking and his oxygen was running low. Moreover, he was stiff and bruised from the concussion of exploding underwater charges. Alas, when he reached the *Olterra* he found that during the night's manoeuvrings Leone had fallen off the *Maiale* and had been lost. Manisco and Varini pressed on through the patrols and reached the Detached Mole, where they were spotted by a sentry and fired on. Pursued by a number of motor launches, Manisco took the unselfish decision to head out to sea in the hope that the patrols would follow him, thereby making things a little easier for the other two *Maiale*. Eventually, after being chased, fired on and nearly stunned by scuttling charges, the two men sank their SLC and climbed aboard an American merchant ship, where they received an enthusiastic welcome from some Italian-American members of the crew. Manisco and Varini eventually ended up in a PoW camp, but the former's involvement in underwater operations was not yet finished. Both men refused to give anything away under interrogation by British naval intelligence. Eventually, after a good deal of bother, Manisco was persuaded to admit that he had come from the submarine *Ambra* which had released the *Maiale* in Algeciras Bay. This admission, made after such a long interrogation, satisfied his questioners sufficiently. The *Olterra*'s secret was safe.

What of Visintini and Magro? Visintini reached the boom, actually penetrated the inner harbour and was about to select his target when his *Maiale* was spotted. Caught in a searchlight, the little craft was sunk by a barrage of gunfire and scuttling charges. A few days later the bodies of Visintini and Magro were recovered by the British. Both men were buried at sea with full naval honours, among which was a wreath contributed by the men of the Gibraltar Underwater Working Party. The latter organisation had been established in response to the Italians' activities and was responsible for searching ships' hulls for explosives. The unit was commanded by Lieutenant Lionel 'Buster' Crabbe.

The Italians were not discouraged by the result of this operation. Although only one man and one *Maiale* returned, the concept of using *Olterra* as a forward base had been proved sound. So, during the first three months of 1943, two more *Maiale* arrived from Italy along with three full-charge warheads and six half-charge, 150kg warheads. A consignment of twenty clamp mines also arrived from the Italian Embassy in Madrid. Before the end of April *Capitano di Corvetta* Ernesto Notari arrived to take command following the death of Visintini, swiftly followed by three

Maiale crews. Notari had flown into Spain disguised as an employee of the Italian civil airline while the *Maiale* men were smuggled in through Irun on Spain's Atlantic coast, whence they were taken to Algeciras.

Notari had a more relaxed attitude to security than Visintini for he allowed the *Maiale* men to come up on *Olterra*'s deck during the day—something which Visintini had never permitted. Furthermore, he allowed the *Maiale* crews to test their craft in Algeciras Bay on 6 May. This was in preparation for Operation 'BG.6', launched on the night of 7/8 May. Three *Maiale* were involved, crewed by Notari with *Sc Palombaro* Ario Lazzari as his Number 2; *Tenente Genio Navale* Camillo Tadini with *Sc Palombaro* Salvatore Mattera; and *Sottotenente AN* Vittorio Cella with *Sc Palombaro* Eusebio Montalenti.

This attack was a complete success. All three *Maiale* were back inside *Olterra* by 0415 on 8 May, having left their charges secured to three merchant ships in the harbour. Further to deceive the British, Italian agents acting on Pistono's orders scattered odd items of diving equipment liberally around the beach at Algeciras. The *Maiale* men were returned to Italy as quickly as possible by the same route they had come. Although on this occasion the *Maiale* were each fitted with two 150kg charges, the operators appear to have left both charges on the one ship. The results of this attack were impressive: three ships totalling 19,000 tons were damaged: the *Pat Harrison* (7,191grt), the *Mahsud* (7,540grt) and the *Camerata* (4,875grt). P. J. Jackson was the *Mahsud*'s Second Officer:

> During my watch on the night of 7/8 May 1943 I saw and heard nothing suspicious although of course it was impossible to hear or see anything under the water. We had not run a wire along the bottom of the ship to see if any mines had been attached because nothing of the kind had occurred for a very long time and we were inclined to regard this precaution as a little unnecessary. Throughout the night we could hear patrolling motor launches dropping depth charges from time to time and we were confident that adequate steps were being taken against underwater attack. Next morning, however, at 0610, while anchored in 34 fathoms, the ship was damaged by the explosion of a sabotage mine. I was sleeping in my room when I heard a violent explosion which sounded like a colossal rumble of thunder. I was thrown to my knees; the Chief Engineer was thrown out of his bunk. Everything movable was scattered about my room. I rushed up on deck, where I discovered that the explosion had taken place under the centre of No 4 hold. The ship settled immediately by the stern with a slight list to port and appeared likely to sink rapidly.[14]

Encouraged by this operation, Notari began plans for another. He returned to *Olterra* at the end of July with the same team as had participated in Operation 'BG.6' except that *Sottocapo Palombaro* Andrea Gianoli replaced Lazzari as his Number 2.

The last *Maiale* operation took place on the night of 3/4 August. Cella and Montalenti placed their mine under the 9,444grt tanker *Thorshovdi* while Tadini and Matera attacked the 5,975grt *Stanridge*. Notari and Gianoli attacked the 7,176grt

Harrison Grey Otis but their attack was marred by the loss of Gianoli. The two men found a new hazard hanging beneath the ship—razor wire. Nevertheless, Notari manoeuvred the *Maiale* beneath the hull while Gianoli prepared to secure the warhead. Having secured the clamp to the port bilge keel, however, Gianole dropped the second clamp so that the warhead was hanging from the port bilge keel by one line. Just then Notari started to lose control of the *Maiale*, which started to rise. He opened the valve to the quick-diving tank but did so too rapidly. The *Maiale* sank like a stone down to 34 metres—three times its test depth—before rushing to the surface. When he reached the surface he was amazed that he was not spotted but found that Gianoli had disappeared. The latter had come to the surface on the other side of the ship and was eventually picked up and taken ashore. All three ships were damaged when the mines exploded, and all had to be beached. A member of the Gibraltar Underwater Working Party had a lucky escape: as he was about to enter the water to inspect the hull of the *Harrison Grey Otis* the mine exploded beneath him.

The success of this attack encouraged Notari to work towards what would be the biggest attack yet on Gibraltar. He planned to secure two *Maiale* beneath the hull of the water carrier *Blossom*, which made the daily journey from Gibraltar to Algeciras and back. *Gamma* men went under *Blossom*'s hull and found that it was possible to secure the *Maiale* via clamps attached to the ship's bilge keels. Since *Blossom*'s speed far exceeded that of a *Maiale*, special shields would be provided to protect the operators during the journey. The plan was elegant in its simplicity: *Blossom* would carry the *Maiale* into Gibraltar harbour, thereby surmounting the problem of getting them through the boom. At the same time the *Decima Mas* planners at Boca di Serchio were working on a more inventive scheme. The submarine *Murena* would release three MTR assault boats which would attack shipping in the Bay. In the confusion resulting from this attack, a number of SSBs (improved versions of the SLC) would penetrate the harbour and attack the warships secured there. Both of these plans were audacious and would have undoubtedly given the British a good deal of trouble. However, the announcement of the Italian armistice on 8 September caused the cancellation of all such plans.

The net had been closing in on *Olterra* and her secret activities for some time. Colonel Medlam, the Defence Security Officer at Gibraltar, had been spending a good deal of money in Spain trying to obtain intelligence on where the attacks were being launched from. His efforts produced a good deal of random information but nothing that was conclusive. The Villa Carmela was definitely suspected. In May 1943 Lieutenant W. Baily, one of the Gibraltar Underwater Working Party, made a covert reconnaissance around Punta Mayorga and spoke to a number of agents who confirmed that the Villa Carmela was where the attacks were launched from. The finger of suspicion continued to wander over the *Olterra*. On 26 August 1943 Medlam wrote: 'The possibility that the attacks may be launched from the tanker and not from the foreshore is one that we have often considered.'[15] Lieutenant Frank Goldsworthy, an intelligence officer at Gibraltar, later recalled that Crabbe was convinced that *Olterra* was the source of the attacks. He proposed that the Gibraltar Underwater Working Party give the Italians a little of their own medicine and mine the *Olterra*. According to Goldsworthy, the proposal went as far as the War Cabinet, where it was rejected on the grounds that such an action would infringe Spanish neutrality![16]

As a last resort, Medlam established beach patrols between Algeciras and La Linea and other watchers were placed on Spanish fishing boats operating close inshore at night. If any of these watchers saw anything suspicious such as a frogman or an 'infernal machine' (as Medlam referred to the *Maiale*), they were to signal to the motor launch patrol using four long flashes sent by an electric light supplied for the purpose. At the same time Medlam recruited more agents to watch known Italian sympathisers ashore and the SIS set about intercepting signals sent from the Italian Consulate in Algeciras to their embassy in Madrid.

In the event, the armistice solved the problem for the British: by August 1943 the Spanish government realised that an Axis victory was a remote possibility and decided to assert its country's neutrality. On 5 August 1943, just after Notari and the others had left for Italy, *Olterra* was boarded by a Spanish naval officer who imposed a strict quarantine on all those on board: no one was to leave the ship. On 15 August the Spanish ordered all the crew to leave except for Amoretti, the Master, who had married locally, and Denegri. The *Guardia Civilia* detachment on board the ship was replaced by a Spanish naval party. On 22 September the Spanish naval officer returned and told Denegri that all traces of *Olterra*'s role as a *Maiale* base were to be destroyed and that these instructions came from the highest authority in Madrid. In order to speed up the work, the Italians conscripted two *Gamma* men who had been based at Huelva (their activities are recounted elsewhere in this book) and a working party from the destroyer *Ugolino Vivaldi*, which had been interned at Cartagena. However, the Spanish were unhappy with the speed of the work, whereupon Pistono left for Madrid and talks with the Italian Embassy. Pistono argued that the local Spanish authorities in Algeciras were losing their heads. If they handed over the *Olterra* intact to the British, the latter could not fail to be convinced by the ingenuity of the arrangements and think that the Spanish had nothing to do with the affair. This argument was accepted. Demolition work stopped on the *Olterra* almost immediately. However, this deception was rendered useless by Denegri's decision to tell the full and unexpurgated story to the British Vice-Consul at Algeciras. On 11 October 1943 *Olterra* was towed out of Algeciras and moored in the commercial harbour at Gibraltar, where her secrets were revealed. As Goldsworthy recalled,

Of course there was then a big inquest as to why we had not discovered the truth sooner. I went through all the agents' reports but, apart from one concerning the arrival of the boiler tubing, there was nothing to link *Olterra* with the attacks. The secret had been well kept.[16]

Decima Mas operations at Gibraltar had been a most successful campaign. Though the operations lacked the overwhelming success achieved at Alexandria, their presence had exerted a continual pressure on the British for nearly three years. Moreover, the use of the Villa Carmela and *Olterra* (while displaying a complete contempt for Spanish neutrality) demonstrated a determination to lose no opportunity in taking the war to the enemy.

Chapter 4

From the Black Sea to the Hudson River

Worthy upholders of the traditions of the assault unit of the Italian Navy—Commander Ernesto Forza, on *Decima Mas* personnel who participated in the Anglo-Italian attack on La Spezia.

After operations against Alexandria and Gibraltar, the *Decima Mas* planners turned their attention to the island of Malta. Malta was a thorn in the side of the Axis. Ships, submarines and aircraft based on the island were taking a significant toll of shipping supplying the Axis armies in North Africa. A plan was drawn up by Commander Vittorio Moccagatta, the commanding officer of *Decima Mas*, for an attack on the harbour of Valletta using MT-type explosive motor boats (this type of craft had already been successfully used in an attack on the British cruiser HMS *York* at Suda Bay on 26 March 1941).

The MT (*Motoscafo Turismo*) boat was a carvel-built, mahogany craft measuring 5.62m by 1.65m by 0.4m and powered by a 6-cylinder, 95hp Alfa Romeo engine which could drive the boat at a top speed of 33kt for a distance of eighty miles. The engine was connected to a one-piece combined rudder/propeller unit mounted on the stern, rather similar to an outboard motor fitting. The single operator sat at the stern on a wooden seat fitted with a back rest which could be ejected from the craft at the pull of a lever. The operator aimed the craft at the target, locked the steering and threw himself overboard on his seat when about 100m from the target. When the craft hit the target a cushioned fender round the bow of the boat split the craft in two. The 330kg Tritolital explosive charge was fitted with a hydrostatic fuse (although an impact setting was also available): when the charge reached its preset depth it exploded. The operator protected himself from the blast by getting on top of his wooden seat.

The entrance to Valletta was well defended. The passage across the mouth of the harbour between Fort St Elmo and Fort Ricasoli was protected by a boom swung from the two breakwaters. The breakwater on the Ricasoli side was constructed from rubble but that on the St Elmo had a 70m gap in it for the passage of small boats. This gap was spanned by a steel bridge supported by one brick pillar. The gap in the St Elmo bridge was protected a stout, steel torpedo net which was hung from the bridge and descended to the harbour bottom.

At first there was no role for the *Maiale* in the attack. Breaking through the net on the St Elmo bridge seemed the easiest way to enter the harbour. The plan was, therefore, for the first MT boat to blast through the net to make a passage for the others. However, Major Teseo Tesei, one of the pioneers of the *Maiale*, argued that using a *Maiale* to hole the net would be far better since the craft could approach the net undetected, lay her charge and make her escape. Despite some opposition, Tesei's plan was adopted. Meanwhile a second *Maiale* would make for the submarine base in nearby Manoel Creek and leave the charge beneath a trot of British submarines secured there. It was felt that, since the British rafted their submarines alongside one another, one 300kg charge would be sufficient for all of them.

The *Maiale* were crewed by Major Teseo Tesei, one of the pioneers of this sort of warfare, with *2o Capo Palombaro* Alcide Pedretti as his assistant. The second SLC was crewed by *Tenente di Vascello* Franco Costa with *Sergente Palombaro* Luigi Barla. Frankly Tesei was unfit for the operation. Years of diving under hazardous conditions had weakened his heart and lungs to a considerable degree. However, he persisted, and, despite being banned from diving by the *Decima Mas*' medical officer, succeeded in persuading Moccagatta to include him. Tesei's spirit was such that no amount of medical advice would deter him from what he considered his duty.

After two false starts the operation was set for the night of 27 July 1941 when the lack of a moon offered good concealment. At 2300 on 25 July the attack force, which consisted of the sloop *Diana* carrying nine MT explosive motor boats, an MTL boat carrying the two *Maiale* in davits, *MAS451* and *MAS452* and one MTS command boat, hove-to in sight of the island. Almost immediately there were problems when Costa's SLC was found to be defective. Tesei spent nearly an hour trying to fix the craft and in the end ordered Costa to return to the MTL and sink the SLC.

The Italians believed that the darkness would shield them from the eyes of lookouts ashore, but, unfortunately for the attackers, the defences of Malta were equipped with the all-seeing eye of radar. By cruel luck on the night of 25/26 July temperature inversion made the radar waves curve slightly over the horizon, thus giving a longer range, and as early as 2230 on the 25th No 502 RAF Radar Station had detected a strong echo 72km north-east of Malta. *Diana* was tracked on her inward journey and the defences were stood to. At about 2300 the echo was seen to move back to the north-east, leaving behind a small indeterminate echo which then faded. The retreating echo was *Diana* moving off after leaving the MT boats, which produced the indeterminate echo. By themselves they were too small to give a good radar return, but grouped together they would produce an echo of the kind observed. As the boats slowly drifted apart this echo, too, would have faded away. The guns' crews were stood down but told to remain at their posts.

Tesei set off around 0300: nothing more was heard from him. Out to sea the MT boats were waiting for the explosion which would tell them that the net had been destroyed. By 0430 no explosion had been heard and Giobbe, the MT force commander, gave the order for Frasetto and Carabelli to use their MT boats to blow up the net. Shortly after 0445 the two boats made their attack. Frasetto threw himself overboard when 50m from the net but his MT boat was not going fast enough to break up the boat and detonate the charge. Carabelli observed what had happened, set his fuse to 'impact' and steered his boat directly into the net. Carabelli did not abandon his craft and was blown up with his boat, the explosion of which also set off the charge in Frasetto's boat. The double explosion more than brought down the net: the right-hand span of the bridge collapsed into the water, blocking the entrance far more effectively than any net.

The defences were now on the *qui vive*. The MT boats ran into a hail of gunfire and all but two were sunk. When Giobbe heard the gunfire he realised that the worst had happened and gave the order to retire. Day broke on the 26th to find the survivors harried by aircraft. Both MAS boats, the MTL carrier boat and the MTS command boat were sunk by RAF aircraft. Most importantly, the entire command of *Decima Mas* had been killed in *MAS452*. What had happened to the SLCs?

Nothing more was heard from Tesei. After the attack a mask similar to that worn by *Maiale* crews was found near the St Elmo bridge with human flesh and hair attached, so it seems reasonable to suppose that Tesei reached his target. One theory is that Tesei and his Number 2 were killed in the double MT boat explosion. After the explosion of Carabelli's boat, Sergeant Zammit, in St Elmo's Fort, saw a small object running awash towards the bridge. He fired one round at a range of 300 yards with his 6pdr gun and the object exploded. This was probably Tesei's *Maiale*. Tesei would have been about one hour behind schedule, having tried to mend Costa's *Maiale*, and because of an offshore westerly current his *Maiale* would have ben taken further out to sea. Either way Tesei died as he would have wished—at sea and in the service of his country. There is a suspicion that he had a premonition that he would be killed in this operation. A latter dated 17 July to a friend concluded that

> By the time you receive this letter I shall have attained the highest of all honours, that
> of giving my life for the King and the honour of the Flag. As you know, this is the
> supreme desire of the soldier and the most sublime joy he can experience . . . [1].

However, his death, along with that of Moccagatta and Giobe, was a grievous loss to the *Decima Mas*. Moccagatta was succeeded in command of the *Decima Mas* by *Capitano di Fregatta* Forza, while Borghese took over command of the underwater division.

The Anglo-American landings in Algiers in November 1942 offered further opportunities to the *Decima Mas*. Air reconnaissance of the port of Algiers showed a massive concentration of naval and merchant shipping. It was, therefore, decided to send the submarine *Ambra*, the sole surviving *Maiale* carrier, to Algiers with three *Maiale* embarked together with ten *Gamma* assault frogmen. Merchant ships were the main target for this operation and therefore the explosive charges carried by the

Maiale would not need to be so large. Accordingly the 300kg warhead was modified to become two 150kg charges.

Ambra, still under the command of *Capitano di Corvetta* Mario Arillo, left La Spezia on 4 December. The *Maiale* crews were Giorgio Badesi, Carlo Pesel, Guido Arena, Ferdinando Cocchi, Midshipman Giorgio Reggioli and Colombo Pamolli; a reserve crew consisted of Augusto Jacobacci and Amando Battaglia. Jacobacci had another role in this operation—to act as a guide for the frogmen. He would leave the submarine via the escape hatch and swim up to the surface. He was equipped with a telephone, connected to the submarine by a waterproofed cable, and would report on the location of targets before the frogmen emerged so that the submarine could be placed in the most advantageous position. This was a new development for the *Decima Mas* and obviously reflected the difficulties experienced by the frogmen in locating targets. The 'guide' was also to assist the *Gamma* and *Maiale* men in regaining the submarine after the operation.

The operational plan was for the *Gamma* men to attack shipping in the outer harbour while the three *Maiale* would press on into the inner harbour. *Ambra* would wait until 0200 on 12 December for the *Maiale* and *Gamma* men to return before beginning the trip back to La Spezia.

By the evening of 11 December *Ambra* was approaching the outer harbour at Algiers and Jacobacci was sent up to the surface. He reported that the submarine had still some way to go, so *Ambra* moved off at slow speed, taking Jacobacci with her. At 2145 Jacobacci reported that the submarine was nicely positioned in a group of six merchant ships. The first *Gamma* man left the submarine at 2230 and by 2300 all ten were out. They were followed by the three *Maiale* crews. Jacobacci now returned to the submarine, but shortly after 0230 on the 12th he returned to the surface to guide the swimmers back. It was now long past the time by which *Ambra* should have retired, but since the assault teams had left the submarine late owing to difficulties in getting into their equipment, Arillo had decided to stay longer. When he got to the surface Jacobacci could hear some of the *Gamma* men calling for him, but he was unable to make contact with them. Reluctantly he returned to the submarine and at 0300 *Ambra* headed for home, arriving back at La Spezia on 15 December.

Badessi and Pesel found they had a faulty *Maiale* and were unable to carry out their attack. Badessi then tried to locate Jacobacci but failed. Instead, he and Pesel headed for the shore, collecting Lugano on the way. Lugano was exhausted, having failed to find a target. On making their way up the beach all three men were promptly arrested by a French patrol. Arena and Cocchi had better luck, despite Arena's feeling extremely nauseous. Each *Maiale* crew had been assigned two targets in order to place the two warheads carried by each craft. During his approach run Arena heard, and felt, depth-charge explosions together with engine noises from fast motor boats. He nevertheless decided to proceed with the operation, but he placed his charges under one ship. Like Badessi, Arena could not find Jacobacci, so he headed for the shore together with the *Gamma* men Luciani and Ghiglione. These two men had not found targets and each was still carrying his limpet mine. The four men were arrested by Scottish troops almost as soon as they struggled up the beach.

The last *Maiale* team, Reggioli and Pamolli, carried out a text-book attack. Reggioli laid his first charge under a 9,000 tanker—the ship had no bilge keels, so the charge was left on the bottom—and his second charge was secured to a freighter. While looking for Jacobacci he was picked out by a searchlight and had a few bursts of machine gun fire sent in his direction, although without effect. However, like the other two *Maiale* teams, Reggioli could not find Jacobacci, so he was obliged to swim to the shore. He and Pamolli were temporarily incarcerated in the depot ship HMS *Maidstone* before being taken to a prisoner-of-war camp. While he was cooling his heels aboard *Maidstone* Reggioli had the satisfaction of hearing his charges explode:

> The explosions began at 5 and continued until 7 o'clock. From the place where we were we could see nothing owing to the darkness and a light sea mist. The same day, from aboard the auxiliary cruiser *Maidstone* to which we had been taken, we noticed near the entrance to the harbour a certain amount of wreckage at the point where we had attacked the first ship, and while we were on the road from Algiers to Camp 203 we saw the motorship which we had attacked [No 59, flying the flag of the United States] stranded on the beach with her stern carried away.[2]

As to the *Gamma* men, Morello, Botti and Feroldi all placed their mines on one ship, as did Rolfini, Evangelisti and Boscolo. Lucchetti was unfortunate to be captured and taken aboard the very ship which Morello had just mined. Luciani, Lugano and Ghiglione all became exhausted while trying to find a target and were brought ashore by the *Maiale* men. All the *Gamma* swimmers were captured.

Obviously the Italians had no idea of the identity of the ships they were attacking so it is extremely difficult to ascribe a shipping loss to a particular team. The results of the night's work were that four merchant ships were badly damaged—*Ocean Vanquisher* (7,174 tons), *Berto* (1,493 tons), *Empire Centaur* (7,041 tons) and *Harmattan* (4,558 tons). Four ships damaged was not a particularly significant result for an operation involving three *Maiale* and ten *Gamma* frogmen.

One controversial area of *Decima Mas* operations was selected strikes on Allied merchant shipping using bases covertly established in Portugal, Spain and Turkey, thereby showing a blithe disregard for the neutrality of these countries. Such bases were established at Huelva, Malaga, Barcelona, Lisbon and Oporto. Each base was usually established in an interned Italian merchant vessel, as in the case of the *Olterra* at Algeciras. *Gamma* men worked from the ship to plant mines on British merchant vessels. One such base, that at Huelva, was set up on board the *Gaeta* and a number of ships were attacked. It is not recorded whether any ships were lost to these ventures, but, following the attacks at Gibraltar, the British implemented a rigorous system of hull examination for any ship arriving from a Spanish destination. The attitude of the Spanish government to the activities of the *Decima Mas* has already been discussed, but Turkey and Portugal were a different matter.

The most outstanding example of this sort of activity took place at the eastern end of the Mediterranean at the ports of Alexandretta and Mersina, where British ships loaded cargoes of chromium, an important strategic commodity. The attention of the *Decima Mas* planners was drawn to Alexandretta by *Tenente* Giovanni Roccardi, a naval intelligence officer working at that port under cover as clerk to the Italian Consul. Roccardi pointed out that merchant ships would lie offshore while loading cargo, which was brought out to them by lighter. While anchored offshore the ships presented an easy and tempting target for the attentions of the *Decima Mas*.

Sottotenente di Vascello Luigi Ferraro, an outstanding swimmer, was selected for the operation. He was provided with diplomatic papers (without the assistance or connivance of the Ministry for Foreign Affairs) which appointed him to the Consulate at Alexandretta for 'special duties'. The Vice-Consul, who had no knowledge of the operation, was requested to give his new assistant all the help he might need. Along with Ferraro came four extremely heavy suitcases all prominently marked with the Italian diplomatic seal and thus immune to customs inspection.

Ferraro arrived in Alexandretta in the middle of June and set about introducing himself into the town's small but extremely curious diplomatic community: the United States, Britain, Greece and France all maintained missions in the town. On the evening of 30 June 1943, after a long game of bowls on the beach, Ferraro slipped into his diving suit and, carrying two limpet mines, swam out to the 7,000-ton *Orion* lying offshore. He fixed the mines to the ship's bilge keels and then returned to the shore. The mines used by Ferraro were fitted with a propeller which activated the detonator when the ship had travelled a certain distance. That way there would be no embarrassing explosions in neutral harbours and, with any luck, the British would think that the ship had fallen victim to a conventional submarine attack or had been mined. On 30 June the mine on the *Orion* duly exploded and the ship, loaded with chromium, sank like a stone. The 4,914-ton *Kaituna* and 7,000-ton *Fernplant* were sunk in a similar fashion on 9 July and 1 August respectively. However, only one of the mines on the *Kaituna* exploded and the ship was beached in Cyprus, where the second device was found. The system of inspecting the hulls of merchant ships was extended to those outward-bound from Turkish ports, and this is what undoubtedly saved the 5,000-ton *Sicilian Prince*.

After the attack on the *Fernplant* Ferraro had used up all his mines and so, following the onset of a convenient attack of malaria which required his repatriation on medical grounds, he returned to Italy. His activities had resulted in the sinking of two ships and the damaging of a third, together with the loss of their valuable cargoes.

Low-key but extremely successful, this was one of the most effective *Decima Mas* operations.

Back in the Central Mediterranean, the reaction of the *Decima Mas* to the invasion of Sicily was to launch an attack on invasion shipping anchored off the port of Syracuse. The *Ambra*, now commanded by *Tenente di Vascello* Ferrini, was selected for this operation. Instead of SLCs, the containers on her casing held three high-speed MTR-type torpedo boats each operated by one man. Ferrini made a skilful approach along the coast of Sicily, but on surfacing off Syracuse he was detected by an aircraft and given a severe depth-charging. Although *Ambra* made her escape, the depth-charging had distorted the doors on the cylinders containing the MTRs so badly that they could not be removed. Reluctantly Ferrini abandoned the operation. This was the last submarine-launched operation by *Decima Mas*.

In addition to the craft operated by *the Decima Mas*, the *Regia Marina* operated two other types of midget submarines, which were employed in more conventional forms of warfare. These were the CA/CB type craft which were constructed by the firm of Caproni and which aroused sufficient interest in the *Regia Marina* for orders to be placed. Four of the CA type and twenty-two of the CB type were constructed between 1938 and 1943 although seventy-two of the CB types had been ordered. Four CA class boats were built in two groups, *CA1–2* and *CA3–4*. Both were similar in size but *CA1* and *CA2* had dual diesel/electric drive while *CA3* and *CA4* were fitted with just an electric motor. The first two were equipped to carry either mines or torpedoes, but the second pair could only carry eight 100kg explosive charges or twenty 2kg charges.

The role of these craft was harbour defence and patrolling coastal waters. The CA class were highly secret and were not entered on to the Italian Navy's order of battle. As far as is known, none saw any active service. However great things were planned for *CA2*. She was modified to be carried by the submarine *Leonardo da Vinci* and used in an attack on New York in the winter of 1943, an operation which is described later and which was frustrated by the Italian armistice. At the time of the armistice in September 1943, *CA1*, *CA3* and *CA4* were at La Spezia and *CA2* was at Bordeaux. All were scuttled, although *CA2* was raised in 1949 and broken up.

The CB class were somewhat larger and fitted with diesel/electric propulsion. Externally they differed from the CA boats in that they were fitted with a fairing around the upper hatch for the commander to stand while the boat was on the surface. The armament of two 450mm torpedoes was carried in external cages on top of the craft, flush with the casing. This arrangement, which was extremely practical, meant that the craft did not have to be removed from the water in order for the weapons to be fitted.

The CB class were constructed in two groups. Boats 1 to 6 were all built in Milan by Caproni and delivered to the *Regia Marina* between January and May 1941. There

CA Type (First Series) Two-Man Midget Submarine

Displacement: 13.5/16.4 tons
Length: 10.0m
Beam: 1.96m
Propulsion: Single shaft, 1 x 60bhp MAN diesel; 1 x 25hp Marelli electric motor
Speed (surfaced): 6.25kt
Armament: Two 17.7in torpedoes, in exterior cradles (*CAI* later modified to carry eight 100kg explosive charges)
Crew: 2
Number delivered: 2

CA1: Built in 1938 by Caproni at Milan. Modified in 1941 and scuttled at La Spezia on 9 September 1943.
CA2: Built in 1938 by Caproni at Milan. Modified 1941–42. Was to have been used with large submarine *Leonardo da Vinci* in operations off East Coast of USA. Scuttled at Bordeaux in 1944, refloated in 1949 and broken up.

CA Type (Second Series) Three-Man Midget Submarine

Displacement: 12.8/14 tons
Length: 10.47m
Beam: 1.9m
Propulsion: Single shaft, 1 x 21kW Marelli electric motor
Speed (surfaced): 7kt
Speed (submerged): 6kt
Armament: Eight 100kg explosive charges and twenty 2kg charges

Crew: 3
Number delivered: 2

CA3, CA4: Built in 1942 by Caproni at Milan. Both scuttled at La Spezia on 9 September 1943.

then followed a two-year halt in the programme until the next boat, *CB7*, was delivered on 1 August 1943. The remaining fourteen units were delivered throughout 1943. Undoubtedly the threat of invasion following the collapse of Axis forces in North Africa stimulated the revival of interest in the programme.

The wartime service of the CB class was varied. Boats *CB1*, *2*, *3*, *4*, *5* and *6* were transported by road and rail to the Romanian port of Costanza on the Black Sea, where they arrived on 2 May 1942. Operating from Costanza, they supported the right flank of the German Army and enforced a naval blockade of Sevastopol throughout the summer of 1942. On 15 June 1942 *CB3* (*Tenente di Vascello* Giovanni Sorrentino) attacked a Soviet submarine without success, but three days later *Sottotenente di Vascello* Attilio Russo in *CB2* attacked and sank the Soviet submarine *SC-208*. On 25 August 1934 *CB4*, commanded by *Tenente di Vascello* Armando Sibille, attacked and sank the Soviet submarine *SC-207* south of Tarahankut. On the debit side, *CB5* was sunk in an air raid on 13 June 1942 when she was torpedoed at Yalta.

The five survivors of the Black Sea boats were handed over to Romania in September 1943, only to be taken over by the Soviets on 30 August 1944 when that country surrendered. The boats are reported to have remained in Soviet service until 1955. Of the remaining boats, *CB8*, *9*, *10*, *11* and *12* were all surrendered intact to the British at Taranto in September 1943. *CB7* was at Pola, where she was captured by the Germans, transferred to the Italian Social Republic (Mussolini's German-backed regime in northern Italy) and then cannibalised for spare parts in order to complete *CB13*. *CB13*, *14*, *15* and *17* were all destroyed in air raids in 1945. *CB16* was transferred to the Italian Social Republic and put into service. On 1 October 1944 she grounded near Sennigallia on the Adriatic coast, where she was captured by British forces. *CB18* and *19* were broken up after the war in Venice. *CB30* was captured by Yugoslav partisans at Pola and her subsequent fate is unknown. *CB21* was rammed and sunk by a German MFP (motorised transport ferry) en route to Ancona to surrender to the Allies. Lastly, *CB22* was captured at Trieste at the end of the war: for many years her hull lay derelict on a quayside but in 1950 she was transferred to the Trieste War Museum, where she is on display today. The CA/CB types were an entirely workable design. They proved effective during operations in the Black Sea and, had they been available in any numbers at the time of the invasion of Italy, they might have acquitted themselves well and disrupted the landings.

At the beginning of September 1943 the situation facing the Italian government was grim. Axis forces had been defeated in North Africa and it was plain for all to see that, following the invasion of Sicily , which began on 10 July 1943, mainland Italy would be next. In the middle of July 1943 Mussolini was urged to tell Hitler that Italy could not prosecute the war for much longer; in the event, Mussolini could not summon the strength to do so, but that did not alter Italy's position. However, on 25 July Mussolini was overthrown and placed under arrest. A new government headed by Marshal Pietro Badoglio promptly entered into negotiations with the Allies and an armistice was signed on 3 September.

The signing was greeted with dismay in the *Decima Mas* command. Borghese had taken over command from Forza in May 1943 when the latter returned to sea. An

---

CB Type Four-Man Midget Submarine

Displacement: 35.96/45 tons

Length: 14.99m

Beam: 3.0m

Propulsion: Single shaft, 1 x 50–80bhp diesel; 1 x 80hp Brown-Boveri electric motor

Speed (surfaced): 7.5kt

Speed (submerged): 6.6kt

Armament: Two 17.7in torpedoes carried in external cradles, or two mines

Crew: 4

Number delivered: 22 (all built by Caproni at Milan)

Career Details of CB Type Midget Submarines

No	Delivered	Fate
CB1	27.01.41	Transferred to Romania after 08.09.43; scuttled in Black Sea 08.44
CB2	27.01.41	As CB1
CB3	10.05.41	As CB1
CB4	10.05.41	As CB1
CB5	10.05.41	Sunk 13.06.42 at Yalta (torpedoed by Soviet aircraft)
CB6	10.05.41	As CB1
CB7	01.08.43	Captured by Germans at Pola 12.09.43; transferred to Italian Social Republic and cannibalised
CB8	01.08.43	Scrapped atTaranto 1948
CB9	01.08.43	As CB8
CB10	01.08.43	As CB8
CB11	24.08.43	As CB8
CB12	24.08.43	As CB8
CB13	1943	Captured by Germans at Pola 11.09.43 while fitting out; transferred to Italian Social Republic and completed with parts from CB7; sunk by Allied air attack at Pola 23.03.45
CB14	1943	Captured by Germans at Pola 11.09.43 while fitting out; transferred to Italian Social Republic and destroyed in air raid 1944–45
CB15	1943	Captured by Germans at Pola 11.09.43 while fitting out; transferred to Italian Social Republic and destroyed in air raid 1944–45
CB16	1943	Captured by Germans at Pola 11.09.43 while fitting out; transferred to Italian Social Republic; grounded 01.10.44 near Senigallia; captured by British; subsequent fate unknown
CB17	1943	Captured by Germans at Trieste while fitting out; transferred to Italian Social Republic and renumbered CB6; sunk by Allied aircraft 03.04.45 off Cattolica
CB18	1943	Captured by Germans at Trieste 10.09.43 while fitting out; transferred to Italian Social Republic; sunk 31.03.45 off Pesaro; raised 1946 and subsequently broken up at Venice
CB19	1943	Captured by Germans at Trieste 10.09.43 while fitting out; transferred to the Italian Social Republic; broken up at Venice 1947
CB20	1943	Captured by Germans at Trieste 10.09.43 and transferred to Italian Social Republic; probably captured by Yugoslav partisans at Pola late 04.45.
CB21	1943	Captured by Germans at Milan 09.43; taken by train to Pola and transferred to Italian Social Republic; rammed and sunk by German MFP (naval transport) 29.04.45 en route to Ancona to surrender.
CB22	1943	Captured by the Germans at Milan 09.43; taken by train to Pola and transferred to Italian Social Republic; never completed (wreck lay on jetty at Trieste until c.1950 when acquired by the Trieste War Museum)

energetic and ruthless commander, Borghese appreciated that, given the critical fuel situation affecting the majority of the Italian surface fleet, the *Decima Mas* was effectively the sole offensive arm of the Navy. At once he set about preparing further schemes for confounding the enemy, of which the mining of merchant ships in neutral harbours referred to earlier was just one. At the same time larger attacks on Gibraltar were planned using new weapons, one of which was the SSB, an improved version of the SLC in which the operators sat inside the craft in a cockpit. Three new submarines, *Grongo*, *Sparide* and *Murena*, fitted with containers for carrying SLCs, SSBs or the MTR torpedo boat, were fitting out and would shortly be available for operations.

It was inevitable that the *Decima Mas* would take an interest in the CA/CB craft even though they were not designed for special operations. However, by the summer of 1942 harbour defences in the Mediterranean were at such a high state that it would be almost suicidal to use a craft which had not been operationally proven. Accordingly the planners at the Boca di Serchio cast their eyes further afield to where the eastern seaboard of the United States beckoned. Not only did this area offer an abundance of targets, but it had not experienced an attack by underwater assault units. Consequently defences (in the United States, port defence was the responsibility of the US Army) were not a patch on anything encountered in the Mediterranean. A successful attack on an American port like New York would have immense political and psychological consequences and force the Americans to devote considerable resources to harbour defence. Borghese decided on the employment of one CA class submarine and a number of *Gamma* frogmen. *CA2* and the frogmen would be released some way outside the harbour. The frogmen would help the submarine through any nets and into the Hudson River, after which they would attack such targets as presented themselves.

But how to convey the tiny CA craft across the Atlantic? The obvious solution was to carry it on the deck of another larger submarine. The *Leonardo da Vinci* was chosen and had a well constructed on her casing forward of the conning tower in which the CA craft settled snugly, being held down by retaining clamps which could be operated from within the submarine. At this stage the Italians asked if the Germans would like to contribute a U-boat so that two CAs could be employed. After due consideration Dönitz refused. However, he did offer the Italians full cooperation in providing up-to-date intelligence on the defences on America's East Coast.

In July 1942 *Leonardo da Vinci* (*Tenente di Vascello* Gianfranco Prioroggia) successfully made the passage through the Straits of Gibraltar and arrived at Bordeaux, which was where *CA2* had been sent by rail. The modifications to her hull were carried out at Bordeaux under the supervision of *Maggiore del Genio Navale* Fenu before she was ready for trials in September. The trials took place at La Pallice and Verdon and were a complete success. It was found to be quite safe to release the

CA when the *da Vinci* was at a depth of twelve metres. The smaller craft, being positively buoyant, simply rose to the surface, where she was boarded by her crew who transferred over in a rubber dinghy. To recover the CA, the *da Vinci* positioned herself underneath the midget, observations being taken through the periscope, and slowly surfaced. It was a manoeuvre requiring some dexterity and skill and was personally supervised by none other than Borghese who had assumed command of *da Vinci* for the purposes of the trials. Unfortunately for the Italians, while further training was taking place and while adjustments were being made to *CA2*, *Leonardo da Vinci* was lost on 25 May 1943 in a depth-charge attack by the British destroyer HMS *Active* and the frigate *Ness*. There was no time to convert another submarine for the role before the armistice brought all operations to a halt.

On 8 September 1943 Borghese was stunned by the announcement that the war was over:

> We were intent on these preparations when, on the evening of 8 September, while I was at Flotilla HQ in La Spezia, I switched on the radio to hear the war news; like a bolt from the blue the announcement of the armistice already in force crashed down on our projects, our activities and our hopes . . . None of my numerous superiors, direct or indirect, had considered it necessary to give me prior warning, even with due reservations, of the fact. I thought it queer.[3]

The armistice put the officers and men of the *Decima Mas* in a difficult position. The legal government of Italy headed by Marshal Badoglio was now negotiating with the Allies and on 13 October would declare war on Germany. This decision (similar in sentiment to that taken by the Italian government in the First World but now made in radically different circumstances) was taken in the hope that Italy would be treated favourably in any post-war settlement. In the event, Italy was never accepted as a full partner in the Anglo-American alliance; rather she was merely regarded as a 'co-belligerent'. The Germans, having rescued Mussolini from captivity on 12 September, established him in northern Italy as head of the Italian Social Republic. This was the dilemma facing the men of the *Decima Mas*: whether to stay with the Badoglio government and find themselves ranged against their former allies or join Mussolini in the north. Either way they found themselves aligned against their own countrymen. Many went for a third option—disappear, and wait for events to sort themselves out. Borghese moved north and joined Mussolini, leaving those who opted to stay with the Badoglio government to be commanded by *Capitano di Fregatta* Ernesto Forza. Interestingly enough, the ranks of the pro-Badoglio forces were to be swelled by officers and men released from prisoner-of-war camps who included the redoubtable de la Penne.

The operations of the pro-Mussolini elements of the *Decima Mas* can be swiftly disposed of. In their flight north, they had abandoned most of their equipment. Their operations were confined to few ineffectual fast motor boat attacks against Allied shipping, their schemes continually frustrated by Allied attack and by partisan activity. On the other hand, the operations of the pro-Badoglio element of the *Decima Mas*, known as *Mariassalto*, involved the officers and men in a new field of activity: cooperation with their former enemies. The Italian armistice did have the effect of bringing together Italian and British practitioners of underwater warfare. It had not escaped the attention of the British that in the *Mariassalto* they possessed a unit of unparalleled knowledge and experience, and Forza was not averse to displaying this proficiency to his former enemies. On the British side, there were also the Chariots and their operators, who had been relatively unemployed since their beach reconnaissance work prior to Operation 'Husky'. An operation against the Italian Fleet, appropriately named 'Bottom', was in the planning stage in September 1943 but was cancelled. A critical factor in the development of Anglo-Italian operations of this type was the realisation that the land front would shortly advance to the ports of Leghorn (Liverno) and, possibly, La Spezia on Italy's west coast. The use of these ports would be of considerable importance to the Allies and therefore it was imperative that the Germans not be allowed to block the harbours before they made their retreat. Photographic reconnaissance indicated that the Germans were preparing blockships for use at Leghorn and La Spezia for this very purpose.

Forza proposed his plan to Flag Officer Western Italy (FOWIT) with the suggestion that explosive motor boats and *Gamma* swimmers be used to destroy the blockships. However, FOWIT was keen to involve the British Charioteers, then based at Taranto, so Commander Heathfield RN was detached from Algiers to advise on this aspect of the operation. Final approval for the operation was given by the Commander-in-Chief Mediterranean, Admiral Sir John Cunningham, who assigned the following target priorities: first, the blockships at Leghorn; secondly, the blockships at La Spezia; and thirdly, submarines based in Muggiano Creek, also at La Spezia. However, during the planning phase Leghorn was dropped from the target list since Allied bombing had already accounted for the blockships before they could be sunk. Instead, a combined operation was proposed using British Chariots against the cruisers *Bolzano* and *Gorizia*, which were to be sunk as blockships at La Spezia, and *Gamma* men against the submarines at Muggiano.

The operation was given the undignified title of 'QWZ'. The forces involved were the Italian destroyer *Grecale* (*Capitano di Fregatta* Benedetto Ponza di San Martino), which would act as headquarters ship for the entire operation. The two British Chariots would be crewed by Sub-Lieutenant M. R. Causer and Petty Officer Cook Conrad Berey, with Able Seaman Harry Smith and Stoker Ken Lawrence as their respective Number 2s. The two Chariots would be carried in *MS74* (*Tenente di Vascello* Pietro Carminati), an MS II series MTB specially adapted for carrying Chariots. *Grecale* would also carry two MTSM boats, one of which would convey the three *Gamma* men. Overseeing this side of the operation were none other than

Tenente di Vascello Luigi de la Penne and *Guardiamarina* Girolamo Manisco, fresh from their prisoner-of-war camps.

The operational plan proposed that *Grecale* sail from Bastia in Corsica at 1700 on 21 June and head for a position near La Gorgona. From there at 2030 the MTSM boats and *MS74* were to proceed alone to a position three miles south of the breakwater, where the Chariots would be launched. The two MTSM boats would proceed to within 400 yards of the breakwater before dropping the *Gamma* men. *MS74* and the two MTSM boats would then re-join the *Grecale*, which would be patrolling up and down the coast. After the operation the British Charioteers were to proceed to the western shore of the Gulf of La Spezia, where it had been arranged for an MTSM boat to pick them up on the following night. The *Gamma* men were to be left to their own devices were but were told how they could contact the nearest partisan unit.

At 1730 on 21 June *Grecale* and *MS74* left Bastia and arrived at the lowering position at 2030. *Grecale* had been delayed by boiler trouble but had made up the lost time by increasing speed. The MTSMs were put into the water and the Charioteers, dressers and Commander Heathfield transferred from *Grecale* to *MS74*. While *Grecale* began her patrol off the coast, the three small craft headed off towards La Spezia at 23kt. As they neared La Spezia speed was gradually reduced to 6kt. The Chariots were launched at 2350. The British Charioteers had been extremely impressed with the way that their Chariots had been launched by *MS74*'s crew through cutaway ramps in the stern. Meanwhile the MTSM boats proceeded to within 300yd of the breakwater to drop off the *Gamma* swimmers. De la Penne released the men at 2350 and on his way back to *Grecale* had passed the Chariots running in.

The Charioteers believed that they had been dropped further out than intended. In fact they had been dropped in the correct place, but their Chariots' batteries were not fully charged and thus they were not travelling particularly fast. Causer and Smith made what amounted to a textbook attack, securing the warhead beneath the hull of the *Bolzano*. Causer recalled:

> Shortly afterwards we could distinguish clearly, by looking up, the shape of the *Bolzano* ... In a few moments we came scraping along the underside of the huge hull. We switched off the motor, clamped on with the magnets and immediately began to pull ourselves and the Chariot along the ship's hull, moving the magnets one at a time. We continued this progress underneath the ship until I reckoned we were half way along and, as far as I could assess, under the boiler rooms. Once settled in this position, I proceeded to stick magnets on the ship's bottom without myself getting off the Chariot. The loose ends of the lanyards hanging from the magnets I secured to the torpedo warhead. As soon as several of these were safely made fast I got off my saddle. That was a mistake in the circumstances as I was holding one heavy magnet it my hand. The weight of this was such that I immediately started on my way to the bottom, so I

quickly let the offending item slip out of my fingers and rose up again on my slightly positive buoyancy. Smith by this time was also off his seat and was up alongside the warhead, making sure it was properly secured. These things could not be too well checked. As it was almost 4.30 a.m., when we decided the charge was well and truly fast, having exchanged the thumbs-up with a fair degree of swagger about the gesture, I turned the handle of the time fuse setting until I felt two distinct clicks. Two clicks two hours, so the balloon should go up as near as dammit at 0630. Back to our seats, therefore, a final check of everything, and then I pulled the release gear that freed the warhead from the Chariot.[4]

Meanwhile Berey had failed to find the entrance to the harbour and, as dawn was breaking, reluctantly decided to scuttle his Chariot. Because they had taken so long on their run-in to the target, both teams failed to make the rendezvous with the MTSM set for 23 June. Instead, they made their way ashore and, by a remarkable coincidence, succeeded in joining the same band of partisans. Berey managed to cross the River Arno in August 1944 and re-join British forces, but Lawrence, Causer and Smith were all captured while trying to make the same crossing.

Forza and Heathfield knew nothing definite of what had been achieved until Berey came through the British lines but had to rely on photographic interpretation. Following a sortie flown on the morning after the attack, 'PRU photographs taken at 221015 showed *Bolzano* capsized at her moorings. Claim this the result of combined British and assault unit timed about 220100.'[5] However, it was apparent that *Gorizia* and the submarines in Muggiano were undamaged. In is report after the attack, Commander Heathfield wrote:

Observing that, from the time of launching the craft at Taranto for the first time to that of loading on board the MS for the operation, less than a week has elapsed and that the craft were definitely 'second hand', great credit is due to the maintenance party who worked by day and night in order to get the craft ready. It is customary to give these weapons a depth test but time was so limited that this was not possible. There was no sign, however, of any of the operators wanting to withdraw from the operation on this account.

Intelligence showed that La Spezia was an extremely well defended port, and I can only emphasise once again that the two crews showed great keenness and daring and it is hoped that these qualities will be suitably rewarded.

As far as the *Gamma* men are concerned ... I would like to state that they too showed great keenness and bravery in undertaking the operation In view of the fact that, if caught, they knew they would almost certainly be shot, they are also deserving of great praise.[6]

In his own report of the proceedings, Forza concluded, quite correctly, that all who took part were 'worthy upholders of the traditions of the assault unit of the Italian Navy'.

Nearly a year was to elapse before the next and last operation by Italian underwater assault units in the Second World War. This was Operation 'Toast', carried out at Genoa in April 1945. The target was the incomplete Italian aircraft carrier *Aquila* which the Allies feared the Germans would sink as a blockship. This was to be an all-Italian operation since all available British divers were either employed in port clearance in north-west Europe or were heading out to the Far East. Once again Forza did the planning, but he was aided by intelligence supplied by the British SOE[7] who not only provided up-to-date intelligence on the harbour defences but managed to find a sympathetic harbour official who was willing to be smuggled out of Genoa and flown south to Florence. SOE also provided details of friendly partisan bands in the Genoa area and of 'safe houses' in the city.

The attack force was similar to that used against La Spezia and consisted of the destroyer *Legionario* which would carry two MTSM boats, *MTSM230* and *MTSM232*. Each of the MTSMs carried one British Chariot, since *Mariassalto* had no SLCs at its disposal. Acting as escorts were *MS74* and the British *MTB177* (Lieutenant B. H. Smith DSO RNR). There were a number of changes to the way this operation would be handled as a result of experience gained in the operation against La Spezia. While the *Legionario* patrolled off the coast, *MTB177* and *MS74* would proceed to the launching position, each towing one of the MTSMs. To avoid any inaccuracy in navigation, *MTB177* would use her radar, accepting the risk of detection by radar countermeasures, to ensure that the force was in the right position before launching the Chariots. The MTSMs would then tow the Chariots to within a mile of the harbour. From there the Chariots were on their own, but he MTSMs would stand off to await their return.

The force, known as the *Forzamento del Porto di Genova* (Mission Against the Port of Genoa), left Leghorn on the afternoon of 18 April 1945. The force reached the launching position at 2330: the Chariots were put into the water and the MTSMs towed them away into the dark. The first Chariot, manned by *Guardiamarina* Girolamo Manisco and *Sottocapo Palombaro* Dino Varini, broke down half a mile from the harbour. Using a shaded hand signal lamp, Manisco contacted the MTSM and was picked up. The other Chariot, crewed by *Sottotenente di Vascello* Nicola Conte and *Sc Palombaro* Evolino Marcolini, succeeding in getting through the net at the eastern end of the harbour, where they found that the net was holed in places and badly maintained. During the planning phase for this operation, Forza had been advised to send the Chariots through a convenient gap in the sea wall. This advice he rejected on the grounds that it was 'too simple' and that there might be hidden problems. Conte found the *Aquila* berthed alongside the Canzio Wharf without difficulty. However, the two men were unable to attach the charge to *Aquila*'s hull, so they left it on the bottom, about three metres down and slightly to port of her keel. The men then left the harbour the same way they had come and re-joined the MTSM by midday on 19 April. In technical terms Conte and Marcolini had carried out a flawless attack.

The charge was set to go off at 0700 on the 19th, but when the first set of aerial photographs arrived it was clear that *Aquila* was still at her berth and afloat, a fact confirmed by oblique photographs taken later that day. A British diving and salvage officer, Lieutenant Frank Goldsworthy, had the unpleasant task of telling Forza that the attack had been a failure. Forza refused to accept this and suggested that *Aquila* had in fact sunk in shallow water on an even keel. Goldsworthy then asked Conte if he was sure that he had placed the charge under *Aquila* and not some other ship, but the Italian indignantly replied that he knew the difference between a merchant ship and a carrier. The possibility that the charge had failed to explode was investigated, but Forza discounted it on the grounds that such a thing had not happened before. Whatever the cause, it was too late to do anything about it for on 27 April advance elements of the 5th Army entered Genoa.

Goldsworthy was determined to find out what had happened. In the meantime he found that the Germans had moved *Aquila* so that she blocked the entrance to the new harbour. This had been done on the night of 23/24 April. However, she had not been sunk, nor were there any explosives on board. A German officer told him that the charge had indeed exploded on the morning of the 19th, but that the force of the explosion had been absorbed by the anti-torpedo bulge on the port side. On examination, this feature of the ship's design did show extensive damage.[8]

With the conclusion of Operation 'Toast' the story of *Decima Mas/Mariassalto* comes to an end. On 8 May the German government surrendered at Rheims and the war was over. In the three years in which the *Decima Mas* had been engaged in operations against the Allies, they had shown themselves to be masters of the art of underwater warfare, demonstrating not only courage of the highest order but also considerable inventiveness in devising ever new and ingenious ways to confound the enemy. Yet it must be said that their efforts had little effect on the overall course of the war. Why was this so, particularly when at one stage the *Decima Mas* had virtually eliminated the Royal Navy from the Mediterranean? The answer lies in Italy's economic inability to wage total war. The relationship between the *Decima Mas* and the Italian Navy as a whole can be compared to that of a football team. It is no use having one star player if the other ten are not up to scratch. The star player can score as many goals as he can, but unless all eleven men play together the cause is ultimately lost. None of this, however, detracts from the fact that the reputation of the *Decima Mas* as the first and most successful practitioners of underwater warfare is secure.[9]

Chapter 5

In the Land of the Rising Sun

All naval writers speak highly of the Japanese handling of submarines and of the sacrifices they are prepared to make.—Captain M. D. Kennedy RN, 1928

On the other side of the world, the Imperial Japanese Navy (IJN) had been pursuing the development of midget submarines since 1918. The First World War shattered the cosy relationship which Japan had hitherto enjoyed with the West. Moreover, at the 1922 Washington Conference on naval limitation, Japan was forced to accept a quantitative discrepancy between her forces and those of Britain and the United States. The Navy General Staff seized upon the midget submarine as one means whereby the imbalance could be rectified. The Japanese thought of war with the United States in terms of a climactic action between their two battlefleets—a battle on the same lines as Tsu-Shima and Jutland. In this context midget submarines would be used to whittle down the American advantage before the two fleets met. For this purpose they could be carried to the operational area in special vessels and used as the opportunity allowed. It followed that their success depended on the enemy being unaware of their deployment, and thus secrecy was essential at all stages of their design, construction and deployment.

The Japanese midget submarines, the *Ko-Hyoteki*, were in a class of their own in terms of development. However, in operations they were not particularly successful and as the course of the Second World War turned against Japan they were withdrawn from offensive operations and employed in harbour and local defence. This role was contrary to their purpose—midget submarines are offensive weapons of surprise—and they incurred considerable losses at the hands of American air and naval patrols. It was a sad end for a force which had promised much and which had not been used to its full potential.

Although the Washington Naval Treaty of 1922 and the London Naval Treaty of 1930 imposed on the IJN quantitative limits of 60 per cent of capital ship, aircraft carrier and cruiser tonnage and 70 per cent of light cruiser and destroyer tonnage relative to the Royal and US Navies, the Japanese were allowed parity in submarine tonnage. There were many in Japan who resented this state of affairs, and as Japan's policy in China throughout the 1920s and 1930s led to a cooling in relations with Britain and the United States, there were those who considered how this situation could be circumvented. The construction of ships which covertly breached treaty limits was one solution, while the policy of constructing ships with maximum offensive power on minimum displacement was another. The development of naval air power, which was not covered by the disarmament treaties, was a third option, and a fourth was the adoption of unique tactics and weapons allied to rigorous training in manoeuvres.

Japanese plans for fighting the Americans envisaged the US Navy coming across the Pacific to fight a decisive action with the Japanese in its home waters. Since the Americans possessed a superior number of ships, the Japanese planned a series of attritional engagements using surface and submarine torpedo attack in order to reduce the numbers. The Japanese then planned to intercept the Americans in an area to the west of the Ogasawara Islands and destroy them in a decisive gunnery duel. In the night before this great battle, the Americans would be subjected to yet more torpedo attacks to shift the balance still further in favour of the Japanese and disrupt the American formation. There were two products of this strategy. The first was improved torpedoes, capable of being fired from great distances, the best known of which is the Type 93 or 'Long Lance'; and the second was the *Ko-Hyoteki* midget submarine.

The development of a midget submarine was the idea of Captain Yokoo Takeyoshi IJN. Yokoo drew upon his experience of the Russo-Japanese War and considered that piloted torpedoes would be of considerable value in sinking ships inside a defended anchorage. His idea was seized upon by Captain Kishemoto Kanji, who was in charge of the Second Section of the First Main Division of the Navy Technical Department (responsible for torpedo development): he turned a theoretical proposition into reality. Undoubtedly some of the inspiration for the *Ko-Hyoteki* concept came from a craft called the *Devastator*, conceived by a British submariner, Lieutenant Godfrey Herbert RN. Little is known about *Devastator*, largely because much of the discussion concerning her design took place across the wardroom bar at HMS *Dolphin*. However, she was small and capable of delivering a one-ton explosive charge. *Devastator*s were to be used as part of the great fleet engagement which dominated naval thinking during the First World War. They would be carried by capital ships and launched into the water in huge numbers just before the two fleets came within gun range.

The *Devastator* was not a suicide weapon, though the chances of survival for its operator were not high. The operator, sitting in a detachable buoyant compartment, set the craft on its course and then released a clip which ejected the compartment by means of compressed air, leaving the rest of the craft and warhead to proceed to their end. It was hoped that a destroyer would then turn up and hoist the chamber and operator aboard. It was a fantastic proposal and wholly unworkable. Nevertheless, in 1923 the idea was given a new lease of life by Captain Max Horton, then Captain (S) of the Second Submarine Flotilla. Horton had been an enthusiastic collaborator of Herbert's on the original *Devastator* project (he probably wanted to ride the thing himself). However, the proposal was turned down for any number of reasons, including that of expense, and because of the innate conservatism of an organisation still firmly wedded to the big gun. The idea was not lost for ever. Britain and Japan were still in the last throes of the Anglo-Japanese alliance, and Japanese naval officers were still accepted on courses in the United Kingdom. A pencilled note on Horton's paper by an officer on CinC Portsmouth's staff remarked, 'This paper is not marked Secret'. Although there is no direct evidence for the link, there is every possibility that the Japanese got wind of Horton's proposal, for the *Ko-Hyoteki* concept mirrored the *Devastator* in all but name.

Kishemoto put his proposal to Commander Asama Toshihide, a specialist in torpedo development, and ordered construction to begin in great secrecy. In brief, Kishemoto's proposal was for a 'mother' torpedo which would close with the enemy battle fleet and attack at high speed and at short range. After consideration it followed that the weapon had to have the following basic characteristics: first, to be effective it had to have a speed 1.5 times that of the mean speed of the American battle fleet—in other words, it had to have a speed of 30kt while dived; secondly, it had to be armed with two torpedo tubes; thirdly, the weapon's range was dictated by the distance between the gun ranges of the two fleets (that is, it had to be outside the range of the IJN battle fleet's main armament) and was therefore set at 35 nautical miles; and fourthly, the craft had to have sufficient habitability to remain in the area of operations to be recovered afterwards.

The upshot of this brief was the production of a research vehicle which was expected to achieve a speed of 30kt using small, light, high-capacity batteries and an electric motor of similar characteristics. Tests using this unmanned vehicle were successful, and in the summer of 1932 Kishemoto had the opportunity to present his plan to the Chief of the Navy General Staff, Admiral Fushimi-no-miya-Hiroyasu, brother of the Emperor Hirohito. Approaching the professional head of the Navy directly was unusual, but Kishemoto felt compelled to do so in order to maintain the secrecy of the project and to gain sufficient backing in order to drive it through the Navy's bureaucracy.

Fushimi gave his approval after noting that the crew had to be provided with a means of escape. At this stage it would be well to note that these weapons were not dedicated suicide weapons or, in Japanese parlance, *Tokko Heiki* (Special Attack Weapons). Suicide was an integral part of the Japanese military code, but was to be resorted to only cases of supreme urgency to avoid the disgrace of failure or the dishonour of capture. It was only when defeat was staring the Japanese government in the face in the summer of 1944 that suicide weapons were adopted as a means of halting the American advance.

Fushimi's approval meant that the design of a prototype could begin. Vice-Admiral Sugi, head of the Navy Technical Department, was ordered to assemble a committee which was to meet in conditions of extreme secrecy with Kishemoto as the chairman. The four members of the committee were Commander Katayama Arika, responsible for hull development; Commander Asama Toshihide, assigned to torpedo development; and Commanders Nawa Takeshi and Yamada Kiyoshi, with responsibility for propulsion development. It is interesting to note that all these officers subsequently attained flag rank.

The design team were soon confronted with a number of difficulties, to counter which they had no body of experience to resort to. How could the deadly battery exhaust gases be vented? How could the steering mechanism be simplified? How could submerged trim be maintained? These were just some of the problems the team had to solve. Nevertheless, in what is now the amazingly short time of two months, the team had worked out the parameters for the prototype: a battery-driven, torpedo-shaped craft with a top submerged speed of 25kt and a radius of action of 60km.

By August 1933 the prototype, built by the Torpedo Experimental Division at Kure, was ready. Tests were carried out in the Inland Sea amid conditions of considerable secrecy. At first the trials were unmanned, the craft being controlled by an automatic depth-keeping mechanism. Performance was satisfactory, with a speed of 24.85kt being recorded.[1] This was, and still is, the highest speed ever recorded by a battery-powered midget submarine.

In October Lieutenant-Commander Kato Ryonosuke and Engineer Sub-Lieutenant Harada Shin became the first naval personnel to operate the craft. The trials continued throughout the winter of 1933 and into the summer of 1934 and proved that the craft had considerable potential. However, there were some problems which needed to be sorted out: the periscope depth had to be increased since the craft tended to broach when in this condition; the depth-keeping machinery was unreliable; and both operators felt that an increase in range was desirable. The first problem was overcome by constructing a conning tower to the torpedo-shaped hull and by lengthening the periscope. However, the fitting of the conning tower also had the effect of increasing resistance and taking two knots off the top submerged speed. Improvements were made to the depth-keeping machinery but the cruising radius remained the same. The trials were finished in December 1934. The prototype was taken ashore and stored at the Torpedo Experimental Division in a sealed warehouse. All documents and plans relating to the project were likewise stored in sealed safes. The Navy had decided to re-test the performance of the craft by building a second series and then comparing the results.

At the same time, the Navy was refining the tactical doctrine under which the boats would be employed. The original concept of the craft delivering massed torpedo attacks from short range was declared valid but the problem remained of how the craft were to be transported to the operational area. The solution lay in the construction of ships specially configured to carry the midgets. These ships would accompany the battle fleet but would deploy at the appropriate time. Three such ships were ordered under the Second Fleet Replenishment Plan of 1934; a fourth was added in the Third Replenishment Programme of 1937 but her construction was altered and she was completed as a seaplane tender. The three original ships were named *Chitose*, *Chiyoda* and *Mizuho* and were declared to be seaplane tenders, which excluded them from the limitations set down in the Washington Naval Treaty. The fourth ship was named *Nisshin*. Each ship could function in the role of seaplane tender but a quick conversion programme would enable each to carry twelve of the midget submarines. As each submarine carried two torpedoes, totalling 96 torpedoes in all, this should have been adequate to do enough damage to whittle down the American superiority.

Meanwhile the trials continued. The Admiral Superintendent at the Kure Naval Yard was given nothing but the merest details of the craft despite the fact that all the tests were carried out at the Torpedo Experimental Division, an organisation of which he was nominally in charge. Only selected personnel could enter the building, and those authorised to do so were issued with passes containing their photograph and fingerprints. Documents concerning the project were never sent by post, only by reliable courier. During tests in the Inland Sea no officer below the rank of Commander took part, so great was the desire to ensure secrecy.

At times this secrecy almost gave the game away. The craft had to be called something, so a number of cover names were introduced such as *TB Mokei* (TB Model), *Tokushu Hyoteki* (Special Target), *A Hyoteki* (A Target) and *Taisen Bakugeki Hyoteki* (Anti-Submarine Bombing Target). This last name nearly had unforeseen consequences:

> Unfortunately the designation came to the notice of the staff of the First Air Fleet, who saw in it a perfect vehicle for their air crew to practise attacks on submarines. Accordingly a demand for the craft made its way through the Navy's bureaucracy and it was only after some difficulty that the aviators were persuaded to withdraw their request.[2]

The result of the first and second series of tests on the two prototypes was that the Navy General Staff adopted a five-point programme for future development:

1. On the basis of the prototype trials, two more test boats were to be constructed at Kure to conduct trials under as near operational conditions as could be replicated.

2. If these trials were successful, then the crews should work up the methods used to launch the craft from the carriers.

3. All being well, 48 such craft should then be constructed as quickly as possible.

4. Facilities for the storage and maintenance of the craft were to be constructed at Kure, secrecy being of paramount importance.

5. Selection and training of personnel should begin at once to provide a pool of trained operators.

However, it was to be nearly four years before any further significant developments took place in the programme. By then Japan's position in the international community had altered dramatically. Japan had resigned from the League of Nations, had given notice of her intention to abandon the system of naval limitation by treaty and was continuing her campaign of conquest in China—to considerable but ineffective international disapproval. Simultaneously the IJN was engaged in an urgent and radical reconstruction programme following the loss of the destroyer *Tomozuru*,[3] the 'Fourth Fleet Incident' in September 1935 and the failure of the medium-pressure turbine blades in the destroyer *Asashio* in December 1937. In other words there was not much in the way of time or resources for midget submarine construction.

It was not until the summer of 1939 that the Navy Minister ordered the two experimental boats from the Navy Yard at Kure. The first was launched in April 1940 and the second at the end of June. Trials began at once in the Inland Sea, with Lieutenant Sekido Yoshimitsu and Engineer Lieutenant Hori Toshio forming the crew. Following these, the next stage was the launching trials from *Chiyoda*, which had completed in December 1938. While the two experimental craft were nearing completion, *Chiyoda*'s stern was modified, very like a whaling factory ship, to form a launching ramp. The craft would be rolled down this ramp, stern first, into the water. First trials at Iyo-Nada in Hiroshima Bay proved satisfactory, and from July to the end of August 1940 attack trials were carried out in the rougher waters of the Bungo Strait.

To begin with, more than ten launches were made off *Chiyoda*'s stern with an unmanned craft before Sekido and Hori undertook the first manned launch. The trials were a complete success. *Chiyoda* launched the craft in various sea states and while steaming at speeds of between twelve and twenty knots. On each occasion a comparatively flat angle of entry into the water was measured, the craft emerged about 1,000m astern of the 'mother' ship and was seen to move away under its own power.

However, Sekido was critical of certain aspects of the craft's performance. Many of the instruments did not appreciate the rough nature of the launch and he noted that, at periscope depth in a running sea, pitching and rolling was very evident, making target acquisition very difficult. The craft also showed a regrettable tendency to broach at the most inappropriate moment:

> ... the conning tower was always exposed, which cannot in fact be called submerging ... for me the impression did not disappear for a long time that an attack on the ocean was very, very difficult.[4]

Nevertheless the observers, including Vice-Admiral Toyoda Soemu, Chief of the Navy Technical Department, were favourably impressed. Toyoda had hitherto been unreservedly sceptical of the whole project, but after seeing the trials from *Chiyoda* he revised his opinion considerably.

One feature of the Japanese programme was constant modification, and the period after the *Chiyoda* trials was no exception. Improvements were carried out to the hydroplane motors to improve submerged control, instruments were made more robust and there were a host of other alterations. However, at this stage there was a certain degree of conflict between the technicians and the operators. The technicians pressed for further improvements and modifications which would have required an increase in size and displacement; the operators argued that any increase in size would have considerable 'knock-on' effects on the mother ships, on stowage, on launching and in a host of other areas. Moreover, the world situation did not permit the trials period to be extended for purely academic grounds: this was a weapon, and it was required at sea.

The operators won. On 15 November 1940 the craft were formally adopted by the Navy and given the name *Ko-Hyoteki*. Things now moved apace. On 10 October 1940 a further ten boats were ordered, Nos 3 to 12, and in December Nos 13 to 26 were ordered. Enough *Ko-Hyoteki* were now on order for three carriers to be converted and armed. At the same time training for the officers and men began, directed by Commander Kato Ryanosuke under the overall command of Captain Harada Kaku, commanding officer of the *Chiyoda*.

The first group of thirteen officers and petty officers reported to *Chiyoda* in November 1940 and practical sea training began in January 1941, the intervening time being occupied with classroom instruction. By March 1941 the training was complete and the second group of twenty-two officers and petty officers, together with twelve mechanicians, arrived in April. At the same time the instruction was moved to Karasukojima near Kure. Theoretical instruction was given at the Torpedo Experimental Division of Kure Navy Yard while instruction in tactics and deployment was given at the Submarine School. Basic sea training aboard the tug *Kure Maru* then followed before the operators moved to the real thing, operating from *Chiyoda* or *Nisshin*, now working in her original role. The second group's training was completed in August. At this stage the pace of the programme was suddenly increased owing to the deterioration in relations with the United States, and three *Ko-Hyoteki*, configured solely for training, were ordered to meet the acceleration.

But what was this craft, which they had kept so secret and on which so much effort had been expended? Externally it resembled a torpedo with tapered ends surmounted by a conning tower amidships. Apart from the conning tower there was no superstructure of any kind. To reduce water resistance, the only fittings on the hull were a number of cleats cut from 12mm steel and welded to the surface. Forward and aft the torpedo tubes and propellers were fitted with shields to protect them, while a 9.5m ballast keel was welded to the underside of the hull.

The *Ko-Hyoteki*'s single pressure hull was manufactured from 8mm cold-rolled steel plates of MS44 quality. Weight reduction was extremely important in all stages of the craft's construction, and Commander Katayma Ariki proved to be resourceful and ingenious in achieving this without compromising either the operational effectiveness of the craft or safety standards. All-welded construction was one way Katayama saved weight. Another was the use of 2.6mm steel in non-pressure bearing parts of the structure instead of 8mm steel. The internal bulkheads which divided the *Ko-Hyoteki* into several compartments were gas-tight but not watertight, since the panels between the stiffeners were only 1.2mm thick. The *Ko-Hyoteki* was built to very fine tolerances and, despite the necessity to reduce weight, the collapse depth was still calculated as 200m and the safe diving depth as 100m. These parameters gave a safety coefficient 1.4 times greater than that of other Japanese submarines.

Compared to the trials version of the craft, the length increased by 6cm and the interior diameter in the control room section by 2.6cm. Increased hydrodynamic performance was obtained by drawing in the sides of the bow to produce an oval as opposed to a circular shape. The forward and after ends of the pressure hull were closed by convex bulkheads, beyond which was one external compartment, bow and stern. At the bow this compartment was used for the main ballast tank and the reserve ballast tank, but the compartment at the stern was a free-flooding space.

The hull was divided into three sections in order to facilitate construction and fitting out. The forward section contained the *Ko-Hyoteki*'s *raison d'être*—two 45.7cm torpedo tubes mounted one above the other. The prototypes had been fitted with 53.3cm tubes for the Type 89 torpedo but the introduction into service of the 45.7 cm Type 97 oxygen-driven torpedo seemed to afford another opportunity for saving weight and so was adopted. The torpedo tubes were 5.4m long, roughly the length of the compartment, and were of a most unusual design. Unlike conventional torpedo tubes, which are fitted with bow and stern caps, those in the *Ko-Hyoteki* were simple tubes with a spherical casting riveted to the rear end in place of the breech which contained a tail stop with a thick rubber baffle and a fitting for the air impulse check valve. There was no bow cap: the torpedoes were merely slid into place tail-first. The simplicity of the design meant that the tubes were free-flooding, so there was no need for complicated flooding and venting arrangements (another weight saving) while the warhead of the torpedo projected about 30mm from the forward end of the tube, thus providing a streamlined finish.

The gyro angle and depth setting of the torpedoes were adjusted from within the control room by means of mechanical linkages and shafts connected to the gyro and depth-keeping spindles in the torpedo tubes, while indicators in the control room monitored the adjusted angles. The torpedoes were fired by air pressure, each tube having a firing tank containing 69.4 litres of air. There was only one problem with the firing arrangements, and this was the subject of bitter complaint by the crews:

since there were no arrangements to vent the tubes internally, a stream of bubbles appeared on the surface each time a torpedo was fired—hardly ideal for a craft engaged in covert operations, but a inevitable result of the need to save weight in the design.

The *Ko-Hyoteki*'s main ballast tank formed the space around the two torpedo tubes. This contained 1,336 litres of water. The tank was usually filled in the depot ship before launch because the small size of the inlet valve made it very difficult to flood the tank while at sea. When the main ballast tank was blown, the bow of the *Ko-Hyoteki* came up very quickly while the stern remained unmoved—unsurprising given that the stern had no ballasting arrangements and contained the weight of the motor. Due to this extreme bow-up angle, it was usually some time before the conning tower broke surface. To deal with this problem a 416-litre emergency tank was fitted under the control room.

Behind the compartment containing the torpedo tubes and their associated firing tanks was that containing the reserve ballast tank, a tank which automatically filled when the torpedoes were fired, to compensate for the loss of weight. However, the size of the inlet valve was not large enough to permit quick filling, and it was all too often the case that a *Ko-Hyoteki* would bob to the surface after firing. Crews tried increasing speed on firing but the *Ko-Hyoteki* still came up—another source of complaint.

The centre-section of the boat was divided into three separate compartments, the forward battery room, the after battery room and the control room and conning tower. Unlike many types of midget submarine in other navies, the *Ko-Hyoteki* used electric power for both submerged and surface propulsion. The main battery was thus the boat's sole source of power. It consisted of 192 trays, each cell consisting of two 2V cells. The cells were connected in parallel-series combinations: 136 trays (75 per cent of the battery) were installed in the after battery compartment and the remaining 56 in the forward compartment. The trays were arranged along the sides of the craft to facilitate inspection and maintenance while under way. Battery ventilation was provided by sucking the air from the forward battery compartment, forcing it through a cell containing a hydrogen absorption agent and then discharging it into the after battery compartment after cooling and mixing with HP air. This was not the ideal hydrogen absorption system but it was considered acceptable since the boat would only have to be at sea for a few hours. When the battery was charged ashore or aboard the depot ship a port in the *Ko-Hyoteki*'s side provided additional ventilation.

The forward and after battery compartments also contained the trimming tanks, a 357-litre tank forward and a 257-litre tank aft. Flooding and pumping out was done via the bilge pump, but this had the unfortunate effect of clogging the system with mud. An additional pump, driven by the periscope motor, was fitted. Trimming was difficult because the distance between the two tanks was comparatively short. To

Ko-Hyoteki Type A Two-Man Midget Submarine

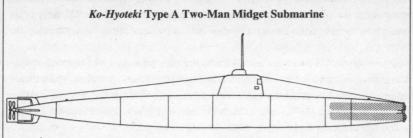

Displacement (submerged): 46 tons
Length: 23.9m
Beam: 1.8m
Propulsion: 1 x 600hp electric motor; one shaft (but fitted with two contra-rotating propellers).
Speed (surfaced): 23kt
Speed (submerged): 19kt
Range (surfaced): 80nm at 2kt
Range (submerged): 55nm at 19kt
Armament: Two 457mm torpedoes
Crew: 2
Number delivered: 20

Production: Two unnumbered prototypes then *HA-1* and *HA-2*, *HA-3–HA-44*, *HA-46–HA-61*. Built from 1934 onwards by Kure Dockyard and then by a special factory solely for their construction at Ourazaki near Kure.
War losses: Five off Pearl Harbor on or about 07.12.41; three at Diego Suarez on 30.05.42; four at Sydney Harbour on 31 May 1942; eight off Guadalcanal 1942; three in Aleutians 1942–43.

correct this, 1,421kg of lead was carried in the forward battery compartment on trolleys which could be shifted manually to compensate for changes in the boat's weight. There were also two balance tanks, one forward and one aft, holding 232 and 180 litres respectively. The forward tank was located under the torpedo tubes, the after one under the main motor.

The control room was located between the two battery compartments and directly beneath the conning tower containing the single access hatch. It contained all the controls for the *Ko-Hyoteki* such as the automatic and manual depth control gear, the helm, the master gyro compass and the directional gyro indicator, the firing controls, the periscope motor, the trim pump, the HP air manifold, a small crystal radio set, the hydrogen detector and the periscope.

The periscope was a marvel of miniaturisation, produced by the Japan Optical Manufacturing Company to a design of the Naval Technical Laboratory. The all-pervasive secrecy surrounding the project required that the device be named *Toku Megane* (Special Glasses). The periscope was 3.05m long and had a diameter of 92mm. It had magnifications of x1.5 and x6. It was enclosed in a periscope casing about 30cm high, streamlined to reduce resistance. In addition to the periscope the *Ko-Hiyoteki* was also fitted with an echo sounder (the use of which would have been a complete giveaway, so it is difficult to see why this was fitted in a craft intended for covert operations) and a primitive, non-directional hydrophone. The only other concession to navigation was the fitting of a tiny chart table. Nevertheless, the periscope, hydrophone and chart table were sufficient for covert operations in confined waters. Above the control room was the pressure-tight conning tower, which consisted of two vertical cylinders arranged one behind the other. The forward cylinder was the access hatch while the after cylinder contained the periscope. At the after end of the conning tower was the aerial for the UHF radio; this could be raised to a height of 8m by worm gear in the control room.

A number of *Ko-Hyoteki* were converted to training boats and were slightly modified. The size of the after battery was reduced and the space saved was used to provide accommodation for two instructor officers and a class of six or seven trainees. An additional tank was fitted, to compensate for the loss of weight due to the removal of the battery. The size of the conning tower was also increased and a second periscope was fitted for the use of the instructor.

The stern section was separated from the after section by an insulated bulkhead and contained the single electric motor. The motor was manufactured by the Toshiba Corporation and weighed about 1.5 tons. At 1,800rpm, the motor produced 600hp and was operated from the control room by manual switches. Depending on battery combinations, the motor drove the *Ko-Hyoteki* at a maximum speed of 24kt and a half speed of 12kt; astern power at 5kt was also available. Reduction gears in the ratio 5:5:1 transmitted the revolutions to the single propeller shaft. The gearbox was located aft of the motor room in the free-flooding space at the stern. At the end of the shaft were two contra-rotating propellers, the forward one turning in a left-handed cycle and the after in a right-handed cycle. The forward screw was slightly larger than the after one—1.35m in diameter as opposed to 1.25m. Vertical and horizontal stabiliser fins with vertical rudders and horizontal hydroplanes were installed just forward of the propellers. The whole assembly was carefully thought out and designed so as not to offer any projections which could snag in a net.

The *Ko-Hyoteki* were possibly the most sophisticated and best-designed midget submarines used by any of the belligerents in the Second World War. The designers were working to a clear and precise operational requirement, which they fulfilled. Naturally there were some shortcomings in the design: poor submerged control and lack of internal venting for the torpedo tubes were two such aspects. However, no design ever manages to meet in total the requirements of its designers and its operators: conflicts were inevitable. The comparison is often made, unfavourably, with the British X-Craft. The comparison is unfair for X-Craft were designed for long-range extended operations, whereas the *Ko-Hyoteki* were designed for a short and decisive naval engagement and this is reflected in the design. The construction of this craft constituted as important a technological achievement for the Imperial

Navy as the super battleships *Yamato* and *Musashi*, also under construction at the time.

Even as late as the spring of 1941 the *Ko-Hyoteki* planners were still thinking in terms of the craft's being used in a decisive battle at sea. However, on 1 February 1941 Admiral Yamamoto Isoroku first put forward his plan for an air strike on the American base at Pearl Harbor. What role would there be for the *Ko-Hyoteki* if the American fleet were to be sunk at its moorings?

Chapter 6

The Birth of a Legend

The first blow is half the battle.—Japanese proverb

While Western Europe became embroiled in the Second World War, an uneasy peace reigned in the Far East. Japan was pursuing a policy of outright conquest in China—which had turned her into an international pariah. In turn the Americans applied economic pressure to Japan which threatened to deprive her of essential imports, particularly oil. The worsening diplomatic situation coincided with the rising influence of the military, especially that of the Army, in Japanese policy-making. The hard-liners in the Army increasingly saw the seizure of economic assets in South-East Asia and war with America as the only way of resolving Japan's position. In the event of war with the United States, the Imperial Navy would be in the forefront and thus it was fortuitous that on 1 February 1941 Admiral Yamamoto Isoruku took command of the Imperial Japanese Navy's Combined Fleet.

Born in 1884, Yamamoto had been educated in America and had also served as Naval Attaché there. As a result, he was familiar with the country, her people and, most importantly, the awesome but latent industrial muscle possessed by America which Japan could never hope to equal. Consequently he opposed, at the risk of his life, the more radical elements in the Japanese Army who saw war with America as the only solution to Japan's position. Indeed, his appointment as Vice Navy Minister had been abruptly terminated and he had been packed off to the Combined Fleet to protect him from assassins who were formulating government policy by bullet or knife. But, whatever his misgivings, Yamamoto was an officer of the Imperial Navy and he devoted all his considerable ability to planning for victory. When confronted with the possibility of planning for war with America, he realised that Japan could not afford to wait for the climactic engagement which the country had long hoped for. The American Pacific Fleet had to be destroyed at its moorings by a swift and overpowering strike. Of this realisation was born the plan for the carrier strike on Pearl Harbor.

Thus, at a stroke, the *Ko-Hyoteki* seemed to be redundant, since the circumstances in which they were designed to be employed would not now occur. However, the determination which had carried the designers and operators through the development and trials programme would not simply go away. Sub-Lieutenant Iwasa Naoji, one of the operators, considered the possibility of employing the *Ko-Hyoteki* in attacking warships in defended anchorages. Why, he reasoned, could not the *Ko-*

Hyoteki attack American ships at Pearl Harbor, Manila, San Francisco and a host of other bases? Iwasa discussed his ideas with Commander Ryonosuke Kato, in charge of *Ko-Hyoteki* training, who passed the plan to Captain Harada.

The next stage was for Iwasa to request an interview with Yamamoto, and it says much for the latter that he was prepared to devote time to hearing the earnest Sub-Lieutenant out. However, despite Iwasa's eloquence and obvious enthusiasm, Yamamoto turned the plan down, not because he doubted the potential of the craft but because did not believe that the operators could be rescued. The *Ko-Hyoteki* men were not disheartened. In September 1941 Harada moved *Chitose* to the Sea of Aki in the Inland Sea, an area which bore a superficial resemblance to Pearl Harbor. Here the *Ko-Hyoteki* were put through their paces, entering a simulated defended harbour and returning to a blacked-out *Chitose*. Although the exercises were a success, it was realised that the short range of the craft meant that *Chitose* could not be risked near to a hostile shore: her presence would be a clear sign of an impending attack and, armed with only four 5-inch guns, she was hardly in a position to defend herself.

The solution lay in carrying the *Ko-Hyoteki* on the casing of a C1 class submarine.[1] The *Ko-Hyoteki* rested, facing aft, on a cradle constructed on the casing aft of the conning tower. This was not an unusual method of carriage for a midget submarine: Italy, Britain and Germany used similar methods, and, indeed, it is extremely logical to use another submarine as a carrier, thus taking advantage of the submarine's inherent stealth qualities. The uniqueness of the Japanese arrangement lay in the design of a mating collar between the *Ko-Hyoteki* and the parent boat. Two close-fitting cylinders enabled access between the midget and the carrier while the latter was submerged, thereby allowing maintenance to be carried out while the submarine was on passage to the target area—a very important consideration. Most importantly, the *Ko-Hyoteki* could be launched while the submarine was dived, since all the restraints and clamps holding the midget to the casing could be released from within the submarine's control room. In any other navy, the fact that the parent submarine had to surface in order to launch a midget made it very vulnerable at that point in the operation. Harada, Ryosunoke and Iwasa had neatly side-stepped this problem.

It was the employment of submarines as carriers which finally won Admiral Yamamoto over. At a series of staff conferences on board the fleet flagship *Nagato* between 11 and 13 October, Yamamoto gave his permission for the *Ko-Hyoteki* to take part in the attack on Pearl Harbor—indeed, they would spearhead it. Yamamoto remained adamant that the *Ko-Hyoteki* men were to do their utmost to complete their mission and then return to their parent submarine.

The crews of the five submarines, which had only just been completed, were placed in a state of virtual house arrest. At the same time workmen from the Arsenal at Kure began to strip away areas of the after casing and install cradles and securing bands. It was clear that the submarines were going to be carrying 'something':

On 6 November these modifications were complete and all five submarines proceeded to Kame-Ga Kubi near the Torpedo Experimental Establishment outside Kure. After we secured, a barge came alongside each submarine. The barges were carrying strange objects heavily screened by black cloth and guarded by armed sailors and police. The objects were hoisted on to the casing and secured in the cradles—still wreathed in their coverings. We, the ship's company, were not informed what the objects were. It was only when we proceeded to sea for trials in the Sea of Aki that we learned what we were carrying. The morale on the submarine was incredible.[2]

The submarines were now formally called the First Special Attack Corps and on 28 November all slipped quietly out to sea and headed for Hawaii. The Senior Officer was Captain Hanku Sasaki in *I-22*. The crews of the midget submarines were:

I-16   (Commander Kaoru Yamada IJN)
         Sub-Lieutenant Masaharu Yokoyama IJN
         Petty Officer 2nd Class Sadamo Ueda

I-18   (Commander Kiyonari Otani IJN)
         Sub-Lieutenant Shigemi Furuno IJN
         Petty Officer 1st Class Shigenori Yokoyama

I-20   (Commander Takashi Yamada IJN)
         Sub-Lieutenant Akira Hiro-o IJN
         Petty Officer 2nd Class Yoshio Katayama

I-22   (Senior Officer: Captain Hanku Sasaki IJN; Commanding Officer:
         Commander Kiroi Ageta IJN; Staff Officer Operations: Sub-
         Lieutenant Keiu Matsuo IJN)
         Lieutenant Naoji Iwasa IJN
         Petty Officer 1st Class Noakichi Sasaki

I-24   (Commander Hiroshi Hanabusa IJN)
         Sub-Lieutenant Kazuo Sakamaki IJN
         Petty Officer Kiyoshi Inagaki

Soon after leaving Japanese waters, the submarines' commanding officers briefed their ships' companies on the operation. There was now, after all, little point in the all-pervasive secrecy which had so far governed the operation.

The trip to Hawaii was not without incident. Rough weather made maintenance of the tiny *Ko-Hyoteki* extremely difficult and on *I-24*'s midget one of the torpedoes was damaged. This was one problem which could not be rectified by using the access tunnel between the two craft: *I-24* would have to surface. The task of withdrawing the torpedo and substituting it with another on the heaving casing of a submarine in the North Pacific would daunt any submariner. For Sakamaki and Inagaki, however, the thought of entering the Americans' principal Pacific anchorage with only one torpedo was an even more appalling prospect. *I-24*'s torpedo party turned to: the damaged torpedo was withdrawn and dropped over the side and replaced with one from the submarine's own supply.

On 3 December, the coded signal 'Climb Mount Niitaka' was received, indicating that the Japanese government had given up on the prospect of achieving a negotiated settlement with the Americans and that war was inevitable. The actual declaration of war was to wait till 1300 (Washington time) on 7 December (0800 Hawaiian time), when the two Japanese envoys in Washington would present an ultimatum. By then Yamamoto's carriers and the *Ko-Hyoteki* would be in position. Although the Japanese government had planned a surprise attack, they were determined to adhere to diplomatic protocol.

As regards reconnaissance and intelligence about the target, the *Ko-Hyoteki* crews were superbly supplied. Seldom have the participants in a special operation been so well briefed about their objective in the days before spy satellites. The key to this aspect of the operation lay in Japan's extraordinary network of agents in Hawaii. Moreover, two *Ko-Hyoteki* operators had visited Hawaii as late as the end of October to gather last-minute details before sailing for Yokohama on the liner *Tatsuta Maru*. One of these officers, Lieutenant Keiu Matsuo, had interrupted his *Ko-Hyoteki* training to take part in this reconnaissance and as a result he was not judged sufficiently competent to command a *Ko-Hyoteki* in action. Instead he became Staff Officer (Operations) and was responsible for the last briefing before the attack.

Shortly after midnight on 6 December all five submarines were in position eight miles from the narrow entrance to Pearl Harbor. One by one the crews entered their submarines and, after last-minute checks and wishes for success from the parent submarine, the telephone connections were cut, the clamps were released and the small *Ko-Hyoteki* moved away. The plan was for the mother submarines to move to a point off Lanai Island, eighty miles east of Pearl Harbor and wait for the their small charges there. If the rendezvous was made, then the *Ko-Hyoteki* would be scuttled and the submarines would return to Japan. In truth, however, the officers and men of the parent submarines realised that they would not likely see the *Ko-Hyoteki* men again. They were not on a suicide mission, but on the other hand their chances of survival were small. In any case, death held no terrors for these men. To die in action represented the ultimate sacrifice as expressed in the *Bushido* creed: 'It is true courage to live when it is right to live and to die when it right to die'. They had all made their wills and left small parcels of hair cuttings and nail clippings for their relatives in the event of their failing to return. What then happened to the five midgets is unclear. Three were definitely attacked and sunk by US naval forces, and the fates of the other two are unknown.

At the entrance to Pearl Harbor three 'Bird' class minesweepers, *Condor*, *Crossbill* and *Reedbird*, were making routine sweeps of the area, which was off limits to civilian fishing and pleasure craft. At 0357 *Condor* (Ensign R. C. McCloy USN) sighted a stick-like object near the harbour buoy heading west towards

Barber's Point. At 0357 he signalled his sighting to the USS *Ward* (Lieutenant William W. Outerbridge USN), which was patrolling a two-mile square outside the harbour entrance. *Ward* closed the *Condor* to conduct a sonar search but found nothing, so the hunt was called off. Later, at 0508, the anti-submarine boom was opened to allow *Condor* and *Crossbill* to enter harbour. The gate should then have been closed, but for convenience's sake it was left open since the repair ship *Antares* was expected from Palmyra towing a 500-ton steel barge.

Antares neared the boom just after 0605. As she did so, Seaman H. E. Raebig aboard *Ward* noticed an object moving through the water at a steady pace between *Antares* and her tow. As dawn broke the object became visible as a weed-encrusted drum with a stick coming out of the top of it, but moving at a steady five knots. *Ward* was joined by a Catalina which began circling *Antares*: neither the aircraft pilot, Ensign William Tanner, nor Outerbridge particularly liked what they saw.

Outerbridge was in two minds about what to do. The 'object' might be some new device of which he was not aware, and if he sank or damaged it his first command would be his last. Alternatively, he knew that the fragile bottom plating of his ship would most likely not survive a ramming. Whatever his doubts, at 0645 he ordered *Ward*'s crew to General Quarters and bore down on the object at 25 knots while opening fire with the forward 4in gun.

The first shot went over, but as *Ward* closed the target Number 3 4in gun on her deckhouse was brought to bear and scored a direct hit at the base of the conning tower:

This was a square, positive hit. There was no evidence of ricochet. The submarine was seen to heel over to starboard. The projectile was not seen to explode outside the hull of the submarine. There was no splash of any size that might result from an explosion or ricochet.[3]

The midget rolled over and began to sink, hastened on her way by four depth charges set for 100ft. In the resulting depth-charge boil, quantities of oil and wreckage were observed. *Ward*'s reporting of the attack was received in the Operations Room in the 14th Naval District at 0711. It was a Sunday morning and, despite the ominous diplomatic situation, the report was treated with a lack of urgency. Rear-Admiral Claude C. Bloch, Commandant of the 14th Naval District, discussed the matter with his Chief of Staff, Captain James B. Earle USN. Both men believed that the sighting must have been a false alarm but concurred with the decision taken by the duty officer Lieutenant Harold Kaminsky—on his own initiative—to alert the standby destroyer, USS *Monaghan*, and order her to sea to support the *Ward*.

Reports of midget submarines were now coming in thick and fast. USS *Chew* reported sinking one while a Navy plane reported sinking another just off the harbour entrance. *Ward* reported attacking another contact just after 0700. Meanwhile

Kaminsky's signal to *Monaghan* reached her just after 0750, just as Commander Mitsuo Fuchida, commander of the air strike, was reporting that complete surprise had been achieved.

It was not until 0827 that *Monaghan* got under way, and by this time the air battle was in full swing. Smoke was rising from Schofield Barracks ashore and the other destroyers in *Monaghan*'s 'nest' were engaging Japanese aircraft. As *Monaghan* headed down the channel she sighted the seaplane tender *Curtiss*, which was flying a submarine alarm signal, while seamen were seen firing at an object in the water at close range. Those on *Monaghan*'s bridge could see the submarine which was partly broached, and at 0840 it fired a torpedo which ran up the North Channel and passed between *Curtiss* and the light cruiser USS *Raleigh* before exploding on the Pearl City shoreline. As *Monaghan* turned in to ram, the midget fired a second torpedo which exploded against Ford Island.

Monaghan struck the submarine a glancing blow and the midget then passed down her starboard side with her bow raised high out the water. As the midget fell astern Chief Torpedoman G. S. Hardon dropped two depth charges set shallow: he was just about to release a third when he felt *Monaghan* go aground. As the charges went off, debris and oil came to the surface. Elsewhere in the harbour the destroyer *Blue* reported sinking a submarine outside the harbour entrance, while the cruiser *St Louis* reported being narrowly missed by two torpedoes.

It is difficult to assess just what was happening in terms of the *Ko-Hyoteki* operations given the pandemonium the air attacks were causing. In assessing just what occurred it is best to discuss what was found after the war. Some weeks after the attack a midget was raised by the Americans. Examination showed a 5-inch hole in the conning tower and a deep gash inflicted by ramming. This would suggest, therefore, that this was the craft dispatched by *Monaghan*. The two-man crew were still inside the submarine but were crushed beyond recognition. No attempt was made to investigate further and this *Ko-Hyoteki* was unceremoniously buried, with its crew, in the foundations of a breakwater then under construction. She thus became a very solid part of the base she had tried to destroy. Shortly after the attack, the sleeve of a uniform jacket laced in the Japanese fashion for a Lieutenant's rank, was recovered from the harbour. As the only officer of that rank in the First Special Attack Group was Lieutenant Naoji Iwasa, it would appear that *I-22*'s midget was successful in entering the anchorage. Perhaps this was the craft which fired at the *St Louis* and which was sunk by the *Blue*. We shall never know. The sleeve was returned to Japan in 1947 and is now at the Yasukani shrine.

Fifteen years later scuba divers found a fourth midget off Keehi Lagoon inside Honolulu Harbour in 76ft of water with its bow pointed at Diamond Point. The craft was raised and found to be in good condition though covered in marine growth; there was even power left in the batteries. There was no sign of the two-man crew and the conning tower hatch was found open and unclipped from the inside, which would suggest that the *Ko-Hyoteki* was abandoned, possibly after becoming unserviceable (the scuttling charge was not set) and that the two crewmen attempted to swim to the shore but were swept out to sea or drowned, possibly of their own accord in a final and honourable act of suicide. A more fanciful suggestion is that the crewmen reached the shore and managed to blend in with the Japanese population in Hawaii. The submarine itself was subsequently returned to Japan, where it is now preserved at the Naval Academy at Etajima.

Thus one of the five *Ko-Hyoteki* was sunk by *Ward* at the entrance to Pearl Harbor; another two—one of which was commanded by Lieutenant Naoji Iwasa—succeeded in entering the harbour, and both of these were sunk; and a fourth was found off Honolulu. What of the fifth? This craft, commanded by Ensign Kazuo Sakamaki, is the only one about which definite information exists. After parting from *I-24* Sakamaki encountered severe problems in maintaining trim. Both he and Petty Officer Inagaki were fully occupied in shifting to iron ballast on the deck to keep the submarine stable. As if this were not enough, the gyro compass began to give trouble. This was a fault which had been noted during the voyage from Japan and it was not a problem which could be dealt with by *I-24*'s engineers. Sakamaki was determined to go ahead despite the compass, but, now, every time he raised his periscope he found that the submarine was pointing in a different direction and he was forced to proceed with his periscope raised.

The mechanical problems meant that the midget was late in entering the harbour and thus it is probable that this was the craft which was attacked by *Ward* just after 0700. The boom was still open as he neared the entrance channel. The smoke and fires from the air attack were clearly visible and Sakamaki and Inagaki were jubilant, but as they planned their approach the *Ko-Hyoteki* went aground on a coral reef near the harbour entrance and became fully exposed. The destroyer *Helm* was proceeding to sea when she sighted the midget and engaged her with her 5in gun. Sakamaki and Inagaki had to make superhuman efforts to shift the trimming ballast over the batteries, which gave off powerful electric shocks, but eventually the craft slipped off the reef. However, both torpedoes had been damaged in the collision and chlorine gas from the battery now began to fill the submarine. Despite these problems, Sakamaki and Inagaki tried to continue their mission. But it was hopeless. By now the two men were ill from inhaling the chlorine gas and both Sakamaki and Inagaki lapsed in and out of a coma. Throughout 7 December the craft drifted out to sea with both men insensible inside.

By nightfall on 7 December they had drifted to a point off Kaneohe Naval Air Station, where the midget went aground for the final time. No amount of manoeuvring could get the craft free, the battery was exhausted and so the scuttling charge was set and both men abandoned the submarine. Inagaki was swept out to sea and drowned but Sakamaki was carried ashore to a beach near Bellows Field where he was captured by Corporal David Akui, ironically a Japanese-American. The brave but luckless Sakamaki had done more than could be expected of him. Had he been a British, Italian or German operator, his determination would have been rewarded with the highest honour: in Japanese eyes Petty Officer Inagaki was both more fortunate and more honoured for having drowned. Sakamaki thus had the dubious distinction of being the first Japanese prisoner-of-war. Despite his repeated requests to take his own life, Sakamaki remained a prisoner-of-war and he was returned to Japan in 1945.

What had the First Special Attack Group achieved? In actual results we shall never know. It is quite possible that one or more torpedoes fired from the two craft which entered the harbour found a target: in the confusion generated by the air attacks it is possible that such a hit went unnoticed amid everything else that was going on. The Japanese propaganda machine claimed that the American battleship *Arizona* was sunk by a midget submarine—a claim that was bitterly disputed by the naval aviators. The way in which the *Ko-Hyoteki* operators had gone about their work and the way in which they, save one, had met their deaths caught the collective imagination of the Japanese people. In some ways the Japanese are very much like the British, in that a glorious defeat is almost as good as a victory. No matter that the craft had not fulfilled their expectations: their operators had gone into action and met their deaths in true *Samurai* fashion. Each of the dead was rewarded with a posthumous two-rank promotion and all were dignified with the status of war gods. Postcards were printed showing the nine (the unfortunate Sakamaki was deemed not to have existed) gathered round a view of Pearl Harbor. The five boats of the First Special Attack Group may have failed, but they were the birth of a legend.

Chapter 7

From Madagascar to Sydney

*Theirs was a courage which is not the property, or the tradition or the
heritage of any one nation.*—Rear-Admiral G. C. Muirhead-Gould, on the
Japanese midget submarine crews killed in the attack on Sydney, June 1942.

The annihilation of the First Special Attack Unit did not inhibit further operations.
A planned raid on Singapore was rendered unnecessary by the British capitulation
there in February 1942. However, it was known that at least one craft had been
captured by the Americans, so a number of modifications were carried out in order
to forestall any likely American countermeasures.

The control of rudders and hydroplanes was changed from HP air to hydraulic.
This was a big step forward since the battery trays which had been removed from the
boats used against Pearl Harbor could be replaced and underwater speed increased
again to 19kt; another advantage was that the hydraulic transmission was a good deal
less noisy than when using HP air. Other modifications included the fitting of bow
caps to the free-flooding torpedo tubes and of runners to the bow to enable the craft
to creep along the sea bed and to surmount obstacles. Some minor improvements
were made to make the craft more habitable, though its small size meant that little
could be achieved here apart from such minor points as improving the seats.

Admiral Yamamoto now planned two simultaneous attacks by the Second Special
Attack Group, then engaged in intensive training in the Inland Sea. One group would
attack Allied warships in Sydney harbour in Australia while the other would range
along the east coast of Africa looking for suitable targets. The western 'half' of the
operation was under the command of Rear-Admiral Noboru Ishizaki flying his flag
in the submarine *I-10*. Ishizaki had an astonishingly wide brief: he was to range
westwards into the Indian Ocean and seek out targets along the east coast of Africa
and the Arabian peninsula. The advance base for the Western Advance Flotilla was
Penang on the west coast of Malaya, where the seaplane tender *Nisshin* had arrived
with a number of *Ko-Hyoteki* for the operation.

The three submarines selected for the raid into the Indian Ocean were *I-16*, *I-18*
and *I-20*, all veterans of Pearl Harbor. Each carried a *Ko-Hyoteki* submarine, crewed
as follows:

> *I-20* (Commander Takeshi Yamada IJN)
> Lieutenant Saburo Akeida IJN
> Petty Officer Masami Takemoto

I-18   (Commander Kiyonari Otani IJN)
I-16   (Commander Kaoru Yamada IJN)
         Ensign Katsusuke Iwase IJN
         Petty Officer Takazo Takata

They were accompanied by the submarines *I-10* and *I-30*, each of which carried a Yokosuka E14Y floatplane for reconnaissance purposes. Additionally, *I-10* was configured as a headquarters submarine for the operation and flew Ishizaki's flag. The submarines would be supported by two armed merchant cruisers, *Hokoku Maru* and *Aikoku Maru*, which would act as auxiliaries for the submarines but could be released for commerce raiding on their own account should the opportunity arise. All in all it was a compact force, not quite the equal of Admiral Chuichi Nagumo's carrier forces which had ranged across the Bay of Bengal in April 1942 but one that was powerful, self-sustaining and possessing its own organic long-range reconnaissance.

The Western Advance Flotilla left Penang on 29 April and battled through the swells of the Indian Ocean, fuelling from the AMCs on 5, 10 and 15 May. The aircraft-carrying submarines *I-10* and *I-30* had preceded the assault submarines and were conducting reconnaissance northwards up the east coast of Africa, beginning on 7 May. The searches proved fruitless, although a large number of merchant ships were sighted in Durban. However, these were of little interest to Ishizaki: in accordance with Japanese doctrine, he was more interested in sinking warships, even though this might mean passing up a promising opportunity. On 29 May the plane from *I-10* returned from a reconnaissance of Diego Suarez at the north end of the island of Madagascar with the news that a *Queen Elizabeth* class battleship, together with other warships and merchant ships, was anchored in the north-east corner of the harbour. This one reconnaissance alone fully justified the value of aircraft-carrying submarines like *I-10*. The *Ko-Hyoteki*-carrying submarines were alerted and Ishizaki made the decision to attack Diego Suarez.

It was something of a coincidence that, as Ishizaki's force swept westwards, the British were launching their own campaign against Madagascar. Madagascar was nominally a French possession, but the rapid advance of the Japanese in Malaya and Java brought the island's strategic position into sharp relief. Diego Suarez lay roughly equidistant from Cape Town, Colombo and Aden, and it was felt that it was here, if anywhere, that the Germans and Japanese would join hands. Despite extensive commitments to the Middle East, Churchill ordered that the island be captured and forces were gathered together under the command of Rear-Admiral E. N. Syfret CB. The landings took place on 5 May 1942. There was some resistance from the Vichy garrison, but the French governor capitulated two days later.

By 24 May Rear-Admiral Syfret was satisfied that the military and air forces were well established ashore and the port was were running as well as could be expected.

However, there were no underwater defences yet in place. Since all the ships involved in the operation had dispersed to their various commands except the battleship *Ramillies* and three 'L' class destroyers, Syfret felt that he could turn over command to the GOC ashore and proceed to Durban in *Ramillies*. This course of action was approved by the Admiralty, with the proviso that the destroyers be placed under the command of the Commander-in-Chief East Indies Station, Admiral Sir James Somerville. Somerville lost no time in ordering the three destroyers, *Laforey*, *Lightning* and *Lookout*, to join him in the Seychelles but offered Syfret *Duncan*, *Decoy* and *Active* as replacements—hardly a fair exchange! This adjustment in forces meant that for the period from 29 May to 4 June 1942 the only anti-submarine screen available at Diego Suarez was provided by the 'Flower' class corvettes *Genista* and *Thyme*.

By the evening of 29 May the submarines had reached their drop-off point outside the harbour of Diego Suarez close to the thickly wooded hills of Cape Amber. The floatplane from *I-10* was launched to conduct a final reconnaissance of the harbour. The plane flew over the harbour at around 2230 but made off after giving the incorrect reply to a challenge from *Ramillies*. Though a number of people had seen the floatplane, its identity could not be established. Though it was suspected that the aircraft may have come from a German raider, it was concluded that it was probably Vichy and engaged in a reconnaissance in advance of a submarine attack. Accordingly, *Ramillies* weighed anchor and steamed slowly round the harbour until daybreak, when she anchored and air patrols by South African Air Force aircraft commenced. Nothing suspicious was sighted and precautions were relaxed.

The British seem to have been extraordinarily lax in their treatment of the aircraft sighting. The Japanese were known to possess aircraft-carrying submarines and were known to have employed midget submarines at Pearl Harbor. Moreover, the Royal Navy had suffered more than most on account of midget submarine operations (see Chapter 2) and ought to have been more aware of the likelihood of attack. True, *Ramillies* was not the most impressive battleship in the Fleet, but she was nonetheless a valuable unit.

The plan was for the *Ko-Hyoteki* to be released some nine miles from the harbour entrance on the evening of 30 May. Following the successful completion of their attacks, the crews would abandon their submarines and make for a rendezvous point near to the town of Hellville,[1] where the carrier submarines would wait for two days before departing for commerce raiding operations in the Indian Ocean. At this stage the *Ko-Hyoteki* on *I-18* obstinately refused to start: it had been damaged in heavy seas during the crossing of the Indian Ocean. The repairs were beyond the capability of *I-18*'s engine-room department and so Otani had to abandon his part of the operation. The *Ko-Hyoteki* were released just after 1700 on 30 May. The four men had all made their wills and left hair and nail clippings behind. Akeida had been one of the pioneers of *Ko-Hyoteki* operations and had few illusions about his chances. In a letter to his wife he promised that, if he were unable to return to the parent submarine, he would fight with his sword until it turned to scrap. Takemoto, a quiet, capable man, wrote two letters, one to his father and the other to his wife. Iwase and Takata made similar preparations on board *I-16*.

Circumstantial evidence suggests that it was the *Ko-Hyoteki* from *I-16* which was lost shortly after launching: the cause is unknown, but flooding or battery explosion are the most likely reasons. It was the *Ko-Hiyoteki* from *I-20*, that commanded by Lieutenant Akeida, which made the long passage down the winding channel leading to the inner anchorage—a considerable navigation feat in its own right.

The night of the 30 May was clear, with a full moon. In Oronjia Pass *Thyme* was on patrol, while at anchor at Port Nievre lay *Genista* at short notice for steam. Suddenly, at 2025, the harbour was rocked by an explosion in *Ramillies*: the battleship had been torpedoed. The torpedo struck on the port side abreast 'A' turret. Three minutes later the tanker *British Loyalty* reported sighting a submarine. There was now a certain amount of pandemonium as *British Loyalty*'s gunners opened fire, joined by *Thyme* and *Genista* and *Ramillies*' picket boat which began dropping depth charges at random around the harbour. While all this was going *British Loyalty* was hit aft by a second torpedo. She had just got under way and she sank rapidly by the stern, her bows remaining above the water.

All attempts at finding the culprit were unsuccessful, but *Ramillies* had been hit hard. There was no electric power below decks and she had assumed a 4.5-degree list to port. However, engineers succeeded in raising steam so that she could be moved into shallow water near Port Nievre should the flooding increase to a dangerous degree. Her draught was 43ft forward and 29ft aft. The 4in HA magazine and 'A' 15in magazine and shell room were flooded, together with all compartments between bulkheads 42 to 58 above main deck and 27 to 42 below it; compartments 27 to 42 and 58 to 72 above the main deck were also flooded. It was a remarkable amount of damage from one 17.7in torpedo.

During the night the flooding was kept under control and no further leaks developed. The next day divers were sent down and reported a hole about 20ft in diameter extending from stations 33 to 43, the highest part being 22ft below the forecastle deck. One plate of the bulge, about 20ft long, was projecting on the foremost side of the damage. On this and succeeding days steps were taken to shore up 27 and 58 bulkheads and to lighten the ship forward in order to reduce the trim by the bow. Since both 'A' magazine and shell room were flooded, it was decided that 'B' magazine and shell room should be emptied together with all 6in and 2pdr ammunition and about 600 tons of fuel and stores in the forward part of the ship.

Duncan and *Active* arrived on 1 June and at once carried out an A/S search of the area but, not surprisingly, found nothing. *Decoy* arrived on the 2nd carrying

Constructor Captain H. S. Pengelly RCNC, Fleet Constructor Officer Eastern Fleet, who pronounced *Ramillies* fit to sail for Durban and more permanent repairs. She arrived on 9 June after an uneventful passage. In his report, Syfret noted that

> ... the excellent work performed in making the ship seaworthy reflects very great credit on all; in particular, the tireless efforts of the engine-room, shipwright and electrical departments are deserving of much praise.[2]

Following the operation Akeida and Takemoto ditched their craft, although the scuttling charges failed to explode, and headed for the hills. On 1 June they were spotted by a native near the village of Anijabe, who reported their presence to the British authorities. A patrol of Royal Marines was sent after the men, who covered 48 miles over rough country until the morning of 2 June, when they were spotted on a hill above the isthumus of Anovondrona within sight of the sea. The Marines called on the Japanese to give themselves up but the two men refused, firing on the patrol with pistols while one of men, probably Akeida, leapt forward with a sword.

The two Japanese never stood a chance. Surrender was out of the question and both men sought an honourable death. After being stripped of their clothing and effects, Akeido and Takemoto were ignominiously buried in an unmarked grave near where they had fallen. The clothing and effects of the two men yielded a rich haul. The war diary for the East Indies Station recorded that

> The clothing found on the two Japanese was such as might have been used by aircraft or submarine crews, but did not include any goggles or flying helmets. One page of notes written on a scrap from a notebook was recovered, as well as a watch and packets of cigarettes, all of which had naval markings. When translated it was found that the above-mentioned notes were a rough log of a successful torpedo attack at Diego Suarez.[3]

The notes were hurriedly translated by a Japanese-speaking naval officer flown in for the purpose and it was learned that they were addressed to Commander Takashi Yamada of *I-20*—proof that it was Akeida and Takemoto who had succeeded in this audacious attack. On the same day that Akeida and Takemoto died, a body wearing Japanese naval uniform was washed up on the beach outside Diego Suarez Bay. After being stripped of clothing and effects, this too was buried unceremoniously.[4]

The graves of Akeida and Takemoto, and that of the unknown member of *I-16*'s *Ko-Hyoteki*, were never marked or found. A memorial near the spot was put up after the war and in 1976 a Japanese businessman, Masayoshi Iijima, had a stone cairn erected in their memory.

The initial British supposition that the attack was the responsibility of a Vichy French submarine meant that no warning was issued to other commands about the danger of Japanese midget submarine attack. Thus, when the boats assigned to attack Sydney harbour surfaced seven miles east of Sydney Heads at dusk on 31 May, they found the harbour brightly illuminated.

The force assigned to attack Sydney was commanded by Captain Hanku Sasaki IJN, who had led the attack on Pearl Harbor, and consisted of four carrier submarines, *I-27*, *I-22*, *I-24* and *I-28*. However, *I-28* was torpedoed by the American submarine *Tautog* on 19 May 1942 off Truk. Also assigned to the force were the submarines *I-21* and *I-29*, which carried the Yokosuka E14Y floatplane for reconnaissance. The crews of the *Ko-Hyoteki* assigned to the operation were:

I-27	(Lieutenant-Commander Iwao Yoshimura IJN)
	Lieutenant Kenshi Chuman IJN
	Petty Officer Takeshi Omori
I-22	(Commander Kiyoi Ageta IJN)
	Lieutenant Keiu Matsuo IJN
	Petty Officer Masao Tsusuki
I-24	(Commander Hiroshi Hanabusa IJN)
	Sub-Lieutenant Katsuhisa Ban IJN
	Petty Officer Momoru Ashibe

Unlike Ishizaki, Sasaki had a much more restricted brief: he was solely to attack warships reported to be in Sydney harbour; he had no wider commerce-raiding brief. On 20 May *I-29*'s floatplane had reported the presence of a number of warships including 'cruisers and battleships'.[5]

On 19 May *I-24* came to the surface to begin a battery charge and the opportunity was taken to carry out some essential maintenance on Yamaki's midget. As *Yamaki* entered the midget, followed by his Number 2, Petty Officer Shizuka Matsumoto, there was a strong smell of chlorine. Matsumoto turned on the interior light to investigate and there was a terrific explosion. Matsumoto was blown out of the hatch like a cork and went overboard. His body was not found, despite a four-hour search. Yamaki was badly burned, so Hanabusa decided to return to Truk. There the damaged midget was exchanged for that which had been intended for *I-28*. Sub-Lieutenant Katsuhisa Ban, who had been left behind at Truk on account of *I-28* having been sunk, was given another chance to take part in the operation. Years later Yamaki was to visit Sydney and regret that it was Ban who perished in the harbour and not him.

There was a world of difference in attacking the undefended harbour at Diego Suarez and attacking Sydney. The Royal Australian Navy had taken steps to protect Sydney harbour and there were, in effect, three layers of defences. The first was an electronic indicator loop laid in deep water well outside Sydney Heads. It formed a defensive half-circle which stretched from North Head to Bondi. The cable was divided into six sections, and 'tails' from each section were led ashore to the main loop station on Outer South Head. The indicator loop was able to detect the passage of surface or submerged craft, the event being recorded on a stylograph. If a contact could not be identified, an alarm would be triggered. The main disadvantage to this indicator line was that it only registered large targets; a small target like a *Ko-Hyoteki* would pass over it unnoticed. Further inside the harbour lay the second barrier. This comprised two, more sensitive indicator loops, one running between Inner South Head and Outer North Head (No 11) and the other between Inner South Head and Middle Head (No 12). These two loops could detect a midget submarine but, obviously, much depended on the alertness and competence of the operators. In a busy harbour like Sydney, where there was a constant level of harbour traffic, operators had to be very alert to distinguish legitimate from suspicious movements. The final layer of defence was an anti-torpedo boom. Boom defences for Sydney harbour had been proposed as early as 1941 when a plan was mooted to construct a double anti-torpedo net between Middle Head and Inner South Head, which constituted the narrowest point of the harbour entrance. However, there were not enough nets for such an ambitious project, so as an interim measure a single anti-torpedo net was constructed between George's Head and Green Point on Inner South Head.

Work began in January 1942 with the sinking of forty clusters of dolphins to support the net. The design of the net allowed for the incorporation of two gates, one across the western channel entrance and the other at the eastern channel. The gates were made from nets suspended from floats as opposed to strung from the dolphins and could be pulled open by boom defence vessels. By May 1942 the fixed centre section of the net was complete but the two gates were not. Thus at the western end of the net there was a gap of 236m while at the eastern end there was a gap of 230m.

On 30 May Warrant Flying Officer Susumo Ito took off in his Yokosuka E14Y from the submarine *I-21*, which was cruising 35 miles north-east of Sydney. He flew low over the anti-submarine boom to sketch it and noted the gaps at the western and eastern ends. He then flew up the harbour, passing the famous Harbour Bridge and flying as far as Cockatoo Island dockyard before returning. The plane overturned on landing and had to be sunk, but Ito and his observer were saved. His reconnaissance enabled Sasaki to issue his final operational order, Telegraphic Order No 4, at 1800 on 30 May. The date for the operation was confirmed as 31 May and on the evening of that day the three parent submarines gathered outside the Sydney Heads. The weather was overcast and the sea rough with a fair swell running. The parent submarines were disposed in an arc around the entrance to Sydney harbour well outside the detection range of the outer indicator loop, whose existence the Japanese suspected but might not have been aware of. *I-27* was disposed nearest the shore, six miles south-east of the harbour. Roughly in the centre was *I-22*, while *I-24* was positioned seven miles north-east of South Head. The *Ko-Hyoteki* were launched while each parent submarine was submerged. The three pairs of crewmen climbed up through the access trunk from the submarine into the *Ko-Hyoteki*, pulling the heavy steel hatch cover up behind them. A control wheel on the inside of the hatch released the three lugs which bound the *Ko-Hyoteki* to the submarine. Actual release was achieved by blowing a small amount of HP air into the ballast tank while going ahead on the motor. At 1721 Lieutenant Matsuo set off from *I-22*, followed at 1728 by Lieutenant Chuman from *I-27*, with Sub-Lieutenant Ban setting off from *I-24* at 1740. Before departure all six men had partaken of a special meal, said prayers before the Shinto shrine in each submarine and made whatever private arrangements each man desired.

Although Matsuo was the first to release his *Ko-Hyoteki*, the plan called for Chuman's craft to proceed first, since he was released nearest the shore, with the others following at twenty-minute intervals. Even though the sky was overcast, the *Ko-Hyoteki* commanders were able to navigate by the measured sweep of the Macquarie lighthouse which, unbelievably, remained lit—despite it being war-time—and provided an ideal operational reference point.

Of the three *Ko-Hyoteki* operations mounted by the Japanese Navy, the attack at Sydney is the best documented, largely because two of the three craft were recovered. It is therefore possible to trace the courses of the craft individually as they went about the operation. Lieutenant Chuman's craft was the first to enter the harbour. He passed undetected over the first indicator loop and then made a sharp turn to port to take up towards the harbour. In the heavy seas and the strong southerly current, Chuman was making slow progress: in fact, he was nearly an hour behind schedule.

At 2001 Chuman passed over the second indicator loop. This time the signature of his crossing was recorded on the stylograph, but no action was taken even though the ratings on duty had standing instructions to raise the alarm if the stylograph registered a contact which was not consistent with harbour traffic. Chuman now headed for the western channel, following a ferry, where, he had been briefed, there was a gap in the boom. Here his luck ran out. For some reason his craft veered off course and, instead of passing safely through the net, ploughed straight into the centre, fixed section. Chuman tried to drive his way through the net in the hope that the serrated teeth on his bow guard would slice through, but all his efforts were in vain and by 2005 the midget was firmly entangled in the net in a bow-up attitude with the ends of the two torpedo tubes protruding slightly above the water.

A Marine Services Board watchman, James Cargill, was on duty at the western end of the fixed section of the net when he noticed what appeared to be a launch without lights alongside the net. He knew that craft without lights were not allowed near the net, so he rowed over to investigate. He found a structure which he thought looked like two oxy-acetylene bottles and resembled a mine or a submarine. A very worried Cargill rowed back to the *Yarroma*, one of two patrol boats on duty by the net that evening. *Yarroma* was commanded by Sub-Lieutenant H. C. Eyres, who had been a shipping clerk before the war. Eyres had *Yarroma*'s searchlight trained on the object, which he dismissed as naval wreckage. He was extremely indifferent about Cargill's sighting, an attitude which the official report on the incident subsequently condemned as 'deplorable and inexplicable'. He refused to take *Yarroma* over to investigate or accompany Cargill in his skiff, confining himself to reporting that a 'suspicious object' had been sighted in the nets. However, he did agree to let one of *Yarroma*'s crew accompany Cargill. When the two men returned just after 2210 they confirmed that the object was a submarine.

In the meantime another harbour defence craft, the *Lolita*, commanded by Warrant Officer Herbert Anderson, had arrived on the scene. Anderson examined the object with the aid of an Aldis lamp and had no difficulty in recognising it as a submarine. The craft's periscope was raised and rotating, causing the Aldis lamp's beam to reflect off the prism. Anderson decided on a fairly drastic measure for dealing with the submarine. Instead of opening fire with his 0.303in machine gun, which would probably have penetrated the thin hull of the craft, he dropped three 350lb depth charges. Fortunately the water depth was insufficient to activate the charges' hydrostatic fuses, otherwise, when combined with the sympathetic detonation of the submarine's two torpedoes, the result would have been an apocalyptic end for *Yarroma*, *Lolita*, the submarine and anyone else in the vicinity. Inside the submarine Chuman and Omori realised that their position was hopeless and that *Jibaku* was the only honourable path open to them. At 10.35 they fired the scuttling charge which blew off the forward section of their small craft. There was a vivid orange flash and a surge of water which nearly swamped the *Lolita* and debris was hurled high into the air.

Meanwhile the second *Ko-Hyoteki*, commanded by Sub-Lieutenant Ban, was inward bound. At 2148 it too passed over the inner indicator loop unobserved (the crossing was noted on the stylograph but no action was taken) and shortly after 2200 glided through the eastern gate in the anti-torpedo net as Cargill was returning for his second look at Chuman's midget. Ban headed up the harbour towards the warships lying at anchor. Even though a submarine alarm had by this stage been reported, there was no black-out and the American cruiser *Chicago* was brightly silhouetted against the floodlights on a large graving dock on Garden Island. However, at 2052 Ban's submarine was spotted by an alert seaman on board *Chicago*. Ban was evidently having trouble in depth-keeping and his craft kept porpoising, for his wake was seen although the shape of his small conning tower was barely visible. *Chicago* illuminated the area with her searchlight and the submarine was sighted. *Chicago* was only at a modified Condition III state of readiness, with most of her ship's company ashore enjoying the pleasures of Sydney. The sole 5in gun's crew, closed up, could not bring their weapon into action because it would not depress far enough, but a quadruple 0.5in machine gun did open fire. The submarine was held in the searchlight's beam and as it drew forward of the beam the range opened and the 5in gun could engage. A veritable hail of 5in and machine-gun ammunition was fired in the general direction of Fort Denison.

Ban continued to head up the harbour, although he had probably already selected *Chicago* as the most profitable target available. He was still finding it hard to keep the craft on an even trim, and as he passed the north-west tip of Garden Island his submarine was sighted by the two corvettes, *Geelong* and *Whyalla*. Seamen on these two ships saw the wake left by the submarine's jumping wire and opened fire with 20mm Oerlikons. Fortunately Ban and Ashibe now managed to position the ballast weights correctly for the submarine submerged. Ban realised that he had come too far up the harbour so he turned around and headed back towards Bradley's Head on the north side—an ideal position from which to torpedo the *Chicago*.

What was the reaction of the command in Sydney to the sighting of two submarines in the harbour? Rear-Admiral Muirhead-Gould had been at a dinner party but shortly after 2230 he decided to visit the boom where Chuman's midget had been scuttled to see for himself. From his demeanour it was clear that he was sceptical about the sightings, asking facetious questions of *Lolita*'s commanding officer and coxswain. The fact that he had been at a party and had eaten and drunk well may have contributed to his relaxed attitude, for it was not until 1114 that he ordered all ships in the harbour to douse their lights and not until 1225 that he ordered the lights on the Garden Island graving dock to be switched off. Even so, ferries continued to run: Muirhead-Gould considered that the more craft there were about the more likely any submarines in the area would keep their heads down.

By 1229 Ban was in position 800m from the *Chicago*, which, although no longer illuminated by the dock lights, was lit by the moon and clearing sky. Smoke was coming from her two funnels and Ban, not unnaturally, assumed that she was under way. Accordingly, when aiming the torpedo he made allowances for what he considered *Chicago*'s speed to be. However the cruiser was still firmly secured to her buoys and the torpedo missed ahead. It passed under the Dutch submarine *KIX* and the harbour ferry *Kuttabul*, now serving as an accommodation ship, to explode against the harbour wall on the eastern side of Garden Island. The blast lifted *Kuttabul* out of the water, killing twenty-one ratings sleeping on board. *Kuttabul* subsequently sank at her moorings. The blast echoed round the harbour. One witness told the *Sydney Morning Herald*:

> I saw the whole ferry lift as though she were on top of an enormous wave and then settle down again, sinking by the stern. I saw pieces of wood flying through the air. Half the steering wheel was blown away.[6]

Ban's submarine lost trim after firing and he had to struggle for some minutes before launching his second torpedo. This missed for the same reason as the first and ran aground on the east shore of Garden Island. Ban now headed for the open sea and the fate of his craft is unknown. At 0158 on 1 June the indicator loop recorded an outward crossing, which, the Official History concludes, may have been Ban heading for the recovery position off Port Hacking.

Ban and Ashibe never made the recovery. Some have suggested that the six *Ko-Hyoteki* operators had agreed a mutual suicide pact in that if they managed to carry out the operation and exit from the harbour they would not try and contact the parent submarines for fear of giving their position away. Speaking many years later, Captain Yamaki supported this theory:

> Admiral Yamamoto told us, 'You must come back. You must take care of your life, never waste it.' But it was very difficult to come back to the mother submarine. We talked over this problem. We made up our minds that if we successfully escaped from the harbour after the attack, we would not return to the mother submarine because that meant using the wireless and revealing the position of the mother submarine. For the sake of two men's lives, the lives of 100 would be put at risk.[7]

However, a more realistic scenario is that Ban's midget ran out of power. Although the craft had a nominal endurance of 80nm at 6kt, Ban had almost certainly exhausted this in his high-speed manoeuvring up and down Sydney harbour. In these circumstances, Ban's midget may have drifted out to sea once the battery was drained. Once the realisation dawned that there was no hope of making the rendezvous, Ban and Ashibe probably fired the scuttling charge.

The third *Ko-Hyoteki*, commanded by Lieutenant Keiu Matsuo, was beginning his run in. While approaching the Heads it was spotted at 1052 by the patrol vessels *Lauriana* and *Yandra*. The latter tried to ram the submarine but merely struck it a glancing blow before dropping a full pattern of six depth charges. When there was no further sign of the submarine those aboard *Yandra* thought their attack to have been successful. In fact, Matsuo had probably headed for the bottom and safety, using his passive hydrophone to indicate when it was clear to move.

Some four hours later Matsuo's craft came off the bottom and headed inwards. He was spotted by the cruiser *Chicago*, which was heading out to sea, at 0300 and at 0301 an inward crossing was recorded on No 12 indicator loop. At 0350 the armed merchant cruiser *Kanimbla*, lying at her buoy, opened fire on what appeared to be a submarine. Nearly an hour later the launch *Sea Mist* (Lieutenant Reginald Andrew RANVR), which was patrolling around the western gate of the anti-torpedo boom, observed a dark object off Taylor's Bay.

Andrew had only been in command of *Sea Mist* for two days and although by his own admission he did not feel ready for command, his actions were very creditable. A red Very light was fired while *Sea Mist* went over the spot where the submarine had been seen to dive and dropped a depth charge. The charge was set to explode at 15m, which gave the *Sea Mist* only five minutes to get clear. As it was, the small craft was thrown forward on a surge of water as the depth charge exploded.

Right: An excellent re-creation of Bushnell's *Turtle* now on display in the Royal Navy Submarine Museum at Gosport. (Royal Navy Submarine Museum)

Below left: The battleship *Viribus Unitis* sinking at Pola on 1 November 1918. This operation was the inspiration for subsequent Italian developments in this field.

Below right: Captain Raffaele Paolucci, the pioneer of Italian underwater assault units. (Museo Storico Navale, Venice)

Above: A *Maiale* on display at the Naval Museum in Venice. The craft is shown with a 300kg warhead attached. (Museo Storico Navale, Venice)

Below: *Tenente di Vascello* Birindelli's *Maiale* at Gibraltar after being recovered from the harbour by the British.

Right, upper: An informal group of *Decima Mas* officers and senior rates at the Boca di Serchio in 1941. Rear row (left to right): Martellotta, Notari, Forza, Borghese, Cella, Chersi and Feltrinelli. Fron row (left to right): De la Penne, Spaccarelli, Manisco, Magello and Marceglia.

Right, lower: The submarine *Ambra* at La Spezia in April 1942 showing the arrangement of SLC containers on the casing.

Right: Keeping up appearances: Admiral Sir Andrew Cunningham takes the salute at the morning ceremony of 'Colours'. The photograph was taken for the benefit of the Press and hid the fact that his flagship, HMS *Queen Elizabeth*, was resting on the bottom.
Below: An aerial reconnaissance photograph of Gibraltar showing warships at anchor within the harbour and merchant shipping at anchor in Algeciras Bay. Note how the proximity of the Spanish coastline made the Italians' task extremely easy.

Above: The Italian tanker *Olterra* at Gibraltar in September 1943 following the armistice.

Below left: The hidden trapdoor in *Olterra*'s forepeak used by *Maiale* to leave and re-enter the tanker. The trapdoor would normally be below the waterline: this photograph was taken by the British when the *Olterra* had been trimmed by the stern to give up her secrets.

Below right: *Sottotenente di Vascello* Licio Visintini, who was responsible for the conversion of the *Olterra* as a forward base for *Decima Mas* operations.

Left, top: A view looking landwards from the beach at Punta Mayorga showing the Villa Carmela (A) and the stream (B) along which the *Gamma* men went to and from the beach.

Left, centre: A view from the beach at Punta Mayorga showing the stream flowing into Algeciras Bay. All the *Gamma* men had to do was to swim out to the shipping seen in the distance.

Left, bottom: Lieutenant Lionel Crabbe, commanding officer of the Gibraltar Underwater Working Party. (IWM A.23270)

Above, left: *CB5* at Costanza on the Black Sea in May 1942.

Above, right: A rare photograph of *CA2* under trials at the secret testing establishment on the Lac d'Iseo in 1942.

Left, upper: The 'bed' made in the casing of the submarine *Leonardo da Vinci* in order to carry a *CA* class submarine across the Atlantic for an attack on shipping inside the harbour New York.

Left, lower: A cutaway model produced by the Admiralty showing the internal layout of a Japanese *Ko-Hyoteki* midget submarine. The craft's armament was composed of the two torpedoes seen in the bow.

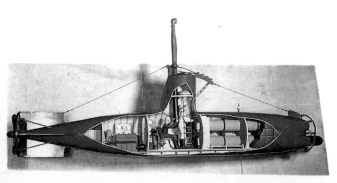

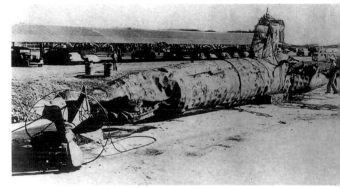

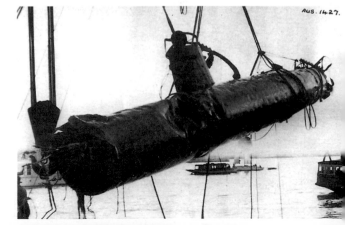

Above: *HA-19* washed
ashore on the island of Oahu
after the Japanese attack on
Pearl Harbor on 7 December
1941. *HA-19* was attacked by
the destroyer *Ward* before
striking a reef and drifting
ashore; her commanding
officer, Ensign Kazuo
Sakamaki, was captured and
became America's first PoW.
Right, upper: One of the
Ko-Hyoteki salvaged at Pearl
Harbor. This specimen was
subsequently entombed in a
breakwater.
Right, lower: Four days
after the attack on Sydney,
Matsuo's *Ko-Hyoteki* is
raised from the harbour.

Above: The seven *Ko-Hyoteki* crew who took part in the attacks on Sydney and Diego Suarez, photographed on board *Chiyoda* in early 1942.

Left: The interior of Matsuo's *Ko-Hyoteki* after it had been raised for examination by the Australian authorities. The view shows the control room looking forward, with the periscope and periscope well in the centre. (AWM)

Right, upper: HMS *Ramillies*, the largest victim of Japanese *Ko-Hyoteki* attacks. (IWM A.25722)

Right, lower: *Ko-Hyoteki* abandoned in the Aleutians in June 1943. These craft were not successful when used in a defensive role.

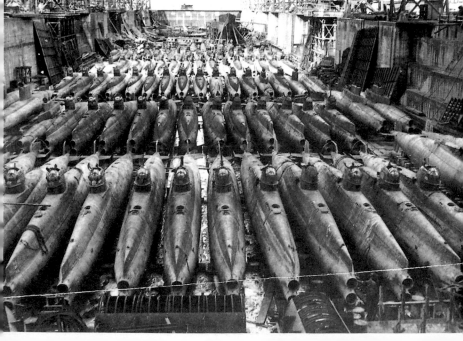

Left, upper: A pall of smoke marks the spot where a *Kaiten* found its mark at Ulithi on 20 November 1944. Of the five *Kaiten* launched, only one found a target—the oiler *Mississinewa*. (USN)

Left, lower: A graving dock at Kure packed with Type D *Ko-Hyoteki*—best known as *Koryu* (Scaly Dragon)—in 1945. These craft could be built at a rate of 180 a month but American bombing and a shortage of raw materials meant that of the 540 ordered in June 1944 only 115 were completed.

Right, top: A *Kaiten* (Heaven Shaker) is launched over the stern of the specially adapted cruiser *Kitakami*

Right, centre: *Kaiten* mounted on the casing of the Japanese submarine *I-370* as he sails to attack US shipping on 20 February 1945. The *Kaiten* crews, wearing their traditional *Hachimaki* headbands and carrying swords, are standing in their craft. Six days later *I-370* was sunk off Iwo Jima by the destroyer *Finnegan*, her *Kaiten* unused.

Right, bottom: A Japanese two-man *Kairyu* abandoned at Kure in September 1945.

Above: The Chariot was the British response to the activities of the *Decima Mas*. It was virtually identical to the Italian *Maiale*, having been copied from one fished out of Gibraltar harbour.

Left: The driver's position in a Chariot, showing the controls. The 'helm', which operated the rudder and hydroplanes, is in the centre with the magnetic compass fitted in front; the switches to the left and right of the helm are for the ballast pumps, while the handle behind the helm is for the main motor. The censor has obliterated the markings of two of the gauges i

e interests of security.

bove: The British also
veloped the Mk II Chariot,
own here, in which the
erators sat back to back in a
ckpit rather than astride the
aft. Mk II Chariots were used
an attack on two Italian-flag
erchant ships at Phuket in
ailand on 27 October 1944.

ight: A Charioteer being
essed in his diving suit (the
aden suit, after Commander
offrey Sladen who designed it,
t better known as the 'Clammy
eath' suit). The breathing
paratus, visible on the diver's
est, was based on the Davis
bmarine Escape Apparatus in
neral use throughout the Fleet
d relied on oxygen being
ycled through a Protosorb
it.

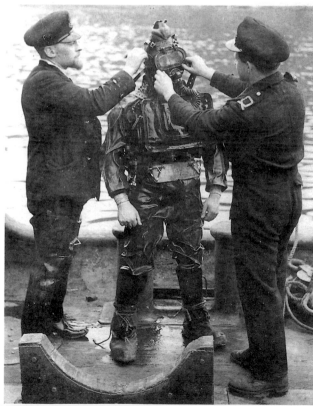

Above: A very rare photograph of either *X3* or *X4*, the prototype X-Craft. The differences in layout between these and the operational craft are easy to spot: they concern the hatch for the W&D in the centre of the craft and the night periscope fitted in the bow.

Below: An X-Craft, one of the *X5–X10* series, out of the water at HMS *Varbel* for maintenance. Note the side cargo fitted to port.

But the damage was done. In the centre of the boil the submarine was seen to surface with her twin propellers rotating slowly before sinking again. Andrew dropped another depth charge on the spot and this time the shock of the explosion wrecked one of *Sea Mist*'s engines, reducing her speed to 4kt. But help was on the way. The patrol craft *Yarroma* and *Steady Hour* were soon on the scene and for the next three and a half hours dropped over seventeen depth charges on the spot. Matsuo's position was hopeless. At some time in the early morning of 1 June Petty Officer Tzuzuku was either killed by Matsuo or shot himself using Matsuo's 8mm Taisho service pistol. Matsuo then turned the gun on himself.

On the morning of 1 June divers located Matsuo's craft in 18m of water but it was not until 4 June that it was brought to the surface. The guard at the bow was badly buckled and the protective bow caps were crushed. On the starboard side amidships was a dent in the hull which may have been made by *Chicago* on her way out of the harbour or by one of the depth charges. Australian naval personnel entered the craft and found Matsuo's body in the control room while Petty Officer Tzuzuku lay in the motor room. Matsuo was wearing his *Senninbari* belt, while his ceremonial sword was found hanging in the control room. The next day the Australians raised the mangled remains of Chuman's craft. The centre section had been completely obliterated by the detonation of the scuttling charge. Nevertheless, both torpedoes were intact and had to be made safe.

The bodies of Matsuo, Tzuzuku, Chuman and Omori were cremated on 9 June at Sydney's Eastern Suburbs Crematorium. A naval guard of honour was paraded, the traditional three volleys fired and the last post sounded. The ashes of the four were returned to Japan in the repatriation ship *Kamikura Maru*, where they were accorded the equivalent of a state funeral. Muirhead-Gould came in for a considerable amount of criticism for the honours accorded the Japanese. He defended his decision in a radio broadcast and his words were a fitting tribute to four brave men:

I have been criticised for according these men military honours we hope may be accorded to our own comrades who have died in enemy lands. But I ask you—should we not accord full honours to such brave men as these. It must take courage of the very highest order to go out in a thing like that steel coffin. I hope I shall not be a coward when my time comes, but I confess that I wonder whether I would have the courage to take one of those things across Sydney harbour in peacetime. Theirs was a courage which was not the property or the tradition or the heritage of any one nation: it is a courage shared by brave men of our own countries as well as of the enemy, and however horrible war and its results may be, it is a courage which is recognised and universally admired. These men were patriots of the highest order. How many of us are prepared to make one thousandth of the sacrifice that these men made?[8]

Some have suggested that the broadcast was a calculated play on Japanese emotions to try and win better treatment for British and Australian prisoners-of-war in Japanese hands. If so, it was a dismal failure, for there was no amelioration in their conditions.

The four parent submarines waited off Port Hacking for the midgets to return. When it became obvious that the craft were not returning, they engaged in a brief and unspectacular commerce-raiding campaign off the east coast of Australia, sinking six ships totalling 29,000grt. Additionally, *I-24* engaged in a bombardment of Sydney and *I-21* did the same at Newcastle. The Japanese were unaware of what had been achieved in the attack, although it was obvious from searchlight activity in the harbour that the midgets had been detected. It was not until the Press announced that the *Kuttabul* had been sunk that any definite news was known of the attack. It was hardly spectacular. Six submarines had been committed to an operation in which an elderly ferry had been torpedoed. But it was pure bad luck that the operation did not meet with greater success. Ban would not be the first submarine commander to credit a target with more speed. Given the stress and conditions under which he was operating, his error was understandable and hardly surprising.

In any case, the Australian authorities had little to congratulate themselves about. The three *Ko-Hyoteki* had all passed through defences established to prevent such an occurrence. As the Official History of the Royal Australian Navy concluded:

> Luck was certainly on the side of the defenders and was undeserved in the early stages where inactivity and indecision were manifested.[9]

The remains of Chuman's and Matsuo's *Ko-Hyoteki* were joined together and sent around Australia as an attraction to boost war savings. The submarine now rests outside the Australian War Memorial in Canberra, where the ravages of the fierce climate have taken their toll. In 1968 the mother of Lieutenant Matsuo visited the submarine and poured a libation of *saki* over the craft in her son's memory. In a gentle and touching ceremony, marred only by the xenophobic outpourings of Australia's gutter press, she was presented with her son's *Senninbari* belt.

Chapter 8

Midget Mortality

Would that I could be born seven times, and
  sacrifice my life for my country
Resolved to die, my mind is firm and again
  expecting success,
Smiling I go abroad.
—Commander Takeo Hirose IJN

The attack on Sydney was the last occasion in which *Ko-Hyoteki* were used offensively. Since there was no possibility of the decisive naval engagement on which the Japanese had pinned so much hope taking place, other means of employment had to be found for these craft. Harbour defence was one such role; another was attacking shipping at anchor. These roles assumed increased importance with the American landings in the Solomon Islands on 7 August 1942. Here, in theory, was a theatre in which the *Ko-Hyoteki* could be profitably employed. There was a surfeit of targets in terms of both warships and transports and the Japanese possessed bases nearby from where the attacks could be launched. Equally important was the fact that because the attacks would always take place relatively close to land, the parent submarines would be freed from the obligation of having to wait to recover the *Ko-Hyoteki*.

In November 1942 the Third Special Attack Flotilla, under the command of Captain Shinosuke Ota IJN, was ordered to Indispensable Strait for operations against American transports in the Lunga anchorage at Guadalcanal. The Flotilla consisted of the veteran submarines *I 16*, *I-20* and *I-24*; no aircraft-carrying submarines were included. However, there were no more experienced *Ko-Hyoteki* crewmen available.

The Third Special Attack Flotilla enjoyed relative success. On 7 November *I-20* released a midget commanded by Sub-Lieutenant Nobuharu Kunihiro IJN at the transport anchorage at the southern end of Savo Island. Kunihiro fired both his torpedoes at the 2,227grt transport *Majaba*, which was lying at anchor. The transport was badly damaged and had to be beached as a constructive total loss. Despite a counter-attack by American destroyers, Kunihiro and his Number 2 were successfully recovered. They were the first *Ko-Hyoteki* crewmen to survive an operation, not, of course, counting the unfortunate Sakamaki who was languishing in an American PoW camp.

A few days after Kunihiro's success, Sub-Lieutenant Teiji Yamaki, who had been unable to take part in the operation against Sydney, was launched by *I-16*. On this occasion the usually reliable *Ko-Hyoteki* malfunctioned—the rudder jammed—and Yamaki scuttled the craft. He and his Number 2 swam several miles to the shore and recovery. On 28 November a midget commanded by Sub-Lieutenant Hiroshi Hoka, with Petty Officer Shinsaku Ikuma as his crewman, fired a torpedo at the 6,200grt US Navy transport *Alchiba*. The torpedo hit started a fire which threatened to spread to the ship's cargo of explosive and drummed petrol. While some members of the crew fought the fire, others hastily removed the explosives. Five hours later what was thought to be a torpedo exploded on the bottom beneath the ship. Either Hoka had returned for a second shot or another midget was in the area whose launch has not been recorded. *Alchiba* was beached, and fires on board burned for four days before being extinguished.

Hoka and Ikuma did not survive this operation. The cause of death is not known, but their craft was salvaged by the Americans in June 1943 and yielded a wealth of intelligence information, including instructions for carrying out an attack:

> Upon receiving a report that the enemy has been discovered, the attack will be carried out with the least possible delay. Do not lose your opportunity because you vainly delayed and thereby allowed the enemy to escape into a strongly defended harbour. Two *Hyoteki* will customarily be used against a powerful enemy ship. Four or more will not ordinarily be used simultaneously at one spot . . . It is essential that the attack be carried out from a firing position which is sufficiently close to ensure a direct hit. The basic firing position is from 70° to 110° at 500 metres.[1]

Eight of the *Ko-Hyoteki* were lost during the Guadalcanal campaign.

Harbour defence as a role for the *Ko-Hyoteki* presented itself particularly from 1943 onwards as the Americans assumed the offensive. The adoption of such a role meant that substantial modifications to the craft were required. However, it proved impossible to incorporate these modifications within the hull of the Type A *Ko-Hyoteki*, so a variant known as Type B was constructed. The Type B differed in several major respects, and comparative dimensions are given in the accompanying table.[2]

The Type B was not much bigger but contained a third crewman who was to be an Engine Room Artificer or Chief Engine Room Artificer—a reflection of the need for proper management of all the equipment on board. The addition of a third member of the crew coupled with the minimal increase in size and increase in endurance meant that conditions would be very cramped indeed, and this must have had an effect on operational efficiency. The other significant alteration was the addition of a 40hp/25kW generator and a 0.6 ton fuel tank. The generator would permit the charging of the battery while at sea (although this took an unacceptable eighteen hours) and would also permit direct drive while the boat was on the surface, thus increasing the endurance to 300–350 miles at 5–6kt. However, the weight of the generator meant a reduction in maximum submerged speed from 24 to 18.5 knots.

Comparative Data for *Ko-Hyoteki* Types A, B and C

	Type A	*Types B/C*
Design begun	1938	1942
First boat completed	1939	1943
Length (oa)	23.9m	24.9m
Beam (max)	1.8m	1.88m
Depth (CT to keel)	3.1m	3.1m
Displacement (submerged)	46 tons	50 tons
Main battery (type/no of cells)	Special D/224	Special D/224
Main motor (hp)	600	600
Max submerged speed	19kt	18.5kt
Diving depth	100m	100m
Torpedo tubes	Two 457mm	Two 457mm
No of torpedoes	2	2
HP air flasks (litres capacity x no)	430 x 2	430 x 2
Periscope length	3.05m	3.05m
Generator	–	40hp/25kW x 1
Crew	2	3
Endurance	Negligible	1–2 days

The Type B was a prototype, but it went into production as the Type C *Ko-Hyoteki*. Some 36 of these boats were built at Ourazaki near Kure before the autumn of 1944.[3]

Although the *Ko-Hyoteki* never fulfilled the hopes their designers had for them, the Japanese never really gave up with the weapon. Methods were tested for the recovery of *Ko-Hyoteki* by a submarine after an operation, even though operational experience indicated that the return of a *Ko-Hyoteki* crew was an unlikely event. The submarine *I-18* was fitted with a recovery apparatus and successfully launched and recovered *Ko-Hyoteki* while submerged and under way in 1943. However, the system was never used in combat. Development did not stop there. A minelaying *Ko-Hyoteki* called *M-Kanamono* was built in 1944 and carried four Type 2 or Type 3 submarine-laid mines instead of two torpedoes. Only one of these craft was constructed. Even writing with all the benefits of hindsight, the failure to proceed with this project represented a considerable lost opportunity for the Japanese. As a covert minelayer the *Ko-Hyoteki* would have been quite successful and would have caused a good deal of trouble to the Americans; the Germans were to make the same mistake with their *Biber* one-man submarine.

For the remainder of the war *Ko-Hyoteki* were employed in the Aleutians, in the Philippines, off Saipan and at Okinawa, without success. Three were lost in the Aleutians, eight in the Philippines and five at Saipan. At Okinawa at least ten were destroyed, although it is difficult to be sure of the exact number deployed and lost.

The only time a *Ko-Hyoteki* came close to achieving a significant success was when No 82 attacked the American cruiser *Boise* as the ship was passing through the Mindanao Sea, heading for the Lingayen Gulf and the invasion of Luzon. To sink a cruiser would have been achievement enough, but on this occasion *Boise* was carrying General Douglas MacArthur and his staff. The *Ko-Hyoteki* fired both torpedoes, the tracks of which were spotted by the USS *Phoenix*. Prompt evasive action by *Boise* saved the ship—and MacArthur—while the *Ko-Hyoteki* was rammed by the destroyer *David W. Taylor*.

Why did the *Ko-Hyoteki* have so little success? The answer is twofold. First, their crews were hopelessly inexperienced. The most seasoned *Ko-Hyoteki* operators had been killed at Pearl Harbor, Diego Suarez and Sydney and there was no pool of operational experience in war or peace for the new men to draw on. Secondly, the *Ko-Hyoteki* were acutely vulnerable to the comprehensive measures deployed against them by the Americans. However gallant their crews, the craft was no match for an enemy which enjoyed superiority in almost every field.

The *Ko-Hyoteki* never justified the hopes of their designers. Their effectiveness was compromised when their original role was changed to that of a covert attack weapon. The torpedo is never the best weapon for a craft operating covertly, since the craft has to compromise its position by coming near the surface in order to aim the weapon. Who knows how effective the *Ko-Hyoteki* would have been if used as their designers had intended? At the very least they would have given the opposing fleet commander a good deal to worry about. The *Ko-Hyoteki* was a craft of excellent design and construction, manned by very brave men, but one whose operational deployment was unsuited to it.

As the tide of the war turned against Japan, desperate measures were advocated to reverse the position. There was little the Japanese could do to counter America's awesome level of wartime production or her technical lead established in areas such as radar. Instead, they looked back and sought inspiration from their own military traditions. Suicide in battle, which had always featured in the Japanese military tradition (and, indeed, the Western tradition) as a means of avoiding capture and thereby disgrace, was now specifically recommended in the hope that individual courage and valour could prevail over American quantitative and qualitative superiority. The inauguration of Special Attack Units, better known by the Japanese term of *Kamikaze* after the 'Divine Wind' which had saved Japan from invasion by the Mongols in 1281, was confirmation that the policy of suicide had official approval (although not everyone in the Japanese High Command was enamoured of it), and the first *Kamikaze* attacks were made by aircraft during the Philippines Campaign at the Battle of Leyte Gulf.

This development did not pass unnoticed in the Japanese submarine service, where officers had been chafing under the restrictions placed on their *modus operandi*. This is not the place for a discussion of the employment of Japan's submarine fleet, but suffice it to say that there was dissatisfaction at submarines being employed on transport duties or attacking landing forces instead of being released against the long American supply lines. Captain Keenosuke Toriso, a submarine commanding officer who in the latter part of 1944 was an operations officer on the staff of the Sixth Fleet, recalled how Japan's submariners viewed their position:

> ... strenuous studies and efforts had been made in the homeland on how to save the ever deteriorating submarine situation. Typical among them was a human torpedo project which was originally advocated by two young submarine officers, Lieutenant Hiroshi Kuroke IJN and Sub-Lieutenant Sekio Nishina.
>
> Kuroke and Nishina, both graduates of the Naval Academy, hated to see the deterioration of the submarine fleet and they decided to do what they could by volunteering to man a large torpedo themselves and ram an enemy ship.[4]

The upshot of this conversation was the development of the *Kaiten* (Heaven Shaker) human torpedo. This was a derivative of the famous Type 93 'Long Lance' torpedo[5] which had caused such execution among Allied ships in the early stages of the war. See accompanying table.[6]

The operator, who was often a trainee naval aviator, sat in a fully enclosed position containing a fixed periscope, gyro compass and controls. The *Kaiten* would be carried on a parent submarine in a fashion similar to the *Ko-Hyoteki*, or in specially converted warships, although in the end only one ship was modified for *Kaiten* operations. The light cruiser *Kitakami* had already been converted to a fast transport with a reduced armament (four 5in, eighteen 25mm AA, eight 24in torpedo tubes) to carry six 14m Daihatsu landing craft when she was torpedoed by the British submarine *Templar* in the Strait of Malacca on 27 January 1944. Though the ship was badly damaged, she was not beyond repair and was subsequently rebuilt as a *Kaiten* carrier. Her torpedo tubes were removed, her AA armament was increased to sixty-seven 25mm and she was fitted with launching rails to carry eight *Kaiten* and a stern ramp to launch them from, in the same way as the *Ko-Hyoteki* were to have been launched from the seaplane carriers. Evidently the Japanese had not given up on the idea of launching *Kaiten* as part of a decisive fleet engagement against the Americans—even though such an engagement was but the stuff of dreams.

Sixteen submarines were converted to carry *Kaiten*. The number varied from class to class and the conversion usually involved the removal of deck guns and hangar/catapult arrangements if fitted (see table). Submarine-launched *Kaiten* would be carried in cradles on the casing. Each craft would be connected to the 'mother' submarine by a flexible tube which would allow the operator to board after receiving his final instructions from the submarine's commanding officer. A telephone linked the operator with the control until the last moment. After release the *Kaiten* ran for

Kaiten (Heaven Shaker) One-Man Human Torpedo

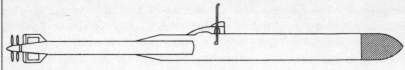

Displacement (submerged): 8.2 tons
Length: 14.75m
Beam: 1.0m
Propulsion: 1 x single-shaft 550bhp liquid oxygen torpedo motor
Speed (surfaced): 30kt
Range (surfaced): 12.5nm at 30kt
Armament: 1,550kg explosives
Crew: 1
Number delivered: About 400

Figures are for a *Kaiten* Mk 1. The Mk 2 version was similar but powered by a hydrogen peroxide engine giving a top speed of 40kt, but production problems prevented more than a handful being completed. The *Kaiten* Mk 3 was an experimental craft which never went into production, while the *Kaiten* Mk 4 reverted to the liquid oxygen engine but carried a larger, 1,800kg warhead. The total production of *Kaiten* Mks 2 and 4 is believed not to have exceeded 20. About 50 *Kaiten*, of all types, were used operationally. Hundreds were found in Japan after the war and broken up.

a period of time at a depth of 6m on a course pre-set on the *Kaiten*'s gyro by the parent submarine's navigator and then surfaced; the operator was now on his own.

Operating a *Kaiten* was extremely difficult. The operator might elect to approach the target submerged on a hitting track, in which case he had no idea of the situation on the surface. Moreover, the high speed of the *Kaiten* meant that the slightest mistake on the controls would have potentially disastrous consequences. During trials of the weapon in Tokuyama Bay in the autumn of 1944, one *Kaiten* went out of control while diving: at 30kt it, and the operator, went straight to the bottom of the bay with no hope of recovery. On the other hand, the operator could choose to make a dash to the target at periscope depth, in which case his periscope wash would be visible and his speed would be limited to no more than 12kt. In theory the operator was supposed make his exit through the access hatch when he was sure that the *Kaiten* was going to hit the target. This would imply that the operator would begin to make his exit when the craft was 100m away from impact and be clear at 50m. However, no one took this provision seriously: all *Kaiten* operators intended to remain with their craft until the end. In any case, a man in water close to the explosion of a 1,550kg warhead had few chances of survival. If the operator missed the target he could go round again for another attempt, although steering the craft at its top speed of 40kt must have been extremely difficult. The warhead could be exploded by an electric switch with two fuses activated by the operator, although an impact inertia switch was also fitted.

The thinking behind the operational employment of the *Kaiten* was very muddled. Some saw the weapon being employed in that fleet action which the Japanese desired so much; another option was to view the weapon as a last-ditch means of defence; while others, including many in the submarine service, saw the *Kaiten* as a substitute for professional competence. Captain Kennosuke Torisu remembered that

It seemed likely to me that a manned torpedo could be released from a submarine and carry out its attack far enough away from the submarine to allow the releasing vessel to remain undetected.[7]

Torisu had endured a punishing counter-attack by British destroyers off Ceylon in 1942 and had no wish to repeat the experience. Even so, this last option represented an appalling waste of men and *matériel* when a little more imagination in the employment of Japanese submarines might well have paid dividends. A couple of stiff sessions in an attack teacher, if the Imperial Navy possessed such a thing, would probably have been far more useful.[8]

As a drowning man will clutch at a straw, so the Japanese expected great things from the suicide weapons. Yet the *Kaiten* could never have the effect that their name would suggest. They were incapable of independent operation. Their relative lack of endurance and non-existent habitability for the single operator meant that they could only be used once a target had been found and identified. Moreover, the *Kaiten*'s oxygen-driven propulsion system required extensive and skilled maintenance.[9] The *Kaiten*, therefore, could not be deployed to isolated bases in the same way as the *Ko-Hyoteki* could be. They depended on the support services provided by the mother ship, be it cruiser or submarine.

One idea governing *Kaiten* employment was for flights of these weapons to be launched against American invasion fleets. Yet there were never enough carriers to

	***Kaiten*-carrying Submarines**	
Class	*Boats*	*No of* Kaiten
KD3	*I-118*	2
KD3b	*I-1156, I-1157, I-1159, I-1160*	2
KD4	*I-1162*	2
KD5	*I-1165*	2
J3	*I-8*	4
B1	*I-36*	6
	I-37	4
B2	*I-44*	4
B3	*I-56, I-58*	4; subsequently 6
C2	*I-47, I-48*	4; subsequently 6
C3	*I-53*	4; subsequently 6

deploy a significant number of *Kaiten* to the operational area: only one cruiser and sixteen submarines were fitted to carry them. Making allowances for refit/repair and time spent on passage between Japan and the operational area, it becomes clear that it was impossible to deploy the weapon in any numbers. Moreover, the carriers were vulnerable to American attack while on passage. It was extremely doubtful that the cruiser *Kitakami* could have got into a position to launch her *Kaiten* without being detected and sunk herself. The submarine carriers were no less vulnerable, being large and unwieldy with a slow diving time.

After the first use of the *Kaiten* there was a divergence of opinion on how the weapons should be used. The 'staff solution' was for them to be employed in more attacks on defended anchorages and American forces engaged in amphibious operations. Torisu, on the other hand, argued that the *Kaiten* be given more flexible employment at sea against American convoys. He argued that, following the attack on Ulithi, the Americans would be alerted to the possibility of a *Kaiten* attack and would be prepared for such an eventuality. The argument went against Torisu and preparations were made for a second attack on Ulithi, the Kossol Passage and Seeadler Harbour in the Admiralty Islands in January 1945. Six submarines carrying 24 *Kaiten* were employed in the attack and on 12 January all *Kaiten* were released as planned.

The dilemma facing the Japanese in their use of the *Kaiten* was perfectly expressed by a *Kaiten* operator who took part in the first attack on Ulithi on 20 November 1944:

> Daylight observation disclosed over a hundred ships at anchor in Ulithi. Though this provides a golden opportunity for the use of our human torpedoes, there are but two submarines and eight human torpedoes—a very regrettable matter.[10]

There was also the question of production. *Kaiten* were quite complicated to build, with the liquid oxygen/petrol powerplant requiring special attention. It would take time before stocks of the weapon were ready for operations, and there was an argument for withholding operations until sufficient *Kaiten* were available for them to make an impact. Commander Torisu recalled:

> My voice, however, was not strong enough to persuade other staff members to share my idea of employing manned torpedoes in raiding operations at sea. As soon as a dozen of the weapons were readied, it was decided to launch the first torpedo attack on Ulithi Atoll.[11]

Training of the *Kaiten* pilots was initially conducted at a secret base established at Otsujima, an island off the town of Tokuyama on Honshu, and some thirty prospective *Kaiten* pilots reported there in August 1944, followed by a class consisting of 200 prospective pilots who had volunteered for this assignment. The first *Kaiten* unit, named *Kikumizu*, was formed on 8 November 1944 and consisted of the submarines *I-36*, *I-37* and *I-47*. There was barely any time for training before the boats sailed for the first operation against American shipping. *I-36* and *I-47* were to attack shipping at Ulithi while *I-37* proceeded to Palau via the Kossol Passage. All three submarines carried a full load of Type 95 torpedoes for more conventional attacks against US ships once the *Kaiten* had been launched. The prospects for the operation looked good: Japanese aerial reconnaissance had reported that the lagoon at Ulithi, large enough to accommodate 800 ships, was crowded with warships and auxiliaries of all sizes.

I-36 and *I-47* stood-to at the entrance to the lagoon on the morning of 20 November. On board the two submarines the final religious ceremonies were arranged for the *Kaiten* pilots, who had already made their wills and left last messages for their families. At this stage of the war not all the parent submarines were fitted with the access tubes which permitted the *Kaiten* to be boarded while the submarine was dived, so both boats had briefly come to the surface to allow two of the pilots to enter their craft (the other two craft were fitted with hatches). The submarines then dived, leaving the two *Kaiten* men to wait for nearly three hours before launch.

Shortly after 0400 on 20 November the *Kaiten* were released. *I-47* launched her craft successfully, one of which was piloted by Lieutenant Sekio Nishina (one of the 'founders' of the *Kaiten*), but only one of the four carried by *I-36* was launched. The other three were defective: two would not release from the parent submarine after their engines had started, while the third refused to start because sea water had leaked into the craft. The three 'unsuccessful' *Kaiten* operators demanded that the submarine's commanding officer should surface to allow the specialist *Kaiten* maintenance parties embarked to work on the craft. The commanding officer wisely refused: his submarine would have been extremely vulnerable if caught on the surface with technicians swarming all over her cargo.

Soon after 0500 *I-47* detected a loud explosion on her hydrophones, followed a few seconds later by another. *I-36* heard similar explosions at 0545 and 0605. Both submarines then returned to Japan. Three days later the lagoon at Ulithi was surveyed by Japanese aircraft and the evidence from this flight, coupled with the patrol reports from the submarine commanding officers, led to the astonishing conclusion that three aircraft carriers and two battleships had been sunk!

There was, of course, no way in which the submarine commanding officers could know what results had been achieved. They were too far away from the attack area. It was easy to classify any explosion heard after the *Kaiten* had been launched as a successful hit—although it should be pointed out that this failing was one which submarine commanders of all nations have been guilty of at one time or another. News of the attack was received with jubilation by those *Kaiten* pilots under training. Ensign Yutaka Yokuta was one of these officers:

The meeting broke up in bedlam, every shouting, congratulating and cheering the *Kaiten* plan . . . Three aircraft carriers! And two battleships! That should give the enemy something to worry about.

I said a short prayer, giving thanks for the success of Nishina and the others. The *Kaiten* was now a proven weapon. It had shown what it could do. If luck smiled on me, I too would strike a blow at our nation's enemy. I too would send a carrier to the bottom of the sea.[12]

Just what had been achieved by the operation? The actual damage inflicted at Ulithi was far less than that claimed by the Japanese. One *Kaiten*[13] struck the large fleet oiler *Mississinewa*, which was carrying 400,000 gallons of aviation spirit. The oiler blew up and sank with the loss of fifty of her crew. It is almost certain that the other four *Kaiten* entered the lagoon. They attacked two cruisers but were sunk by gunfire and depth charges dropped by a USMC aircraft, while one was rammed by a destroyer.

What of *I-37*? She never launched her four *Kaiten* for on 19 November she was detected and sunk by the destroyer-escorts *Conklin*, *McCoy* and *Reynolds* north-west of the Kossol Passage. Thus in exchange for the sinking of a fleet oiler, the Japanese had expended nine *Kaiten* and one fleet submarine. It was not exactly an auspicious start.

Planning for the second *Kaiten* operation proceeded with increased vigour as news of the first attack's 'results' became known. Vice-Admiral Shigeyoshi Miwa, Commander-in-Chief of the Sixth Fleet, drew up plans for more ambitious missions while the number of officers and men under training increased, their ranks swelled by aviators for whom aircraft were not available. The second *Kaiten* operation, code-named '*Kongo*', would be a strike by six submarines carrying 24 *Kaiten* in all against Ulithi, Hollandia, the Kossol Strait, the Admiralty Islands and Guam. The disposition of the submarines was as shown in the accompanying table.

The *Kaiten* were scheduled to be launched on 11 January 1945 except for those from *I-48*, which would make the second strike against Ulithi nine days after the first. All the submarines assigned to the operation are believed to have reached their operational areas, despite the array of American anti-submarine forces deployed against them. *I-36*, *I-47* and *I-58* launched their *Kaiten*. *I-53* reached the Kossol Strait and began to release her *Kaiten* but only two of the four got away: one refused to launch from the parent submarine while the other exploded shortly after release. *I-56* approached her target off Manus in the Admiralty Islands but found the defences very much on the alert so abandoned the operation and returned to Japan with her *Kaiten* intact. Lastly, *I-48* was sunk by the destroyer-escorts *Conklin*, *Corbesier* and *Raby* 25 miles north-east of Yap in the Caroline Islands on 23 January 1945.

In the subsequent debrief, the staff of the Sixth Fleet concluded that the '*Kongo*' group had accounted for as many as eighteen vessels, including a battleship sunk at

Ulithi. These claims were nowhere near the mark. Once again the submarine commanders, the staff of the Sixth Fleet and the pilots of the reconnaissance aircraft were guilty of over-exaggeration. In fact, for the loss of one fleet submarine and nineteen *Kaiten*, no American ships were sunk or damaged.

At this stage the Sixth Fleet staff began a reappraisal of the effectiveness of *Kaiten* operations. Although the *Kikumizu* and *'Kongo'* operations were believed to have resulted in impressive successes, the American forces were advancing remorselessly on Japan. Moreover, as shown by *I-56*'s experience off Manus, American anchorages were becoming heavily defended and it was more and more difficult for a submarine to approach a launching position without courting destruction.

Accordingly the emphasis for *Kaiten* attacks was switched from anchorages to ships at sea, preferably in areas where there would be fewer escorts. For the third operation, the American supply route to Iwo Jima was selected as an area likely to yield good results. This operation was code-named *'Chihaya'* and involved the submarines *I-368*, *I-370* (each carrying five *Kaiten*) and *I-44* (carrying six). *I-368* and *I-370* left port on 20 February (by coincidence the day on which American troops landed on Iwo Jima), followed by *I-44* on 23 February. If the Japanese hoped that this operation would be any easier, they were cruelly mistaken. Both *I-368* and *I-370* were detected and sunk by American forces, the latter on 26 February by the USS *Finnigan* 120 miles south of Iwo Jima and the former on 27 February by aircraft from the USS *Anzio* 35 miles west of Iwo Jima. Japanese sources indicate that *I-370* did manage to launch her *Kaiten*, but no hits were recorded.

The third submarine, *I-44*, stayed at sea for just over two weeks before returning to port on 9 March, her *Kaiten* unexpended. The commanding officer, Lieutenant-Commander Genbei Kawaguchi IJN, explained to a furious Admiral Miwa (who subsequently relieved him of his command) that American opposition had been too tough. Every time *I-44* had come to the surface to launch her *Kaiten* she had been detected. Opposition was so widespread that *I-44* could not surface to charge the battery properly, so Kawaguchi gave up. The third mission had been a complete failure—two submarines and ten *Kaiten* expended for nothing in return.

Disposition of Japanese Submarines for Operation *'Kongo'*

Submarine	Kaiten	Target
I-36	4	Ulithi
I-47	4	Hollandia, New Guinea
I-48	4	Ulithi
I-53	4	Kossol Strait
I-56	4	Admiralty Islands
I-58	4	Apra Harbour, Guam

Two submarines had now returned from an operation with their *Kaiten* unexpended—*I-56* from *Kongo* and *I-44* from *Chihaya*. The strain on the *Kaiten* crews caused by their unexpected return was immense. They had already undergone the ceremonial rites of a Japanese warrior about to face death and were psychologically prepared to give their lives. The disappointment caused by the cancellation of an operation was terrific, and seeing men to whom they had already said 'farewell' walking around the base three weeks later had an appreciable effect on the morale of those in training

The fourth *Kaiten* operation, named *Shimbu*, was no more successful than its predecessors. *I-36* returned with engine problems, having proceeded no further than the Bungo Strait. The other submarine, *I-58*, had her orders changed while on passage. She was ordered to provide a radio beacon for *Kamikaze* aircraft about to attack Ulithi on 11 March. When the signal was received, *I-58* (Commander Hashimoto Mochitsura IJN) was actually in the process of beginning an attack run. Her passive radar receiver had picked up transmissions from American warships and Hashimoto was heading towards them with his *Kaiten* manned and ready for launch. When the signal was received he wrote:

It is maddening to be turned back on the enemy's doorstep—I could hardly believe it. There was no question of replying by signal as that would have led immediately to our discovery. While I was weighing up the possibility of going on to launch the *Kaiten* before obeying the signal, a personal message came from the Chief of Staff Combined Fleet: 'Operation HA [the *Kamikaze* attack on Ulithi] is very important and your orders must be followed without fail. Report programme and expected time of arrival off Okinoshima.' There was nothing for it but to conform.[14]

Accordingly, Hashimoto ordered the *Kaiten* to be ditched, much to disgust of their operators, made a fast surface passage to the beacon position and did not return to port until 16 March. When he got back to port Hashimoto remonstrated with the staff, only to be told that the staff had not realised that he had progressed so far.

After the conquest of Iwo Jima, the Americans pressed on to their next target, the Ryuku Islands, south of Japan and only 340 miles from the Japanese home island of Kyushu. The date set for the invasion of the main island of Okinawa was 1 April 1945, but before then, as part of the preparatory operations, the islands were subjected to a series of air attacks and bombardments to 'soften up' the defences.

The Japanese command were convinced that the *Kaiten* were sinking ships at a rate of one per craft: therefore, it could only be a matter of time before *Kaiten* attacks, coupled with those made by suicide aircraft, brought the American advance to a halt. The battle for Okinawa witnessed some of the fiercest fighting of the Pacific War. *Kamikaze* aircraft took a fearful toll of American ships[15] and accounted for 164 out of the 371 American vessels sunk before the islands were secured and for 27 of the 36 ships damaged. *Kaiten* were also employed, but, owing to the comprehensive anti-submarine measures adopted by the American command, they were totally unsuccessful.

The boats employed against Okinawa were *I-44*, *I-47*, *I-56* and *I-58*, carrying a total of twenty *Kaiten*. The operation was given the name *'Tatara'*. The submarines sailed from their bases between 29 March and 3 April, yet no sooner had they left the relative safety of the Inland Sea than they encountered American anti-submarine forces. The combination of air patrols and surface hunting groups proved deadly. *I-56* was dispatched on 18 April by the destroyers *Collett*, *Heerman*, *McCord*, *Mertz* and *Uhlmann*, assisted by aircraft from the USS *Bataan*, 160 miles east of Okinawa. *I-44* lasted until 29 April, when she was sunk by aircraft from the USS *Tulagi*. *I-47* kept trying to find a way through the defences but was attacked several times and was eventually forced to return to port with her *Kaiten* damaged and unused. The last boat in the group, *I-58*, was ordered to rendezvous with the battleship *Yamato*, heading south to Okinawa on her own suicide mission. The Japanese plan was for the battleship's attack to be coordinated with *Kamikaze* and *Kaiten* strikes in one massive assault on the invasion forces. But it was not to be. The long arm of Admiral Marc Mitscher's TF.58, the fast carrier group in the American Fleet, reached out and sank *Yamato* on 7 April almost before she had started on her mission. Commander Hashimoto, *I-58*'s commanding officer, kept heading south in an attempt to outflank the anti-submarine screen, but to no effect. Hashimoto had, reluctantly, to return to Japan.

None of the twenty *Kaiten* carried by the submarines of the *Tatara* group was launched against the Americans. Moreover, two of the four parent submarines involved had been sunk. An attempt to use land-based *Kaiten* at Okinawa was also unsuccessful. Eight *Kaiten*, their operators and maintenance crews, were deployed to Okinawa. This method of using the *Kaiten* might have worked had they been pre-positioned before the American assault. As it was, the transport carrying the *Kaiten* to the island was sunk by US aircraft.

The losses suffered among the *Kaiten* carriers caused the Japanese command to reassess how the craft were being employed. This change of policy coincided with a change of command, Vice-Admiral Daigo Tadashige replacing Vice-Admiral Miwa as Flag Officer commanding Sixth Fleet. Daigo decided to employ the *Kaiten* against supply lines further away from the combat zone, where, it was hoped, opposition would be less intense. Consequently the *Tembu* group, consisting of *I-36* and *I-47* each carrying six *Kaiten*, left Japan on 26 April 1945. *I-36* attacked a convoy on 27 April and prepared to launch her six *Kaiten*. However, only four got away because the release gear on the other two was faulty. *I-36*'s hydrophones subsequently picked up the sound of four detonations, reported that four explosions had been heard and claimed to have sunk four ships. In fact, no ships were sunk in this attack, although one of the convoy's escorts reported two *Kaiten* as having been sunk. The explosions heard by *I-36* were most likely the depth charges deployed as countermeasures.

I-47 also found a convoy on 1 May but on this occasion the submarine's commanding officer, Lieutenant-Commander Zenji Orita IJN, decided to employ more traditional submarine weapons. He fired four torpedoes and heard three explosions. As in *I-36*'s attack, no ships were sunk and the explosions were most likely the torpedoes detonating at the end of their run. On 2 May *I-47* launched four *Kaiten* against a convoy but no hits were scored. The seventh *Kaiten* operation, code-named '*Shimbu*', consisted of the submarine *I-367* carrying five *Kaiten*. This operation was no more successful than any of the others. Off Okinawa targets were sighted but, owing to mechanical defects, only one of the *Kaiten* would run. Although the Japanese claimed one ship sunk on 27 May, there is no record of such a loss in American records. However, the destroyer *Gilligan* was damaged on that day by a torpedo which may have been a *Kaiten*.

The Japanese were not downhearted and continued to proceed with *Kaiten* operations. The *Todoroki* group consisted of *I-36*, *I-361*, *I-363* and *I-165* carrying a total of eighteen *Kaiten*. Only *I-36* managed to launch her *Kaiten*, to no effect, on 22 and 28 June. A number of detonations were heard, and as the ARL *Endymion* was damaged in that area on that day, her damage may have been the result of this attack. Only *I-36* and *I-363* returned to Japan, the former badly damaged and narrowly avoiding a salvo of four torpedoes fired by an American submarine at the entrance to the Inland Sea. Of the other two boats, *I-361* was sunk on 30 May by aircraft from the USS *Anzio* (the most effective American anti-submarine carrier in the Pacific), while *I-165* was sunk on 27 June by two PV Ventura bombers east of Saipan.

The was only one more *Kaiten* operation before the end of the Second World War and, perversely, this was the most successful. This was also the largest operation using *Kaiten* which had been mounted to date. The operation, by the *Tamon* group, involved six submarines, *I-53*, *I-47*, *I-58*, *I-363*, *I-366* and *I-367*, carrying a total of 33 *Kaiten*. *I-53* was the first submarine to sail on 14 July 1945 and was followed by the other boats over a three-week period. Mechanical problems caused the return of *I-47*, *I-363* and *I-367* but the remainder carried on. On 21 July 1945 the assault transport *Marathon* was damaged off Okinawa by a conventional torpedo: both *I-47* and *I-367* were in the area at the time. More concrete success came on 24 July when *I-53* (Lieutenant-Commander S. Oba IJN) attacked a convoy of eight LSTs loaded with battle-weary troops of the 96th Infantry Division who were returning to Leyte from Okinawa with the destroyer *Underhill* (Lieutenant Robert M. Newcomb USN) as the escort. The convoy had been sighted by a Japanese aircraft that morning and the Americans subsequently believed that the aircraft had vectored the submarine on to the LSTs. At 1500 on the same day, what was identified as a mine was sighted dead ahead of the convoy. While the LSTs made a 45-degree emergency turn to port,

Underhill bore down on the 'mine' to destroy it. While doing so, the destroyer's sonar detected multiple underwater contacts, which must have been the launch of all six *Kaiten* by *I-53*. *Underhill* started to drop depth charges and was rewarded by a terrific explosion. Moments later a torpedo was sighted heading straight for *Underhill*'s port bow. The torpedo was avoided, but at the same time an object, identified as a submarine, was sighted dead ahead. There was no time for avoiding action and *Underhill* ploughed straight into the submarine, with cataclysmic results. The whole forward part of the ship was blown off, as far back as the forward boiler-room bulkhead. Ten officers and 102 enlisted men were killed. The after part remained afloat till the evening, when it was sunk by gunfire.

Three days later *I-58* launched a pair of *Kaiten* against a tanker and heard explosions after approximately an hour. No tanker was sunk, but the destroyer *Lowry* was damaged, possibly as the result of a *Kaiten* attack. On 30 July *I-58* scored the Japanese submarine service's single biggest success of the war when she sank the cruiser *Indianapolis* using the conventional Type 95 torpedo.

On 10 and 11 August *I-58* and *I-366* launched two and three *Kaiten* respectively but scored no hits. The final *Kaiten* attack came on 12 August when *I-58* launched two against what Hashimoto thought was a seaplane carrier. In fact his target was the LSD *Oak Hill*. The *Kaiten* scraped down the side of the LSD but did not explode and was sunk by depth charges from an escort, the USS *Thomas F. Nickel*. In turn the *Nickel* was missed by a second *Kaiten* which passed down her port side and exploded when some distance away. Hashimoto heard the two explosions and claimed the 'seaplane carrier' as sunk. He and the crew of *I-58* were elated by their success, but the elation turned sour on 15 August when a message in cipher was decoded announcing that Japan had surrendered. Hashimoto could not believe it, and thought it a newspaper stunt or Allied radio countermeasures. He ordered the signal destroyed. But when *I-58* docked at Kure on 17 August, there was no doubt of the

---

Koryu (Scaly Dragon) Five-Man Midget Submarine

Displacement (submerged): 58.4 tons
Length: 26.25m
Beam: 2.04m
Propulsion: 1 x 150bhp diesel; 1 x 500hp electric motor; one shaft (but two contra-rotating propellers)
Speed (surfaced): 8kt
Speed (submerged): 16kt
Range (surfaced): 1,000nm at 8kt
Range (submerged): 320nm at 16kt

Armament: Two 457mm torpedoes
Crew: 5
Number delivered: 115
Production: 540 of this class were ordered, with the first, *HA-77*, completed in January 1945. Production problems and the effects of American bombing meant that only 115 were completed. None saw action and all were broken up in the post-war period.

Kairyu (Sea Dragon) Two-Man Midget Submarine

Displacement: 18.94/18.97 tons	**Armament:** Two 457mm torpedoes or
Length: 17.28m	one 600kg explosive charge
Beam: 1.30m	**Crew:** 2
Propulsion: Single shaft, 1 x 85bhp	**Number delivered:** 212
diesel; 1 x 80hp electric motor	**Production:** It was planned to have 760
Speed (surfaced): 7.5kt	*Kairyu* ready for operations by Septem-
Speed (submerged): 10kt	ber 1945 but only 212 were ready by
Range (surfaced): 450nm at 5kt	the end of August. All were broken up
Speed (submerged): 36nm at 3kt	after the Japanese surrender.

veracity of the message. The war was over. The *Kaiten* had failed and the cost had been high. Eight submarines and 900 Japanese officers and men were killed in *Kaiten* operations for the loss of two ships, the oiler *Mississinewa*, sunk on the first *Kaiten* operation, and the destroyer *Underhill*, which was sunk on the last. A US commentator wrote what is the most apt epitaph for the *Kaiten* programme: 'the Imperial Navy did a lot better with torpedoes before the human guidance system was added.'[16]

Even at the end of hostilities the Japanese Navy was working on new designs of midget submarines. These were suicide weapons, conceived in the vain hope that self-sacrifice could turn back the Allied forces ranged against Japan. As such, these weapons joined the band of other Japanese last-ditch devices—frogmen armed with explosive charges and schoolchildren armed with bamboo pikes. The *Koryu* (Scaly Dragon) was a development of the *Ko-Hyoteki* and was armed with two 18in torpedoes. However, a shortage of torpedoes meant that most were fitted with a single explosive charge. Of the 540 ordered, only 115 were completed when the war ended: most were found in a vast graving dock at Kure which had in better days held the Japanese Navy's battleships. The *Kairyu* (Sea Dragon) was a three-man suicide craft armed with an explosive warhead on account of the shortage of torpedoes. Over 200 had been completed by the end of the war, but none saw service.

Japanese midget submarine operations never justified the high hopes of their proponents. Why did the Japanese midgets, of all kinds, achieve so little and at such great cost? Given the paucity of Japanese official records, that question is likely to remain unanswered for a long time. Overwhelming American superiority above, on and under the sea is one answer. Yet, as Saburo Akeida showed, it was possible for determined, well-motivated men to succeed. Poor planning and ignorance of the operating limitations of these small by craft by the staff is a more likely reason. Japanese midget submarine crews were a group of brave and dedicated men, well-equipped but badly trained and poorly led.

Chapter 9

Jeeps and Chariots

Go away and build me a Human Torpedo . . . I'm busy, but get on with the job right away and report to me as soon as you have got something.—Vice-Admiral Max Horton to Commander W. R. 'Tiny' Fell RN

Britain was the country least likely to take an interest in midget submarines of any kind. Even though the Royal Navy was numerically smaller than it had been at the apogee of its greatness in 1914, Britain was still the pre-eminent maritime power, with battle fleets deployed in the Atlantic and Mediterranean and smaller squadrons worldwide. The midget submarine was the weapon of the weaker power, designed for covert attacks on targets such as capital ships, which, even in 1939, were regarded as the arbiters of naval power. Britain had more to fear from the operations of these craft than she had to gain by developing them herself.

The German occupation of Norway in 1940 presented the Royal Navy with a new and perplexing situation. From February 1942 the *Kriegsmarine* maintained a powerful surface task force in various Norwegian fjords centred around the 42,000-ton battleship *Tirpitz*, or 'The Beast' as she was referred to by Churchill. Though this force hardly ever put to sea, it exercised a wholly baleful influence on the conduct of British maritime operations. The German ships were placed to break out into the Atlantic and posed a continual threat to the convoys taking supplies to the Soviet ports of Murmansk and Archangel.[1] Their mere presence, safe behind the nets and booms of their Norwegian lairs, was sufficient to keep large numbers of British ships in home waters when they could have been more profitably employed elsewhere. In short, a significant proportion of the Royal Navy was employed in guarding against a threat which never materialised. Moreover, the German ships were relatively safe in the Norwegian anchorages: they could not be assaulted by conventional ships, and submarines stood no chance of penetrating the fjords. Until the development of precision bombing by the RAF, air power stood no chance of sinking these ships either. They appeared invulnerable.

It was the exploits in the Mediterranean, already recounted, which encouraged the British towards the development of midget submarines. Nothing succeeds like success, and the British were thoroughly irritated by the activities of the Italians, which, of course, had culminated in the crippling of the battleships *Valiant* and *Queen Elizabeth* at Alexandria on the night of 20/21 December 1941. Winston Churchill was never one to have his thinking restrained by conventional dogma and on 18 January the familiar 'Action this Day' docket landed on the desk of General Sir Hastings Ismay, Secretary to the Chiefs of Staff Committee:

> Please report what is being done to emulate the exploits of the Italians in Alexandria harbour and similar methods of this kind. At the beginning of the war Colonel Jefferis had a number of bright ideas on this subject which received very little encouragement. Is there any reason why we should be incapable of the same kind of scientific aggressive action the Italians have shown? One would have thought that we would have been in the lead.[2]

In due course the requirement landed on the desk of Vice-Admiral Max Horton, Flag Officer Submarines. Horton sent for Commander W. R. 'Tiny' Fell, a submariner and old acquaintance, and ordered him to

> Go away and build me a Human Torpedo . . . I'm busy, but get on with the job right away and report to me as soon as you have got something.[3]

Horton was a commander who never wasted a moment on complicated staff requirements. The job needed to be done and, having delegated, he expected results. The outcome was the Chariot.

Fell was a submariner who had thought that his submarine days were over when he handed over command of *H31* in August 1939. However, shortly after the declaration of war he was appointed to command the submarine *H43*, which, together with the trawler *Tamura*, spent the winter of 1939–40 in a fruitless and uncomfortable search for U-boats suspected of lurking in Irish territorial waters.[4] Thereafter he had been employed in combined operations and he had seen service at the raids on Vaagsøy and Florø. Though he found combined operations exciting, he was casting about for a return to his beloved submarine service when Horton sent for him.

Fell proceeded to HMS *Dolphin* at Gosport, the home of the Submarine Service, where he joined Commander Geoffrey Sladen, an experienced submarine commanding officer who had just relinquished command of HMS *Trident* after a very successful commission in Arctic waters. Sladen concentrated on the development of a flexible underwater suit with air supplied by an oxygen bag similar to the Davis Submarine Escape Apparatus in general use throughout the Navy. The breathing apparatus was a closed-cycle system, that is, the air was recycled within the equipment and not vented where it would leave a trail of bubbles, thus giving the game away. The breathing bag contained a cylinder which supplied the wearer with pure oxygen. On exhaling, the air was passed through Protosorb crystals which removed most of the carbon dioxide. The dangers of breathing pure oxygen were not fully appreciated by the British, although the Italian *Decima Mas* men were well aware of such problems. British interrogation of Italian operators put this caution down to poor training.[5] This was not the case: the Italians were more aware of the dangers of breathing pure oxygen as the result of some singularly brutal experiments. The suit became known as the 'Clammy Death' suit and consisted of a one-piece rubber body overall and hood. Early models had individual eye goggles but later versions were fitted with a single visor over which a pair of night vision glasses could be fitted. One problem that had to be solved at the beginning concerned the type of underclothing to be worn, a type which would keep the wearer warm without encumbering him too much. Various combinations were tried and the favoured arrangement was silk underwear next to the skin, woollen underwear over this and kapok padded jerkins and trousers under the suit. No satisfactory means could be found of keeping the Charioteers' hands warm. No gloves seemed up to the task and eventually Sladen left each man to make his own choice. Most opted for bare hands with a liberal measure of heavy-duty grease. Whatever the apparent glamour of serving in a special unit, Charioteering was never a pleasant experience:

> With nose tightly clipped for hours, swollen and raw from the previous day's dive, with gums cut and puffed from constant gripping of the mouthpiece, and with hands cold to the point of numbness, cut and torn from each day's diving . . . And when one surfaced, and hands thawed out while one undressed, there was the feeling that all hell had broken loose with the remaining circulation.[6]

Meanwhile Fell was building the first prototype out of a twenty-foot log of wood, ably assisted by Engineer Commander Stan Kerry, the base Engineer Officer. Fortunately Fell and Kerry had plans and photographs of an Italian *Maiale* captured at Gibraltar. Building a Chariot[7] did not present any serious engineering problems and after a number of experiments on the wooden prototype—dignified by the name *Cassidy*—the first powered craft was ready in June 1942. The machine was 7.65m long and resembled a standard 21in torpedo except that the positions for the two crewmen had been built on top and the nose had fittings to hold the 600lb detachable warhead. The 60V lead acid battery containing 30 chloride cells drove the 2hp motor along at 4kt for four hours and at just under 3kt for six hours. In theory this provided for an operational range of 18 miles. The battery also supplied the power for the ballast and trim pump motors.

The pilot—'Number 1'—sat forward behind a breast-high screen which covered his rudimentary instruments—a depth gauge, compass and clock. Between his knees was the helm which operated the rudder and hydroplanes (one set mounted aft). To the left and right of the helm were switches controlling the ballast and trim pump, while behind was the main motor switch. Number 1's back rested against the main ballast tank, which also served as protection for the diver, Number 2 straddling the after end of the machine. In turn Number 2 rested against a locker containing net cutters, ropes and two spare breathing apparatuses.

The initial trials at Portsmouth were successful, but it was not easy to work up the craft in that crowded harbour with all sorts of interested (friendly or otherwise)

Chariot Two-Man Human Torpedo

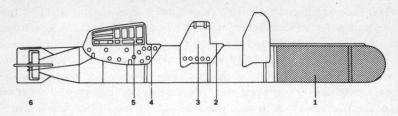

6   5   4   3 2   1

Displacement: 1.5 tons
Length: 7.65m
Propulsion: 60V lead-acid battery driving 2hp electric motor
Speed: 4kt
Range: 16nm at 4kt; 17.4nm at 2.9kt
Armament: One 600lb charge
Crew: 2

Key to drawing:
1. Position where 600lb warhead would be attached.
2. Driver's ('Number 1') position.
3. Ballast tank (also served as back rest for Number 1).
4. Assistant's ('Number 2') position.
5. Locker containing net cutters, magnets, ropes and two spare breathing sets (also served as back rest for Number 2.
6. Propeller and control surfaces.

War Losses

V	Reported 06.44 as being in accident off west coast of Scotland
VI	Lost 31.10 42 during Operation 'Title' (unsuccessful attack on *Tirpitz*)
VIII	As *VI*
X	Lost 02.01.43 with HM Submarine *P311* during Operation 'Principal' en route for attack on Maddalena
XI	Reported 06.44 as abandoned at Malta
XII	Lost 19.0143 during Operation 'Welcome' (sinking of blockships in Tripoli harbour)
XIII	As *XII*
XIV	As *XI*
XV	Lost 03.01.43 during Operation 'Principal' in attack on Palermo
XVI	As *XV*
XVII	As *XI*
XVIII	As *X*
XIX	As *XV*
XX	As *XI*
XXI	As *XI*
XXII	As *XV*
XXIII	As *XV*
XXIV	As *XI*
XXV	As *XI*
XXIX	As *XI*
XXXI	As *XI*
XXXIV	As *XI*
LII	Jettisoned 22.11.43 due to heavy weather during attack on German shipping in Norwegian fjords
LVII	As *LII*
LVIII	Lost during attack on La Spezia 22.06.44
LX	As *LVIII*
LXXIX	Lost during raid on Phuket harbour 28.10.44.
LXXX	As *LXXIX*

spectators. Consequently the Chariots and operators moved north to Scotland, first to Erisart (found unsuitable) and then to Loch Cairnbawn. The ancient depot ship HMS *Titania* was allocated to support the Chariots, but her commanding officer, Commander Robert Conway RN, was less than impressed with his new charges: news that the Charioteers had held a party underneath the train while waiting to depart from Euston and had only been dissipated by the arrival of Admiral Horton, who was, coincidentally (and unfortunately), taking the First Lord of the Admiralty,[8] the Hon. A. V. Alexander (a singularly humourless character at the best of times) to visit the Submarine Flotillas in Scotland.

Once the Charioteers were in Scotland, training began with a vengeance. The Boom Defence Department laid on various types of net for them to work with and gradually their skills were perfected. The curriculum established by Sladen and Fell was by no means confined to the aquatic aspect of the task in hand: there was always the prospect of his men being forced to escape overland after an operation. As a result, he suggested to the local Home Guard commander that they run an escape and evasion exercise. The result was pure unadulterated mayhem, the climax of which was the passing of a calcium flare, which had just been dipped in water, through the letter box of the local police station.

The climax of all this training was a series of exercises against a 'live' target. The battleship HMS *Howe* was obligingly loaned by the Home Fleet, and after the ship's arrival in Loch Cairnbawn she was immediately surrounded by a several layers of nets supplemented by hydrophones rigged out on booms and suspended from the ship's side. Additionally, *Howe*'s boats would patrol between the ship and nets and would be carrying Aldis lamps to use as searchlights. Seven teams of Chariots left *Titania* at fifteen-minute intervals with the simple instruction from Fell and Sladen, 'Get your charge under the *Howe* and get away undetected'. It was a very tall order: the defences were much tougher than anything the Charioteers had faced to date, the loch was littered with pockets of fresh water and, unknown to Sladen and Fell, *Howe*'s draught was deeper than the safe depth for men breathing oxygen under pressure.

The exercise was a complete success. Three of the Chariots planted their charges and returned. A fourth was spotted by the launch on the way out. The other three Chariots were all forced to withdraw for various technical reasons, but none was spotted. Had the attack been a real one, there was no doubt that *Howe* would have been sunk. However, the exercise revealed some hazards of 'Charioteering': Lieutenant S. F. Stretton-Smith RNVR and Leading Seaman Rickman hit an unexpected pocket of fresh water, crashed some seventy feet to the bottom and had to be rested for several days to allow their ears to recover from the ordeal. The operation was repeated on the following night: four machines were used and all four planted their charges, although two were spotted on the way out. Again, had the attack been a real one, *Howe* would have been sunk. The second exercise was enlivened by Lieutenant D. C. 'Taffy' Evans RNVR and Petty Officer W. S. Smith placing their charge underneath the accommodation ladder leading up to the quarterdeck under the very eyes of the Officer of the Watch.

There was time for one more exercise before *Howe* had to sail for more conventional duties. Before the last exercise the Chariots ran up and down the line of hydrophones to provide information about the noise they generated. During these trials, carried out in daylight, *Howe*'s upper deck was cleared of all but those whose duties were concerned with the working of the ship or the trials themselves. On the third attack, tragedy struck. It was perhaps too much for all to have gone so well without a serious accident. While underneath the 35,000-ton battleship fixing his mine, Sub-Lieutenant Jack Grogan SANVR passed out. His Number 2, Able Seaman 'Geordie' Worthy, acted quickly by taking control and moving forward and out from underneath *Howe*'s hull and thence to the surface. For all his efforts it was too late: Grogan was dead, probably as a result of oxygen poisoning. One death and the various *matériel* failures were to be expected given the hazardous and experimental nature of 'Charioteering'. In a real operation there would certainly be greater losses.

The decision to use Chariots against *Tirpitz* was made on 26 June 1942 and given the code-name Operation 'Title'. The Chariots, together with their crews, were to be taken to the approaches of Trondheim Fjord in a small fishing boat. On arrival off Trondheim they would be put over the side and secured beneath the boat, which would sail up the fjord, passing the various German controls en route. The Chariots and their crews would then be transferred to a local fishing vessel, less likely to attract attention, for the final approach to the target. However, this last element of the plan had to be amended when the local SOE operative in Trondheim was unable to acquire a suitable local craft. The new plan cut out the transfer to a local craft altogether; instead, the trawler would proceed all the way up the fjord. The operation was jointly commanded by Admiral Sir Max Horton, Flag Officer Submarines, who was responsible for the purely naval aspects of the plan, and Lieutenant-Colonel J. S. Wilson OBE of SOE, who handled the deception plan and also the arrangements for the escape of the crews to the safety of neutral Sweden once the attack had taken place. Meanwhile steps had to be taken find a suitable fishing vessel for the operation, and the Norwegian trawler *Arthur* was finally selected.

The Chariot team was commanded by Lieutenant Jock Brewster RNVR with Able Seaman Jock Brown as his Number 2. Sergeant Donald Craig of the Royal Engineers and Able Seaman Bob Evans made up the other crew, with Able Seamen Malcolm Causer and Bill Tebb as spare crew and dressers. *Arthur*'s crew was commanded by Lieutenant Leif Larsen of the Royal Norwegian Navy, who was an expert in penetrating the German coastal defences.[9] Engineer Bjornøy and Seaman Kalve were the other two Norwegian members of the crew.

Arthur left the Shetland Islands on 26 October 1942 but encountered very heavy weather during the passage across the Norwegian Sea. However, she managed to make her landfall on 29 October as arranged and on the following day she proceeded to a berth on the island of Hitra where storm damage was made good and the Chariots hoisted out and secured beneath her hull. *Arthur* then proceeded up Trondheim Fjord and successfully negotiated the security checks. A German patrol vessel came alongside the *Arthur*. German seamen scrutinised her papers and made an inspection of the ship herself but found nothing: the Chariots, trimmed heavy, were securely slung beneath *Arthur*'s hull while their crews were concealed behind a false bulkhead.[10] The various false papers, made by SOE's forgers in Baker Street, passed muster, for the Germans issued *Arthur* with a pass permitting her to enter the security area surrounding the *Tirpitz*.

So far so good. But, on rounding Rodborget, *Arthur* ran into heavy seas and the Chariots were heard bumping against her hull. Nothing could be done until *Arthur* was under the lee of Tautra ,when a quick inspection showed that both Chariots had broken adrift and sunk. Lieutenant M. K. Brewster subsequently confessed:

> We were ten miles from the pride of the German Navy: all our obstacles were behind us; and we might have been at the North Pole. Looking back, I don't remember one single curse. We were all too unhappy for that.[11]

There now remained nothing more to do but to get the Charioteers and *Arthur*'s crew to the relative safety of Sweden. *Arthur* was scuttled on 1 November off the island of Frosta, after which the Norwegians and British personnel split into two groups: Larsen, Craig, Evans, Tebb and Strand in one party, with Brewster, Brown and Causer together with the Norwegians Bjornøy and Kalve in the other.

Brewster's party succeeded in reaching Sweden, although all five men were suffering badly from frostbite and were existing on nothing other than benzedrine tablets. Once in Sweden they found that Larsen's group had already arrived, though without Evans. In a small town on the Norwegian side of the border the five men had been stopped by German soldiers (although some sources say that Norwegian Quislings were responsible). When the five could not adequately vouch for themselves they were told to proceed under escort to the local police station, where further checks would be made. At this point Tebb, who was the only one of the party still carrying a weapon, resolved to take the two Germans on. As they turned a corner, he turned and fired killing both, but not before Evans was felled by a burst of automatic fire. Larsen and Craig tried to carry Evans with them but he was a large man weighing over fourteen stone. As he appeared to be dead he was, reluctantly, left lying in the street while the others made their escape. Evans was not dead but badly wounded. He was given such medical attention as to make him fit for interrogation before he was shot by special order from OKW.[12] Evans was the only midget submariner from any belligerent nation to meet his end in such a fashion, which contravened all international law (though not dressed in uniform, he was wearing his Royal Navy identity discs at the time of his capture). Evans' murder was but one of the reasons why *Generalfeldmarschall* Wilhelm Keitel, Head of the *Oberkommando des Wehrmacht*, mounted the gallows on 16 October 1946 following the Nuremburg trials.

Operation 'Title' was the last use of Chariots in home waters, although there was a brief resurgence of interest at the end of 1943. *Arthur* had not been a particularly effective way of delivering the Chariots to their operational area, so a number of other means were investigated. Among these was flying-in the Chariots slung underneath a Sunderland flying boat. Trials—known as Operation 'Large Lumps'—proved the method to be practicable, though it was never used operationally. A simpler method involved two Chariots being carried in davits on *MTB675*, a Fairmile D type motor torpedo boat. In October 1943 *MTB675* sailed for the island of Askvoll, seventy-five miles north of Bergen, where an agent had to be landed to establish an observation post. The plan was for the MTB, and her charges, to lie up in a concealed berth. When a likely looking target appeared, the Chariots would be released for an attack. Unfortunately the plan went awry when a *Verpostenboot*[13] took too close an interest in the island and the commanding officer of *MTB675* decided to abandon the operation. However, in the return trip across the North Sea thirteen out of the boat's complement of forty-four were killed or wounded and the craft herself was badly damaged in a series of air attacks. A number of other such operations were planned but, continually frustrated by the bad winter weather, these were eventually abandoned, never to be revived. The MTBs of the Royal Norwegian Navy were quite capable of causing mayhem among German shipping using the coastal route without the added encumbrance of having Chariots to look after.

It was the submarine which offered the best means of delivering the Chariot to its target. Three 'T' class submarines, *Thunderbolt*, *Trooper* and *P311*, were fitted with pressure-tight containers on their casings in which the Chariots would be carried. *Thunderbolt* and *P311* carried two Chariots forward and aft of the conning tower, but *Trooper* carried three, one forward of the conning tower and two aft, disposed between the after external torpedo tubes.

The launching drill would be for the submarine to surface, after taking all the usual precautions that it was safe to do so. The Charioteers would already be dressed in their 'Clammy Death' suits and, accompanied by their dressers, would clamber up and out of the conning tower and down on to the casing—no easy task when thus encumbered. The submarine would then trim down to bring the containers awash. The dressers would open the containers and drag the Chariots out. As they came clear, the Charioteers would climb on and proceed. It sounds very simple but it was an extremely dangerous time for the submarine. There was constant risk that she might be surprised on the surface with the containers open and all manner of people stranded on the casing. Everything depended on the vigilance of the look-outs, for although an listening watch would be kept on the asdic, that apparatus would be next to useless given the background of sea noise. Although submarines like *Thunderbolt* were fitted with the fairly basic Type 291W air warning radar, its performance was indifferent at the best of times. Moreover, there were fears that the Italians possessed radar warning receivers. A refinement of this technique, developed in June 1943, was for the Charioteers to use the two-man escape chambers fitted in the 'T' class to leave and re-enter the submarine while she remained dived, thus removing the need for the boat to surface. Although an ingenious idea, it proved impractical when tried in HMS *Truant*. There was barely enough space in the chamber for two men wearing normal clothing, let alone a Charioteer and his dresser wearing diving suits. Nevertheless, the experiment paved the way for the development of exit/re-entry compartments which are so common in modern submarines.[14]

It was the Mediterranean which beckoned for further Chariot operations. Apart from the climate being a good deal more favourable than that in the North Sea, the theatre offered targets aplenty in the shape of battleships and cruisers of the *Regia Marina*, which, following their drubbing at Matapan in March 1941, had not ventured forth. By December 1942 eight teams of Chariots were ready to be dispatched to Malta. The target allocated to these Chariots, in an operation code-named 'Principal', was shipping gathered at the ports of La Maddalena in Sardinia, Palermo and Cagliari, although at the last moment Cagliari was dropped in favour of a concentration on Palermo. It might be thought curious that the large Italian battle fleet was not selected for an attack. In his postwar memoirs, Commander G. W. 'Shrimp' Simpson, who was then Captain (S) 10 at Malta, remembered that intelligence reports indicated that the Italian battle fleet was virtually harbour-bound on account of fuel shortages. Hence it was decided to seek other targets.

The Chariots had been joined in Malta by *Thunderbolt*, *Trooper* and *P311*, which had all made the passage through the Straits of Gibraltar on the surface at night so that any curious watchers would not note the strange ungainly containers on their casings. The boats departed from Malta at intervals from 28 December 1942. *P311* (Lieutenant R. D. Cayley RN) was sent to Maddalena and, because the passage of the Sicilian Channel was thought to be as dangerous as the operation itself, *Trooper* and *Thunderbolt* were held back until Cayley had reported that he was safely through. His signal was received at 0130 on 31 December, giving his position as 38° 10' N, 11° 30' W. This was the last ever heard from *P311* and her remarkable commanding officer, who had previously commanded HMS *Unison* with such distinction. There is no evidence that her Chariots were ever launched and she was most likely caught in the maze of minefields that guarded the approach to Maddalena.

Trooper and *Thunderbolt* had better luck. The two boats dispatched their five Chariots outside Palermo on the night of 2/3 January 1943 and then withdrew, leaving the submarine *Unruffled* behind to rescue the crews afterwards. Three of the machines ran straight into trouble. One had to abandon the attack owing to a defective breathing bag; her crew, Sub-Lieutenant H. L. H. Stevens RNVR and Leading Seaman Carter, were subsequently picked up by *Unruffled*. Another suffered a battery explosion; one of her crew, Able Seaman W. Simpson, was drowned but the other, Petty Officer Miln, swam ashore, where he was taken prisoner. The driver of the third team, Lieutenant H. F. Cook RNVR, became critically ill with seasickness and had ripped his suit open on nets. His Number 2, Able Seaman Worthy, drove the craft ashore, left Cook and then carried on alone. However, he found the craft too difficult to control and abandoned it in deep water. He then swam back to where he had left Cook, but failed to find him. Probably Cook had opened his visor while too far from the shore and then had stumbled and drowned. Like Miln, worthy was taken prisoner. However, the remaining two Chariots, *XXII* (crewed by Lieutenant R. Greenland RNVR and Leading Seaman A. Ferrier) and *XVI* (crewed by Sub-Lieutenant R. G. Dove RNVR and Leading Seaman J. Freel), were more fortunate.

After leaving *Thunderbolt*, Greenland made his approach in fairly uncomfortable seas until he came under the lee of the land. Two nets were negotiated without difficulty, the first by the simple expedient of pushing the Chariot's nose underneath it and then blowing ballast. The Chariot rose, taking the net with it, and the two men were able to slither underneath. Coming to the surface after passing beneath the second net, they came upon the unmistakable bulk of their target, the brand new cruiser *Ulpio Traiano*. The 600lb warhead was clamped to the cruiser's hull and then Greenland and Ferrier set about distributing the four 5lb limpet mines, which were stowed in the after locker, among a group of merchant ships and escorts rafted up nearby. Moving with impunity among the ships, they mined the destroyer *Grecale*, the torpedo boat *Ciclone* and the merchant ship *Gimma*. Greenland then headed seawards at maximum revolutions and cleared the first net by simply charging straight at it. Then things began to go wrong. They cannoned into a darkened merchant ship and the compass, which had given trouble earlier in the evening, was now completely useless. Undoubtedly both men were by this time exhausted and suffering from oxygen poisoning: they had been breathing pure oxygen for a long time, some of it under pressure, and their judgement must have been impaired. Greenland realised that he was going round in circles and, appreciating that it was nearly 0430 (the time beyond which *Thunderbolt* would not wait for them), decided to ditch the Chariot in deep water and make for the shore. The two men had accomplished more than they could possibly have hoped for.

Meanwhile Dove and Freel had penetrated the harbour and fixed their charge under the hull of the 8,500-ton liner *Viminale*, which was being used as a troopship. They too were suffering from exhaustion and consequently did not use their limpet mines but sank the Chariot and swam ashore. The Italians were unaware that the attack had taken place and it was not until the charge under the *Viminale* exploded at dawn that the alarm was sounded. Even then the Italian authorities were extremely dilatory in ordering a bottom search on the hulls of the other ships in the harbour, and at 0800 the charge under *Ulpio Traiano*'s bows went up. Greenland and Ferrier were still at liberty at the time and they were able to watch the spectacle. The mines planted by Greenland and Ferrier did not explode, either because they were found and made safe by Italian clearance divers or, as one Italian report suggested, because the two Charioteers neglected to arm the mines after securing them to the target's hull.

The four Charioteers were eventually captured and incarcerated in a prisoner-of-war camp. Shortly after their capture they were interviewed by none other than Borghese, who did not think much of their equipment as a whole but was impressed with the various escape and evasion devices which the Charioteers carried (miniature compasses, counterfeit money and the like). According to Borghese, one of the Charioteers (sadly unidentified) volunteered to join the *Decima Mas*! When Italy capitulated in September 1943 the prisoners were moved to the German *Marlag* at Westertimke, where they were liberated in May 1945. On their release they found out that, in what can only be described as a calculated act of meanness by a parsimonious government, their special pay for Chariot duties had been stopped from the day they became prisoners-of-war. The usual practice in the case of submariners, air crews and others entitled to special pay was for the allowance to be continued while the officer or rating concerned was a PoW. This mean gesture saved the nation some £1,300.

The results of Operation 'Principal' are open to question. The Italians lost a new cruiser (which would probably never have done anyone any harm) and had a valuable troopship damaged. However, in return, the British lost *P311* and her experienced ship's company, together with another 'T' class submarine, HMS *Traveller*, (Lieutenant-Commander D. St Clair Ford RN), which had been mined off Taranto on or about 4 December 1942 during a reconnaissance of the base. At a time when the Commander-in-Chief of the Mediterranean Fleet, Admiral Sir Andrew Cunningham, said that 'Every submarine is worth her weight in gold', these losses could not be afforded. Moreover, at the time that 'Principal' was sanctioned, the campaign in North Africa was entering a critical phase. Every Allied ship, submarine and aircraft was engaged in sinking vessels taking supplies to sustain the Axis armies in North Africa. To withdraw five submarines for a special operation was a dangerous distraction for little gain. As the Naval Staff History succinctly commented,

> . . . the diversion of submarines for Chariot-carrying and recovery duties gravely interrupted their normal patrol activities at a time when there were many valuable targets at sea on the Axis supply lines to North Africa.[15]

This opinion was shared by Commander Simpson, who, as commanding officer of the 10th Submarine Flotilla (the 'Fighting Tenth'), was responsible for the prosecution of the submarine war in the central Mediterranean:

If it [Operation 'Principal'] only resulted in the sinking of a light cruiser not yet in commission and an 8,500-ton transport, then the prolonged use of three T-Class submarines exclusively for Chariot work, and the loss of one of them, seems a disproportionate price to have paid.[16]

There were two other Chariot operations in the Mediterranean. On 18 January 1943 two craft launched by HMS *Thunderbolt* were sent to sink merchant ships at Tripoli on the North African coast. It was feared that the Germans might use the ships to block the harbour. One Chariot was defective, but Chariot *XIII*, driven by Sub-Lieutenant H. Stevens RNVR and Chief ERA S. Buxton pressed on. They arrived off the harbour just as the Germans were sinking the first of the ships. Nevertheless Stevens managed to attack his secondary target, the merchantman *Guilio*. Both men were subsequently captured and after a series of adventures sought refuge in the Vatican City, where they enjoyed a civilised and restful lifestyle until the Fifth Army arrived fifteen months later and liberated them.

The other Chariot operation in the Mediterranean was a new departure for these craft in that they undertook reconnaissance of the beaches before the invasion of Sicily in May and June 1943. For these operations one Chariot each was carried on the casing of the 'U' class submarines *Unrivalled*, *Unseen* and *Unison*. The operations yielded extremely useful hydrographic data but, as Captain G. C. Phillips RN, Captain (S) 10 noted,

It is hoped that these reconnaissances are of real value to the planners. It has become clear from recent results that submarines engaged on reconnaissance work fall off in efficiency for offensive patrols.[17]

Beach reconnaissance prior to the invasion of Sicily marked the end of Chariot operations in the Mediterranean (except for the unique Anglo-Italian operation in June 1944 whose story is told in Chapter 4). Amazingly, new Chariots and more personnel were sent out to the Mediterranean even when it was clear that there was no employment for them. A good deal of time was spent preparing grandiose schemes for blocking the Corinth Canal and for attacking the Italian battle fleet at Taranto, but with the Italian capitulation in September 1943 all these schemes came to an end.

There was but one more Chariot operation in the Second World War. This took place in the Far East against two Italian liners, the *Sumatra* (4,859 tons) and the *Volpi* (5,292 tons), lying at Phuket, north of Penang. On the night of 27 October two Chariots were successfully launched from the submarine *Trenchant* (Lieutenant-Commander A. R. Hezlet RN). These Chariots were the Mk II or 'Terry' Chariot, in which the two men sat back to back in an enclosed cockpit which afforded much greater protection from the elements. Both teams planted their mines, returned to *Trenchant* and were able to observe the results of their handiwork through the periscope the next morning. Potentially the Far East offered considerable opportunities for Chariot operations in view of Japan's large naval and mercantile fleets. After due consideration, however, the Admiralty decided that they should be withdrawn from the theatre, since

> . . . although targets exist, they do not afford that reasonable prospect of escape for Charioteers which is essential when dealing with an inhuman enemy.[18]

The Phuket operation marked the end of the Royal Navy's involvement with Chariots. The experience was not wholly wasted, since the knowledge gained was applied with equal success to the rapidly expanding field of assault frogmen and clearance diving. However, it is doubtful whether the Chariots repaid their inventor's hopes or the investment in terms of *matériel*. They had been built to take on the *Tirpitz*, and, following the failure of the sole operation against that target, they were flung willy-nilly at whatever target presented itself. Their exploits in the Mediterranean, gallant though they undoubtedly were, were hardly war-winning stuff and the loss of two conventional submarines in support of Chariot operations was certainly not an acceptable exchange. Chariots were an imaginative but ill-conceived response to a particular threat.

The Royal Navy's foray into the world of midget submarines did not end with the Chariot. Hidden in remote Scottish lochs while Chariots were undergoing trials was the X-Craft—a four-man midget submarine and undoubtedly one of the most potent and versatile vessels ever constructed for the Royal Navy.

Chapter 10

A Most Potent Weapon of War

*Taking command of an X-Craft for the first time was rather like being given a
toy train set for Christmas.*—Commander Richard Compton-Hall RN

There was no doubt that the X-Craft was the most potent and effective of all midget
submarines employed during the Second World War. Though it lacked the technical
sophistication of the Japanese *Ko-Hyoteki* and the Italian CB craft, this was more
than compensated for by the versatility of the vessel. A brief summary will show the
many uses to which the X-Craft could be put: attacks against targets in defended
harbours; attacks against the enemy's strategic communications; beach reconnaissance; and employment as navigational beacons. Had the war lasted longer, who can
say what other uses would have been found for these craft? Before proceeding to
discuss the many and varied operations in which X-Craft were employed, some
discussion of their design, construction and *modus operandi* will be of interest.

Following the Admiralty's decision to take over the design and production of a
midget submarine from the Army at a Controller's meeting in July 1940,[1] the War
Office—in a rare example of inter-service cooperation not evident in subsequent
Army midget submarine projects—agreed to lend the services of Colonel Jefferis
MC, who had produced the original idea, to assist in the establishment of a Staff
Requirement for the craft. This was defined as a small submarine capable of laying
a magnetic mine in shallow and confined waters where more conventional means of
minelaying were not appropriate. At the beginning of the project an important
principle was established. Though an immensely secret project, the craft would be
built under the supervision of the Director of Naval Construction to ensure that it
complied fully with constructional standards and requirements. This would not be
a covert project carried out by individuals where enthusiasm took precedence over
reality. From the beginning, X-Craft would be part of the Royal Navy's Submarine
Service.

The project was first known as 'Job 82' and the first two prototype craft were given
the Dockyard job numbers D.235 and D.236. The project was under the supervision
of Commander C. H. Varley DSC RN, a retired submariner who possessed access
to engineering facilities at his own Varley-Marine Works near Southampton, and
Commander T. I. S. Bell RN. Varley had already long been interested in midget
submarines and human torpedoes, so his appointment was a fortuitous one. He was
a larger-than-life personality, of whom it was written:

'Crom' Varley was a typical naval officer of the best type, and readily identified as such without the aid of uniform, by his breeziness, geniality and good-natured consideration for others. He easily became the centre of any company in which he found himself. He had a great deal of the forthrightness of his ancestor the Lord Protector, while he conspicuously lacked the less attractive characteristics of that great man.[2]

As the design progressed, the submarines became known, almost by accident, as X-Craft. As there had already been an *X1* in the Royal Navy it was decided that the two prototypes should be numbered *X3* and *X4*. Very many changes were made from the Army design, but in March 1942 *X3* was ready for trials, swiftly followed by *X4*. The general characteristics of the craft, together with the subsequent six boats of the *X5* group, are shown in the accompanying table.

In terms of general appearance, the craft resembled the early Holland boats, which had been the first true submarines in the Royal Navy. Owing to the secrecy under which the craft were built, and because different builders were used for *X3* and *X4*, there were minor differences between the prototypes, but these were no more than cosmetic. *X3* and *X4* were never used operationally. Instead they rendered long and valuable service for trials and experiments of all kinds and at the same time provided early and essential training for personnel. Finally their hulls were surrendered to the Ship Target Trials Committee (STTC) at the end of 1944 for a Promethean end.

The results of the early trials with *X3* and *X4* were very encouraging and the design of the production craft now had to be finalised. The main requirements were for a vessel similar to *X3* with a surface speed of 6kt, a dived speed of 5kt and an endurance of eighty miles at 2kt. The craft had to be able to carry two 4-ton side charges together with sufficient food and water to last the crew for ten days. It also had to be fitted with appropriate towing arrangements since intelligence indicated that German patrols and air reconnaissance would preclude launching the craft from a depot ship off the Norwegian coast as originally envisaged. However, on being asked to produce the sketch design resulting from this requirement, the Submarine Section of the Directorate of Naval Construction indicated that they were fully occupied with conventional submarine matters and so the work was given to the Design Section of Vickers at Barrow. This was approved in July 1942 and an order was placed for twelve craft.

The X-Craft were, of course, intended for use against the *Tirpitz*, safe in her Norwegian lair. For a successful attack certain conditions of moon and hours of darkness were required—conditions which occur only twice a year. Since the Admiralty wanted to use the X-Craft against the *Tirpitz* in March 1943, Vickers were asked to employ all their skill, facilities and experience to ensure that at least six craft were delivered as soon as possible to form the Twelfth Submarine Flotilla based at HMS *Varbel*[3] at Port Bannatyne on the Isle of Bute. At the same time the contract for the second six was placed with Broadbent Group of engineering firms.

Vickers were as good as their word. The first boat, *X5*, was laid down in September 1942 and the last, *X10*, was delivered in January 1943. This, given the strained circumstances of Britain's wartime economy, was a remarkable achievement, especially so because at the time Vickers was being criticised by the Admiralty over long delivery times for submarine construction.[4] All five craft were transported by rail from Barrow to Faslane on the Clyde, from where a floating dock took the craft in one lift to Port Bannatyne. There the craft and their crews embarked on a period of intensive training. However, the time scale was simply too tight for an attack to

Particulars of X-Craft

	X3	X4	X5–10
Length	43ft 6in	45ft 0in	51ft 7½in
Beam	5ft 6in	5ft 6in	5ft 9in
Draught (fwd)	5ft 1in	5ft 1in	5ft 3in
Draught (aft)	7ft 0in	7ft 0in	7ft 5in
Displacement (surface)	22 tons	23 tons	27 tons
Displacement (dived)	24 tons	25 tons	29.7 tons
Weight of side cargo	4 tons	4 tons	4 tons
Explosive charge	4,480lb	4,480lb	4,480lb
Surface speed (max)	6kt	6kt	6.25kt
Surface speed (cruising)	4.5kt	4.5kt	4kt
Endurance at 4.5kt	1,400 miles	1,300 miles	1,860 miles
Dived speed (max)	5kt	5kt	5.75kt
Dived speed (cruising)	2kt	2kt	2kt
Endurance at 2kt	85 miles	85 miles	82 miles
Pressure hull	8lb	8lb	10lb 'S' steel
Operational diving depth	200ft	200ft	300ft
Number of hatches	1	1	1
Builders	Varley-Marine	HM Dockyard, Portsmouth	Vickers, Barrow
Engine makers	Gardner	Gardner	Gardner
BHP at 1,800rpm	32	32	42
Main motor makers	Keith Blackman	Keith Blackman	Keith Blackman
HP at 1,650rpm	32	32	30
Type of battery cell	Ediswan	DP BSV/A	Exide 20SP
No of cells	96	106	112
Capacity at 5hr rate	350 amp hrs	370 amp hrs	440 amp hrs
Gyro compass	Browns A	Browns A	Browns A
Auto-helmsman	Browns	Browns	Browns
Magnetic compass	Not fitted	ACO Mk XX	
Direction indicator	Not fitted	AFV 6A/602	AFV 6A/602
Crew	3	3	4

be mounted in March, so it was put back to September. The operation, code-named 'Source', is covered in the next chapter.

The craft ordered from Broadbent were numbered *X20* to *X25* and incorporated experience gained in the construction and trials of the *X5* series. This caused some delay in their production and it was not until the autumn of 1943 that the first of the craft were ready. After the twelve operational craft had been ordered, Admiral Horton proposed that a non-operational type of X-Craft be built for training purposes and to free the number of submarines employed as anti-submarine targets for

Particulars of X20-, XT- and XE-Craft			
	X20 group	*XT class*	*XE class*
Length	51ft 7in	51ft 4in	53ft 1in
Beam	5ft 9in	5ft 9n	5ft 9in
Draught (fwd)	5ft 3in	5ft 11in	5ft 10in
Draught (aft)	7ft 5in	6ft 11in	7ft 1in
Displacement (surface)	26.8 tons	26.5 tons	30.3 tons
Displacement (dived)	29.8 tons	29.6 tons	33.6 tons
Weight of side cargo	4 tons	n/a	4.8 tons
Explosive charge	4,700lb	n/a	3,700lb
Surface speed (max)	6.25kt	6kt	6.6kt
Surface speed (cruising)	4kt	4kt	4kt
Endurance at 4kt	1,860 miles	500 miles	1,350 miles
Dived speed (max)	5.75kt	5kt	6.09kt
Dived speed (cruising)	2kt	2kt	2.5kt
Endurance at 2kt	82 miles	80 miles	88 miles
Pressure hull	10lb	10lb	10lb
Operational diving depth	300ft	300ft	300ft
Builders	*See table on page 137*		
Engine makers	Gardner	Gardner	Gardner
BHP at 1,800rpm	42	42	42
Main motor makers	Keith Blackman	Keith Blackman	Keith Metro-Vickers
HP at 1,650rpm	30	30	30
Type of battery cell	Exide J380	Exide J380	Exide J418
No of cells	112	112	112
Capacity at 5hr rate	440 amp hrs	440 amp hrs	484 amp hrs
Gyro compass	Browns A	n/a	Browns A
Auto-helmsman	n/a	n/a	n/a
Magnetic compass	ACO Mk XX	ACO Mk XXI	ACO Mk XXII
Direction indicator	AFV 6A/602	AFV 6A/602	AFV 6A/602
Crew	4	3	4

operational duties. Originally known as Z-Craft, they were subsequently reclassified as XT-Craft. In May 1943 orders for six such craft were placed with Vickers and for twelve with Broadbent. The Vickers boats, *XT1* to *XT6*, were delivered by March 1944 and were usefully employed as 'targets' in anti-submarine exercises for coastal forces base HMS *Seahawk*, at Loch Fyne, where two craft at a time were employed for over a year. XTs were also based at Campbeltown, Portsmouth and Harwich. The experience gained in working with the XTs was of tremendous value when the Royal Navy had to deal with the menace posed by German midgets in the English Channel following the Normandy landings. The twelve XTs ordered from Broadbent, *XT7* to *XT19*, less *XT13*, were all cancelled. Six were cancelled in March 1944, to be replaced by XE craft, while the final six were cancelled in September 1944 when it became clear that the six XTs already in commission were sufficient for training purposes. The XT craft differed substantially from the operational craft. No cargo release gear nor night periscope were fitted, while the induction mast, which could be lowered in the operational craft, was made a fixed structure.

The final development of the genre was the XE class. These were intended for operations in the Far East and thus considerable attention had to be paid to habitability—an area which had received scant attention in the X and XT series. Particular attention was also paid to the electrical installation, given that conditions in the Far East would be extremely humid. Eighteen XE craft were ordered in early 1944: *XE1* to *XE6* from Vickers and *XE7* to *XE19* (again excluding number 13) from Broadbents. At the end of the year the Vickers six were ready and formed the Fourteenth Submarine Flotilla. After working up, they then departed for the Far East with their depot ship HMS *Bonaventure*; their subsequent adventures are covered in Chapter 14. Only five, *XE7*, *XE8*, *XE9*, *XE11* and *XE12* of the Broadbent craft were delivered before the end of the war caused the cancellation of the rest. Of these, *XE11* was returned to Broadbents for virtual reconstruction after she had been rammed by a boom defence vessel; she was subsequently broken up. The remaining craft saw extensive and varied peacetime service before they were replaced by the post-war *X51* class.

That describes the production schedule of the X-Craft and their various deriva-tives. But just how were these craft constructed and how did they work? The operational and XT boats were of all-welded construction using 10lb 'S' steel. Although there was a nominal diving depth of 300ft, post-war trials using one of the *X20* series showed that the hull would not collapse until the craft had reached nearly 600ft.[5] The hull was constructed in three sections, bolted together internally through flanges. The central section was cylindrical, the bow and stern sections conical. This meant that the craft could be parted on the occasion of a major refit or the replacement of a main engine or motor. Depot ships and shore bases supporting X-Craft would carry a complete spare stern section for rapid replacement while the defective section was being repaired. Otherwise there was no need for the craft to be parted since all the other equipment could be removed or maintained by using the existing hatches.

In such a small craft the efficient running and safety of the electrical installation was of major importance. In such a confined space the main battery is far more likely to produce dangerous levels of hydrogen than in a larger submarine. In the prototype craft the battery consisted of 96 individual cells which were stowed in two layers and required individual ventilation. A catalyst system was designed by the Admiralty chemist at Portsmouth and proved so efficient that it was fitted to all subsequent classes. The battery exhaust gas was first passed through a container of soda lime and charcoal to remove the acid and then through a heated catalyst of palladised asbestos. Subsequent trials and operational experience showed that the hydrogen concentrations never rose above 0.8 per cent—a very safe figure. In *X5* and subsequent classes the battery was stowed forward with general ventilation arrangements, though the same catalyst system was fitted. One hundred and twelve Exide J.380 cells were fitted in the X and XT craft while the XE craft had the same number of Exide J.418 cells which were designed for the higher temperatures found in the Far East.

Carbon dioxide exhaled by the crew was absorbed by Protosorb. In the prototypes, Protosorb trays were simply left on the deck but this was found to be too cumbersome in such small craft. In the X and XT classes the substance was carried in 6lb canisters which were placed in the ventilation trunking. In the XE class 10lb canisters were carried. Oxygen was carried in cylinders—XEs had three of these, totalling 4.5 cubic feet—in the control room, the gas being released when required through a control valve.

The X-Craft used conventional diesel propulsion when on the surface and electric drive when dived. The diesel engine, either a 32bhp or 42bhp Gardner, mounted on a sound insulated raft, proved exceptionally reliable. The engine was the same as that used in London buses, and, to quote one authority, 'proved just as reliable running up Norwegian fjords as it did on the streets of the metropolis'.[6] The engine naturally had to be adapted for marine use and was fitted with a freshwater cooling system which in the XE craft could be topped up from the Freon distillate tank. If this cooling system failed it was possible to use sea water from the Wet and Dry (W&D) compartment. Air was drawn down to the engine by means of a folding induction mast (although this was a fixed structure in the XT class), while the exhaust gases were expelled by a muffled, drowned exhaust. The main motor, of conventional design, evolved from the open 30hp Keith Blackman motor fitted to *X3* to the fully enclosed, water-cooled model designed by Metro-Vickers for the XE class. The switch gear was of the drum type and was specially proofed against damp.

The control systems replicated those of a conventional submarine except that they were in miniature. Since there was but a small crew, only one set of hydroplanes was fitted at the stern in order to save space and weight. The prototypes experienced some problems in submerged control and these were investigated in the Admiralty Experimental Tank at Haslar. They showed that with only one screw fitted the hydroplanes lacked sufficient power to control the craft. The solution was to extend the surface of the hydroplane aft so that the rudder had to split into upper and lower sections in order to allow both to benefit from the slipstream. Initially power-operated steering was fitted, with emergency hand steering. However, the power steering was removed in the *X20* class for buoyancy reasons; the hand steering gear was found to be so effective that it was retained.

Despite the elementary nature of the X-Craft's controls, the boats handled very well when dived. As the Technical Monograph on the X-Craft noted:

> Whereas the orthodox submarine cannot do more than hold a stopped trim in certain favourable circumstances, X-Craft could be manoeuvred astern submerged, backed and filled and raised or lowered while stopped without difficulty by a skilful crew. This attribute was of the greatest advantage when the technique of accurately laying the charges beneath the target was developed.[7]

The X-Craft possessed navigational instruments of considerable sophistication, given the small size of the vessel. A gyro compass was fitted since it was considered impossible to position a magnetic compass far enough away from the hull to ensure sufficient accuracy. The gyros gave endless trouble: three of the six craft engaged in Operation 'Source' suffered gyro failure, while *X24*'s gyro gave out on both her operations against targets in Bergen. In the second raid, Operation 'Heckle', *X24* was proceeding up the Hjeltefjord with her gyro in pieces in the control room being reassembled by a very harassed ERA. A magnetic compass was subsequently fitted outside the hull in the top of a periscopic pinnacle, an image of which was projected on to a screen in front of the helmsman. In the operational X-Craft the binnacle, Type ACO Mk XX, could be raised and lowered as required, but in the training XT series the Mk XXI binnacle was fixed in the 'up' position. For the XE series a more sophisticated version was produced, the Mk XXII, which included compensating arrangements for the degaussing equipment. Although the magnetic compass was a satisfactory back-up under normal conditions, it was totally useless during the form of attack in which the X-Craft specialised—harbour penetration. The raised binnacle was likely to become fouled on nets, it took too long to raise and activate if the gyro compass failed and it was liable to damage while the X-Craft was manoeuvring under the target. Even if all man-made hazards failed to upset the compass, it was found that the distortion in the Earth's magnetic field caused by the presence of the target was sufficient to send it completely haywire. It was therefore necessary to find some non-magnetic means of navigation for this phase of the operation. A variety of mechanical direction indicators were evaluated, and eventually an Air Ministry Model, AFV 6A/602, was chosen. This could be pre-set either by eye or from the gyro and was liable to a maximum 'wander' of 5 degrees either side of the set course in twenty minutes. It was not, therefore, especially accurate, but it was sufficient for what was required. However, on one occasion, when the device was most needed, it malfunctioned with potentially disastrous consequences. As *X10* (Lieutenant K. Hudspeth RANVR) was retiring down Altenfjord following her commanding officer's decision to abandon the attack on *Scharnhorst* during Operation 'Source', both gyro and magnetic compasses were wandering. Hudspeth decided to dive and use the direction indicator, but on surfacing for a routine 'guff through' he found that the device had turned the craft through 180 degrees and he was heading back up the fjord.

While the X-Craft was making its submerged run-in toward the target it was, naturally, 'blind': periscope observation of the target would be impossible. In an effort to improve navigation during this most important part of the operation, two blind navigation devices were tested but eventually discarded. The first was a 'Course Indicator', which consisted of a long, flexible arm which was stowed alongside the keel but could be lowered so that it rested on the bottom. Riding on a hinge and pivoted so that it showed the deviation from a fore-and-aft line on a pointer inside the craft, it was designed to show the true course made good over the ground. Fitted along this, a measuring device consisting of twenty miles of special fine wire wound on to a bobbin gave the actual distance run along the bottom. Both devices were fine in theory but in practice it was found that they caused the navigator far more work than their results justified, and although they had been fitted to *X5–X10* they were removed before Operation 'Source'. Other navigational aids consisted of a Chernikeeff log (a device for measuring distance) and an echo sounder, described later. A small chart table was fitted, although the cramped conditions in the X-craft meant that the chart always had to be folded (and, invariably, the fold always lay in the part of the chart which was being used!).

Hydrophones were first fitted to X-Craft as a safety measure while the craft were in training, to warn of the approach of any traffic which might have unwittingly entered the training area. This was a sonic tank-type device on either bow which was connected to a switching apparatus so that the operator could either maintain an all-round watch or listen alternately to the port or starboard hydrophones. However, during the trials process it became abundantly clear that something more sophisticated was required. In particular, there was a need for a directional hydrophone to monitor the movements of harbour patrol craft so that avoiding action could be taken. The equipment selected was similar to the Type 129 set used in conventional submarines, but in order to give the same performance the diameter was reduced from 15in to 5in, while the frequency was increased to 30kc from 10kc. A quartz hydrophone was mounted on, and rotated with, the night periscope, while a simple battery-powered amplifier and headphones completed the installation. In trials using the prototype *X3* in Loch Striven, good bearings within 2 degrees of the day periscope readings were obtained despite the jerky rotation. During practice attacks it was found that the low-frequency noise emanating from the target vessel's auxiliary machinery (which would be running continuously whether or not the vessel in question was under way) could be used by the X-Craft as a means of homing in. The idea seemed fine in principle and a low-frequency hydrophone was developed for this purpose. However, trials of this instrument showed that, although a general increase in noise was detected from the vague direction of the target vessel, it was not of a sufficient level to aid navigation. Moreover, the hydrophone was extremely susceptible to noise from passing small craft. As these were precisely the conditions under which the set would have to perform in an enemy harbour, the project was abandoned.

The relative failure to use low-frequency sound emanating from the target led to the development of a high-frequency hydrophone which would indicate when the X-Craft was directly under the target. Originally it was proposed simply to invert an echo-sounder, but this was rejected on the grounds that the impulses would be easily detectable. The Mine Department at the Admiralty then stepped in and proposed the use of a magnetic detector. It was found in trials with X3 that the magnetic detector did not give a very definite indication of the precise position of the target, so attention reverted to the hydrophone.

To reduce the risk of detection, the impulses from the hydrophone had to be very high—300kc. This was ten times higher than the frequency at which any known enemy hydrophone could operate and produced such a sharp vertical beam that interception was considered highly unlikely. The echoes were displayed on a cathode ray tube and the method had the additional advantage that it was possible to calculate the draught of the target so that mistakes in attacking shallow-draught vessels could be avoided.

The development of the set, called the Type 151 target indicator, was accorded a high priority and trials took place in X8 in June 1943. Unfortunately, no sooner had the device been fitted than X8 collided with the target vessel and the apparatus was damaged. Subsequently refitted in X5, the set gave very good results: during trials it proved possible to use it to recognise nets and other obstructions as well as the target. Six sets were ordered and fitted in the six craft destined to embark on Operation 'Source'. The quartz oscillator was mounted flush with the casing and protected by a metal grid. The entire installation, comprising transmitter, receiver, cathode ray tube, oscillator and pressure hull gland weighed only 53lb—a master-piece of miniaturisation. The usefulness of the Type 151 was further extended by fitting a second oscillator face down in the keel. A selector switch connected either oscillator to the depth meter and this meant that 'soundings' of up to 100ft either way could be obtained.

Experience gained during Operation 'Source' and subsequent operations off the Norwegian coast showed that there was a need for a short-range underwater

Career Details of X-Craft

X3, X4	Built by Varley-Marine (*X4* completed by Royal Dockyard, Portsmouth); broken up in 1945
X5	Vickers, 1942; possibly sunk *c.*22.09.43 during Operation 'Source'
X6	Vickers, 1942; scuttled 22.09.43 after placing charges beneath *Tirpitz* during Operation 'Source'
X7	As *X6*
X8	Vickers; abandoned 16.09.43 during outward passage on Operation 'Source'
X9	Vickers; broke tow 16.09.43 during outward passage on Operation 'Source' and not seen again
X10	Vickers; scuttled 23.09.43 during Operation 'Source' after multiple defects prevented her reaching her operational area
X20	Broadbent, 1943; extant until 10.45
X21	Broadbent, 1943; extant until 10.45
X22	Markham, 1943; rammed and sunk by HMS/M *Syrtis* in Pentland Firth 07.02.44
X23	Markham, 1943; extant until 07.45
X24	Marshall, 1943; preserved at Royal Navy Submarine Museum
X25	Marshall, 1943; extant until 10.45
XT1–XT6	Vickers, 1943–44; *XT1*, *XT2* listed until 10.45, remainder until 07.45
XT7 XT19	(Less *XT13*) Broadbent, cancelled 1944; listed until 07.45.
XE1–XE6	Vickers; broken up Australia 1945
XE7, XE8	Broadbent; *XE7* broken up in 1952; *XE8* preserved by Imperial War Museum
XE9, XE10	Marshall; *XE9* broken up in 1952; *XE10* cancelled while under construction
XE11, XE12	Markham; *XE11* rammed and sunk by boom defence vessel 06.03.45, salved and broken up; *XE12* broken up 1952

communication system to be used while the X-Craft was being towed, dived, by the parent submarine since the previous method of using a telephone cable secured to the tow-rope had proved unreliable. Moreover, there was a need for communication between the submarine and the X-Craft after the tow had been slipped or if, for some reason, the tow parted. The equipment became known as the Type 713 hydrophone and was based on the submarine's Type 129 asdic in which the set was switched to transmit, the transmission being used as a carrier and modulated by voice. Good speech was received at ranges of up to 1,000yd, but if the X-Craft were directly astern of the submarine it was found that the sound beam was blanked by her ballast keel. This disadvantage led to the development of the Type 156 underwater telegraphy set. This consisted of a combined transmitter and receiver with an oscillator working on 10kc fitted in the forward ballast tank. The parent submarine used her Type 129 set in the normal manner for SST communication. The equipment proved of immense use, particularly in the Far East, when on one occasion the tow broke and the auxiliary tow had to be passed. A special hydrophone set was fitted to *X20* and *X24*, which were tasked with the reconnaissance of the invasion beaches in Normandy prior to the D-Day landings in June 1944. These two craft were fitted with a standard small-boat echo-sounder together with a chemical recorder. This latter had to be carried, despite its considerable bulk, as it was necessary to bring back permanent records for analysis by the invasion planners.

The armament of the X-Craft will be described later, but another feature of the craft was the Wet and Dry Compartment (known as the 'W&D'), whereby a diver could leave and re-enter the craft for the purpose of placing underwater charges, cutting nets or clearing obstructions. The compartment was placed in the centre of the craft, surrounded by No 2 ballast tank, with hatches leading forward into the control room and aft into the engine room. The exit hatch led up on to the casing. To leave the craft underwater, the diver entered the W&D, shut the hatches behind him and, using a telephone link, informed the First Lieutenant that he was ready. The latter then applied LP pressure to No 2 ballast tank, the Kingstons being shut, so that water began to enter the W&D, the displaced air venting into the control room. The LP air was shut off when the compartment was nearly full and the inboard vent shut when water spilled out. While the W&D flooded up the diver was subjected to the slow increase in pressure, an unpleasant sensation grimly known as the 'Squeeze'. Meanwhile the diver opened the equalising cock in the hatch and emerged, shutting the hatch behind him in case he failed to return. Before the diver returned, No 2 ballast tank was vented inboard ready for the diver's return.

These arrangements proved satisfactory but cumbersome. In particular, the position of the W&D in the centre of the craft made passage from the control room to the engine room difficult when the W&D was dry and impossible when it was flooded. Consequently, in *X5* and subsequent craft the W&D was placed forward of the control room so that only the battery compartment was isolated. Other improvements included the fitting of a silenced W&D pump to replace the rather noisy LP blower, cross-connected to the compensating pump in case of failure. In the early craft a number of cable runs, ventilation shafts, trunkings and water pipes had to be led through the W&D and the fluctuating air and water pressure played havoc with the glands. In the XE and subsequent craft all these services were passed over the top of the W&D. One feature of the W&D remained impervious to all change or modification: it was the only place on board where the WC could be located. The latter was a cramped, hand-pumped inconvenience with the ever-present hazard of 'getting ones own back'.[8] The latter phenomenon was bad enough in an ordinary submarine: in an X-Craft it was nothing short of catastrophic.

Allied to the role of the diver was the provision of net cutters to allow him to carve a way through net defences. The first net cutters were simple hand-held shears recovered from Italian *Decima Mas* operators captured at Gibraltar. These were useless against the type of wire mesh nets thought to be protecting *Tirpitz*, so something more effective was required. The advice of the Director of Boom Defence at the Admiralty was sought and he produced three versions of an air powered cutter, Mks I, II and III, which, though capable of cutting through thick nets, were awkward to operate, requiring the use of both hands, and, being air-powered, left a trail of bubbles on the surface. The comparative failure of the air-powered cutter led to the decision that the firm of Starkie Gardner (who made standard net cutters for the Navy) should be indoctrinated as to why powerful cutters were required. Though the security officers frowned, it proved a wise decision. Starkie Gardner produced the Mk IV, which was little more than an improved Mk III except that it could be operated by one hand, before introducing the Mk V. This was a radical departure in that it was hydraulically powered, leaving no tell-tale stream of bubbles. Further refinements produced the Mk VI cutter, which was the version finally adopted by the Admiralty. This was a one-handed device looking like an outsize tree pruner and which could cut through 3.5in FSWR with enough fluid in the reservoir for twenty-two cuts. Two such cutters were carried by each X-Craft stored in lockers in the casing. So much work had gone into the design and development of the Mk VI cutter that it was immediately classified 'Secret'—and remains so.

The time of entering a net was planned so that the X-Craft would be running against the tide. This enable the Captain to manoeuvre the craft at a depth of around 25ft into and through the net while maintaining full submerged control. The diver would then start cutting at the base of the X-Craft's keel, making a slit upwards in each successive strand so that the craft gradually pushed through. It sounds simple, but in the cold waters of a Scottish loch or a Norwegian Fjord, it was easy to amputate a finger without noticing the loss—and not just in cold northern waters. During the cutting of the Hong Kong to Singapore underwater telephone cable in 1945 by *XE5* the diver, Sub-Lieutenant B. G. Clarke RNVR, accidentally cut his thumb off. While trying to enter the W&D he became entangled with a Portuguese man o' war and was very badly stung (owing to the high ambient water temperature he was not wearing a suit). Eventually he made it back into the W&D and was hauled out, thrown down on the control room deck and given a shot of morphine in his backside, vigorously administered by *XE5*'s commanding officer, Lieutenant H. P. Westmacott RN. Before the drug took effect he was heard to mutter, 'My God, what next!'[9]

Given that the Royal Navy paid little attention to the subject of 'acoustic housekeeping' in its submarines, the attention paid to this matter in X-Craft was remarkable. At first it was thought that, although lack of space prohibited the fitting of any 'defensive' weapon, the small size of the X-Craft would be its protection, early trials with the prototypes showed that the craft were incredibly noisy. The result was a hasty programme of silencing and of noise reduction of all machinery on board.

Special attention was paid to the design of the propeller to avoid cavitation and thrash at speeds below 3kt, while 'singing' was avoided by thinning the edges of the propellers. Similar work was done with the reduction system, although a supposedly silent chain system fitted in *X21* proved more noisy than the meshed gears and was quickly removed. *XT5* was built 18in longer than her sisters to allow the main motor and diesel to be mounted on a common, sound-insulated bed connected to the hull by special clips. The installation proved most successful and was subsequently fitted to the boats in the XE class. The one seemingly insoluble acoustic problem was the transmission of pump noise through the water in the system. This proved especially difficult to deal with and was only partially solved by the fitting of special filters and flexible pipe connections. Other aspects of acoustic housekeeping included the removal of all unnecessary external fittings.

At trials held at the submarine sound range on Loch Goil—which was conveniently situated close to the X-Craft base at Kames Bay—a 'detectability range' of 500 yards was set, and reached, for all machinery used during an attack An idea of the progress made can be gauged from the fact that the *X5* to *X10* class were restricted to 1,000rpm when within 10,000yd of the target for fear of cavitation and thrash while a year later *XE5* ran her motors at 1,000rpm and was undetectable until she was within 1,000yd. The gyro, battery fan, W&D pump and other machinery could be run with impunity 500yd from the sensitive hydrophones used for the test.[10] Noise reduction was a continually monitored process. In every depot ship where X-Craft were employed special monitoring equipment was embarked, together with an officer specifically charged with making sure that each craft was as quiet as possible.

It seemed that no aspect of X-Craft's *modus operandi* was beyond the Navy's attention. The advent of radar during the Second World War led to the fear that an X-Craft might be thus detected while on the surface. Accordingly, the silhouette was kept as low as possible, despite the disadvantages this caused, although early plans to give the craft a collapsible conning tower were quickly shelved. The 'step' on the casing in the X and XT classes was removed in the XE class since it was found to be very distinctive at night. Furthermore, the bow and stern of the XE class were rounded down to make them even harder to spot. Camouflage was another matter to which considerable attention was paid. After a number of schemes, including 'Mountbatten Pink', had been tested, it was decided to adopt the standard submarine scheme of grey sides and black upper surfaces, although the XE class were painted black overall. The only exception to this rule were the two X-Craft which operated off the French coast prior to Operation 'Overlord'. These were painted yellow ochre, stone and Hooker's green for protection from air observation when operating close to the shore in daytime. Other passive defence measures included the fitting of degaussing equipment and net detectors and coating the hull in anti-magnetic paint to counter magnetic indicator nets.

The X-Craft lacked sufficient range to reach the target under its own 'steam', so it was usually towed for part of the voyage. Towing was not the first method selected but was adopted by force of circumstance when it was realised that no depot ship could approach to within launching distance of the target without being detected and therefore achieve the advantage of surprise. The favoured option was then to use a fishing trawler, and trials were successfully conducted in February 1943 using the *Bergholm*. However, to have the X-Craft towed by another submarine was the best method, and the 'T' class submarine HMS *Tuna* was allocated for trials in March 1943. These trials were equally successful, with *Tuna* towing a craft at speeds of up to 10kt, dived and on the surface, without any significant problems of control: the X-Craft, in the words of *Tuna*'s Commanding Officer, 'followed like a lamb'.[11]

The question of the tow rope proved an intractable one. Manila was initially selected: 100 fathoms of 4.5in constituted the tow rope, into which was woven a telephone cable. However, the Manila tow ropes were prone to breakage after between 60 and 80 hours of use. Consultation with salvage experts, who had to be fully briefed on the project in order that their expertise could be profitably employed, showed that frequent large stresses imposed on a waterlogged tow rope as the X-Craft surged up on the tow caused the structure of the rope to disintegrate and that a critical period of 70 hours was reached, when, under a sudden strain, the tow rope would part. Towing trials with *X20* in rough but bright weather showed the X-Craft surging forward on the tow, which then curled back like a whiplash over the little submarine. The rope could not be seen as the strain came on, but this undoubtedly was the moment when the damage was done.

The alternative was to use a nylon tow rope. The use of nylon for towing purposes had been developed by the Air Ministry in connection with gliders, and after some debate—for nylon was a valuable material: an X-Craft tow rope contained enough nylon to make, for example, 20,000 pairs of stockings—the Air Ministry agreed to part with 600lb. The first test rope endured over 3,500 miles of towing with no appreciable sign of wear and tear. So impressed was he with the nylon rope that Lieutenant Donald Cameron RNVR insisted on having one for *X7* in Operation 'Source'. His decision was well-founded: *X8* broke her tow en route and foundered, probably dragged down by the weight of a sodden rope. So successful was the nylon rope that, like the net cutter, its details are still classed as 'Secret'.

There was one aspect of the X-Craft to which little or no attention was paid, and that was habitability. Conditions on board were unbelievably squalid and could not be endured by anyone who was not wholly dedicated to the task or who had not previously experienced life at a British public school (or Britannia Royal Navy College, Dartmouth). Each X-Craft had a crew of four, Commanding Officer, First Lieutenant, engineer and diver. Trials with the craft soon showed that it would be beyond the endurance of one crew to take it across the North Sea, carry out an operation and then return. Accordingly each boat was allocated a passage crew who would operate it during the outward passage and exchange with the operational crew when the tow was slipped. The passage crew had the same composition as the operational crew less the diver. The role of the passage crew was unenviable:

> Their craft was submerged [for] most of the tow, during which they had to make sure everything was on top line for the operational team, who would have, naturally, most of the excitement and the rewards.[12]

Right forward in the craft there was a bunk placed on top of the battery cells. Even if the occupant managed to avoid dragging a sleepy hand across the terminals, he was likely to awake with a splitting headache and lungs full of hydrogen. As a result, the preferred place for a sleep was on a foreshortened couch in the control room or curled around the periscope. Needless to say, there was no galley on board. A single vessel in the control room served as a cooker. The first four tins which came to hand were emptied into the pot, stirred and heated. Understandably, even the hardiest appetite faded after a day or so of 'Potmess'.

The armament of an X-Craft consisted of two large side charges each containing two tons of amatol. Tests showed that the original amatol charge did not detonate completely, although a charge composed of Amatex did so; moreover, the original casings leaked at depths below 200ft and had to be redesigned. In the final Mk XX charge (which was made negatively buoyant by the addition of free-flooding ballast chambers so that it would sink and not embarrassingly come to the surface) the total weight was 5.5 tons, of which 3,700lb constituted the Minol charge with a 10 per cent cyclonite addition. The charges would be laid directly below the target and fitted with a variable time fuse to allow the X-Craft to clear the area. X-Craft could also carry limpet mines stowed in the casing which could be planted on the target's hull by the diver. In order to keep the X-Craft stationary while the diver placed the mines, all the boats from the XE series onwards were fitted with three special hinged, spring-loaded antennae which could be raised from within the craft. Once the X-Craft was beneath the target, the antennae were raised and then slight positive buoyancy was applied so that the craft rose gently upwards until it rested securely against the target's hull. The antennae left sufficient room for the diver to leave and re-enter the W&D.

After placing the charges or mines, the X-Craft would clear the area as quickly as possible. The risk of detection increased with time, and it was unwise to linger when the side cargoes or limpets detonated. There then remained the long journey out to the rendezvous with the parent submarine, the exchange of recognition signals and the welcome appearance of the passage crew for the return journey.

That, then, was the X-Craft—a most potent weapon of war. There are two points of interest when considering its design. First, the craft was an integral part of the submarine service and its construction and equipment were based on sound submarine practice rather than the enthusiasm of a special forces establishment. Secondly, as in the case of the tow rope and the net cutter, the Admiralty were prepared to risk compromising the programme by enlisting the best advice available—even from civilian contractors. This is an important point which applies to all such craft and which is not generally appreciated: their construction had to be grounded in reality and experience.

Chapter 11

Cool Courage and Determination

Have you seen an Englishman? There are four standing outside the
regulating office at this moment!—German seaman on board *Tirpitz* on the
morning of 22 September 1943.

By the summer of 1943 all was ready for the operation against the *Tirpitz*. The
techniques had been practised and perfected in exercises against capital ships 'on
loan' from the Home Fleet, protected by the most formidable obstacles the Boom
Defence Organisation could provide. The responsibility for much of this training
rested on Commander D. C. Ingram DSC RN, a distinguished submarine commander who had torpedoed the battlecruiser *Gneisenau* in 1940. Training is the key
to any mission, and those involved in the training are as often as not overlooked when
the rewards and medals are distributed. Not in Ingram's case: in his follow-up report,
Rear-Admiral C. B. Barry[1] commented:

> By his leadership and ability Commander D. C. Ingram DSC RN, as officer in charge
> of training, inspired all officers and ratings alike and achieved that high standard of
> fitness which was so essential. He was responsible that the crews were at the peak of
> their efficiency at the time the operation began.[2]

Special security measures were implemented at Loch Cairnbawn. From 1 September no home leave was given and only a select number of officers and men were
allowed to leave the area. Meanwhile detailed plans for the operation were being
prepared by Barry's staff in London. The operation had to be completed before the
onset of bad winter weather (which would make the tow across the Norwegian Sea
impossible), but while there was sufficient winter darkness to provide some cover
for the X-Craft and their towing submarines. A certain amount of moonlight to assist
the X-Craft in the navigation of the fjords was also desirable. When these three
factors were considered, the period 20–25 September 1943 was selected as the most
suitable period for the operation. 'D-Day'—the day on which the X-Craft would be
slipped from the towing submarines—was fixed for 20 September.

Tirpitz was known to be in Kaafjord, a branch of Altenfjord, but in the event of
her moving, alternative operational orders were prepared. The key to the operation
lay in air reconnaissance of the operational area up the last practical moment so that
the most up-to-date intelligence could be supplied. Altenfjord lay beyond the range
of Mosquito aircraft making a return trip from the United Kingdom, so arrangements
were made for them to fly on to Murmansk in North Russia and thence back home.

For last-minute photo-reconnaissance, PR Spitfires were deployed to North Russia: three Mk IXs from 'A' Flight, No 543 Squadron, flew from RAF Benson to the Soviet naval air base at Grasnaya. In the event the Mosquito reconnaissance did not take place owing to bad weather, but, as Admiral Barry noted in his report, the Spitfires, which arrived at Vaenga on 3 September and flew 31 missions, more than made up for the shortfall in material:

> The subsequent reconnaissances flown by this unit were invaluable. Full details on the dispositions of the enemy units and net defences were signalled from Russia and given to all personnel taking part before they left harbour. The first photographs taken by this unit did not arrive until a few hours after the X-Craft had sailed; but this did not in fact matter as the relevant information was complete in the signalled report.[3]

The essence of the operational plan was as follows. Six operational submarines each towing an X-Craft were to proceed independently to a position 75 miles west of the Shetlands and then to follow routes twenty miles apart until they reached a position some 150 miles from Altenfjord. From there they would head for a position from which to make their landfall. The changeover between passage and operational crews was to take place any time from D–3 (17 September) onwards.

Each submarine had been allocated a sector to seaward of the declared minefield off Sorøy Sound in which she was to remain after making her landfall. The X-Craft were to be released at positions two to five miles from the minefield after dusk on D-Day (20 September). They would cross the mined area on the surface and proceed to Altenfjord via Sterjnsund, spending the daylight hours of 21 September on the bottom. All five aimed to arrive off the entrance to Kaafjord at dawn on 22 September. They would then, as the Official History simplistically described it, 'enter the fleet anchorage and attack the target for which they had been detailed'. Target allocation would be done by signal while the X-Craft were on passage in the light of the most recent intelligence, since it would take nearly ten days for the X-Craft to reach their operational area.

While the X-Craft were operating independently, the towing submarines were to remain in their areas. For the recovery of the X-Craft, such as survived the operation, positions were established in each sector. Should an X-Craft fail to make this rendezvous, then an alternative location had been established in a desolate bay on the north coast of the island of Sorøy which would be searched by one of the towing submarines on the nights of 27/28 and 28/29 September. As a last resort, any X-Craft which were not recovered from Sorøy were to make their way independently to the Kola Inlet where the SBNONR[4] had arranged to have a minesweeper stationed at the entrance from 25 September to 3 October as a look-out.

The plans were made and slowly the various elements involved came together. On 30 August HMS *Titania* (Commander W. R. Fell OBE DSC RN) arrived at Loch Cairnbawn to act as depot ship for the submarines taking part. Forty-eight hours later she was followed by the towing submarines, *Thrasher, Truculent, Stubborn, Syrtis, Sceptre* and *Seanymph*. The submarines had all been fitted with the towing bracket and but case of equipment failure or accident two more similarly fitted boats, *Satyr* and *Seadog*, stood by at Scapa Flow.

Towing trials and practice at transferring the passage and operation crews were carried out between 1 and 5 September. Then, after final swinging of compasses, each X-Craft was hoisted on board the depot ship *Bonaventure* to have their side charges fitted.

At this stage it was by no means clear where *Tirpitz* was anchored. On 3 September a Soviet aircraft had spotted her in Altenfjord, together with *Scharnhorst* and *Lützow*. However, on 7 September the first Spitfire sortie from Vaenga found only *Lützow*. In fact *Tirpitz* and *Scharnhorst* were at sea that day, engaged in a rather futile bombardment of Spitzbergen. They were back in Altenfjord on 10 September. Although the British SIS had established an agent in Altenfjord, he was not able to send reports to London at this stage. It was not until a German naval signal was decoded on 10 September that news of *Tirpitz*'s return was received—and the return was confirmed by air reconnaissance that day.

The location of the ships in Kaafjord meant that the submarines would have to sail immediately if they were to reach Altenfjord by 22 September, the most favourable time for an attack. Accordingly, on the evening of 11 September HMS *Truculent*, towing *X6*, was the first to sail, followed by *Syrtis* towing *X9*, *Thrasher* towing *X5*, *Seanymph* with *X8* and *Stubborn* with *X7*. *Sceptre* and *X10* did not sail until 1300 on 13 September. For the record, the nominal list of officers and men involved in Operation 'Source' is given in the accompanying table.

From 11 to 14 September the passage was uneventful. Three or four times in every twenty-four hour period the X-Craft would surface to 'guff through' and ditch gash. Good speed was made, the two 'T' class boats attaining 10kt and the smaller 'S' class 8.5kt. On 14 September the photographs taken by the Spitfires of No 543 Squadron arrived in Britain. The pictures showed *Tirpitz* and *Lützow* secured in Kaafjord while *Scharnhorst* lay a little distance away in Altenfjord. Various options had been prepared in the event of one or more of the German ships being away or all three being widely dispersed. The plan which most suited this disposition of the German ships was 'Target Plan 4', which was duly signalled to the submarines at sea together with the latest information on net defences. The big effort would be directed against the *Tirpitz* which was allocated to *X5*, *X6* and *X7*; *X8* was allocated to *Lützow* and *X9* and *X10* were allocated to *Scharnhorst*.

It was almost inevitable that something should go wrong, and early on 15 September the tow between *Seanymph* and *X8* parted. *X8*'s passage crew surfaced almost immediately but could see nothing of *Seanymph* although visibility was around five miles. Undaunted, Lieutenant Smart set off on a course of 029°. The loss

Officers and Men involved in Operation 'Source'

Operational Crew   *Passage Crew*

X5, towed by HM Submarine *Thrasher* (Lt A. R. Hezlet DSC RN)

Lt H. Henty-Creer RNVR   Lt J. V. Terry Lloyd SANF
Mid D. J. Malcolm RNVR   Act Ldg Smn B. W. Element
Sub-Lt T. J. Nelson RNVR   Sto 1 N. Garrity
ERA 4 J. J. Mortiboys

X6, towed by HM Submarine *Truculent* (Lt R. L. Alexander DSO RN)

Lt D. Cameron RNR   Lt A. Wilson RNVR
Sub-Lt J. T. Lorimer RNVR   Ldg Smn J. J. McGregor
Sub-Lt R. H. Kendall RNVR   Sto 1 W. Oakley
ERA 4 E. Goddard

X7, towed by HM Submarine *Stubborn* (Lt A. A. Duff RN)

Lt B. C. G. Place DSC RN   Lt P. H. Philip SANF (V)
Sub-Lt L. B. Whittam RNVR   AB J. Magennis
Sub-Lt R. Aitken RNVR   Sto 1 F. Luck
ERA 4 M. Whitley

X8, towed by HM Submarine *Seanymph* (Lt J. P. H. Oakley DSC RN)

Lt B. M. McFarlane RAN   Lt J. Smart RNVR
Lt W. J. Marsden RANVR   Act Ldg Smn A. H. Harte
Sub-Lt R. Hindmarsh RNVR   Sto 1 J. G. Robinson
ERA 4 J. B. Murray

X9, towed by HM Submarine *Syrtis* (Lt M. H. Jupp DSC RN)

Lt T. L. Martin RN   Sub-Lt E. Kearon RNVR
Sub-Lt J. Brooks RN   AB A. H. Harte
Lt M. Shean RANVR   Sto 1 G. H. Hollett
ERA 4 V. Coles

X10, towed by HM Submarine *Sceptre* (Lt I. McIntosh RN)

Lt K. Hudspeth RANVR   Sub-Lt E. V. Page RNVR
Sub Lt B. E. Enzer   ERA 4 H. J. Fishleigh
Mid G. G. Harding RNVR   Act PO A. Brookes
ERA 4 L. Tilley

of the tow was not noticed in *Seanymph* until some two hours later when the submarine surfaced to let *X8* 'guff through': Oakley accordingly reversed course and spent the rest of the day in a fruitless search for the missing X-Craft.

At 1213 *Stubborn* sighted a U-boat and promptly dived, and remained so for over an hour. At 1550 the tow between *Stubborn* and *X7* parted, and while the ancillary tow was being connected *X8* hove in sight. It was quite possible that the 'U-boat' sighted earlier had been *X8* looking for *Seanymph*. The motley flotilla of *Stubborn* towing *X7* and with *X8* in company now set off to find *Seanymph*. At dusk the situation was reported to Admiral Barry, who was able to pass the information to *Seanymph*.[5] However, *X8* became separated during the night of 15/16 September, having misread an order to steer 046° as 146°. By 0300 on the morning of 16 September *X8* had disappeared again, but *Seanymph* was sighted. After giving her all the relevant information, *Stubborn* proceeded to the northward, leaving *Seanymph* to search for her errant charge, which she eventually found at 1700. By 2005 the tow was connected and, since conditions were favourable, the exchange of passage and operational crews had taken place, so *Seanymph*, with *X8* firmly secured, was resuming her interrupted passage.

X8's troubles were by no means over. On the morning of the 17th the craft began to experience difficulty in maintaining trim. Air could be heard escaping from the starboard side cargo. By 1630, in order to keep the craft level, both the compensating tank and No 2 ballast tank were fully blown. MacFarlane decided that the starboard charge would have to be jettisoned. The charge was set to 'safe' and dropped in 180 fathoms just after 1635. However, the 'safe' setting malfunctioned, for the charge exploded fifteen minutes later when about 1,000 yards astern of *X8*. The port side cargo then showed signs of leaking, so it was decided that this should be jettisoned as well. This time MacFarlane set the charge to explode two hours after release in order to let *X8* and *Seanymph* get clear. The charge was released at 1655 but 1840 it exploded with colossal force. The Wet and Dry compartment in *X8* was flooded and considerable shock damage done to pipework. *X8* was in no state to continue and so it was decided to scuttle her to avoid compromising the operation.

Meanwhile disaster had overtaken *X9*. At 0120 on 16 September she had dived after a routine period on the surface to ventilate boat. *Syrtis* then increased speed to 8.5kt. At 0855 speed was reduced and *X9* ordered to come to the surface by means of firing a number of small underwater charges. But on surfacing it was found that the tow had parted. *Syrtis* then returned on a reciprocal course and at 1545 a well-defined oil slick running along the submarine's track was sighted. Jupp continued the search until 0145 on 17 September and then reluctantly broke off and steered to the northward to report the loss of *X9* to London. His signal was never received and it was not until the evening of 2 October that London learned of *X9*'s demise. What had happened to *X9*? Undoubtedly her tow rope, which was a Manila one, had reached its breaking point and parted. The weight of the waterlogged rope hanging from *X9*'s bows had dragged the small craft into the depths and destruction.

The two 'T' class boats, towing *X6* and *X5*, both made their landfalls off Sorøy without incident on 17 September; *Sceptre* and *Syrtis* made their landfalls on 19 September, while *Stubborn* was catching up and would make hers on the 20th. In doing so, *Stubborn* had a most alarming scare. At 0105 on 20 September a drifting mine was sighted which passed clear of the boat but became entangled in the tow rope and travelled down to bump gently on *X7*'s bows. Displaying great presence of mind, Lieutenant Place sheered the mine off by some deft footwork and then bumped it down *X7*'s side until it drifted aft.[6] A couple of hours later *Syrtis* sighted a U-boat 1,500yd away and in a perfect position to be attacked. However, Jupp's orders forbade him attacking anything other than a German capital ship for fear of compromising the operation, so he had to watch while the intruder slipped away.

Thus, by the early afternoon of D-Day, 20 September, the four submarines with X-Craft in tow were ready to slip their charges. The exchange between passage and operational crews had been completed and between 1830 and 2000 the four tiny vessels moved off independently for Sorøy Sound, their parent boats withdrawing seaward. In his diary Lieutenant Cameron wrote:

> I have that just-before-the-battle-mother feeling. [I] wonder how theory will bear up under fire for the first time and how I will behave, though not under fire for the first time ... If I were a true Brit, the job would be the thing, but I can't help thinking what the feelings of my next of kin will be if I make a hash of it.[7]

The passage crews must have been relieved to gain the comparative comfort of the towing submarine. Their role was unsung but vital to the success of the operation. The discomfort which these crews endured was immense. Apart from the crowding caused by three men living in a very confined space for ten days, the disparity in size between the towing submarine and the X-Craft meant that the latter would porpoise up and down by as much as 60ft. Then there was an unremitting routine of maintenance and preparation to be carried out so that when the craft was handed over it was in tip-top condition.

The X-Craft crossed the mined area off Sorøy during the night of 20/21 September, making the passage on the surface. They then dived at daybreak on the 21st to proceed up Stjernsund during the day in order to reach Altenfjord by dusk. After charging batteries in a position south of the Bratholme group of islands, the X-Craft had only four miles to go before reaching the entrance to Kaafjord. In order to allow all the craft ample time to reach Kaafjord and to prevent an early assault compromising the entire operation, attacks were forbidden before 0100 on 22 September. After that each commanding officer had a free hand. Informally the commanders had decided to make their attacks between 0500 and 0800, setting their charges to explode at 0830, by which time they hoped to have withdrawn from the area.

Tirpitz was protected by a layered series of net defences supplemented by patrols and hydrophone surveillance of the area. Across the mouth of Kaafjord was a 48m deep net stretching from Auskarneset on the north side to Jemeluftneset on the south side. A 400m wide gate was fitted in the southern side which could be closed by a movable boom. However, on account of the frequent movements of local and naval traffic, this gate was invariably left open and only closed in the event of a submarine alert. Additionally a patrol boat fitted with hydrophones was stationed at the gap and all vessels entering or leaving were stopped and checked.

Inside Kaafjord *Tirpitz* lay in a net enclosure at Barbrudalen. The enclosure consisted of a 15m deep net with a secondary net 36m deep. Information on the net defences was gathered by RAF reconnaissance and from the observations of the Norwegian resistance, particularly two very brave men, Torstein Raaby and Alfred Henningsen. However, neither the eagle eye of the RAF Spitfire nor the close observations of the Norwegians revealed a third net suspended beneath the secondary net, giving a total coverage of 72m. A 20m gap lay on the side nearest the mouth of the fjord (roughly on *Tirpitz*'s port bow). It could be closed by a boom from which hung a 36m net. This boom was to be closed at night, but on the night of 21/22 September it was inadvertently left open, although the gap was still covered by a patrol craft and by observation and hydrophone watch from *Tirpitz*.[8] Frequent exercises were held to test the defences and it seems that these had induced a state of over-confidence among the ship's crew. Interestingly, given that the Germans knew that the British would use underwater weapons to sink the *Tirpitz* (presumably they knew all about Operation 'Title' from the unfortunate Evans), they made no attempt to keep sufficient steam raised to move the ship in a hurry—nor did they adopt any simple precautions such as keeping the propellers turning slowly to generate a wash which would make things extremely difficult for divers.

X6 and *X7* dived between 0145 and 0215 on 21 September to commence their run up Stjernsund. Both craft experienced difficulties with trimming as they encountered 'pockets' of fresh water. The passage up the fjord was encountered without difficulty, although occasional patrol craft were sighted. At 1630 Place's *X7* sighted the *Scharnhorst* under the lee of Aarøy island. Place was tempted to attack her but stuck to his original plan. Both craft lay up off Bratholme Island on the night of 21/22 September (though not in contact with one another) and at 0045 on 22 September Place set course for Kaafjord, followed roughly an hour later by Cameron. The weather was in their favour—a dull overcast sky with a wind sufficient to whip up white horses, which was ideal for hiding the wake made by a periscope.

By 0400 Place had gone through the net at the entrance to Kaafjord by blowing the X-Craft's ballast tanks and 'climbing' over the top of the net, but shortly afterwards he was forced to go deep to avoid a patrol craft. In doing so his boat became entangled in a empty square of anti-torpedo netting which had once been used to protect the *Lützow*. It took nearly an hour of blowing and filling to free *X7* and in the process she broke surface though, fortunately, was not observed. By 0600, after fouling another wire with her periscope, *X7* was proceeding cautiously towards the net enclosure at Barbrudalen—cautiously because her trimming pump and gyro compass were out of action following the encounter with *Lützow*'s net.

X6 was also encountering mechanical problems. Her periscope had developed a leak, which made visual observation extremely difficult. Unlike Place, Cameron planned a more orthodox means of penetrating the net at the entrance to Kaafjord. The diver, Sub-Lieutenant R. H. Kendall RNVR, was ordered to get ready to leave the craft and cut a way through. However, just as Kendall was cramming himself into the W&D, Cameron heard the HE effect of a small ship overhead. In a very bold and decisive move he brought *X6* to the surface and nipped through the gap in the net undetected in the wake of a small coaster. *X6* then paused while Cameron stripped and cleaned the periscope in an attempt to make it serviceable. On coming to periscope depth, Cameron found that he had drifted perilously close to the tanker *Nordmark* and a rapid alteration of course was required to avoid fouling her mooring buoy. The periscope then flooded again, and to make matters worse the periscope motor brake burned out: from now on the periscope would have to be raised and lowered by hand. Cameron's feeling can be imagined:

> We had waited and trained for two years for this show and at the last moment faulty workmanship was doing its best to deprive us of it all. There might be no other X-Craft within miles. For all I knew we were the only starter, or at least the only X-Craft left. I felt very bloody-minded and brought her back to her original course . . . It might not be good policy, we might spoil and destroy the element of surprise, we might be intercepted and sunk before reaching our target, but we were going to have a very good shot at it.[9]

Cameron pressed on. By 0705 *X6* was through the boat gap in the Barbrudalen nets with nothing between her and the *Tirpitz*.

On board the *Tirpitz* there were no indications that anything was amiss: 22 September was going to be another routine day. At 0600 the hydrophone watch maintained during the night hours was stood down. At the same time the hands were called and the usual daytime AA and anti-sabotage watches were set. The gate in the anti-torpedo net was opened for the passage of routine craft. All this was to change when, at 0710, what the *Tirpitz*'s log described as a 'long black submarine object' was sighted on the battleship's port beam. This was *X6*, which, after passing through the net gate, had run aground on the north shore. However, the sighting was dismissed as being a porpoise and no action was taken. *X6* was by now in a poor condition. The periscope had flooded and the gyro compass had been put out of action in the grounding. Cameron was groping his way blindly toward the *Tirpitz*, hoping to fix his position by the shadow of the ship. Five minutes later *X6* became caught in an obstruction which was probably one of the two service craft alongside the battleship's port bow. She came to the surface only thirty yards away, and this time there was no mistaking her for what she was. The alarm was raised and a brisk fire was opened using small arms; fortunately, *X6* was so close to her quarry that none of the light flak or medium weapons could depress sufficiently to engage her.

Cameron disengaged *X6* from the obstruction and, realising that there was no escape, backed until her stern scraped *Tirpitz*'s hull abreast 'B' turret, released his charges and scuttled the craft after destroying all classified equipment. As the tiny *X6* started to sink, a launch from *Tirpitz* came alongside and took Cameron and his crew off. The Germans made a half-hearted attempt to take the sinking *X6* in tow, but without success. As *X6*'s crew went up the accommodation ladder to *Tirpitz*'s quarterdeck, Sub-Lieutenant John Lorimer RNVR (*X6*'s First Lieutenant) wondered, with a strange sense of detachment, whether he should salute the quarterdeck and colours of a foreign warship. Sub-Lieutenant Kendall recalled that

As we reached the quarterdeck John [Lorimer] turned to me, conscious as ever of protocol, and said, 'Do we salute the quarterdeck?' It was the last thought that crossed my mind and, besides, I wasn't wearing a cap. I think John 'cut off a smart one'.[10]

The four were treated well, given coffee and schnapps and then separated. Cameron and Lorimer were taken to one compartment while Kendall and Goddard were taken to another and left under guard.

On board the *Tirpitz* the alarm was raised with a vengeance. Divers prepared to go down and examine the hull, steam was raised and the ship prepared to leave the net enclosure. There does seem to have been a certain amount of laxity in the response of the command in *Tirpitz* to the events which were unfolding around the ship. Although *X6* was first sighted at 0707, it was not until 0721 that action stations were sounded and not until 0732 that it was reported that the crew were fully closed up and all watertight doors secured. Further confusion was caused at 0740 by the sighting of a second midget submarine, Place's *X7*. That there were clearly more than one midget submarine on the loose in Kaafjord 'presented the Germans with a picture so little to their liking' (in words of the British Staff History) that they decided to keep *Tirpitz* within the safety of the net but to try to move her as far away as possible from the site where *X6* had sunk. Accordingly, the port cable was veered while heaving in on the starboard cable to swing the ship's bow to starboard.

During all this commotion *X7* was making her attack. Place had decided to go under the anti-torpedo net but was defeated by the net's being much deeper than intelligence estimates had led him to believe. Place made two attempts to go through the net but became stuck each time. Only by violent manoeuvring was *X7* freed from the nets and in the process her gyro compass failed. She also broke surface at one stage in the proceedings (0710) but was unobserved, the attention of those in *Tirpitz* being concentrated on Cameron's *X6*. By this time Place was by no means sure of where he was, so he allowed *X7* to come slowly to the surface for visual observation. The following events are best described in the words of Place's subsequent report:

By some extraordinary, lucky chance we must have either passed under the nets or worked out way through the boat passage, for on breaking surface the *Tirpitz*, with no intervening nets, was sighted right ahead not more than thirty yards away. Forty feet was ordered, and at full speed *X7* struck *Tirpitz* at 20 feet on the port side approximately below B turret and slid gently under the keel, where the starboard charge was released in the full shadow of the ship. Here, at 60 feet, a quick stop trim was caught—at the collision *X7* was swung to port so [we] were approximately down the keel of the *Tirpitz*. Going slowly astern, the port charge was released about 150 to 200 feet further aft—as I estimated, under X turret.[11]

Place now tried to make his escape but was hampered by the lack of a compass. *X7* slithered over the anti-torpedo net at 0740 and this was when she was first spotted by the Germans, who opened fire with machine guns. Place then took *X7* deep, but the little craft veered to starboard and around 0810 she became caught in the anti-torpedo net which she had just surmounted. Almost as soon as *X7* was entangled in the net there was a terrific explosion which shook the little craft out of the net and up to the surface, where, Place noted, 'It was tiresome to see *Tirpitz* still afloat'.

The vigorous manoeuvring in and out of the nets had caused many of *X7*'s control systems to fail. She had no compass, the diving controls were inoperable and she had almost exhausted her supplies of compressed air. Place decided to surface to give him and his crew a chance of escaping. *X7* came to the surface near to a battle practice target and Place was able to step from one to the other without getting wet. His crew were not so fortunate. As *X7* approached the target, Place realised that the bows would dip when she came alongside. Since *X7* had very little buoyancy, he kicked the hatch shut to prevent water entering the craft. However, Sub-Lieutenant Aitken was unaware of this and opened the hatch, allowing water to flood in. *X7* lost her buoyancy and sank. Of the three men trapped inside, only Aitken would survive—and how he did so is a story of cold-blooded heroism:

On the bottom the options of a DSEA[12] escape or getting out on the surface, if we could get *X7* there, were discussed. To do the latter the compressor and pumps would have to be run and it was thought their noise would bring the depth charges closer. It was decided to flood the whole boat. The First Lieutenant would escape from the after hatch, the ERA through the W&D hatch and I, who was at that time next to the W&D, would follow the first one out. We waited until there had been no depth-charging for some time, then strapped on the DSEA sets. We were unable to open some of the valves and the flooding was very slow. In time the water reached the electrics, something fused, the boat filled with fumes and we had to go to oxygen. We then discovered that with our DSEA sets it was impossible to change places, but the ERA signalled he was all right where he was. When I thought the boat was nearly flooded I entered the W&D to try the hatch. It would not open. On my return to the control room I found the ERA slumped on deck. Checking his breathing bag, I found it flat and the two small emergency cylinders empty. Without oxygen he had drowned. I returned to the W&D and tried the hatch again. It wouldn't open. Then my oxygen bottle ran out. I broke open my two emergency cylinders but at that depth they only seemed to give me a couple of breaths, but enough to try the hatch again. It opened and I climbed out by standing on the WC housed in the W&D. As I rose, the pressures reduced, the oxygen in my lungs expanded and I could breathe. My breathing bag inflated and provided the buoyancy required to shoot me to the surface. As I rose the pressure continued to reduce and it was essential to breathe out to avoid bursting a lung. I unrolled the apron under the breathing bag and held it out at arm's length to act as a brake to slow up the ascent. I remember thinking how pleased my instructor would have been to see the correct drill being carried out!

My delight on reaching the surface was short-lived. *Tirpitz* was still afloat and there was no sign of the First Lieutenant. A motor boat picked me up and I was taken aboard *Tirpitz*, stripped, given a blanket and taken below for preliminary interrogation.[13]

Sub-Lieutenant Robert Aitken RNVR had only left school in the summer of 1940. As a footnote to this incident, the Germans raised the midships sections of *X7* in October 1943 and found Sub-Lieutenant Whittam's body, which was buried with full naval honours in the cemetery at Tromsø. Of ERA Whitley's body there was no trace.

Back on board the *Tirpitz*, considerable alarm was caused by the sighting of *X7* and a brisk fire was opened on her and on anything else that moved in the fjord. When, at 0812, the charges exploded, the whole ship whipped viciously, all electric lights were extinguished, any items of equipment not secured fell about and glass from broken scuttles and mirrors cascaded everywhere. Anyone standing up was thrown off their feet. The ship's log recorded that

. . . at 0812, two heavy consecutive detonations to port at 1/10 second intervals. Ship vibrates strongly in vertical direction and sways slightly between her anchors.[14]

A seaman who subsequently served aboard *Scharnhorst* and who survived the sinking of his ship in December 1943 confessed to his interrogators:

We've had torpedo hits, we've had bomb hits. We've hit two mines in the Channel, but there's never been an explosion like that![15]

One consequence of the explosion was the attitude of the Germans towards their British prisoners. *Kapitän zur See* Karl Topp ordered that all four be shot at once, a course of action from which he required vigorous dissuasion. Nevertheless, the mood was ugly and, as Sub-Lieutenant Lorimer recalled, had it not been for the 'distraction' provided by *X7*'s appearance, things might well have ended badly.

It is not clear how many of the four charges laid beneath *Tirpitz* exploded. Post-war hydrographic surveys of the area failed to find any of the charges or even traces of splinters, so it must be presumed that all four detonated simultaneously. Only the decision to move the ship to starboard saved her from greater damage. This action moved her bows further away from *X6*'s two charges and the charge laid by *X7* under 'B' turret. Had the Germans known that a second X-Craft had laid charges beneath *Tirpitz*'s hull, they might have moved her further, for *X7*'s second charge lay right under her engine room.

It was not until the *Tirpitz* was fully surveyed that the extent of her injuries could be established. The damage was extensive. Although her hull remained intact, there was considerable shock damage in the machinery spaces. All turbine feet, propeller shaft plummer and thrust blocks and auxiliary machinery bearers were cracked and distorted. The port turbine casing and condenser casing were fractured. The propellers could not be turned and the port rudder was inoperable on account of the steering compartment having been flooded through a stern gland. The four 38cm turrets had jumped off their roller paths, although 'B' and 'D' turrets were quickly repaired. All the optical rangefinders except those in 'B' turret and the foretop were rendered useless. Three of the four flak directors were out of action and the aircraft catapult was unserviceable. One seaman was killed and forty more injured.

It was clear that *Tirpitz* needed the services of a major shipyard, but her return to Germany was out of the question in the face of determined Allied air, surface and submarine attack. The *Luftwaffe* could not provide the massive air umbrella with which they had protected *Scharnhorst* and *Gneisenau* during the 'Channel Dash', and there were insufficient naval forces to protect *Tirpitz* against the Home Fleet. Hitler agreed that the ship should be repaired *in situ*, with workers and materials being sent up from Germany. Docking was out of the question since the *Kriegsmarine* possessed only one floating dock large enough to take the ship and it was inconceivable that this could be transferred to Norway. Divers repaired the cracks in the ship's hull using underwater cement while a coffer dam had to be constructed around the port rudder to allow the gland to be repacked.

The British learned about the results of the attack by means of Enigma decrypts. A series of signals decrypted between 22 September and 3 October made it clear that complete surprise had been achieved and that the *Tirpitz* had been badly damaged. Enigma was supplemented by visual reports from the SIS agent in Altenfjord, who reported that the battleship was down by the bow and surrounded by small craft. A further series of signals indicated that repairs would be carried out locally, and a signal revealing that *Tirpitz*'s ship's company were to be given home leave in three watches finally convinced the Admiralty that 'The Beast' would not be a going concern for the near future.

What of *X5*? She had last been seen on 20 September off Sorøy by *X7* but no trace of her was found thereafter. At 0843 the Germans sighted a third X-Craft some 500 yards outside the net enclosure. The craft was fired on and depth charges were dropped in the area. Sub-Lieutenant Lorimer noticed what he took to be a periscope from *Tirpitz*'s quarterdeck and saw an explosion followed by a spreading oil slick after the German counter-attack. It may well that this sighting was *X5* but a number of hydrographic surveys of the fjord have not discovered the wreck of a third X-Craft. Although the British Official History declares that *X5* was sunk at 0843, this analysis must be open to doubt.

X10 had the most miserable journey of all. After slipping from *Sceptre*, Hudspeth made good progress and by 2320 on 21 September the craft was on the last leg of her long passage. Then things began to go awry. First the gyro compass failed and then the illumination on the magnetic compass (outside the hull) failed. Worse was to follow: at 0150 on 22 September the periscope motor burned out and Hudspeth was forced to surface in order to ventilate. *X10* had no compass and no periscope, and proceeding with the attack was out of the question. Accordingly Hudspeth elected to spend the 22nd on the bottom in an attempt to sort the defects out. While bottomed he heard the explosion of the charges under *Tirpitz* and realised that at least one of the craft had struck home. He also realised that the defences would now be very much on the alert. Consequently, when darkness fell on the evening of the 22nd, he reluctantly took the decision to withdraw. One author has described this action as a 'gallant and selfless decision',[16] and it was one which was approved of by Rear-Admiral Barry, who commented:

> I consider Lieutenant Hudspeth's decision to abandon the attack was in every way correct. To have made the attempt without a compass and with a periscope which could not be operated and must remain in the fully raised position would have made any chance of success remote indeed.[17]

As it happened, *Scharnhorst* was at sea on the 22nd: her new commanding officer, *Kapitän zur See* Julius Hintze, was not satisfied with the efficiency of his new command and had taken her to sea for full-calibre firings. *Scharnhorst*'s absence was known to the Admiralty by means of Enigma but it had not been possible to inform *X10*. Had Hudspeth persevered, he would have found the net enclosure in the Altenfjord empty. *X10* then withdrew and hid along the coast in increasingly bad weather until 0055 on 28 September, when *Stubborn* was sighted, although it was not until conditions had abated twenty-four hours later that the transfer between passage and operational crew could be effected. Even then *X10*'s troubles were not over, for *Stubborn* experienced difficulty with the tow and the weather was deteriorating. Duff and Hudspeth were loath to abandon the little craft, but at 1807 Duff received clearance from Rear-Admiral Barry to scuttle her in view of the worsening weather. By 2040 the passage crew had been re-embarked in *Stubborn* and five minutes later *X10* sank, her end marking the end of Operation 'Source'.

Apart from the considerable damage inflicted on the *Tirpitz*, the strategic gains from the operation were immense. With *Tirpitz* out of action and with *Lützow* withdrawn to Germany, the *Kriegsmarine*'s battle group in Norway was reduced to the *Scharnhorst*, and she was dispatched by the guns of HMS *Duke of York* on 26 December 1943 in the Battle of the North Cape. A total of sixteen convoys to and from the Soviet Union were run in the 1943 winter season without the threat of interference by the *Tirpitz* hanging over them. The loss of five X-Craft, together with nine officers and men, was not an unduly steep price to pay in return.

Strategic consequences aside, Operation 'Source' was a magnificent example of cold-blooded courage, and the Admiralty showed their appreciation with a liberal award of decorations. Place and Cameron were awarded the Victoria Cross, Lorimer, Kendall and Aitken the DSO, Hudspeth a DSC and Goddard a CGM. As Rear-Admiral Barry summed up in his dispatch,

I cannot fully express my admiration for the three commanding officers, Lieuts H. Henty-Creer RNVR, D. Cameron RNR and B. G. Place RN, and the crews of *X5*, *6* and *7*, who pressed home their attack and who failed to return. In the full knowledge of the hazards that they were to encounter, these gallant crews penetrated into a heavily defended fleet anchorage. There, with cool courage and determination, and in spite of all the modern devices that ingenuity devised for their detection and destruction, they pressed home their attack to the full . . . It is clear that courage and enterprise of the very highest order was shown by these gallant gentlemen, whose daring attack will surely go down in history as one of the most courageous acts of all time.[18]

Chapter 12

Improbable and Unworkable Designs

... the enemy continued the mini-war with ever new ideas.—War Diary of
the German *Gruppe Nord* Command, November 1943.

The British Special Operations Executive was formally set up on 19 July 1940 and
charged with coordinating 'all action by way of subversion and sabotage, against the
enemy overseas'[1]. During the course of the Second World War the SOE operated
throughout Europe, the Middle East and the Far East with varying degrees of
success. In doing so it established its own research and development organisation
which produced a variety of weapons and other aids to resistance fighters in occupied
countries. Research was carried out by SOE's Station IX at a former private hotel,
the Fryth, near Welwyn Garden City in Hertfordshire, while production was the
responsibility of Station XII at Aston House near Stevenage. Some of the inventions,
like the 'S-Phone', a lightweight transceiver for agents in the field, were outstand-
ingly successful; others, such as the explosive turd,[2] did little other than keep their
inventors out of mischief.

The Welman one-man midget submarine definitely falls within the latter cat-
egory. It was the brainchild of the aptly named Colonel John Dolphin, an officer in
the Royal Engineers, who envisaged the craft being used for attacks on enemy
warships inside defended harbours, for the insertion of agents and stores into enemy
country and for beach reconnaissance. Development began at Welwyn (hence the
name Welman: One-Man Submarine made at Welwyn) in June 1942 and trials were
carried out at Vickers' experimental tank at St Albans, the Admiralty experimental
tank at Haslar, near Portsmouth, and in Laleham Reservoir near Windsor.

It was indeed a curious craft which took to the water in January 1943 for
preliminary trials. The first three Welmans were made at the Fryth and their
construction reflected the amateurish nature of the operation. The Welman was a
very simple craft—so simple that it represented the most that could be achieved with
a minimum of resources and it defied all attempts to improve it with what one
operator has subsequently described as 'Thatcher-like arrogance'.[3] Externally, the
craft was low-lying and of cylindrical appearance, with a conning tower pierced by
four armoured glass ports (no periscope was fitted) to enable to single operator to
navigate the craft. Propulsion was by means of a 2.5hp electric motor, which came
from a London bus, powered by a 40V battery of 220amp/hr capacity, although some
early craft's batteries were of only 180amp/hr capacity. There were two ballast tanks,

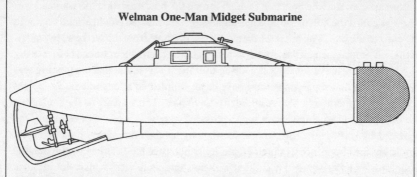

Welman One-Man Midget Submarine

Displacement: 2.5 tons (with charge)
Length: 6.08m
Beam: 1.06m
Propulsion: 2.5hp electric motor
Speed (surfaced): 3kt
Range (surfaced): 36nm at 4kt
Armament: One 540kg charge

Crew: 1
Number delivered: 100+

Fates: *W10* lost in accident 09.09.43; *W45*, *W46*, *W47* and *W48* all lost during unsuccessful raid on Bergen 21–22.11.43; remainder broken up from 1944.

one port and one starboard, which were blown by compressed air but vented by a hand-operated lever. Submerged trim was maintained by a 300lb weight which had to be moved forward and aft as required by hand, although some later craft had proper compensating tanks and arrangements for trimming by pump. The diving depth was supposed to be 300ft, but after a Welman imploded at 100ft while being lowered on a measured wire during an unmanned test dive, orders were issued revising the maximum depth to which one of these craft could be taken.

The single operator sat amidships in a very cramped position on a seat salvaged from an Austin 7 motor car. He was supplied with oxygen via a face mask from a cylinder situated under the control panel, but there was also a tray containing Protosorb CO_2 absorption crystals. His controls were rudimentary in the extreme. A joystick, plundered from a Spitfire fighter aircraft, governed the rudder and hydroplanes. There was only one set of hydroplanes, situated at the stern, which gave poor control when dived, and Welmans always had a tendency to porpoise at the slightest loss of trim. A foot-operated pump was provided for emptying the bilges and for the trimming tanks, where fitted. Other aids included a compass, barometer, ammeter, voltmeter and depth gauge.

The 'weapon' was a 1,200lb charge containing 600lb of amatol secured to the fore end of the craft and held in position by rod gearing. The operator aimed to place his craft underneath the hull of the ship he was attacking. He would then release compressed air into the bow tank, which forced the bow up so that the warhead was resting against the hull of the target. Magnets on the warhead would effectively hold the craft to the hull. The operator then released his craft from the warhead by means of the rod gearing, which was first driven right home to arm the warhead before being unscrewed to achieve separation. During training it was found that the gearing was very stiff and that separation could only be accomplished after some fairly violent action by the operator, which resulted in a lot of noise being made. At the same time the operator had to compensate for the loss of weight as a result of releasing the warhead by shifting the trim weight forward by hand. A time fuse on the warhead would set the charge off five hours later, by which time the Welman would be well clear, although the warhead was fitted with anti-tamper devices which would cause it to explode should it be discovered and an attempt made to remove or defuse it.

Attack instruments were basic in the extreme. A combined clock/stopwatch allowed the operator to time his run in to the target using a gyro direction indicator, also from a Spitfire, set by eye to maintain the correct course. Since the operator was not provided with a periscope, he had to approach his target either by running awash with the conning tower just above the water or by approaching the target dived while 'porpoising' frequently, but briefly, to check the course. Harvey Bennette was an SBA[4] stationed at the Fryth who was involved with the Welman project. He recalled:

> The whole business of having no periscope, which made the craft blind, was something no one could understand. No one came to appreciate why there was no periscope: [this] made the things unusable because they were blind.[5]

Bennette ascribed this astonishing omission to the all-pervasive influence of Colonel Dolphin on the project: the Welman was very much his idea and all outside suggestions were stoutly resisted.

It is clear that a Welman operator would be a very busy man during an attack and this was one of the greatest flaws of the design. In fact, other than having an engine and marginally better instrumentation, the operator's position was little different from that of Ezra Lee in his *Turtle* in 1776. There was simply too much for one man to do for the craft to be effective. Moreover, by making it a one-man craft, the designers denied the operator the moral support which would come from another crew member.

Training in the Welmans was carried out initially at Laleham Reservoir near Windsor. At this stage it was unclear how the craft were to be employed, although strong interest was expressed by Admiral Louis Mountbatten, Chief of Combined Operations. Mountbatten even went so far as to 'drive' a Welman himself. Disaster nearly struck when one of the glass ports gave way when the craft was dived at 30ft, and it was only by releasing the drop keel that Mountbatten was able to surface. After completion of the trials at Laleham, 150 Welmans were ordered on 23 February

Above: The X-Craft were the best-known and most successful British midget submarines. They are shown here under construction at the Huddersfield works of Thomas Broadbent in 1944.

Right: Sub-Lieutenant Robbie Robertson standing on *X24*'s air induction mast (which doubled as a snortmast). The mast was fitted with a safety rail (known as the Hezlet safety rail, after Commander Arthur Hezlet) for the crewmen to hold on to. Forward of the induction mast is the hatch into the W&D, while aft of the mast is the non-elevating night periscope, used when on the surface at night or observing the activities of the enemy. (IWM 22905)

Above: Robertson poses for another publicity photograph, this time in *X24*'s control room. The seat in front of him is for the helmsman, while behind him can be seen one of the release wheels for the side cargoes. (IWM 26932)

Left: The German battleship *Tirpitz*—'The Lone Queen of the North', but perhaps better described by Churchill as 'The Beast'—lying behind her nets at Kaafjord.

Above: A photograph which includes four of the five X-craft commanders who participated in Operation 'Source'. From left to right ~~~e Lieutenant T. L. Martin ~~N, of *X9*; Lieutenant K. R. ~~udspeth RANVR, of *X10*; ~~ieutenant B. M. MacFarlane, ~~ *X8*; Lieutenant Godfrey ~~ace RN, of *X7*, and ~~eutenant Donald Cameron, ~~ *X6*. Missing is Lieutenant ~~. Henty-Creer of *X5*. (IWM ~~21688)

~~ight: Lieutenant K. R. ~~udspeth RANVR, who ~~rticipated in Operation ~~ource', the X-Craft beach ~~connaissance and the ~~ormandy landings—all ~~thin the space of nine ~~onths. (IWM A.19626)

Above: *X24* at Loch Cairnbawn flying her 'Jolly Roger' after a successful mission to Bergen under the command of Lieutenant Max Shean RNVR on 13 April 1944 in which the 7,500-ton merchantman *Barenfels* was sunk. However, Shean's intended target had been the nearby floating dock, so in September 1944 Lieutenant Percy Westmacott took *X24* back to complete the job.

Right: *X23*, commanded by Lieutenant George Honour RNR, returns to the HQ ship HMS *Largs* on 6 June 1944, having, together with *X20* (Lieutenant K. Hudspeth RANVR), preceded the invasion fleet by some 48 hours in order to act as a navigational beacon for the flights of landing craft heading towards 'Juno' and 'Sword' beaches.

Above: *XE6* on trials in Rothesay Bay in August 944. XE-Craft were a variant of the original design roduced specially for service in the Far East. Note ie flush-deck casing—a distinguishing feature of ie type.

3elow: XE-Craft personnel at Rothesay before their leparture for the Far East: (from left to right) AB J.

Magennis, Lieutenant Ian Fraser, Lieutenant B. Carey and ERA R. Maughan. Magennis and Fraser were both awarded the Victoria Cross for the attack on the *Takao*. Carey was killed in a diving accident off the Great Barrier Reef before the two cable-cutting operations. (IWM A.26940)

Above: The Japanese cruiser *Takao*, the main target for *XE1* and *XE3* in Operation 'Struggle'. Allied intelligence over-estimated the ship's seaworthiness. (IWM MH.5935)

Below: HMS *Selene* preparing to take *XE5* in tow at Subic Bay in July 1945. *XE5* was ordered to cut the Hong Kong–Singapore telegraph cable after *XE4* had shown that such an operation could be successful by cutting the Saigon–Singapore–Hong Kong cables on 31 July.

above: A Welman submarine at the Fryth Hotel
near Welwyn Garden City. (IWM HU.56768)
below: Lieutenant Jimmy Holmes in the small

conning tower of a Welman, showing the limited
visibility afforded to the operator and his extremely
cramped position. (IWM HU.56760)

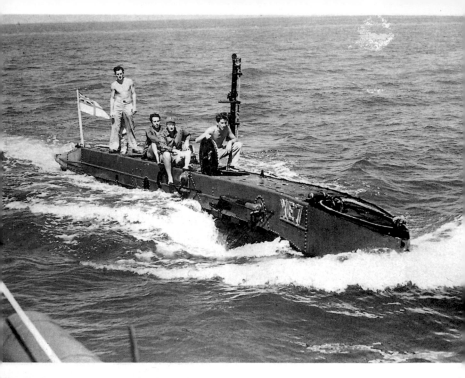

Above: *XE7* under way at
Hampton Roads during joint
USN/RN exercises in 1950.
Note the aft-facing hinged
probe on the starboard bow.
When raised to the vertical
this allowed the craft (with a
slight positive buoyancy) to
rest under target with three
feet of clearance between the
casing and the target's hull,
enabling the diver to leave
and re-enter the submarine.
Left: A diver poses at the
W&D hatch on an XE-Craft.
Leaving the craft was an
uncomfortable experience for
the diver. He sat alone as the
W&D was flooded up from
an internal tank (so as not to
upset the trim), knowing
when the compartment was
full (and the pressure equal
to that outside) by the sudden
pressure exterted on him by
the incompressible water—
an unpleasant phenomenon
known as 'The Squeeze'.

Above: *X52* (HMS *Shrimp*), one of the four *X51* class craft built in the 1950s.

Right, upper: A German *Neger* (Nigger), one of the first such weapons deployed by the *Kriegsmarine*.

Right, lower: The operator sitting in his position in a *Neger*. He was equipped with a closed-cycle Dräger breathing apparatus, a wrist compass, and few rudimentary controls and little else. He sat too low to see his target properly and, in any case, his canopy was usually fouled by oil slicks. His only aids to aiming the torpedo were a graduated scale engraved on the interior of the canopy and an aiming spike in front of him.

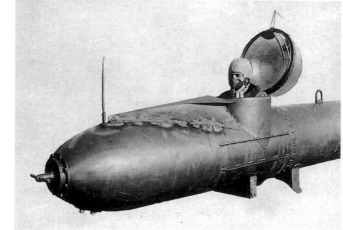

Above: The *Molch* (Salamander) was an electrically driven one-man torpedo carrier. Two G7e torpedoes were slung either side of the craft and the operator sat in a small conning tower at the stern.
Left: The *Biber* (Beaver) was a more sophisticated craft powered by a petrol motor (never an ideal form of propulsion for a submarine) when on the surface and an electric motor when dived. The armament comprised the usual two G7e torpedoes, carried in recesses in the pressure hull. The craft was fitted with a proper periscope, which is here shown camouflaged with a 'nest' in order to disguise the tell-tale 'feather'.

Right, top: The operator's position inside a *Biber*, showing the austere nature of the design. The control wheel is in the centre, with the rudder indicator at lower left and the hydroplane indicator at lower right. Above, from left to right, are the indicators for engine oil pressure, oxygen pressure, battery voltage and LP and HP air. The three armoured glass ports are visible, but the operator was also given a fixed, forward-facing periscope.

Right, centre: *Biber* were first employed off the Normandy beaches on the night of 29 August 1944. They performed but one operation before their base at Fécamp was overrun and the *Biber* were abandoned on the beach as shown here.

Right, bottom: A *Biber* on the stern of one of the U-boats involved in Operation 'Caesar'—a poor photograph but a historically significant one.

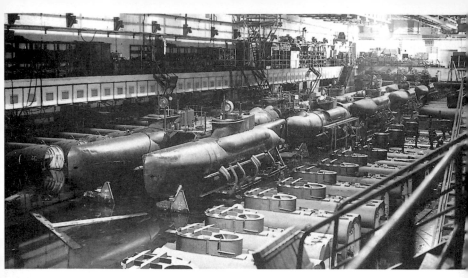

Above: The Type XXVIIB U-boat, better known as the *Seehund*, shown here in series production at DWK's Kiel factory.

Below: Eighteen *Seehunde* at Kiel in the summer of 1945 following the German surrender. (IWM A.289973)

Right, upper: Damage to the bows of HMS *Puffin* after she rammed a *Seehund* on 26 March 1945 off Lowestoft. The shock of the impact caused one or both of the G7e torpedoes to explode. (IWM A.27876)

Right, lower: A crude model of the German *Seeteufel*, a craft which combined a torpedo armament with tracks for land travel. (Royal Navy Submarine Museum)

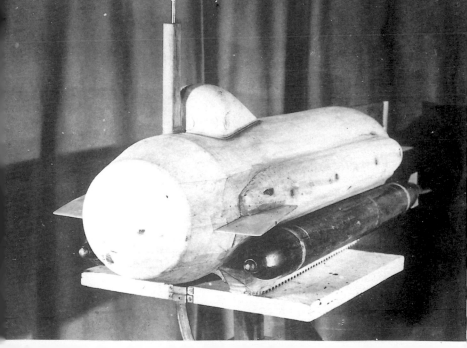

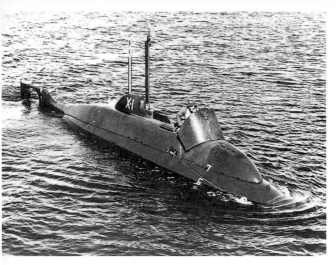

Left, top: *X1*, the only American midget submarine design. The project was abandoned after a series of problems with the hydrogren peroxide propulsion plant.

Left, centre: A boom defence vessel (BDV) laying a net during the Second World War. Such defences can make life difficult for midget submarines, and modern sensors might make nets even more effective. However, the skills required for net-laying and boom defence have now all but been forgotten.

Left, bottom: A Soviet 'India' class rescue submarine with two DSRVs in wells on her after casing. The military applications of this class are obvious.

Right, top: Rear-Admiral R. Bass USN, who was a keen exponent of midget submarines within the US Navy in the post-war period. (US National Archives)

Right, centre: The Yugoslav midget submarine *Soca* on completion. This vessel is now part of the Croatian Navy.

Right, bottom: One of many midget submarines in service with the North Korean Navy. The extended mast at the after end of the conning tower is a combined induction/exhaust schnorkel.

Above and below: Two submarines separated by nearly fifty years and a technological revolution yet with one feature in common—containers mounted on their casings for the carriage of submersibles. HMS *Trooper* (above), was a diesel-electric 'T' class submarine, built in 1942, which carried the British Chariot; and USS *Kamehameha* (SSN-642, below), is a *Lafayette* class nuclear-powered former ballistic missile submarine converted to carry two SDVs in containers mounted on the casing. (Royal Navy Submarine Museum/USN)

1943; production was carried out at the Morris motor car factory at Cowley near Oxford. However, in October 1944 the order was reduced to twenty, yet production could not be stopped until 100 had been completed!

At this stage the Welmans seemed to have been earmarked for Combined Operations for use in beach reconnaissance. In the spring of 1943 the craft and their crews, who at this stage were largely drawn from No 2 Commando of the Royal Marines' Special Boat Service, moved up to Scotland for more advanced training. Their first home was HMS *Titania*, a depot ship moored in Holy Loch. They then moved up to Lochgair, where training in earnest started. After a few weeks the Welmans were transferred to HMS *Bonaventure*, another depot ship with special facilities for handling midget craft, and moved to Port HHX at Loch Cairnbawn, a highly secret establishment where the Royal Navy's midget submarines, X-Craft and human torpedoes (Chariots) were in training. While on the Clyde one Welman, *W10*, was lost in a training accident; the hull was recovered in the 1960s.

It was here that the problem of how to get the Welman to the target area was addressed. Since the craft lacked sufficient endurance to make the journey unaided, it would have to be towed or carried. Towing was out of the question since it would have been unbearable for the operator, but two methods of carrying the craft were evolved. In the first the Welman would be stowed on the upper casing of a submarine in the same way as the Royal Navy's Chariots. A drawing in the Royal Navy Submarine Museum shows HMS *Thrasher*, a Group 2 'T' class submarine, adapted for this purpose, although it is not known whether she actually carried Welmans on exercises. The alternative was to carry the Welman slung in the davits of a destroyer or MTB. The possibility of towing the Welman while mounted in a 'skid' at high speed from an MTB was also investigated but not pursued very far—probably to the great relief of those manning the craft!

In the autumn of 1943—the date is uncertain—Combined Operations decided that the Welman was not suited to their purposes. The decision was probably taken after General Sir Robin Laycock took over Combined Operations after Mountbatten's departure for better things in India as Supreme Allied Commander. Laycock, a professional soldier, clearly had no use for the Welmans which had so obviously appealed to Mountbatten. The SBS personnel were redeployed and the Admiralty found itself the unwilling custodian of these craft. However, Admiral Sir Lionel Wells KCB DSO, Flag Officer commanding Orkney and Shetlands, got to hear of the Welmans and thought that they would be useful for attacks on German shipping using coastal waters inside the Leads off Norway. MTBs of the 30th (later 54th) Flotilla, operating from Lerwick and manned by officers and men of the Royal Norwegian Navy, were already engaged in these operations, and it was thought that the Welmans would be a useful addition to the forces available. They would be carried over to the Leads, the strip of water between the outer islands and the

Norwegian mainland, by the MTBs, which would select a suitable place to hide, usually an uninhabited island. An observation post would be established and the crews would wait until a suitable target presented itself.

Accordingly a base was set up at Lunna Voe in the Shetland Islands, which for security reasons was known as the Advanced MTB Base, and training began in earnest. By the middle of November the conditions of moon, tide and weather were suitable for such an operation, On 20 November *MTB635* and *MTB625* left Lunna Voe carrying Welmans *W45* (Lieutenant C. Johnsen, Norwegian Army), *W46* (Lieutenant B. Pedersen, Norwegian Army), *W47* (Lieutenant B. Marris RNVR) and *W48* (Lieutenant J. Holmes RN). Their targets were shipping and the huge Laksevaag floating dock at Bergen. *W47* and *W48* were assigned to the floating dock while the other two craft were ordered to attack shipping at Puddefjord and the Dokkeskjaer Quay. After planting their charges the Welman crews were to head out to Dyrsviken where they were to sink their craft in as deep water as possible. They were then given 48 hours to make their way to Hindenaesfjord, where an MTB would be waiting. An alternative rendezvous was established at Sordalen.[6]

Initially all went well: the MTBs dropped the Welmans in the water early in the morning of 21 November at the entrance to Solviksund near Bergen before returning to the Shetlands. The plan called for the four men to camouflage their Welmans and hide on the small island of Hjelteholmen, just outside Bergen; intelligence had indicated that Hjelteholmen was only used during the summer. However, throughout 21 November the island was visited by a great number of local fishermen, some of whom spotted the Welmans and came over to talk to their operators. On the advice of Johnsen the party did not attempt to detain the Norwegians, who were allowed to leave the island: Johnsen claimed that he knew and trusted the fishermen and that their absence would be noted should they fail to return home. At this stage the sensible thing to do would have been to pull out on the grounds that the mission was hopelessly compromised. It is interesting to note that on the day after the operation the Germans landed on Hjelteholmen and subjected the island to a thorough search; the possibility that the four Welman operators were betrayed cannot be overlooked. Yet the operators, confident that the Norwegians they had spoken to were 100 per cent loyal, decided to press ahead with their attack on the night of 21/22 November.

Having waited until an inward-bound convoy had passed, they began their run-in at approximately 18.45, leaving Hjelteholmen at fifteen-minute intervals. Pedersen was in the lead, followed by Holmes, Marris and Johnsen. Pedersen's *W46* encountered a net in Westbyfjord and was forced to the surface, where the craft was spotted by the German patrol boat *NB59*. Pedersen, blinded by searchlights, tried to scuttle his craft but was unsuccessful and was captured along with the Welman.

Holmes, in *W48*, found that his craft was making water through the stern gland and decided to return to Hjelteholmen to make repairs. At about 01.30 on 22 November he began his second attempt but his boat continued to leak. He also noticed that the harbour defences were very much on the alert. The searchlights were continually playing and there was much activity from small craft. Holmes decided that he could not continue with the attack so returned to Hjelteholmen, where he hoped he would find Marris or Johnsen. When he realised that he was alone he scuttled his craft and, after making an unsuccessful attempt to make the pick-up point in a borrowed rowing boat, returned to wait at Hjelteholmen.

Marris, in *W47*, found that the searchlights prevented him from making out his position so he decided to abandon his craft near Bratholm. Johnsen, in *W45*, had a similar experience and abandoned his craft at Vindnes. Johnsen then went into hiding at Sordalen and was intrigued when a local boy told him that he had seen a strange man walking in the hills. Johnsen showed the boy his Ursula suit.[7] When the boy answered 'Yes', Johnsen suspected that it might be one of the others and sent him a note telling the man to come to Johnsen's hiding place after dusk. Sure enough, an exhausted Marris arrived. A week later they encountered Holmes and the three settled down in hiding at Sordalen, where Johnsen knew the daughter of one of the local farmers very well. Meanwhile the arrangements for the pick-up had not gone to plan. The MTB ordered to make the pick-up, *MTB626*, was damaged beyond repair in a petrol explosion at Lerwick on 22 November 1943 and with the approach of the bad winter weather no further attempt was possible.

The detailed adventures of the three men in Norway fall outside of the scope of this article. With the help of the Norwegian Resistance they were able to radio to London to request evacuation, but it was not until 5 February 1944 that weather conditions were suitable. By then the three men had had to move north, their Norwegian hosts fearing reprisals should they be discovered. Eventually the three were picked up by *MTB653* and returned to England. Pedersen survived the war and was lucky in that he was not executed under the provisions of the notorious 'Commando' order.[8] Although the *Kriegsmarine* handed him over to the *Gestapo* at Bergen, he was eventually transferred to a prisoner-of-war camp in Germany. He made two unsuccessful attempts to escape before being liberated by the British Army in April 1945—just as his plans for a third attempt were nearly complete.

W46, now in the hands of the *Kriegsmarine*, was subjected to a minute examination. The War Diary for the *Kriegsmarine*'s *Gruppe Nord* noted that 'the enemy continued the mini-war with ever new ideas'.[9] *W46*'s capture came at a time when the Germans were becoming seriously interested in midget submarines themselves. It is difficult to prove a connection, but there are many similarities between the Welman and the German *Biber* one-man submarine which entered service in early summer of 1944.

The raid on Bergen was the only occasion on which the Welmans were employed operationally. By the beginning of 1944 they were seen as largely irrelevant when compared to the Royal Navy's X-Craft. On 15 February 1944 Laycock formally notified the Admiralty that the Combined Operations Directorate had no further use for the Welman. Rear-Admiral (Submarines), Rear-Admiral Claude Barry, agreed and added that no attempt should be made to find alternative uses for them.

The Welman concept enjoyed a brief revival with the Welfreighter, a four-man submersible which could carry up to two tons of stores. It was originally intended to use these craft in the Adriatic, taking supplies to Albanian partisans, but the war ended before they could be deployed. Instead eight Welfreighters went to the Far East, based at Port Moresby. From there they would take supplies, towed part of the way by 66ft 'Snake' class sailing ketches, to the Malay peninsula where a guerrilla war was in progress against the Japanese. But here, too, the war ended before they could be deployed. After the war the remaining craft were simply abandoned, broken up in the great post-war disposal of naval and military equipment declared surplus to requirements. One survives at the Royal Navy Submarine Museum at Gosport.

The Welman came nowhere near to fulfilling the enthusiastic hopes of its designers. In this it suffered from the same fate as many 'special' or 'secret' weapons conceived by enthusiastic amateurs working in the cloistered atmosphere of a special forces research establishment. It was designed with little or no reference to the professionals in the Royal Navy who were accumulating much experience in midget operations with the X-Craft and Chariots, nor were the operational realities concerned with its employment taken into account. The Welman was the result of a situation where enthusiasm for unorthodox and unusual means of attacking the enemy lost touch with the realities of making war.

Chapter 13

From Bergen to Normandy and Back Again

What a big bastard you are!—Signal from *X24* to HMS *Duke of York*,
flagship of the Home Fleet.

Following the return of the towing submarines and passage crews (and *X10*'s
operational crew) engaged in 'Source' to *Varbel* there was a certain pause in the
tempo of operations since there were no X-Craft available. One consequence of the
five X-Craft being lost in 'Source' was that the victualling and stores staff managed
to account for a good deal of missing equipment by entering against one or other of
the five X-Craft's names as 'lost in action'. Any X-Craft carrying a tenth of the
equipment supposedly on charge to them would have sunk like a stone! But this
pause did not last for long. XT-Craft (*XT1* to *XT6*), the variant specially designed for
training purposes, were arriving from the builders and they were followed by the *X20*
class (*X20* to *X25*) of operational craft. Of the XT series, Lieutenant H. P. Westmacott
(who commanded *XT5* and later *X24* in Operation 'Heckle') wrote:

> The XT Craft was an ideal craft for the purpose of training new-entry personnel. The
> hulls were exactly the same as the *X20* class, the only operational boats in the flotilla,
> some of which were still being built. The main engine and motor was the standard fitted
> in the other classes, [and] the pumping system was the same as was subsequently fitted
> in the XE class. Planes and steering were the same but they had a fixed periscope and
> only a magnetic compass of the projector type instead of a gyro. Lacking the more
> complicated equipment, they were easier to maintain.[1]

With new X-Craft also came an influx of new volunteers from the Submarine
Service to take the place of those killed or captured in 'Source'. Lieutenant Percy
Westmacott was one of these, his previous appointment having been as First
Lieutenant of the *Unshaken*. Westmacott was unusual in that he came to the 12th
Submarine Flotilla from the regular Navy. He evidently did not find the informal life-
style in the 12th Flotilla altogether to his taste:

> I continued, disgusted with my life and my companions. None of my senior officers
> exhibited the slightest claim to my respect and none of my contemporaries or even my
> juniors appeared to even speak my language.[2]

Westmacott soon made his presence felt by insisting that his crew be dressed in
the correct rig of day, and not for nothing did he acquire the nickname of 'Pusser
Percy'. Nevertheless he was a consummate professional who had plenty of experience in conventional submarines on which to build his X-Craft expertise. Soon after

joining *Varbel* he had Lieutenant Max Shean RANVR put together the first completed guide to the X-Craft *modus operandi*. He was evidently well aware of his own abilities for he noted in his unpublished memoirs that it would not take him, an officer in the Regular Navy, nearly as long to master the principles of X-Craft operations as his Reservist colleagues. Despite his straight-laced manner, he had the humour to appreciate that not all training in the 12th was conducted in a manner of which their Lordships would approve:

> Our training with 'Nobby' Clarke, who always took us out, consisted of sloping off to the nearest area which he always allocated to himself, opening main vents, dropping to the bottom without catching a trim, putting the kettle on for mid morning or mid afternoon tea and sitting down to a round game of dice . . . all very wrong and quite inexcusable.[3]

The next operation for the 12th Flotilla was to be the destruction of a giant floating dock in Bergen harbour. The Germans were making increasing use of the 8,000-ton Laksevaag dock for U-boat repairs and the Admiralty believed that, if it were given suitable modifications, the Germans might just be able to put *Tirpitz* into the dock for repairs. Moreover, the dock's plant supplied power for two smaller dry docks. An attack on the Laksevaag dock would therefore have a significant effect on the enemy's ability to maintain and repair ships and submarines in Norwegian waters. An unsuccessful attempt at sinking this dock had already been made the previous year (see Chapter 12) using the Welman one-man craft; now the X-Craft were to go back and finish the job properly. Training started in earnest in January 1944 and was to be completed by the end of April. Before then there were a number of other tasks for the *X20* class, chief among which was testing harbour defences in home waters. The Admiralty were aware that it was not beyond the bounds of possibility that the Home Fleet could suffer the same fate as the Mediterranean Fleet and the *Tirpitz* and wanted to take precautions accordingly. Furthermore, it was not known whether the Germans had recovered any of the X-Craft lost in Operation 'Source'. The testing of harbour defences was to be one of the *X20* class's chief roles.

X24 was scheduled to go north to Scapa Flow to test the harbour defences there but at the last moment dropped out because of mechanical defects. Her place was taken by *X22*, commanded by Lieutenant B. M. McFarlane RAN.[4] *X22* was towed north to Scapa by the submarine *Syrtis*. While crossing the Pentland Firth in bad weather the submarine was 'pooped' by a large wave which washed the Officer of the Watch, Lieutenant C. Blyth RNR, off the bridge. *Syrtis* turned to look for Blyth but in so doing bore down on *X22*. Petty Officer Hugh Fowler, *Syrtis*'s coxswain, recalled:

> Saw the shape of a man then realised it was the X-Craft. Wave smashes her right under the bows of *Syrtis*, crunch, crunch, crunch. She is hit three times and the Captain smells oil fuel.[5]

So *X24*, with Lieutenant Max Shean RANVR in command, went north to Scapa after all. The exercises proved surprisingly successful—from *X24*'s point of view if not from that of the Boom Defence Department. *X24*'s presence at Scapa was kept secret and her daily routes to and from the exercise area took her well away from the body of the Fleet. However, on the final day of the trials she returned to *Bonaventure* through the main anchorage and was the source of considerable interest. Shean and his First Lieutenant very properly decided to render passing honours to the flagship of the Home Fleet, HMS *Duke of York*, and were greatly amused by the sight of nearly 1,000 men on the battleship's upper deck coming to attention as the salute was returned. Not content with this, Shean then signalled to the battleship, 'What a big bastard you are!' using a hand-held Aldis lamp. The signal was acknowledged with the receipt of the signal code group but nothing more. It was, therefore, with no small degree of consternation that the next day Shean discovered that his company and that of his First Lieutenant was requested by Admiral Sir Bruce Fraser, CinC Home Fleet, for dinner on the flagship. This was followed by a visit from Fraser in which he remarked how wet it must have been for the two officers on the casing the previous afternoon but made no mention of the signal. Shean and his Number 1 sat through the dinner in an agony of apprehension until told by Lieutenant Vernon Merry RNVR, Fraser's Flag Lieutenant, that the Admiral had not seen the signal.

The plan for Operation 'Guidance', as the attack on the Bremen dock was known, involved changes in the working of the X-Craft to what had been done previously, Bergen being considerably nearer to home than Altenfjord. The port of departure was Port HHZ, Loch Cairnbawn, from where the passage crew[6] took *X24* to Burra Forth in the Shetlands. There the depot ship *Alecto* had been sent ahead to assist the X-Craft crews with any last-minute maintenance problems. At Burra Forth the operational crew would take over and proceed with the sortie. *Alecto* would wait in the Shetlands until the X-Craft returned.

X24, commanded by Lieutenant Max Shean RANVR,[7] left Port HHZ on 9 April towed by HM Submarine *Sceptre* (Lieutenant Ian McIntosh RN). After a two-day passage in fine weather, they arrived at Burra, where the crews changed over. On 11 April they left the Shetlands and made an uneventful passage to landfall at Feje, the northern entrance to the Bergen Leads. *X24* was slipped at 2050 on 12 April and entered Fejeosen on the surface. *Sceptre* retired to seaward with orders that she was not to attack enemy shipping for fear of compromising the operation. This was a necessary restriction, but it must have been galling for McIntosh to have to watch a U-boat pass across his bows on 13 April at a range of only 500 yards.

Meanwhile *X24* was sailing unmolested down the Leads on the surface. Before the operation Shean had been well briefed by officers in the Royal Norwegian Navy about lights, marks and other navigational data, so that he was well familiar with the area. At 0230 on 13 April the craft dived off Kalvenoes Light with some twelve miles of the journey still to do. On entering West Byfjord, very heavy local traffic was encountered and there was a considerable risk of collision. To add to the problems a German *Verpostenboot* took an unhealthy interest in *X24*'s whereabouts, but fortunately, despite transmitting on her asdic, she failed to find the little submarine.

By 0800 *X24* was in the harbour proper and the target was in sight. The dock was 850 yards away and fully flooded down. In the briefing before the operation, Shean had been cautioned against being too free with his use of the periscope. As a result he made a blind run in at 60ft, grounded, turned and reversed his course. Confident that he could find the target, he took *X24* under what he thought was the dock and released his charges at either end. With the cargoes gone, *X24* headed up the fjord to Feje and the waiting *Sceptre*. *X24* did not surface until 2130 on the 13th, by which time the air in the boat was foul and all four men were suffering from CO_2 poisoning. It was not long before *Sceptre* was located, the tow passed and the operational crew relieved. Both *Sceptre* and *X24* retired across the North Sea without incident and reached Port HHZ on 18 April, where they were accorded a tumultuous welcome.

However aerial reconnaissance of the harbour immediately following the attack showed that the dock was afloat and undamaged. During her second run-in *X24* must have been deflected by currents, for her charges had been laid under the 7,800-ton *Barenfels*, which lay parallel to the dock alongside the coaling wharf. The ship was completely destroyed in the explosion, together with a large portion of the coaling wharf and coaling gantries. The fact that the dock was unscathed did not detract from the success of the operation: for the first time an X-Craft had penetrated a defended harbour, laid her charges and returned undetected, leaving the Germans none the wiser as to the cause of the subsequent explosions.[8]

While *X24* had been working up for the attack on the floating dock, *X20* had been sent south to Portsmouth for an altogether different operation. Preparations for the invasion of Europe were well under way and the Seine Bay had already been selected as the general area in which the troops would go ashore. As part of the preparations for the landings, Combined Operations Pilotage Parties (COPP) had been making a comprehensive survey of the Normandy coastline to determine which beaches were most suitable for an amphibious assault. This work entailed divers going ashore, noting beach defences and obstructions and obtaining soil samples. The first operation was scheduled to take place on New Year's Day 1944 and was to be of the beaches off Courselles. But the plan was vetoed by the Commander-in-Chief Portsmouth, Admiral Sir Charles Little. He considered that the risk of the X-Craft becoming stranded on the Calvados Reef was too great and so the first reconnaissances were carried out using fast landing craft. For the reconnaissance of the beaches at the western end of the Seine Bay, however, there was no alternative but to use the X-Craft: the distance to these beaches was too great for the landing craft to cover in the space of a night.

On 17 January 1944 *X20* left Portsmouth and joined her towing ship, the trawler *Darthema*, in the Channel. *X20* was commanded by Lieutenant Ken Hudspeth DSC RANVR, a quiet, serious Australian who had had such a disappointing time in *X10* during Operation 'Source'. Hudspeth had one other crewman with him, Sub-Lieutenant Bruce Enzer RNVR, and three members of a COPP team, Lieutenant-Commander Nigel Willmott DSO DSC RN, Major Logan Scott-Bowden DSO MC and Sergeant Bruce Ogden-Smith DCM MM.

X20 was to spend four days off the French coast. During the day time was spent in conducting periscope reconnaissance of the shoreline and taking bottom soundings using the echo-sounder installed for the purpose. Occasionally Hudspeth noted small-arms fire directed at his periscope and believed that he had been spotted. However, this was probably nothing more than the German defenders engaging in a bit of routine shooting to break the monotony. Certainly there is nothing in the German records to indicate that *X20* had been spotted. Each night *X20* would close the beach and Scott-Bowden and Ogden-Smith would swim ashore. Each was weighed down with a shingle bag, brandy flask, sounding lead, underwater writing pad and pencil, compass, beach gradient reel and stake, .45 revolver, trowel, auger, torch and bandolier. Each also carried a supply of condoms, not in case of either of them struck lucky with any of the locals ashore, but as a convenient means of storing the soil samples collected on the beaches. The condoms had to be unpacked and specially prepared for the operation. This work was carried out by Wrens using a specially adapted broomstick handle; the Wrens were specially selected for their prudence and rectitude. The demands of modern warfare are many and various, but this task was without doubt one of the strangest.

The divers went ashore on two nights to survey the beaches at Vierville, Moulins St Laurent and Colleville in what would become the American 'Omaha' beach. On the third night they were due to go ashore off the Orne Estuary, but by this stage fatigue (all five men had been living on little more than benzedrine tablets) and the worsening weather caused Hudspeth to cancel the operation and *X20* turned for home. After making their rendezvous with *Darthema* they arrived back alongside at HMS *Dolphin* on 21 January 1944. In his subsequent dispatch to the Admiralty the Commander-in-Chief Portsmouth described the operation as a 'sustained and impudent reconnaissance under the very nose of the enemy'.[9] Hudspeth received a well-deserved Bar to his DSC awarded for 'Source'.

Further beach reconnaissance operations were planned for *X20*, soon to be joined by her sister-craft *X23*. However, the planners decided that, given the lengthening hours of daylight, the risk of compromising the entire operation should the X-Craft be captured outweighed any shortfall in intelligence caused by not sending the X-Craft. Although there were to be no more beach reconnaissances, the involvement of *X20* and *X23* in the forthcoming invasion of Europe was not finished. There existed a requirement for vessels to lie off the invasion beaches and act as markers for the landing craft, whose navigational equipment was minimal and whose shallow draught made them very susceptible to being driven off course by tides and currents. Two of the beaches assigned to the Anglo-Canadian forces, 'Sword' and 'Juno', were of particular concern in this respect since the coastline in these areas was not distinctive in outline.

For this role the two X-Craft had to carry a good deal of additional equipment. The most important items were two small portable radar beacons and three 18ft telescopic masts, together with lights and batteries and taut wire measuring gear; there was a good deal of other equipment, including small arms and ammunition. An unusual item for each of the crew was a set of portrait photographs, to be used in the event of their having to abandon their craft and swim ashore, although, as Lieutenant George Honour commented,

... if possible we were to contact the French Resistance, who would then whisk us away by some unknown means. I personally don't think we would have got far off the beach.[10]

All this extra equipment meant extra weight, so the two craft were fitted with additional buoyancy chambers, similar to the side cargoes, port and starboard. They were also given two CQR anchors to ensure that the craft could be firmly secured in position, and bollards were fitted forward and aft. The purpose of the additional equipment was to enable the X-Craft to act as mobile lighthouses for the invasion fleet, in particular to mark the points at which the DD (Duplex Drive) Sherman tanks could be safely launched into the water. Lights—shaded so that they could not be seen from the land—would be erected on each craft together with a radio homing device. As well as the main light, the COPP members on board would establish secondary lights set up, rather perilously, in dinghies, although, on the day, the bad weather meant that this part of the plan could not be implemented. X23 was positioned off 'Sword' and X20 off 'Juno' beach. X23's sector ran east from the Landgrune to the port of Ouisterham while that marked by X20 ran west from Landgrune to Ver-sur-Mer. Each X-Craft would remain at the outer edge of their sector, so that the incoming force for 'Juno' beach would keep to the left of the light while the invasion force for 'Sword' would keep to the right.

On the evening of 2 June the two craft departed. X20 (Lieutenant K. Hudspeth DSC* RANVR[11]) was towed by the Darthema while X23 (Lieutenant George Honour RNVR[12]) was towed by the trawler Grenadier. By early morning on 4 June both craft had arrived at their positions. When daylight was sufficient to fix their positions accurately, they did so and then sank to the bottom to wait until nightfall. Precisely at 2315 on 4 June both craft surfaced and raised their aerials to receive a coded message which would indicate whether the invasion was proceeding. However, the message received at 0100 on 5 June, 'For Padfoot, unwell in Scarborough', indicated that the invasion had been postponed for twenty-four hours. The radio masts were dismantled and both craft dived to spend another boring and uncomfortable day on the bottom. Lieutenant George Honour, in *X23*, recalled watching the German defenders on the beach enjoy a lazy Sunday afternoon:

> The interesting point was that here were the Germans enjoying a Sunday afternoon's recreation, little knowing what was waiting for them on the Monday.[13]

The reason for the postponement was, of course, the deteriorating weather. General Eisenhower, the Supreme Commander, was faced with a most difficult decision. If the invasion were put off again, then the carefully thought-out timetable would collapse and the whole project would have to be abandoned. At the time of the cancellation some convoys were already at sea, and one convoy of landing craft had to be hurriedly recalled by an aircraft sent out to find them. After listening to his staff and, in particular, the advice of Chief Meteorologist Group Captain J. M. Stagg RAF, Eisenhower gave the final order to proceed on the morning of the 5th.

On the evening of 5 June, when both craft came to the surface, the BBC had a different message for 'Padfoot'. The invasion was on! Lieutenant George Honour recalled that

> On the Monday night we again surfaced and received a message that the invasion was 'on'. So once again we went down and sat on the bottom and at about 0430 on the 6 June we surfaced again, put up all our navigational aids, the 18 foot telescopic mast with a light shining to seaward, a radio beacon and an echo sounder tapping out a message below the surface. This was for the benefit of the navigational MLs as they led the invasion force in.[14]

X20's report noted:

> 0500. Surfaced and checked position in shore fix by dawn light. Rigged mast with lamp and radar beacon.[15]

Thus was the huge Allied invasion fleet, consisting of over 5,000 vessels, guided in towards the beaches by two of the Royal Navy's midget submarines.

To the crews of the X-Craft, the wait before anything happened seemed endless, although there was a stream of aircraft passing overhead. They heard the noise of thousands of ships' engines before they saw the endless waves of landing craft and ships close and pass them by before disgorging tanks and soldiers on to the beach. This was potentially the most dangerous phase of the operation for the X-Craft. They were small and their presence was not widely known. With thousands of armed soldiers pouring past them and flocks of so-called friendly aircraft[16] passing overhead, the X-Craft were very vulnerable to the eager but unwanted attentions of their own side. Lieutenant Honour had taken special precautions in this respect. Dissatisfied with the size of white ensign supplied to *X23*, he purloined an ensign of a size usually flown by capital ships in order that there would be no mistakes.

Their task completed, *X20* and *X23* returned to the headquarters ship *Largs* before being towed back to Portsmouth. In the wardroom bar at HMS *Dolphin*, Hudspeth's and Honour's claim to have led the invasion fleet was met with incredulity! Honour was awarded the DSC and Hudspeth a second Bar to his DSC; Hudspeth's award of a DSC and two Bars for operations covering a time span of less than nine months must constitute something of a record.[17]

Operation 'Gambit', as the beach marking was known, was a success in that the assault forces for 'Sword' and 'Juno' beaches were landed in precisely the right area. The operation also represented a considerable achievement for the X-Craft personnel. Since their departure from Portsmouth on 2 June they had spent sixty-four hours dived. As Admiral Ramsay noted,

> It is considered that great skill and endurance was shown by the crews of *X20* and *X23*. Their reports of proceedings, which were a masterpiece of understatement, read like the deck log of a surface ship in peacetime and not of a very small and vulnerable submarine carrying out a hazardous operation in time of war.

'Postage Able' and 'Gambit' had been new departures in terms of X-Craft operations. They had not gone out to destroy anything but their non-violent role in the planning for, and execution of, the invasion of North-West Europe had been of considerable importance in the final outcome of the operation. Just how important is shown by the American experience at 'Utah'. The Americans had been given a demonstration of beach marking techniques by the X-Craft but had declined their help, trusting to the accuracy of their navigation. On the morning of 6 June the American force heading for 'Utah' beach was driven to the west by strong tides and currents and went ashore in the wrong place.

Following the successful conclusion of operations in Normandy, *X24* and *X20* returned to Rothesay, where attention was once again focused on the Laksevaag floating dock in Bergen which Shean had missed in the spring. For this second attempt *X24* was commanded by Lieutenant H. P. Westmacott.[18] As with the previous operation, the preparation was thorough and included briefings by Norwegian officers familiar with Bergen and its environs. Two Norwegian officers, Lieutenant Kvinge and Sub-Lieutenant Utne of the Royal Norwegian Navy, provided much local knowledge and their contribution was subsequently acknowledged by Westmacott:

> Everything with very minor exceptions, probably due to the limited vision through the periscope, was exactly as they described it. I wish particularly to express my immense appreciation of the pains they took on my behalf.[19]

There was instruction in escape and evasion techniques in the event of *X24*'s crew having to abandon their craft and make for the shore. There was also the priceless gift of names and addresses of friendly Norwegians who could be contacted. Naming no names, Westmacott acknowledged the importance of this information:

Also my thanks to the Norwegian officer who instructed us in evasion. The trust he reposed in us by giving us the information he did was felt to be a compliment beyond words.[20]

After an uneventful passage from Rothesay to Balta Sound in the Shetlands from 3 to 6 September, *X24*, in the tow of 'bring 'em back alive' *Sceptre* (Lieutenant I. S. McIntosh RN) left the Shetlands at noon on the 7th. Westmacott wrote a detailed account of this operation, code-named 'Heckle', which is worth quoting in full:

Our routine was as follows: at 0600, noon and 1800 we surfaced for ten minutes' ventilation and at 2200 we came up for two hours or so to top up the battery. For each of these routine surfaces all hands were called and a meal, which had been cooked by the watch and eaten, was washed up. On diving, the two previously on watch turned in and the other two took on for the next six hours. Life apart from the ventilation surfaces was very easy. The planes and helm needed absolutely no watching, so that the planesman was free to read from a book or cook while the other fellow sorted out stores, topped up RU stowages and mopped and mopped and mopped . . . The condensation and sweating was incredible. We had sorted out the doubtful electrical circuits and practically every one was meggered each six-hour watch, and two, the gyro and periscope circuits, each three hours or even more. We would watch a circuit's insulation drop to perhaps 2–300,000 ohms, then put an electric hair drier on it and bring it up to about two megs. These things we had to do or the machinery would not be available when we needed it. And, just in case the gash hand was idle for a moment, there was the never-ending mopping of decks and bulkheads. With four of us we could keep pace easily enough. Then we would surface and just the ten minutes would beat Beadon, Davison and Purdy. Even I myself was sick one night during the two hours up. However, the trip was to take about four days as *Sceptre* was to do the passage dived, and finally spend one day on the coast reconnoitring. But by the third day we had accumulated so much gash, having been unable to ditch it, it being too bad to get on to the casing, that I had put all the hands to work flattening all the tins to reduce the bulk. I was getting rather desperate about it, and, thinking the weather was easing, I dressed Purdy up for the worst, put him in the W&D, and, warning him that he would probably get a lot of water in with him, told him to ditch the gash. Ye gods! The first wave filled the W&D and the craft sank to about 20ft, and when she came back—no Purdy. *Sceptre* circled round for him But it must have been hopeless in the darkness and the storm.[21]

Westmacott's determination to keep a 'tidy ship' is laudable, but was it worth the loss of one of his crew, who was irreplaceable (Purdy was the diver)? The storm lasted for some eighty hours and it was not until 10 September that Sub-Lieutenant Robinson of the passage crew could be transferred from *Sceptre* to take the unfortunate Purdy's place. Westmacott continues:

About 6 p.m. all hands turned to and we cooked a mighty meal and mopped and dished as best we could, ran up the gyro and generally prepared so that by 2000 all was ready. We surfaced alone in a long oily swell beneath a starry sky with the black shadow of the coast unbroken ahead of me. We slipped the tow and got under way. Shortly I could see the gap between the two islands through which we were to pass, looking quite ridiculously narrow. The gyro repeater system chose this moment to fall over but ace Beadon got it right in a couple of hours—not, incidentally, till we were half way through the first minefield. What with the noise of the engine, and Robby and Beadon shouting ship's heads at one another while sorting out the gyro compass, there was a fair commotion going on below but the essentials were right. On the whole we were off to a flying start, although the compressor was not working[22] and I only had enough air for two surfaces. However I was only looking as far as the next one! I was dressed in an Ursula suit, with a pair of binoculars around my neck and seaboots (full of water) on my feet. My throat was as dry as dust, so I had a dozen cans of orange juice sent up and ranged them on the casing, puncturing one every few minutes and drinking it off. We slid through Fejeosen with Feje Light flashing on the port beam and came round to the south down the Leads for Bergen, still about thirty miles away. Inside the Leads the lights were wonderful—a system of coloured sectors pointing down the fjord. You ran in on the red sector till it turned white, thence down that beam in the white sector of another light and so on.

The Hjeltefjord down which we were now running took us fifteen miles on our way before narrowing to about a mile as you turn into the West Byfjord. By the time we got down to the Narrows at about 1 a.m. the moon, which was about half grown, was shining like a street lamp and I could see cottages ashore without glasses. As the easy swell which had pushed us on our way from the north had ceased, the water was greasy calm and I felt rather like a fly in the middle of a large window. But though there was a large German garrison on the eastern side of these Narrows, nobody saw us, and in another hour I was coasting 50 yards off an uninhabited island, in the shadow, though with myself standing in the W&D with my finger on the klaxon.

So far so good. Realising that there was a corner about seven miles on which I must round dived, which would require daylight to navigate through a periscope, and being well ahead of schedule and with the battery bubbling merrily at full charge, I dived at about 0330. We settled down at 40 feet, rumbling on at about three knots . . . the water became restricted and the traffic denser. The surface was glassy. I was crawling round the deck, poking the periscope about like a billiard cue, prohibited by very necessary caution from showing more than two inches and that for only about ten seconds at a time. This of course was the moment ordained by Practical Jokes Co-ordination Ltd for the periscope to jam up and smoke to start from its works. I was pretty near the dock now, no nets in sight, and shame! nothing in the dock. However, two small ships tied up alongside it.

There was the mast of Maxie Shean's *Barenfels* with a notice hanging from it—*Langsam Fahren* (Go Slow). That's all right, I'm only doing two and a half knots. One last quick tussle as I square up to go under the dock, now about a hundred yards away, with a small motor boat which I'm sure went right over the stern, and we're under. Phew! It was about 0930 when we went astern under the north end of the dock and I let her settle on the bottom while we released one charge, then manoeuvred up two hundred feet under the other end to let go the other. All was done by 1015 and with the boat feeling in my hand like a whippet, I let her go for a thousand yards clear, took one fix, tucked her head down and ran like a racehorse to the entrance of the Byfjord. After the way in and the knowledge that at least we'd done our stuff, the outward journey was a picnic.[23]

The rendezvous was successfully made with *Sceptre*, and three days later *X24* was back at Rothesay. The Admiralty described the operation as 'a fine example of a perfectly planned and executed operation'.[24] Aerial reconnaissance photographs showed four of the six sections of the dock to have been completely destroyed, together with the two merchant ships alongside, the 1,820grt *Sten* and the 914grt *Kong Oscar II*.

'Heckle' was the last operation carried out by X-Craft in home waters: with the sinking of the *Tirpitz* on 12 November 1944 (by the RAF), their *raison d'être* had disappeared. But the Far East theatre beckoned and, with the new and more capable XE-Craft coming off the production line, the future looked promising for more operations.

Chapter 14

Cruisers and Telephone Cables

. . . the little guys with a lotta guts!—Admiral James Fife USN, on the
operations of British XE Craft in the Far East.

With the crippling and subsequent sinking of the *Tirpitz* and the diminishing threat
posed by the German Navy, target opportunities in home waters were becoming few
and far between by the end of 1944. It was natural, therefore, that the thoughts of the
staff of the 12th Flotilla should turn to the Far East, where there was an abundance
of targets and where a British fleet was in the process of forming. Consequently the
depot ship HMS *Bonaventure* was detached to form the 14th Submarine Flotilla
under the command of Captain W. J. R. Fell RN, a distinguished submarine
commander who had been involved in X-Craft development from the beginning. At
this stage no thought was given as to just what the X-Craft would do in the Far East.
In the words of the First World War infantry song, 'We're here, because we're here,
because we're here!'

Bonaventure left Port Ballantyne in Scotland on 21 February 1945. Her destination was Pearl Harbor via the Caribbean and the Panama Canal. Secrecy was
extremely tight during the voyage, so any hopes of shore leave in the West Indies
were quickly dashed. However, the secrecy proved counter-productive. The virtual
quarantine in which *Bonaventure* was kept during her transit of the Panama Canal
aroused such curiosity that rumours circulated that the crew were detained on board
on account of there having been a mutiny.[1] It was not until *Bonaventure* reached Pearl
Harbor that leave was granted. Here Fell received the news that the services of his
Flotilla would not be needed after all: instead, *Bonaventure* would be required for
service with the British Pacific Fleet's logistic train. To have come so far for nothing
was a bitter disappointment:

> Morale fell with a bang but some hope remained as we were told to proceed to Manus
> in the Admiralty Islands. Before we got there we were diverted south to Brisbane and
> arrived with our tails right down, in black despair.[2]

The reasons for the Americans' refusal to employ the XE-Craft are complicated
and do not lie solely in national prejudice as some historians have asserted. The
Americans were winning the war in the Pacific with conventional submarines and
could see little use for the small XE-Craft. They had a point: what could the XE-Craft
sink that could not be sunk just as easily by submarines or by the long arm of carrier
or land-based aircraft?

Fell was not going to give in without a fight: running stores around the Pacific would be the supreme indignity. So after an interview with Admiral Sir Bruce Fraser, CinC British Pacific Fleet, Fell travelled north by air, and without any formal air priority, to Subic Bay, where he obtained in interview with Admiral James Fife, Commander Submarines Seventh Fleet. This was a stroke of luck, for Fife was very familiar with the British submarine service. In 1940–41 he had been attached to the staff of Admiral (Submarines) as an observer and had made a number of patrols in the Mediterranean with British boats. As the Official Staff History commented,

> From every point of view no more suitable officer could have been selected to command a force of submarines to which British and Netherlands submarines were attached.[3]

Fell made a strong and convincing presentation to Fife on the capabilities of the XE-Craft. Fife listened, but

> . . . at the end he showed the most astonishing grasp of what I had said and in words that somehow softened the blow and making his reasons seem so sane . . . the more I saw of this man in the next few months the more my feelings were strengthened that I had met the most sincere, the straightest and the ablest of men.[4]

Fell flew back to Brisbane in a black mood, only to be greeted by the news at a staff meeting on 31 May that there was a chance of a reprieve for his Flotilla. There existed a staff requirement for cutting the submarine telegraph cables carrying Japanese communications between Hong Kong, Saigon and Singapore. Telephonic communications were absolutely secure in that they could not be intercepted, but cutting the cables would force the Japanese command to use radio which, as we all now know, was vulnerable to interception and analysis. The task was, however, difficult: using a cable ship to locate and raise the cable would mean mounting a major fleet operation in waters close to the Japanese-controlled littoral. Moreover, such an operation would leave the Japanese in no doubt as what was going on.

Fell was asked if his XE-Craft could tackle the operation. It was like asking a duck if it could swim. Fell was convinced that his XE-Craft offered the ideal means of cutting the cables. He convinced Fraser, who told him to start training and prove that an XE-Craft could do the job. Two problems had to be solved. First, the cable had to be located: cable positions were clearly marked on charts, and although this information was useful for defining the general operational area, it was not sufficient to find the exact spot where the cable ran. The solution was to tow a grapple behind the XE-Craft along the sea-bed which would, it was hoped, snag on the cable. Cutting the cable posed fewer problems. XE-Craft were already fitted with a powered net cutter and all the divers were trained in its use. After its jaws had been widened, the net cutter could also cut submarine cables. *Bonaventure* moved to an anchorage off the Great Barrier Reef to begin trials which sadly cost the lives of two of the personnel, Lieutenant B. Enzer RNVR of *XE6* and Lieutenant D. Carey RN of *XE3*. No trace was ever found of their bodies, and oxygen poisoning was considered the most likely cause of death.

The trials proved successful and a triumphant Fell flew north to Subic Bay, where he found that not only had Admiral Fife accepted his plan but his staff had been stricken by XE-Craft fever and had prepared plans for a number of operations, including an attack on the Japanese cruisers *Takao* and *Myoko* lying in the Johore Strait. *Takao* had been badly damaged in air attacks in February 1945 and the decision had been taken to moor her and *Myoko* in the Strait as floating AA batteries. Allied intelligence considered the ships fully sea-going, which was why the decision was taken to attack her with X-Craft. Meanwhile *Bonaventure* and the XE-Craft arrived at Subic Bay on 20 July. As the 'T' class submarines fitted with towing bars for XE-Craft were operating from Fremantle, 'S' class boats of the 8th Flotilla were taken in hand and fitted with the necessary modifications.

The plans were now complete. *XE1* (Lieutenant J. E. Smart RNVR) and *XE3* (Lieutenant I. E. Fraser RNVR), towed, respectively, by HM Submarines *Spark* (Lieutenant D. G. Kent RN) and *Stygian* (Lieutenant G. S. C. Clarabut RN), would attack the two cruisers in the Johore Strait on 31 July. *XE4* (Lieutenant M. H. Shean RANVR), towed by *Spearhead* (Lieutenant-Commander R. E. Youngman RNR), was to cut the Saigon–Singapore and Saigon–Hong Kong submarine cables, while *XE5* (Lieutenant P. Westmacott RN), towed by *Selene* (Lieutenant-Commander H. R. B. Newton), was to cut the Hong Kong–Singapore cable. Whatever operation they were assigned to, each of the XE-Craft crews carried an 'escape kit'—items deemed useful if they were forced to abandon their craft and go ashore. Lieutenant Ian Fraser recalled that

> First and foremost was a square of silk with a Union Jack printed on it, surrounded by various expressions in three or four different languages, like, 'I am a friend', or 'I am hungry', or 'Please help me reach British territory'. Another square when unfolded, disclosed a map of the Malay Peninsula and was marked with the best routes for making an escape, or a quick passage to a pick-up position on the coast. Compasses were designed as buttons or pen clips, or sewn into the lining of a cap badge. A file had a hacksaw blade for an edge and a rubber cover for inserting, with considerable discomfort, into the rectum. A packet contained 48hr rations, medical equipment, benzedrine, boxes of matches and various items reckoned to be useful against mosquitoes, leeches and other jungle pests. In addition, each man had a machete, fishing gear and a .45 revolver which took me all my time to lift let alone shoot.[5]

What Fraser did not mention was that the escape kit also contained a suicide pill in the event of the crews' being captured by the Japanese.

Stygian and *Spark*, with the XE-Craft in tow, left Brunei Bay in North Borneo on 26 July. The passage was uneventful and on 30 July the passage crews exchanged with the operational crews. The role of the passage crews was essential but monotonous and often hidden in the blaze of publicity which surrounded the operation. As Captain Fell commented in his Report of Proceedings,

> It is not often realised how big a part these men play in the success of an operation. Towing at high speed (it was sometimes as high as eleven knots) is far from being an easy or even a particularly safe job and is very far from being a comfortable one . . . To a considerable extent the success of an operation depends on the condition in which the craft is turned over to the operational crew. In no sense of the word are the X-Craft passage crews 'maintenance crews'.[6]

At 0600 on 30 July the passage crews exchanged with the operational crews and at 2300 the tows were slipped near Horsburgh Light at the eastern end of the Singapore Strait, some 40 miles from where *Takao* was lying. The towing submarines then withdrew seawards to wait for the rendezvous.

Lieutenant Fraser in *XE3* found the *Takao* with little difficulty:

> We went through the boom, the gate of which was open, at the entrance to the harbour at about 0900 in the morning of 31 July and navigated our way up this channel until we saw the *Takao*. And once I'd sighted it—it was heavily camouflaged, lying very close inshore on the north end of Singapore Island with its stern towards the island.[7]

After letting the three other members of *XE3*'s crew take a look at their target through the periscope, Fraser manoeuvred under her hull for a suitable position to deposit the side cargo. *XE3* was carrying one side charge on her starboard side and six limpet mines in a container on her port side. Things then started to go awry. The tide was falling, and when the diver, Leading Seaman Magennis, tried to leave the submarine he found that the hatch would only open a quarter of its normal way. Undeterred, he deflated his breathing apparatus and wriggled out. His troubles were not over: the curve of the *Takao*'s hull and the fact that her bottom was badly fouled with barnacles and other marine growth made fixing the limpet mines a difficult and tiring task—a task not aided by the fact that Magennis's breathing apparatus was leaking a steady stream of bubbles. Nevertheless, he fixed all six mines to *Takao*'s hull before regaining the safety of the W&D compartment in a state of near collapse.

Fraser released the starboard side charge and then tried to manoeuvre *XE3* out from underneath the cruiser. But he was trapped by *Takao*'s bilge keel, which was coming down on them with the falling tide:

> . . . we couldn't get out because the tide had gone out. We were in a very narrow hole under this thing. There was hardly any room and it took me twenty minutes to get out—I really was a bit frightened then. I was a bit frantic—going full ahead, full astern, blowing tanks, filling tanks, just to nudge a hole in the sea bed so we could climb out. And eventually we did.[8]

Just as Fraser and his men were beginning to think that they would be there when the mines went off, *XE3* shot up and broke surface not fifty yards from the *Takao*.

Within seconds they were back on the bottom, only to find that the port-side limpet mine container had not released and that the little craft was difficult to manoeuvre. Despite his exhausted condition, Magennis donned his suit and after several minutes' work with crowbar, sledgehammer and chisel (the range of equipment carried by XE-Craft catered for all eventualities), succeeded in freeing the container. *XE3* then withdrew to Horsburgh Light to rendezvous with *Stygian* at 0330 on 1 August. It had been an epic operation. From slipping the tow until the rendezvous with *Stygian* the crew of *XE3* had been on duty without sleep for fifty-two hours and had been dived for over sixteen. The coxswain, ERA[9] C. Reed, had been at the helm for over thirty hours without relief.

What of *XE1*? Smart should have gone ahead of *XE3* since *Myoko* lay further up the Strait. However, his passage was delayed by tides and by patrol craft who may have been alerted to what was happening by the banging and scraping as *XE3* got out from underneath *Takao*. As a result Smart arrived off the naval base late and after the time when Fraser would have laid his charges. He was in a dilemma: he could either carry on with the operation against *Myoko* and risk certain destruction from *XE3*'s charges which would explode while he was on his way out, or he could leave his side charge under the *Takao* and ensure her destruction. He chose the latter, but owing to the falling tide he had to be content with leaving the half-ton of amatol alongside the cruiser. Like *XE3*, Smart withdrew to the rendezvous with *Spark* and was picked up at 2215 on 1 August.

The charges exploded at 2130 on the evening of 31 July. Unfortunately the main charge laid by *XE3* did not explode but a number of the limpet mines did. A hole 7m by 3m was blown in the hull to starboard of, and parallel with, the cruiser's keel between frames 113 and 116 and there was some flooding of compartments below the lower-deck level. There was considerable shock damage, including distortion of the roller paths for the ship's main gun turrets and damage to sensitive fire control instruments. Unfortunately, the ship sank in shallow water on an even keel and her upper deck remained above the water. However *Takao*'s days as an operational unit of the Imperial Japanese were over. She was eventually scuttled in position 03 ° 05' N, 100° 41' E on 27 October 1945.

Fraser and the others had heard an explosion at Singapore and had presumed that *Takao* had been disposed of. However, on their return to Brunei Bay they found that the all-seeing eye of Allied air reconnaissance had observed that *Takao* was still there and probably sitting on the bottom with her upper works above water. Fell was annoyed:

[Fell said to me,] 'Well, we've got to do something about this. You'll have to go back and have another go at it.' Well, that really upset me, having done what I thought was a really successful attack, to have to go back again. But nevertheless we said OK and we fixed to go back seven or eight days later.[10]

The other two XE Craft were enjoying equal though less spectacular success. *XE4* sailed from Brunei Bay on 26 July and headed for the approaches to Saigon. The tow was slipped on 30 July at 2120 after an uneventful passage and *Spearhead* withdrew to seaward. During the night, while running on the surface, Shean was washed overboard but managed to cling on to a wire jackstay near the rudder and drag himself back on board. Both the Saigon–Hong Kong and Saigon–Singapore cables were located with the grapple on 31 July. Divers successfully cut the cables and brought back one-foot lengths of each as souvenirs. *XE4* then withdrew to seaward to rendezvous with *Spearhead*. Both arrived back at Brunei Bay without incident on 3 August.

XE5 left Subic in tow by *Selene* on 27 July to cut the Hong Kong–Singapore cable in the approaches to Hong Kong harbour west of Lamma Island. The operational crew took over on the evening of 30 July. During the tow the shackle securing the tow rope to *Selene* broke, leaving the rope dangling from *XE5*'s bows. Eventually the crew found *Selene* and secured the spare tow, but the operation had to be postponed by twenty-four hours. The rendezvous had only been achieved by means of a prodigious expenditure of flares: that both submarines remained unmolested was proof of the supremacy the Americans exercised over the South China Sea at this stage in the war.

The task of cutting the Hong Kong–Singapore cable was complicated by the fact that where the cable entered the sea from Hong Kong Island the bottom shelved very steeply and there was only a strip about 100yd wide where the diver could work: any shallower and he could be seen from the surface; any deeper and he would succumb to oxygen poisoning. *XE5*'s diver, Sub-Lieutenant B. G. Clarke DSC RNVR, soon injured himself using the net cutter, so Westmacott withdrew to rendezvous with *Selene* and transfer the injured officer. Westmacott then returned to Hong Kong harbour where his second diver, Sub-Lieutenant D. V. Jarvis RNVR, spent nearly two days wallowing around up to his elbows in white sludge trying to locate the cable. Though a number of obstructions were encountered which might have been the cable, Westmacott abandoned the operation on 3 August. *Selene* arrived back at Subic on 6 August with *XE5* in tow. Westmacott must have been disappointed, particularly on hearing the exploits of the others, but, when British forces occupied Hong Kong a month later, it was found that *XE5*'s burrowing around in the mud had damaged the cable beyond repair.

A grateful Admiralty was not slow in recognising these operations. Fraser and Magennis were awarded the Victoria Cross, the highest British award for gallantry. Smart and Shean were awarded the Distinguished Service Order, while Westmacott received the Distinguished Service Cross. Other awards totalled one Distinguished Service Order, five Distinguished Service Crosses, one Conspicuous Gallantry Medal, two Distinguished Service Medals, two Orders of the British Empire and eleven Mentioned in Dispatches. The war ended while further operations were being planned: Fraser was preparing to return to the Johore Strait to finish off the *Takao* swhen the two atomic bombs rendered the plans unnecessary. The 14th Flotilla was disbanded with almost indecent haste: the personnel were given other appointments and the XE-Craft were simply dumped on a jetty at Sydney to rust until bought for scrap. It was a sad end.

As a footnote to these operations, Fraser had the unique experience of being shown over the *Takao* while on his way back to Britain to receive his VC from the King. The Japanese

> . . . showed me all over the ship. I went right down to the bottom. They were opening all sorts of hatches and as a matter of fact I was a bit frightened. I thought, Oh God, knowing the Japanese mentality they're going to chuck me down one of these holes and lock me in.[11]

Fraser also learned that at the time of the attack *Takao* had been de-ammunitioned and that the only personnel on board were a care and maintenance party. Consequently, when the limpets went off, the cruiser simply settled on the bottom. The explosion witnessed by Fraser was an aircraft crashing at Changi, coincidentally at the same time as the charges went off.

What had the 14th Flotilla achieved? In simple terms, it could be argued that they accomplished very little. In comparison to the high tonnage of sunken Japanese shipping racked up by American submariners, they sank no ships at all. However, taking the longer-term view, their operations were strategic rather than tactical. The cutting of the submarine cables greatly disrupted Japanese communications at a critical time in the war and forced the enemy to go over to using radio, with all the benefits for the Allied side that that implied. Space precludes a discussion of the intelligence gain from these operations, but considering that at the time the Allies were planning the final invasion of Japan, Operation 'Coronet', any intelligence about the plans and intentions of the Japanese command was of value. Neither the planners nor the XE-Craft crews were to know that the atomic bombs would render their work unnecessary. In reviewing these operations, the Official Historian, Captain S W Roskill, concluded:

> Though it would be impossible to claim that the gallant efforts contributed materially to the defeat of Japan, they confirmed that midget submarines provide very valuable means of penetrating closely guarded enemy waters in order to attack specially important targets.[12]

Therein lies the true value of these operations. The 14th Flotilla gave the Allied command the means of attacking selected high-value targets, quietly and efficiently. In doing so their crews more than earned Admiral Fife's judgement that they were 'the little guys with a lotta guts'.

Chapter 15

The K-Verband

. . . the swift raising of a completely novel unit, equipped with completely new kinds of arms.—Grand Admiral Karl Dönitz, 1944

Germany was the last of the belligerent powers to enter the field of midget submarines. In theory this gave the Germans a position of some advantage in that they could learn a good deal from the experience of their Italian and Japanese allies together with whatever intelligence they had gained of British operational methods and *matériel*.[1] However, despite the efforts of their allies in this field and the known threat posed by the British, it was not until the end of 1943 that the *Kriegsmarine* began a serious investigation of the subject. Even then, it was threat of invasion which provided the stimulus rather than any desire to take the offensive against the Royal Navy.

There had, however, been two attempts to interest the *Kriegsmarine* in midget submarines prior to 1943. In October 1941 a Professor Dräger of the Drägerwerk company submitted a paper to OKM[2] in which he proposed the construction of midget submarines with a displacement of 120 tons. Drager foresaw these craft being used in the defence of the European coastline, to support the *VP-Boote*[3] and for use in mercantile cruisers. Drager's midget was a tadpole-like craft powered by a diesel motor using nitrogen injection. He believed that his craft would be of considerable value in the waters surrounding the British Isles and in the Mediterranean, where their small size would make them difficult to spot. However, his enthusiasm for his invention was not reciprocated by OKM. At the end of 1941 victory for the Axis powers seemed almost assured and Britain was certainly in no position to mount an invasion of Europe. There seemed no conceivable use for the sort of craft that Drager was proposing and on 22 January 1942 he was told by State Councillor Rudolf Blohm:

> Even if the small U-boat can be brought to the point of fulfilling technical require-
> ments, we cannot regard it as adequate for operational purposes because, carrying only
> two torpedoes, it has a minimal armament and because in adverse weather conditions
> heavy seas do not allow such vessels to be used adequately in operations. Furthermore,
> the radius of operation, in the light of the increasing distances over which we are having
> to wage war, is insufficient.[4]

However, in February 1942 *Dipl. Ing.* Adolph Schneeweisse of OKM put forward a proposal for midget submarines which could be carried by Type X or Type

XI U-boats. Schneeweisse had made an exhaustive study of U-boat patrol reports and had come to the conclusion that, as the Royal Navy became more proficient in anti-submarine warfare, so the ability of the U-boats to penetrate escort screens and attack merchant vessels would be greatly reduced. To put this argument forward at a time when U-boats were indulging in the second 'Happy Time' off the eastern seaboard of the United States took a good deal of moral courage. Schneeweisse argued that the considerable sinkings off the American coast were a short-term trend and that eventually the U-boats would have to return to the Atlantic convoys. He proposed that the only way to deal with the convoy escorts was to overwhelm them with massed attacks by small submarines. He therefore proposed the construction of an *Unterwassersturmboot* (underwater assault craft) of about ten tonnes displacement, armed with three F5 or two or three G7a or G7e torpedoes and capable of speeds of 30kt. Three or four such boats could be carried on a Type XB U-boat and two on a Type XI. His preliminary sketch bore a considerable resemblance to the later *Biber* one-man submarine.

At the same time as Schneeweisse was putting forward his idea, by coincidence the German Naval Attaché in Tokyo, Rear-Admiral Wenneker, was requested to obtain details of the Japanese *Ko-Hyoteki* two-man midget submarine and was provided with a list of forty-six questions to ask concerning its construction. After some hesitation by the Japanese authorities, Wenneker and the Italian Naval Attaché were allowed to visit Kure on 3 April 1942 where one of the Type A *Ko-Hyoteki* was paraded for their inspection and Wenneker received the answers to some but not all of his questions. Although Wenneker reported back to Berlin, nothing seems to have come of this initiative.

Schneeweisse's ideas appear to have met the same fate as Dräger's. The *Kriegsmarine* was an intensely conservative force—far more so than the Royal Navy—and was commanded by officers with little or no operational or sea-going experience. The weakness at the top in the *Kriegsmarine* was reflected in the often ham-fisted nature in which naval operations were conducted. Their short-sightedness in not investigating midget submarine designs is extremely hard to understand. It is even harder to understand when one considers that just across the North Sea from the German coastline lay a cornucopia of targets. In the Orkney Islands lay the great harbour of Scapa Flow, further south was the naval base at Rosyth, while even closer to Germany lay the port complexes of the Tyne, Humber and Thames. On the English South Coast—a short trip from the French coast—were the great naval bases of Portsmouth, Portland and Devonport. Seldom can a belligerent have been presented with such a variety of targets so close to hand.

Yet the *Kriegsmarine* does appear to have maintained some momentum in this field, despite the rejection of Drager's and Schneeweisse's proposals. In the summer of 1942 *Capitano di Fregatta* J .V .Borghese, the redoubtable commander of the

Italian *Decima Mas*, visited a German base near Brandenburg to watch the development and training of German assault frogmen. He was not impressed:

> From everything I saw (and my opinion was confirmed by the way the Germans began this particular warfare), I drew the conclusion that they were barely initiated into this sphere of underwater surprise weapons: they had not yet produced anything that would compare with our human torpedo and explosive limpets, but were wasting time in somewhat crude and childish experiments which we had long since discarded.[5]

It was the threat of invasion which finally pushed a recalcitrant *Kriegsmarine* into the field of midget submarine development. As invasion forces massed in England, the fact slowly dawned on the *Kriegsmarine*'s High Command that they had virtually nothing in their armoury with which to oppose a seaborne landing. In order to design and operate such craft, a small unit known as the *Kleinkampfverband* (*K-Verband*, or Small Battle Unit), was established under the command of Rear-Admiral Helmuth Heye. Heye had previously commanded the cruiser *Admiral Hipper* and had since served in a number of staff appointments; at the time of his new appointment he was serving as Chief of Staff to the Fleet Commander. Heye had been Dönitz's original choice for the post but the latter was persuaded by the Chief of Personnel that Heye could not be spared from his current appointment. Accordingly, Vice-Admiral Weichold was given the job. Weichold was not a success, however, and was speedily relieved by Heye, whom Dönitz described as 'a resourceful man, full of ideas'.[6]

Heye's appointment was unique in that he was simultaneously an operational commander, the representative of his service at the high command and the officer responsible for procurement and production. But, as Dönitz commented,

> This dual role was unique and was contrary to every principle of organisation. But in this particular case it was a necessary move, designed to ensure the swift raising of a completely novel unit, equipped with completely new kinds of arms.[7]

Heye established the *K-Verband* at a base at Timmersdorfer Strand near Lübeck and this was where the mangled remains of *X6* and *X7* where brought together with the Welman. Heye was unconventional in his approach to training the men of his new command. He believed in fostering morale as an essential ingredient to success and thus organised his men very much on the Nelsonian 'band of brothers' ethos. There was little formal discipline in the unit, mere lip service was paid to the *Kriegsmarine*'s bureaucracy and rank badges were not worn. There were considerable similarities between the spirit of the *K-Verband* and that of the *Decima Mas*, but any comparison of the two ends there.

Speed was of the essence in constructing and testing a weapon, and Heye was given some formidable powers by Dönitz:

> As speed was essential there was no question of lengthy tests and trials. At my suggestion the Commander-in-Chief gave me considerable powers which enabled me

to short-circuit tedious bureaucratic procedure and to have direct contact with all departments of the Naval Staff and—especially important—with industrial concerns. Unless I had made full use of these powers, the formation and equipment of the K-Force would hardly have been feasible in the short term available.[8]

Heye was under no illusions about the magnitude of the task facing him:

We ourselves possessed no practical experience in this form of warfare. We knew broadly that the Italians and the British possessed several different forms of small battle weapons, but we knew nothing of the Japanese operations with midget submarines.[9]

However, although Heye may have got what amounted to a licence to organise his own production programme, he was handicapped by two restrictions. First, Dönitz would not let him have any men from the U-boat arm: Heye would have to scrape his crews from other sections of the *Wehrmacht*.[10] Heye recruited from all three arms of the *Wehrmacht* and apparently was not particularly choosy about where his men came from. Lieutenant Richard Hale RNVR, of the minesweeper HMS *Orestes*, recalled the interrogation of a *Marder* operator captured on the 8 July 1945 during operations off Normandy:

... the prisoner turned out to be eighteen years old who had been in cells for some crime and had been let out to do his suicide job.[11]

Secondly, the need to produce the new weapons as quickly as possible meant that there would be little time for research and development: the new craft would have to be built from components of existing craft or weapons.

The first German weapon was based on the standard G7e torpedo, designed by *Stabsingenieur* Mohr and developed at the *Torpedo Versuchs Anstalt* (TVA) at Eckenforde. Mohr played a considerable part in the development of the craft, including doing much of the testing, and the name given to the craft, *Neger* (Nigger) was a pun on his own name, Mohr being the German for Moor. The weapon was extremely simple. The G7e torpedo was fitted with a small cockpit covered with a plexiglass dome for the single operator to sit in. The craft was powered by an electric motor similar to that used in the conventional torpedo. It weighed some 5 tonnes and had a range of 30 nautical miles at 3kt. The weapon was a single G7e which was slung underneath it. The craft could not dive but possessed merely sufficient positive buoyancy to support the torpedo. A larger version of *Neger*, called *Marder*, was built which incorporated a diving tank and could submerge to a depth of 25m for very short periods.

The *Neger* operator was provided with rudimentary controls: a wrist compass; a self-contained Dräger breathing set and a crude aiming device consisting of a graduated scale marked on the perspex dome and an aiming spike on the nose of the craft rather like the foresight on a rifle. A handle in the cockpit released the torpedo, which started and ran at a preset depth. One disadvantage of the craft was that on

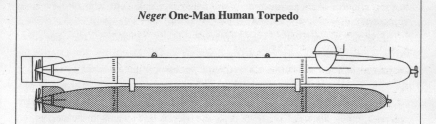

Neger **One-Man Human Torpedo**

Displacement: 2.7 tons
Length: 7.6m
Beam: 0.5m
Propulsion: Single shaft, 1 x 12hp
motor from electric torpedo
Speed (surfaced): 4kt
Range (surfaced): 48nm at 4kt
Armament: One G7e torpedo
Crew: 1

Number delivered: Approx. 200, plus
300 *Marder* which were identical in all
respects except that they had a displacement of 3 tons and a length of 8.3m.
Fates: Approx. 140 of the 200 *Neger*
were lost in action. Of the 300 *Marder*,
the number lost is unclear. Roughly 150
were employed in NW Europe and the
remainder in the Mediterranean.

occasions the torpedo started but failed to release, carrying the upper unit and operator to oblivion.

In theory, and especially in the eyes of the shore-based planners, the vision of a swarm of *Neger* and *Marder* overwhelming an invasion fleet was an attractive one, but in reality the position was very different. The operator was too low to see properly and the perspex dome was easily obscured by oil or other scum in the water, rendering the operator blind. If he opened the perspex lid to get a better view, he risked swamping the craft. These problems meant that in operations the craft would suffer an appalling casualty rate of between 60 and 80 per cent.

A successor to the *Neger/Marder* combination was the *Molch* (Salamander). This was a basically nothing more than a slug-like craft 10m long, a carrier for G7e torpedoes which were slung externally on either side. As with other German designs, it was to use as many existing components as possible. The fore section contained the twelve Type 13 T210 battery troughs which drove the 13hp electric motor. The size of the battery meant that the *Molch* was a comparatively large craft, with a displacement of 8.4 tonnes (without torpedoes) but the device did have a substantial underwater range—50 nautical miles at 5kt was impressive. Behind the battery in the after section was the operator's position. He sat between two trimming tanks whose relatively small size and position must have made them virtually useless in compensating for the weight of the battery. In fact, when the first production model went out on trials, it proved impossible to make her submerge and therefore most *Molch* operations were carried out with the craft running awash. The controls were

187

extremely simple. A magnetic compass was fitted externally, although in some boats an automatic pilot was fitted together with a simple hydrophone. A periscope was fitted but its use was negated by the fact that it could only be rotated 30 degrees either side of the centreline. Finally, behind the operator was the electric motor. Despite the problems associated with *Molch*'s handling, series production was begun in June 1944 and a total of 393 units were completed by the end of February 1945. Production was largely centred at the works of Deschimag AG Weser at Bremen.

An altogether different creature was the *Biber* one-man submarine, whose development arose from the capture of Welman *W46* at Bergen on 22 November 1943. The Welman was a one-man craft of extreme lethality to its operator but it acted as a spur to *Korvettenkapitän* Hans Bartels to develop something similar. In a service not known for eccentrics, Bartels stood out like a beacon. During the 1940 Norwegian campaign he had taken the surrender of a Norwegian destroyer and an entire flotilla of torpedo boats. He then designed and built a minesweeper to his own specification, followed by eleven more, and then invited OKM to pay for them. When Grand Admiral Erich Raeder indignantly refused, Bartels moored one of the minesweepers in a canal opposite German naval headquarters in Berlin where Raeder could inspect the craft. Raeder took a dim view of these proceedings and Bartels was packed off to the destroyer *Z34* to cool his heels in the 'real' Navy.

Bartels evidently found considerable inspiration in the Welman and on 4 February 1944 he began negotiations with Flenderwek of Lübeck for the construction of a similar craft. On 15 March 1944 the first prototype, known as either the *Bunte-Boot*

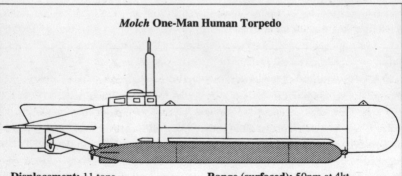

Molch One-Man Human Torpedo

Displacement: 11 tons
Length: 10.8m
Beam: 1.8m
Propulsion: Single-shaft, 1 x 13hp motor from electric torpedo
Speed (surfaced): 4.3kt
Speed (submerged): 5kt

Range (surfaced): 50nm at 4kt
Range (submerged): 50nm at 5kt
Armament: Two G7e torpedoes
Crew: 1
Number delivered: 393
Fates: Accurate figures for the number of *Molch* lost in action are unavailable.

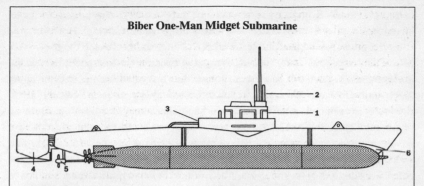

Biber One-Man Midget Submarine

Displacement: 6.3 tons
Length: 9.0m
Beam: 1.6m
Propulsion: Single shaft, 1 x 32hp Opel Blitz Otto petrol engine; 1 x 13hp motor from electric torpedo
Fuel capacity: 0.11 tons
Speed (surfaced): 6.5kt
Speed (submerged): 5.3kt
Range (surfaced): 100nm at 6.5kt
Range (submerged): 8.6nm at 5kt
Armament: Two G7e torpedoes
Crew: 1
Number delivered: 324
Fates: Accurate figures for the number of *Biber* lost in action are unavailable.

Key to drawing:
1. Conning tower containing glass viewing ports
2. Masts (from forward to aft): projector binnacle; single forward-facing periscope; air induction mast
3. Exhaust arrangements, consisting of exhaust valve, exhaust tank and exhaust pipe.
4. Rudder and hydroplanes.
5. Single propeller.
6. Recess for G7e torpedo (port side had similar recess).

(after Director Bunte of Flenderwerke) or *Adam*, was complete. Trials, with Bartels himself doing much of the testing, were run on the River Trave, and on 29 March 1944 the craft was accepted for service. Twenty-four production models were ordered as a first batch out of an eventual run of 324. Deliveries throughout 1944 comprised three units in May, six in June, nineteen in July, 50 in August, 117 in September, 73 in October and 56 in November. Although air raids on Kiel destroyed some components, Allied bombing failed to disrupt production to any appreciable degree.

The *Biber* displaced 6.3 tonnes when armed with its two G7e torpedoes. It was 29ft 6in long, 5ft 3in in the beam and had a draught of 4ft 6in. Surface propulsion was provided by a 32hp Opel Blitz automobile engine which gave a range of 100 nautical miles at a maximum speed of 6.5kt. Reservations had been expressed about the safety of a petrol motor in such a small craft, but these were dismissed by Dr Bunte. Petrol engines were cheap to make and could be supplied in quantity, and an added advantage was that they made very little noise when running. However, the reservations were well founded. Like all petrol engines, the Opel in the *Biber* gave off carbon monoxide in its exhaust. Thus the operator sat in a potentially lethal atmosphere if he ran the engine for any longer than forty-five minutes with the upper hatch shut. Operators were supplied with breathing apparatus and twenty hours' worth of oxygen, but many must have succumbed to CO poisoning while on operations. Three Type T13 T210 battery troughs powered a 13hp electric motor for submerged drive, which gave the *Biber* a range of 8.6 nautical miles at 5.3kt. The hull was made of 3mm sheet steel and gave a safe diving depth of 60ft, although some *Biber* went down to 100ft and more on operations. Four internal bulkheads and three longitudinal ribs reinforced the hull plating. There were no compensating or trimming tanks, just a single diving tank in the bow and another one in the stern. The *Biber* handled well on the surface, but it proved virtually impossible to control when dived, largely because of the absence of any trimming arrangements.

The *Biber* was built in three sections which bolted together. The bow section contained nothing more than the main diving tank. Between the first and second bulkhead was the main compartment where the operator sat with his head poking up into the 28in conning tower. The control panel was directly in front of the operator's seat and was compact and austere. The conning tower was fitted with glass ports which were the operator's principal means of seeing where he was going. A periscope was fitted but it was fixed in a forward-facing direction. Maintaining the craft at periscope depth was almost impossible because of the lack of trimming arrangements. Behind the operator was the compartment containing the engine. In theory this was sealed off from the main compartment but in practice the insidious petrol vapour permeated every part of the boat. The final compartment in the boat contained the after diving tank. There were no facilities for the operator whatsoever. He was given a ration of chocolate which had been 'improved' with the addition of stimulants such as caffeine and cola, but that was all.

The two G7e torpedoes were slung on a rail in semi-recessed positions on either side of the craft. The rail ran from a fitting on the keel to a swinging eyebolt above. There was a pneumatic cylinder to which air was admitted in order to fire the torpedo. The piston in the cylinder then travelled towards the rear, releasing a clamping eyebolt and forcing back a trip lever on the torpedo. The torpedo then started and ran forward under its own power, suspended from the rail by two lugs until it cleared the submarine. The firing arrangements were, if anything, too simple and there were to be serious incidents of 'negligent discharge' in which a number of craft were wrecked and their operators killed. An alternative armament to the torpedoes was the mine. Two GS mines could be carried by each craft, fitted with either magnetic/ acoustic or magnetic/pressure fuses.

Captain W. O. Sheflord RN, an authority in the Royal Navy on all aspects of diving and submarine escape, was responsible for surveying a *Biber* found abandoned in France after the Normandy campaign. In his report[12] on the *Biber* he compared it to the British Welman (which is not much of a recommendation), although it was superior in certain points. He was of the opinion that the torpedo was a superior armament to the explosive charge carried by the British X-Craft, even though use of the torpedo meant that the craft had to risk detection in order to attack its target.

Further developments of the *Biber* were planned which included two-man versions, the *Biber II* and *Biber III*. However, these were nothing more than drawing board projects. Their cancellation came about as a result of a directive issued by OKM at the beginning of 1945 to the effect that work on all craft not in series production should be suspended. However, this directive was largely ignored. The fact that Admiral Heye was virtually independent ensured that work proceeded on a number of designs until the end of the war. Among the most ingenious of these was that for the *Seeteufel* (Sea Devil), which was an amphibious craft fitted with both a single propeller and caterpillar tracks. The requirement for a tracked craft arose from the difficulties experienced in launching *Marder* and *Molch* in the water without dockside facilities: the *Seeteufel* could simply make its own way into the water. As built, the prototype had a two-man crew and was much larger than other midget types. Propulsion was by means of an 80hp petrol engine which could be switched to drive either the single screw or the caterpillar tracks. For submerged drive the boat had a 30hp electric motor, which gave a speed of 8kt—which was very good considering that the *Seeteufel* had the worst underwater resistance of any German midget U-boat. The petrol engine was installed in the bow beneath a fixed *schnorkel* mast which also contained the periscope, a rod aerial and the magnetic compass with lighting transmission. Behind the petrol engine was the crew compartment. All controls were grouped into an aircraft-like column placed forward of the driver's seat beneath a plexiglass dome. Despite the fat shape of the boat, *Seeteufel* handled well under water. The diving depth was 21m. Tests with the craft proved satisfactory except that it was found that on land the engine lacked power and the tracks were too

Seeteufel Two-Man Amphibious Midget Submarine

Displacement: 20 tons	**Speed (surfaced):** 10kt
Length: 13.5m	**Speed (submerged):** 8kt
Beam: 2.8m	**Range (surfaced):** 300nm at 10kt
Propulsion: Single shaft; 1 x Opel Blitz	**Range (submerged):** 80nm at 8kt
Otto petrol engine with one 30hp	**Armament:** Two 53cm torpedoes
electric motor; fitted with caterpillar	**Crew:** 2
tracks for launching and possibly	**Number delivered:** 1 tested by TVA
bottom crawling	but broken up before end of hostilities

narrow. In water, however, the craft handled perfectly well. Heye was impressed and entered into negotiations with the automobile manufacturer Carl Borgward for series production of the *Seeteufel* with a more powerful 250hp diesel engine. However, these plans came to nothing: the prototype *Seeteufel* was taken to Lübeck, where it was destroyed at the end of the war.

Other designs investigated but not put into series production were the *Delphin*, a small streamlined craft which towed a 500kg mine. The craft was quite fast, with an underwater speed of 14kt, and was powered by a 2.5-litre Opel Kapitän closed-cycle engine. Only two craft were built and trials showed some promise, but both were destroyed at Potenitz on 1 May 1945 to prevent their falling into the hands of the British. Another craft was *Schwertal*, a two-man device armed with two torpedoes which bore an uncomfortable resemblance to the Japanese *Kaiten*. *Schwertal* was a development of the Type XXVIIF U-boat whose construction had been halted at the end of 1944. The Type XXVIIF was powered by a closed-cycle Walther turbine and could achieve an underwater speed of 20.4kt with torpedoes slung and 22.6kt unarmed. The use of the closed-cycle drive conferred numerous advantages, including high speed and the ability to dispense with separate systems for surface and submerged drive.

Schwertal was to be a fast and manoeuvrable underwater craft and was intended to have an ASW role as well as an anti-shipping one. She was to be armed with two torpedoes but other suggested weapons included the 500kg towed mine and underwater rockets for use against pursuing ships. The high speed of the craft meant that she could not be fitted with a periscope, and a simple plexiglass dome was provided for surface vision and navigation. An orientation device consisting of a gyro-stabilised aircraft compass with automatic control for lateral movement and depth-keeping was fitted and performed well on trials. The master magnetic compass was fitted externally in a streamlined pod on top of the rudder assembly.

By the end of April 1945 *Schwertal* was ready for trials. All the systems worked in tests ashore and the powerplant had generated the requisite 800hp in test-bed trials. However, at the end of the war the craft was scuttled at Plon to prevent her falling into British hands. She was subsequently raised by the Royal Navy and, after a brief examination, was scrapped at Kiel. A design known as *Schwertal 2* was projected. It was even more streamlined than the original and additionally was fitted with a 25hp electric motor for silent creep speed. *Schwertal 2* never progressed beyond the drawing board.

Despite the ingenious nature of the design, *Schwertal* would have probably been lethal to her operators. The problems of controlling a craft underwater at high speed are considerable—a moment's inattention, and the craft could plunge beneath its test depth to destruction. Furthermore, the Walther turbine was not tested under operational conditions. Post-war British and American experience found that this method of propulsion was not suitable at all for submarine use. A final German project was *Manta*, another high-speed craft with a trimaran hull capable of over 50kt while planing on the surface and a submerged speed of over 30kt, with a Walther turbine and an electric motor for very quiet, submerged creep speed. The central hull contained the compartment for the two-man crew, while the two outer cylinders contained fuel tanks. The propulsion unit consisted of two *Schwertal 2* type units housed in the keels of the outer cylinders. These side units were also fitted with aircraft wheels to allow the craft to launch itself into the water. The armament was four torpedoes, or mines, carried on the wing surface between the outer hulls and the central body.

Manta can only be described as a fascinating design. The whole story of midget submarines is packed with 'what if?' scenarios. That of a *Manta* storming through an Allied convoy at 50kt plus, firing torpedoes or towing the 500kg mine, is definitely one of the best . However, *Manta*, together with *Delphin* and *Schwertal*, are little more than reflections of the desperate position facing Nazi Germany at the end of the war. In such circumstances, rather akin to those facing the Japanese, German designers who had hitherto been sceptical of the value of midget submarines took refuge in any design, however fantastic.

The first operation undertaken by the *K-Verband* was conducted against Allied shipping off Anzio. Following the landings at Anzio on 22 January 1944, forty *Neger* were dispatched to Practica di Mare, were they arrived on 13 April after a difficult journey. Problems finding a launching site—the beaches all had very shallow gradient—meant that some 500 unwilling soldiers had to be conscripted to construct launching ramps and thus it was not until the night of 20/21 April that the attack could be launched. Twenty-three *Neger* were launched but the subsequent attack was a fiasco. At least four were sunk by the defences and one was captured intact, found washed up on the beach. Only thirteen craft returned from the operation, which did not result in the loss of a single Allied ship. It was an ominous portent for the future.

Chapter 16

Desperate Measures

I was standing on the afterdeck of Cockatrice *when I heard the explosion and saw the stern of* Pylades *blown clean off and then the forward part of the ship just tipped and sank almost immediately.*—Able Seaman Fred Holmes in HMS *Cockatrice*, 8 July 1944.

The Allied invasion of Normandy in June 1944 offered the *K-Verband* an outstanding opportunity to strike a significant blow against the Anglo-American forces. Off the Normandy beaches, corralled by the Mulberry harbours, lay over 5,000 warships and merchant ships. Although this armada was well protected, the Germans had the advantage of possessing bases lying on the assault area's doorstep and therefore the time spent by the *Marder* and *Biber* in transit to their operational area would be minimal.

An MEK (*Marine Einsatz Kommando*) of *Linsen* explosive motor boats had already arrived in Normandy and launched three sorties beginning on 25 June. However, bad weather and the poor state of training of their operators meant that no successes were scored and nearly all of the *Linsen* and their control boats were lost. On 30 June *Kapitän zur See* Fritz Bohme reported that no further *Linsen* operations were possible until he was supplied with replacement boats and crews. The next *K-Verband* arrivals in Normandy were a group of forty *Marder* which had left Germany on 13 June. After a long road journey in which much time was lost in avoiding the attentions of the RAF, they arrived at Villers-sur-Mer, a few miles along the coast to the west of Honfleur, on 28 June. The *Marder* were kept under camouflage netting in woods at Favrol while German Army pioneers laboured to construct launching ways on the beach down which the *Marder* could be run into deep water. *Marder* operations were effectively governed by the state of the tide. The tiny craft could only be launched after dark and they needed the ebb tide to help them reach the assault area by low water. They would then make their attacks and return to their base with the flood. There were only three or four days in each month when these tidal conditions could be met. The first of these was on the night of the 5/6 July 1944.

The Allies had already adopted a plan for the defence of the invasion anchorage. Owing to the restrictions placed on the movement of German ships and U-boats by their own minefields and by the Allies' overwhelming air superiority, static defence was adopted. It reduced the risk of collision and kept wear and tear on ships' hulls and machinery to a minimum. Seaward patrols, under the command of Captain A.

F. Pugsley RN, consisted of a line of minesweepers anchored five cables[1] apart, six miles from the shore and parallel to it. The minesweepers were backed up by two or three divisions of MTBs and by a number of destroyers.

Defence from attacks launched from seaward was not really a problem: the real threat came from attacks launched from the land, and in particular from the eastern section of the assault area. There was little threat to the American anchorages in the western section of the assault area following the swift American occupation of the eastern coast of the Cotentin peninsula. On the other hand, in the eastern section, the Germans were still holding the ground to the east of the River Orne in strength, together with the port of Le Havre, and it was from this area that the main threat would come. The defence of the eastern anchorages called for vigorous measures, and it was decided that the current static patrols be strengthened by the formation of the Support Squadron Eastern Flank under the command of Commander K. A. Sellar RN. The squadron consisted of the old China gunboat HMS *Locust* as headquarters ship and seventy-one other craft, mostly LCGs, LCFs, LCSs and motor launches, manned by a total of 240 officers and 3,000 men.

A double patrol line was established running roughly six miles to the north of Ouistreham and from there for two miles in a north-westerly direction until it entered the area where the seaward defence patrols were operating. The first line consisted of the landing craft, anchored 3½ cables apart. The second line consisted of one motor launch to every two craft in the static line. If things were quiet then the MLs simply secured to one of the landing craft. On an alert being sounded, they cast off and patrolled the area between the two craft for which they were responsible. This system was known as the Trout Line. The nightly deployment of the Trout Line was a matter of extremely accurate timing. If the line were deployed too early, then the ships would be shelled from the shore. Retirement in the morning had to be done just before first light for the same reason. The Trout Line was first employed on 28 June and from then until the night of 5 July it enjoyed a quiet existence. The abortive attacks by *Linsen* motor boats are not even mentioned in the Naval Staff History of the campaign.[2]

Twenty-six *Marder* were launched from Villers-sur-Mer but two were forced to turn back on account of mechanical failure. Their attack on the Trout Line opened shortly after 0300 on 6 July and continued until 0630. Despite the earlier capture of a *Marder* off Anzio and the publication of its particulars in the Weekly Intelligence Report dated 9 June 1944, none of this information had reached the Eastern Flank Support Squadron. Consequently the first sighting of a *Marder* came as something of a surprise.

The experience of *ML151* may be taken as typical of that of the ships of the Support Squadron that morning. *ML151* was moored astern of *LCF21* in the static defence line when, shortly after 0300, her attention was called by loud hailer to an object moving on the landing craft's starboard quarter. *ML151* went astern but at 0307 a torpedo passed under her and headed off in the direction of *LCG(L)681*. The ML then tried to ram but was forced to turn away on account of gunfire from *LCF21* and *LCG(M)681*. At 0315 the enemy dived and *ML151* plastered the area with 5lb scuttling charges before proceeding to drop similar charges over a much larger area east of the Trout Line.

This engagement set the pattern for many that night and early the next morning. Petty Officer Len Warland, in HMS *Orestes*, remembered that

> ... action stations was sounded when these strange objects appeared. One ran along our port side and swung towards us, just missing our stern. The Oerlikons were brought to bear on them and rifles were issued to seamen who also let fly ... One torpedo was rammed head-on and disappeared beneath us. One pilot swam to our side and was hoisted aboard and kept under guard in the sick bay. Next day he was transferred to another ship. I remember being told that he told his guard that he was in the German Army and not being a sailor had little stomach for it.[3]

The British were not at all sure what they were firing at and it was not until the morning, when the night's results could be collated and the prisoners taken interrogated, that some kind of sense could be made of the evening's activities. Thirteen of the weapons had been destroyed and a number of their operators taken prisoner. However, the debit side was that the minesweepers HMS *Magic* and *Cato* were both torpedoed in the Northern Defence Line off 'Sword' area at 0353 and 0511 respectively.[4] *Magic* was the first to be attacked and sank with the loss of 25 of her crew. Many of the survivors were taken on board *Cato*, which was attacked shortly afterwards. Twenty-six men were killed in *Cato*. The Germans claimed the operation as a great success, but the loss of half the attack force in return for sinking two minesweepers was hardly an encouraging exchange rate.

The prisoners proved remarkably cooperative and under interrogation revealed that another attack would be launched as soon as the right conditions were met. On the night of 8/9 July twenty-one *Marder* were launched from Houlgate and proceeded westwards along the coast to the assault area. The first sighting of the *Marder* was at 0307 and it some indication of the confusion these small craft could create that between then and 1130 on the 9th there were 31 sightings. Five were definitely sunk and another nine assessed as 'probables'. Many were sighted and attacked by RAF and FAA aircraft, some as much as five miles west of La Heve. In fact, as the War Diary for *Gruppe West* recorded, not one of the 21 Marder returned from this operation. On the other hand, British losses had been minimal. The minesweeper *Pylades* was sunk in the Northern Defence line. Chief ERA Allan Smales in HMS *Pylades* remembered that

> At about 0650 we were hit in the stern by what we later learned was a *Neger*. Fortunately I was ERA on watch in the forward engine room at the time of the explosion

and I was able to get out. I remember having a laugh as I got out of the ship to see a seaman sailing merrily past on one of the Oropesa floats clad only in his vest.[5]

Able Seaman Fred Holmes in HMS *Cockatrice* recalled that:

I was standing on the afterdeck of *Cockatrice* when I heard the explosion and saw the stern of *Pylades* blown clean off and then the forward part of the ship just tipped and sank almost immediately.[6]

Other Allied losses that night included the Polish cruiser *Dragon*, which was so badly damaged that it was decided to sink her as an additional blockship in the Gooseberry Harbour off 'Sword' beach.

From intelligence gleaned from German prisoners and observation of the weather, the British decided that the next night on which the conditions would be most suitable for a *Neger* attack would be 1/2 August. In the event all was quiet on the night of 1 August. On the following night the weather was so bad that an attack seemed unlikely but as conditions improved throughout the night the decision was taken to sound a preparatory alert at 0200 on 3 August.

The attack opened at 0220 when the old cruiser *Durban*, which had been sunk as a blockship to form the easternmost Corncob[7] in the 'Sword' area Gooseberry Harbour, was struck by a torpedo. However, the alarm was not raised as no news of this attack was forwarded to the headquarters of Rear-Admiral J. Rivett-Carnac, Flag Officer commanding the British Assault Area (FOBAA). The main attack developed from 0251 and nearly all the action was concentrated at the northern end of the Trout Line, indicating that the Germans were trying to round the line rather than break through it—proof of the efficiency of the defence.

At 0251 the destroyer HMS *Quorn* was torpedoed. The torpedo struck on the starboard side amidships, the ship assumed a 40-degree list to starboard and less than a minute after the attack she had rolled over on to her beam ends. Although she temporarily righted herself, *Quorn* was broken in two amidships. Both ends sank rapidly until 30ft of the stern and 15ft of the bow were above the water. Four officers and 126 ratings were killed—a very heavy loss of life.[8] Ten minutes later *LCG1* and *ML131* engaged a *Marder* without success. At 0310 a torpedo narrowly missed the destroyer HMS *Duff* and at 0325 the trawler *Gairsay* was torpedoed and sunk. When news of these events reached FOBAA's headquarters a full alert was ordered at 0341. This was just as well, for shortly after 0350 the Germans launched an attack on the Trout Line using *Linsen* explosive motor boats. For the next two and a half hours the *Linsen* tried to break through the Trout Line but were unsuccessful. The support landing craft proved quite capable of dealing with the small *Linsen*, while any that did break through were destroyed by the motor launches. By 0615 the Germans withdrew, having lost sixteen *Linsen* and two of their control craft in return for sinking *LCG764*.

While this furious battle was raging in the centre of the Trout Line, the *Marder* were still trying to creep around the northern flank. On was destroyed by *HDML1049* at 0610 and contact with others continued until 0730 when they withdrew. One *Marder* was captured by HMS *Blencathra* but as it was being hoisted inboard the torpedo exploded, doing considerable damage. However, another was recovered intact and dispatched to the United Kingdom for examination. Those *Marder* which had survived the night were relentlessly harried by Spitfire aircraft of No 132 Squadron on their way back to harbour.

The night's events had been nothing short of a disaster for the Germans. Their total losses amounted to 22 out 32 *Linsen* and 41 out of 58 *Marder*. In return the Germans had sunk the *Quorn*, *Garsay* and *LCG764*. Other casualties that night included the merchant ships *Fort Lac la Ronge* and *Samlong*, which were both damaged. In the case of these two ships it is impossible to say how they were damaged: a *Marder* may have been responsible, but the two ships may have been mined or hit by a *Dackel*[9] (Dachshund) circling torpedo.

There were no further *Marder* attacks on the Trout Line during the night of 15/16 August although *Linsen* boats made their second and last attack. However, during this period there were a number of alarms which kept tension in the Support Squadron at a high level. The Germans deployed decoy devices to supplement the existing hazards presented by mines (of all types and sizes) and the *Dackel*. These consisted of cylinders of various shapes and sizes and 'dummy' *Marder* on which the head and shoulders of a man were painted on a torpedo body. It was clear that measures had to be taken to clear up the anchorage in order to reduce the confusion caused by these objects. A special ML patrol was instituted during the daylight hours and all ships were ordered to post look-outs to sink such objects with rifle fire. At the same time orders were given to clear the harbour of rubbish which could be mistaken for dangerous objects or lead to confusion when searching for them. Lastly, all ships were given large quantities of flares and other illuminants. These measures appear to have been successful, for FOBAA's war diary makes no reference to them after 9 August.[10]

The plethora of German weapons employed in the Seine Bay makes any estimation of losses caused by *Marder* attacks extremely difficult. Between 7 and 11 August (a period when there were no *Marder* attacks) six vessels were sunk or damaged by underwater explosions. The first, the motor vessel *William Darcy*, was damaged near Berth H-34 on 7 August by either a floating mine or a *Dackel*. One and a half hours later the hospital ship *Amsterdam* was sunk near L7 buoy with heavy loss of life.[11] On 8 August the motor vessel *Fort Vale* was damaged south of 56H buoy: she remained afloat and was safely berthed in the 'Juno' anchorage. On 9 August the cruiser *Frobisher*, which had already been bombed and damaged on 18 July, was struck by a *Dackel* while at anchor off Courselles on 9 August. On the same day the

Flotilla No	Weapon	Location
	Disposition of K-Verband units, 1 September 1944	
211	Marder/Linsen	Germany
261	Biber	Ex-Fécamp, en route for Lübeck.
361	Marder/Linsen	Germany
411	Molch	En route for Genoa
412	Molch	Germany

transport *Iddesleigh* had to be beached near Berth H-20 after suffering an underwater explosion. The sixth casualty was the seaplane carrier HMS *Albatross*, which was severely damaged by an underwater explosion on the 11th with the loss of 55 officers and men. Between 12 August and 11 September (with the exception of the attack on 17 August, another '*Marder*-free' period), a further five ships were reported sunk or damaged as a result of underwater explosions. The first was the balloon ship *Fratton*, sunk in four minutes on the morning of 18 August.[12] The next casualty was the SS *Harpagus*, mined on 19 August near the Arromanches approach channel. On 23 August the small tanker *Empire Roseburg* was mined in the 'Gold' area three miles north of Arromanches. The fourth victim was the minesweeper *Gleaner*, mined on the 27th, and the last was the trawler *Kingston Cherysoberyl*, damaged in an underwater explosion on 2 September while at anchor.

The next *Marder* attack, on 15/16 August, was a failure. Only fourteen of the planned 53 craft set out and seven returned, the other seven having succumbed to bad weather. The operation is not mentioned in British records. On the next night all 42 *Marder* were dispatched. At 0632 the support craft *LCF1* was torpedoed while weighing anchor and blew up with the loss of all seventy of her complement. A torpedo also struck the hull of the transport *Iddesleigh*, which had been mined on 9 August and beached; she was subsequently written off as a total loss. These were the Germans' sole successes. Two torpedoes hit the hull of the old battleship *Courbet* which had been sunk as a blockship in the breakwater of No 5 Gooseberry Harbour. As the Official History drily noted,

> This old French battleship exercised an irresistible fascination over the enemy. Lying on the bottom in shallow water and flying an immense tricolour and Cross of Lorraine, she presented an entirely normal appearance. This illusion was deliberately fostered by the Support Squadron, which frequently carried out bombardments from behind her covered by smoke. The ruse met with no small measure of success for the Germans wasted many shells, torpedoes and bombs in an endeavour to destroy her, without in any way impairing her efficiency as an effective blockship.[13]

During this abortive attack the Germans suffered heavy losses. Twenty five of the 42 *Marder* were destroyed while another was captured and brought ashore by

LCS(L)251 after a four-hour salvage effort. Seven prisoners were taken. Never again did the Germans risk making a raid on the Trout Line in such strength.

At the end of August the *Neger* received some reinforcement in the shape of *K-Flotille 261*, equipped with twenty *Biber* one-man submarines and commanded by *Korvettenkapitän* Hans Bartels. It had been intended for the *Biber* to operate from Le Havre, but on 20 August the Anglo-American armies finally broke out of the beach-head. The German Army retired in disorder and Le Havre was surrounded. Undaunted, Bartels pressed on. It took his unit five days to make the journey from their depot in Belgium to the port of Fécamp, which was to be their new base, where they arrived on 28 August.

Once at Fécamp, Bartels gave the *Biber* operators less than twenty hours to make their craft ready for sea. Eighteen *Biber* were launched on the night of 29/30 August and, in contrast to the *Neger* missions, all eighteen craft returned safely. The operation took place in unfavourable weather conditions. The Germans claimed a landing ship and a Liberty ship sunk but these losses are not substantiated by Allied records; indeed, there is, again, no reference to the attack in the official British narrative. On 31 August *K-Flotille 261* was forced to abandon Fécamp in the face of the Allied advance. Most of the *Biber* were destroyed and abandoned and those few which were taken away were subsequently destroyed in a night action with an Allied armoured column. This episode marked the end of *K-Verband* operations in Normandy.

The operations had been decidedly unsuccessful. At a cost of 99 Marder the losses inflicted on the British amounted to one destroyer, three minesweepers, a trawler, two merchant ships and a number of landing craft—in an area packed with transports and warships. The lack of any significant successes reflects on the unsuitability of the *Marder* as an attack weapon. The craft may have been technically reliable, but the single operator was hopelessly overworked. He had to con his craft, sneak past an alert and aggressive defence and then select a target while sitting in an extremely uncomfortable position and able to see only a few inches above the water, the surface of which would have been fouled by oil and other detritus. Most of the *Marder* operators probably fired at the first shadow that loomed up before them.

With the conclusion of operations in Normandy, the *K-Verband* units were re-formed and reorganised. The disposition of the various units on 1 September is shown in the accompanying table. Between the beginning of September and early December there were few operations. This was largely due to the shifting nature of the front, making it difficult to establish an operating base with any degree of security. However, the *K-Verband* planners were not short of ideas for the future employment of their craft. The Channel Islands were suggested as a suitable base. The idea was soon dropped when it was realised that the craft would have to be taken to the islands by air using large, slow transport aircraft and with the probability of horrific losses in the face of Allied air superiority. Moreover, the prospect of the small and unseaworthy *Marder* and *Biber* having to cope with the notorious tides and races around the Channel Islands did not bear thinking about. A more adventurous plan was for the employment of a *Biber* in the Suez Canal.[14] In an operation similar to the British Operation 'Large Lumps',[15] and conceived by a staff officer whose imagination had gone into a shallow glide after a long lunch, the *Biber* would be loaded into a Bv 222 flying boat (the aircraft would require substantial modification) and landed on the Suez Canal. The craft would then be released with the intention of sinking a ship and blocking the Canal. The plan was ingenious but hopelessly impractical. The Bv 222 was the largest operational flying boat in the world with a wingspan of 46m, and its arrival over the Suez Canal would hardly be a low-key affair.

Another use for the *Biber* was an abortive attempt to destroy the road bridge over the River Waal at Nijmegen which had been captured by the US 82nd Airborne Division in September 1944. Assault frogmen had already made an unsuccessful but daring raid on the rail bridge. However, after this incident the defences around the bridges were strengthened by rigging four net barriers across the Waal upstream from the bridge. The operation began on the night of 12–13 January 1945 when the Germans released 240 mines in four waves. These were to destroy the net barriers and were followed by twenty *Biber*, each with their periscopes camouflaged to resemble floating nests. These *Biber* were to fire torpedoes fitted with hooks to catch the nets and blow gaps in them. Finally, four *Biber* towed 600lb explosive charges, which would be released to drift down under the bridge. Each charge was fitted with a photo-electric cell. As the charge floated under the bridge the change of light would trigger the charge and complete the night's work of destruction. The operation was a failure. Both banks of the Waal were held in strength by the Allies and, after the explosion of the mines, the river was raked by gunfire. All four of the explosive charges were destroyed before they passed the net barriers.

In mid-December Heye drew up a comprehensive operational plan for the employment of all *K-Verband* units in the Scheldt Estuary. This area appeared to be very promising. There were numerous inlets and islands amongst which the *K-Verband* could be hidden and the growing use of the port of Antwerp meant that there would be no shortage of targets. The German Navy's *B-Dienst* station on the island of Schouwen was in an excellent position to report shipping movements. However, the operations would be strongly constrained by the weather conditions and the state of the tide. In the first place the wind and sea should not be greater than State 4 on the Beaufort Scale—anything greater and the *Biber* would be unable to operate—and secondly there should be no moon. The *Biber* would sail on the ebb tide so that the forty or so miles to the western Scheldt would be covered fairly quickly and the *Biber* would arrive in the operational area at dusk. The wholly inadequate periscope fitted in the *Biber* meant that periscope attacks at night were impossible. Instead the craft would attack while on the surface.

An advanced base was prepared at Poortershavn and Hellevoetsluis at the head of the Waal/Maas estuary. The main base was Rotterdam, where thirty *Biber* and thirty *Molche* were sent. The *Biber* would be towed down from Rotterdam by units of the Rhine Flotilla to Hellevoetsluis, where their tows would be slipped and the craft would proceed independently. A further 60 *Molche* would arrive at Assens from Heligoland together with thirty *Biber* from Groningen. Sixty more *Biber* would arrive in the area in January 1945.

All this concentration of force achieved little. Eighteen *Biber* sailed from Poortershavn and Hellevoetsluis on the night of 22/23 December 1944. The operation ended in failure. British MTBs surprised the *Biber* while their tows were being slipped and four were lost instantly. One was mined and one returned damaged. The remaining twelve disappeared. No cause has ever been given for their loss, but suffocation from petrol fumes and accidental flooding while proceeding on the surface are the most likely reasons. Only one success was recorded—the sinking of the 4,700-ton *Alan a Dale*.

This operation set the tone for four months of sustained operations by the *K-Verband* in the Low Countries. Night after night *Biber* and *Molche* would be launched against Allied shipping for no result and with most of the craft failing to return. Grand-Admiral Karl Dönitz, Commander-in-Chief of the *Kriegsmarine*, referred to the operators as *Opferkämpfer* (suicide fighters). It says much for the morale of the *K-Verband* that they were prepared to continue with these operations in the almost certain knowledge that they would not return.

The operation was repeated on the nights of the 23rd/24th and the 24th/25th when, respectively, eleven and three *Biber* were sailed. None returned. Thus by the end of 1944 thirty-one *Biber* had been lost in return for one merchant ship sunk. This was hardly an inspiring exchange rate. Only eight of the *Biber* lost were claimed by the Allies, the rest being casualties of operator error or marine accident. On 27 December a force of fourteen *Biber* was preparing to sail from Hellevoetsluis when two G7 torpedoes were accidentally fired into the lock. In the resulting conflagration eleven of the *Biber* were destroyed together with two launches. Undeterred, the three remaining craft set out. None returned but *Biber 90* was found drifting off the North Foreland on 29 December by the minesweeper HMS *Ready* with the operator dead at the controls. *Ready* took the *Biber* in tow and was later joined by a rescue tug which took over the tow. However, the weather quickly deteriorated, and while the tug was trying to enter Dover, the tow broke and the *Biber* sank. It was not recovered until ten days later. A post mortem established that the operator had died of carbon monoxide poisoning.[16] This dismal record convinced many in the *Kriegsmarine* that *K-Verband* operations were a waste of resources and manpower. However, Dönitz disagreed. He had great hopes for the *Biber*, particularly in its role as a minelayer, and for the two-man *Seehund* midget submarines which were just coming into production. However, as the Flag Officer Channel Coast cryptically remarked, since no one had yet returned from a *Biber* operation, their success could not be guaranteed![17]

At the end of 1944 the remaining *K-Verband* units in the Low Countries consisted of 20 *Biber* and 12 *Molche* at Rotterdam with a further sixty *Molche* units held in reserve inland. The *Biber* were nearly all expended in an operation on 29/30 January. Fifteen *Biber* sailed from Hellevoetsluis in bitter conditions. One was sunk following a collision with floating ice while a further five were forced to return with ice damage. One was found beached downstream from Hellevoetsluis after its operator had spent a marathon sixty-four hours at sea looking for a target, while five failed to return. The *K-Verband* bases had not escaped the all-seeing eye of air reconnaissance. On 3 February the *Molch* depot was attacked by Spitfires, while Lancaster bombers of No 617 Squadron attacked the depot at Poortershavn. Although no *Biber* were lost, there was considerable damage to dockside installations which effectively prevented any further *Biber* operations in February. A summary of *K-Verband* operations in January and February shows that during the former month there were fifteen sorties and ten losses and during the latter fourteen sorties and six losses; no successes in terms of Allied ships lost or damaged were achieved in either month.

On 6 March there was a further torpedo accident at Hellevoetsluis when a torpedo was accidentally fired in the basin at Rotterdam. Fourteen *Biber* were sunk and nine more damaged. Nevertheless, on the afternoon of 6 March eleven *Biber* were towed down to Hellevoetsluis. None returned. One was captured by an ML off Breskens, four others were found abandoned along the coastline at North Beveland, Knocke, Domberg and Zeebrugge, one was sunk by gunfire off Westkapelle on 8 March and the other five vanished. There were two further operations in March. On 11/12 March fifteen *Biber* participated in a joint operation with fourteen *Molche*, *S-Boote* and *Linsen*. Again it was a disaster, with thirteen of the *Biber* and nine of the *Molche* failing to return. Of the known losses, an RAF Swordfish sank two off Schouwen on 11th, MLs accounted for four off Westkapelle, shore batteries sank four off Flushing and Breskens on the 12th, a Spitfire sank one off Walcheren on the 12th and the frigate HMS *Retalick* sank one at 0325 on the 13th. On 23/24 March sixteen *Biber* left Hellevoetsluis for the Scheldt. Seven returned, but, as in the earlier operation, no Allied ships had been sunk. As many as four *Biber* were sunk by the *Retalick*, one was found abandoned on Schouwen and one was sunk by a Beaufighter of No 254 Squadron off Goree. The fates of the rest are unknown. Thus in March 1945 there were fifty-six *Biber/Molch* sorties, and 42 of the craft were lost for no result.[18]

By the beginning of April Holland was almost entirely encircled by the British Army and *K-Verband* was finding it increasingly hard to supply the forces based at

Rotterdam, where there were now twenty-four *Biber*, with sixty *Molche* held in reserve at Ammersfoort. There were four more operations in April which involved a total of twenty-four *Biber* and in which nineteen were lost. No Allied vessels were sunk or damaged in these operations.

The *K-Verband* operations in the Low Countries were characterised by considerable bravery and endurance on the part of the *K-Männer* but these virtues were set against a singular lack of success. The reasons for this are legion. Poor equipment and inadequate training account for some of the failures; other factors include bad weather and very aggressive opponents who possessed overwhelming material superiority and who enjoyed complete command of the air.

K-Verband units were also deployed to Denmark and Norway. It was feared that the Allies would use southern Norway or Denmark as a springboard for a drive into the Baltic and Germany's north coast. Accordingly, *Biber* and *Molche* were allocated to this area in some numbers. *Kapitän zur See* Fritz Boehm assumed command of units in Denmark and Norway but his command was later divided between *Kapitän zur See* Duwel in Denmark and *Kapitän zur See* Beck in Norway. The forces deployed in Norway and Denmark were substantial and in November 1944 the proposed organisation was as shown in the accompanying table.

The first *Biber* arrived at Harstad on 22 November 1944 but a proposal to transfer a second flotilla to northern Norway was vetoed by Dönitz on the grounds that the craft were wanted for the defence of the Skagerrak. The organisation was further refined when *Kapitän zur See* Duwel was replaced by *Kapitän zur See* Brandi. The *K-Verband* organisation in Norway was now to consist of one *Biber* flotilla at Kristiansund and one *Marder* flotilla on the Norwegian west coast. Provisional reinforcements included two more flotillas of *Marder*. In the event, all the plans for the deployment of *K-Verband* to Scandinavia came to nothing for the Allies had no need to launch an invasion in that theatre.

However, there was one interesting plan for an attack employing *Biber* based in Norway. The Germans planned to use the *Biber* to attack escorts and merchant ships making up the Russian convoys while they were anchored in Vaenga Bay in the Kola

---

Disposition of K-Verband units, Norway, November 1944

Location	Unit
Northern Norway	60 *Biber*, 60 *Molche*
Southern Norway	60 *Molche*
Denmark	60 *Biber*, 60 *Molche*, 12 Hecht
Heligoland	30 *Molche*
Borkum	30 *Molche*
Ems Estuary	30 *Biber*

Inlet. *K-Flotilla 265* was formed and dispatched to Harstad in Norway in November 1944, although actual planning for the operation had started some time earlier. Like the Japanese, British and Italians, the Germans planned to deliver the *Biber* to the operational area by carrying them on the casings of selected U-boats. Trials had already taken place in the Baltic and the method was found to work. But the Germans failed to learn from the experience of their allies in one respect. The Italians had always carried their *Maiale* in containers secured to the casing to protect the craft from weather damage and to insulate them, to a certain extent, from the vibration of the parent submarine's machinery. The *Kriegsmarine* took no such precautions: the *Biber* would travel on simple chocks mounted on the casing—directly above two large, throbbing diesels in the engine room below.

As might be expected, German preparations were thorough. There was plenty of aerial reconnaissance material available of the area, but in order to obtain precise information arrangements were made to capture some local fishermen, whose subsequent interrogation provided a good deal of data on the defences in the Kola Inlet. The defences were formidable and consisted mainly of patrols by local anti-submarine craft. However, the bay itself was protected by a net and boom on each side of the island of Salny. The date for the operation hinged on the state of the moon. The planners wanted sufficient moonlight to give the operators a sight of their target without necessarily exposing them to discovery. On 8 January 1945, the date favoured by the planners, the tables showed that a half moon would rise at midnight and would still provide enough light by 0300. This was reckoned sufficient to allow the *Biber* to make their run in and carry out the attack.

The likely target for all this endeavour was the Soviet battleship *Archangelsk* (ex-HMS *Royal Sovereign*) but the Germans also hoped that a number of British warships would be present. This presupposed that the attack would be synchronised with the arrival or departure of a convoy. In turn this meant that the operation would have to be launched while the outward convoy was still at sea on its way to Murmansk since the Germans must have realised from aerial reconnaissance that the escorts did not linger in the Kola Inlet—on occasions their stay was no longer than was required to take on ammunition and fuel. There is no evidence that the Germans actually coordinated the operation with convoy operations: that would have required a degree of cooperation with the *Luftwaffe* unfamiliar to the *Kriegsmarine* and would also have risked compromising the operation: it might have been thought suspicious if the *Kriegsmarine* were suddenly interested in warship movements around the Kola Inlet.

The operational plan was for the U-boats to leave Harstad on X–3 and to launch the *Biber* at X–12 hours when forty miles from the enemy anchorage. Thus the *Biber* would have twelve hours to get into position—not long given the underwater speed of the craft. Following the attack, a rendezvous was arranged to seaward of Sjet

Navolok. The *Biber* were to lie on the bottom and make contact with their parent U-boat by SST. The craft would then be abandoned and scuttled and the operators recovered to the parent boat. An alternative rendezvous was arranged for X+1 off the Fischer peninsula. This would have been the more likely pick-up point, for the planners had allowed the *Biber* twelve hours to approach the target but only four to get out. Any operator who missed both rendezvous was instructed to make for Persfjord, ditch his craft and head for Sweden on foot.

Accordingly the three U-boats, *U295*, *U318* and *U716*, departed from Harstad on 5 January, making most of the running on the surface. This was the operation's undoing. In a periodic inspection it was found that in two of the *Biber* the vibration had caused leaks in the petrol pipes. This was easily put right by the U-boat's engineering department and the submarines continued, albeit at a slower speed. However, a subsequent examination of the *Biber* when the force was off the North Cape showed that further leaks in the petrol pipes had developed together with leaks in the stern glands. As a result water had entered the machinery space in some of the craft. Reluctantly the operation was cancelled and the force returned to Harstad. In fact, had the attack gone in on 8 January then the *Biber* operators would have found the anchorage deserted barring local defence craft. Convoy RA.62 had sailed on 10 December 1944 and the next convoy, JW.63, would not arrive until the evening of 8 January. *Archangelsk* herself was safely in the White Sea.

The only other area where *K-Verband* craft were employed was the Mediterranean, where a number of *Marder* and *Molche* units participated in attacks on Allied shipping off Villefranche at the end of 1944. No successes were achieved, and the operations of the *K-Verband* were hopelessly compromised by the confused political situation operating in that theatre at the time.

Chapter 17

Götterdämmerung

Fortunately for us, these damn things arrived too late in the war to do any
damage.—Admiral Sir Charles Little, Commander-in-Chief Portsmouth

On the whole, German midget submarine designs owed more to desperation than to good naval design practice. There was, however, one German design which was a cut above the rest and which, had it not been for the vast array of countermeasures deployed against it, might have made some impact on the course of the war. This craft was the *Seehund* or Type 127 submarine. It was a two-man craft, armed with two torpedoes and capable of extended operations.

The genesis of the *Seehund* (Seal) lay in the recovery of the remains of *X6* and *X7* from the depths of Kaafjord. Subsequently the *Hauptamt Kriegschiffbau*[1] produced a design for a two-man midget submarine designated Type XXVIIA and also known as *Hecht* (Pike). Like the X-Craft, *Hecht* was designed to carry mines to be laid beneath the hulls of enemy ships. However, it was substantially smaller than its British counterpart and differed in a number of significant areas. To begin with, *Hecht*'s designers saw no need for a dual diesel/electric motor propulsion system. It was envisaged that the craft would operate submerged all the time and therefore there was no need for a diesel engine. The powerplant thus consisted of an 8 MAL 210 battery based on five 17T torpedo troughs driving a 12hp AEG torpedo engine. Even so, *Hecht*'s endurance was a paltry 69 nautical miles at 4kt. Since the craft would have to pass through nets and other obstructions it was not originally fitted with hydroplanes or stabilising fins. Instead, adjustable weights on spindles were installed inside the boat. This system proved completely ineffective since the weights could not be moved quickly enough in an emergency to affect the trim of the boat. They were subsequently replaced by hydroplanes and stabilising fins. Even so, submerged control was very poor. Since *Hecht* would be operating dived, it was not fitted with ballast tanks, but two compensating tanks gave the craft sufficient buoyancy to lie awash on the surface.

Although *Hecht* was designed to carry an explosive charge, Dönitz insisted that a torpedo be fitted so that attacks could be mounted on shipping in coastal waters. *Hecht*'s lack of buoyancy meant that only torpedoes without negative buoyancy could be used and these were of a relatively short range. Accordingly, the craft was fitted for both mine- and torpedo-carrying. If a torpedo was carried then a further three battery troughs could be fitted. Externally *Hecht* resembled a British Welman.

In the nose of the craft was the detachable mine. In the forward section was the battery and a gyro compass. *Hecht* was the first German midget submarine to be fitted with a gyro compass, which was deemed essential for navigation if the craft were to be spending so much time submerged. Behind the battery was the control compartment with seats for the two-man crew. Having a crew of two was another new departure for the Germans. The pair could offer each other mutual support and share the watchkeeping/routine maintenance load. The crew sat in seats arranged fore and aft on the centreline, with the engineer sitting forward and the commander aft. The latter was provided with a simple periscope and a plexiglass dome for navigation purposes. Further aft was the electric motor.

On 18 January 1944 Dönitz discussed the new design with Hitler, who expressed his approval for the craft. On 9 March a contract was placed with Germaniawerft for the construction of a prototype, followed by another for 52 boats on 28 March. The boats were built between May and August 1944; none saw active service, but all were employed in the training role for *Seehund* crews.

At the same time as the orders were being placed, numerous variations of the *Hecht* were under consideration. The first was the Type XXVIIB, which had increased range, an armament of two torpedoes and dual diesel/electric propulsion. The initial design was complete by the end of June 1944 and showed a craft which strongly resembled *Hecht* in many ways but which was fitted with a ship-shaped casing, for better seakeeping while on the surface, and with saddle tanks. More room was created inside the craft by placing the battery troughs in the keel, while the two torpedoes were slung externally in recesses in the hull. A 22hp diesel was fitted for surface travel and it was estimated that this would provide a speed of 5.5kt, with a submerged speed of 6.9kt.

A variant of the Type XXVIIB was the *Klein U-boot K*, which differed from the former only in that it was powered by a closed-cycle engine. The proposal came from Chief Naval Construction Adviser Kurzak, who was the *Kriegsmarine*'s representative for closed-cycle propulsion at Germaniawerft. The boat was powered by a 95hp diesel engine commonly used in the *Kriegsmarine*'s small boats and therefore available in quantity. The engine ran off oxygen, 1,250 litres of which were stored in the boat's keel at four times atmospheric pressure. It was anticipated that the boat would have a maximum submerged speed of 11–12kt and a range of 70 miles at that speed; for long-range travel at a reduced speed of 7kt, the boat would have a range of 150 miles. Kurzak presented his design at a meeting chaired by Vice-Admiral Heye on 21 May 1944 and was requested to develop a closed-cycle engine appropriate to such a submarine.

Kurzak's proposal had a considerable influence on the final variant of the Type XXVII, which emerged as the Type XXVIIB5, better known as the *Seehund*. *Seehund* had a boat-shaped hull with a small raised platform amidships containing

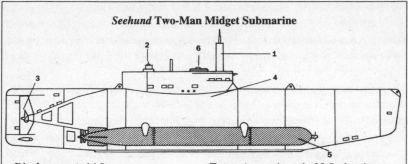

Seehund Two-Man Midget Submarine

Displacement: 14.9 tons
Length: 11.9m
Beam: 1.7m
Propulsion: 1 x 60bhp diesel engine
with one 25hp electric motor
Fuel capacity: 0.5 tons
Speed (surfaced): 7.7kt
Speed (submerged): 6kt
Range (surfaced): 270nm at 7kt
Speed (submerged): 63nm at 3kt
Armament: Two 53cm torpedoes
Crew: 2
Number delivered: 285

Fates: Approximately 35 *Seehunde* are
believed to have been lost while on
patrol to enemy action or as a result of
bad weather and/or accident.

Key to drawing:
1. Housing for periscope
2. Magnetic compass
3. Single propeller and hydroplanes.
4. 'Saddle tanks' for additional fuel.
5 . G7e torpedo (equivalent on port
side)
6. Conning tower hatch

the air intake mast, the magnetic compass, the periscope and a glass dome for observation purposes (which safely withstood pressures down to 45m). The casing contained the ballast tanks and a free-flooding compartment forward. Inside the pressure hull the layout resembled that of the *Hecht*. In the forward part were four of the 7 Mal 210 battery troughs, the other four being stowed in the keel. In the centre of the craft was the control compartment with seats for the two operators. The engineer handled the controls and fired the torpedoes on the word of the commander. During the attack the boat was kept at periscope depth and 'talked' on to the target by the commander. The fixed 10m periscope was of excellent design and incorporated lenses which allowed the commander to search the skies before surfacing. The armament of the *Seehund* comprised the standard two G7e torpedoes slung in recesses under the hull. This arrangement meant that the boat had to be removed from the water before the weapons could be loaded—a tiresome procedure at the best of times.[2]

In the after part of the boat were the diesel and electric motors. *Seehunde* were powered by a 60hp Büssing diesel with a 25hp AEG electric motor for submerged drive. This gave an endurance of 270 nautical miles on the surface at 7kt. If exterior fuel tanks were used, the range rose to as much as 500 nautical miles—although the crew's efficiency during such a long passage would have been doubtful. Submerged endurance was 63 nautical miles at 3kt. These figures were rather disappointing and it was apparent that the design of the hull, particularly when the torpedoes were carried, exerted considerable resistance.

The first contract for *Seehund* construction was placed on 30 July 1944. Enthusiasm for the craft was so great that most of the contracts and hull numbers had been allocated before the design was complete. The Ministerial Programme of June 1944 envisaged a total of one thousand Type XXVII boats in service. Germaniawerft and Schichau at Elbing were to build 25 and 45 boats per month respectively. Other centres involved in *Seehund* production were CRD at Monfalcone on the Adriatic and Klockner-Humbolt-Deutz at Ulm. Like so many other schemes in the Third Reich, reality fell far short of expectations. Dönitz would not consent to the production of the Type XXIII U-boat being held up for *Seehund* construction while raw material shortages, labour difficulties, transport problems and conflicting priorities in Germany's crumbling war economy all combined to reduce *Seehund* production. In the event, production was concentrated at the Konrad bunker under Germaniawerft in Kiel which was no longer required for building Type XXI or Type XXIII submarines. A total of 285 units were actually built: they were allocated the numbers *U5501* to *U6531* and the production schedule comprised three craft in September 1944, 35 in October, 61 in November and 70 in December, with 35 in January 1945, 27 in February, 46 in March and 8 in April.

While the design process was well in hand Chief Naval Construction Adviser Kurzak proposed the incorporation of a closed-cycle powerplant into the design to achieve significant savings in volume and weight. The design of this unit was similar to that for the *Klein U-boot K* described earlier but of slightly larger dimensions. The engine, the Daimler Benz OM67/4 of 100hp (with an electric motor for silent creep speed), was to be mounted on a common frame which could be simply inserted into the stern section for easy access and secured by a few screws. Significantly, attention was paid to reducing engine noise as much as possible. The common frame was mounted on an elastic bedding using four rubber buffers at the edges. It was hoped that noise reduction measures would so effective that the silent creep speed electric motor could be dispensed with altogether, thus making the powerplant extremely simple and light. The closed-cycle *Seehund* would have a submerged range of 69 nautical miles at 11.5kt or 150 nautical miles at 7.25kt.

Development of the closed-cycle *Seehund* was carried out by Ingenieurbüro Gluckauf in Blankenburg and was given the designation Type 227. Contracts for prototypes were awarded to Germaniawerft in Kiel and to Schichau at Elbing and by May 1945 a contract for three operational models, *U5188* to *U5190*, had been awarded to Germaniawerft. These models would have used the standard *Seehund*

Comparison of Type XXVII, *Seehund* and Type 227

	Type XXVII	Seehund	Type 227
Displacement	11.8 tons	14.9 tons	17 tons
Length	10.4m	11.9m	13.6m
Beam	1.7m	1.7m	1.7m
Propulsion	1 x 12hp ET	1 x 60hp D	1 x 100hp diesel
		1 x 25hp E	1 x 25hp electric
Fuel capacity	N/A	0.5 tons	0.6 tons + 0.72 tons O_2
Speed (surface/dived)	–/6kt	7.7/6kt	8/10.3kt
Range (surface)	–	270nm at 7kt	340nm at 8kt
Range (dived)	38 at 4kt	63nm at 3kt	71nm at 10kt
Torpedoes	1	2	2
Mines	1	0	0
Crew	2	2	2

powerplant converted to closed-cycle operation on the grounds that Daimler-Benz engines were not available in any quantity. Tests showed that the Büssing engine could be successfully converted, but the war ended before the craft could go into production. The accompanying table[3] compares the original Type XXVII, the *Seehund* and the Type 227.

The *Seehund* was the most sophisticated of all the midgets which went into production for the *Kriegsmarine*. From the Allies' perspective, its small size made it almost impossible for asdic to get a return off her hull while her very quiet slow speed made her almost impervious to hydrophone detection.

Oberfähnrich Klaus Goetsch was attending the U-boat school in Murwik in October 1944 when his training was abruptly terminated and he was assigned to the *K-Verband*. The nature of his new appointment was a mystery to him: he subsecquently confessed, 'I think that when I joined the *K-Verband*, they were better known to the English than they were to me!'[4] Goetsch was paired with a young *Maschinemaat* who was a first-class engineer and who had been a fitter with Deutsche Reichsbahn before he had been called up for the Navy. Their training lasted eight weeks, culminating in a 2½-day voyage in the Baltic. The training was hard and Goetsch estimated that during his time at Neustadt some twenty crews were lost in accidents. Goetsch and his engineer nearly found themselves on the Roll of Honour when their *Seehund* refused to surface. The battery was low, so the two men, working in near darkness, cross-connected the diesel exhaust to the ballast tanks and started the diesel to drive the boat upwards. It was desperate gamble: the diesel had to put enough gas into the tanks to lift the boat before it consumed all the air inside. As soon as the casing was awash, the two men scrambled up and out to safety. His training complete, Goetsch was posted to Heligoland, where, to his chagrin, he saw no action at all until Germany surrendered.

It was December 1944 before the first *Seehund* were dispatched to Ijmuiden in the Netherlands. Six were sent by road on 24 December followed by a further eighteen, so that by the end of the month there were 24. Their operational début was on New Year's Day 1945 when seventeen sailed to attack an Allied convoy off the Kwinte Bank. Seven were later found beached and two returned. Of the remainder, the destroyer HMS *Cowdray* and frigate HMS *Ekins* accounted for one each, another was found abandoned at Domberg while a fourth was found drifting, without a crew, by an MTB. The remaining four disappeared, probably victims of bad weather. The sole gain from the operation was the sinking of the trawler *Hayburn Wyke*. It was not an auspicious start, but it was better than anything the other *K-Verband* units had achieved. Bad weather interfered with further operations throughout January 1945. A sortie on 3 January had to be called off for this reason, as did another on the 6th. However, on 10 January five *Seehunde* were dispatched to the Kentish coast off Margate. Only one of the ten reached the operational area but this craft later returned to base with her torpedoes intact. Two days later all operations were suspended on account of the weather.

By 20 January reinforcements had brought the number of *Seehunde* available back to 26. On 21 January ten were dispatched to Ramsgate, the North Foreland and the swept channel off Lowestoft. Of these boats, seven returned with defects and two returned having sighted nothing. The story of the other craft constitutes something of an epic. This boat suffered a compass failure, and after attacking a ship in the Thames Estuary on 22 January it was driven northwards by the tides until by the 24th it was off Lowestoft, where it was attacked by *ML153* but managed to escape. However, in so doing the craft had drifted even further to the north and was now off Great Yarmouth—unknown to the crew. When they tried to set course to the east and home, the *Seehund* went aground on Scroby Sands, where it remained for two and a half days. Eventually the exhausted crew fired distress flares and were taken off by the Trinity House tender *Beacon*. This episode illustrates the considerable fortitude displayed by *Seehund* crews. The fact that the craft was found so far from home was not lost on the Admiralty. The final *Seehund* sortie in January 1945 was on the 29th, when ten boats were dispatched from Ijmuiden, five for the area off Margate and the remainder for the South Falls. Only two reached their operational area, the rest returning with mechanical problems.

The *Seehunde* faired a little better in February. Operations on the 5th and 10th were unsuccessful but on the 12th five boats were sent out to the North Foreland. On 15 February the 2,628-ton Dutch tanker *Liseta* was damaged off the North Foreland while in convoy TAM.80. At least two boats were lost in these sorties and several were beached but recovered. A new departure for the *Seehunde* was an attempt to use them in the Scheldt Estuary in a combined operation with *Linsen*. On 16 February four *Seehunde* sailed for the Scheldt, followed by fifteen *Linsen* that night. The operation was a failure: of the four *Seehunde*, two vanished without trace, one beached without having made an attack while the last beached after an abortive attack on a small convoy of landing craft. Since the *Seehunde* were no more successful in inland waters than the *Biber* or *Molche*, they were redeployed back to open waters. On 20 February three boats sailed for Ramsgate and on the 21st four sailed for the South Falls, followed by a fifth on the 23rd. This group had some results: on 22 February LST364 was sunk while in convoy TAM.87 and the cable ship *Alert* was sunk off Ramsgate on 24 February. All eight craft returned, one of them surviving an attack from Beaufighter 'J' of No 254 Squadron east of Orfordness. A summary of *Seehunde* operations in January/February 1945 shows, for January, 44 sorties for ten losses, with one ship of 324 tons sunk, and, for February, 33 sorties for four losses, with two ships totalling 3,691 tons sunk and one of 2,628 tons damaged.

In March 1945 there were a total of twenty-nine *Seehunde* sorties, from which nine boats failed to return. MTBs sank two and the frigate *Torrington* another, three were claimed by aircraft, one was sunk by HMS *Puffin* and the fates of the other two are unknown. The sinking by *Puffin* was a Pyrrhic victory: on 26 March the *Puffin* rammed the *Seehund* off Lowestoft, but in the collision both of the *Seehund*'s torpedoes exploded and the British patrol vessel was so badly damaged that she was not repaired. However, three ships totalling 5,267 tons were sunk: the 2,878-ton *Tauber Park* on 13 March off Southwold, the 833-ton *Jim* on 30 March south-east of Orfordness and the 1,556-ton *Newlands* on the 26th off the North Foreland.

In April the *Seehunde* were the only *K-Verband* craft which could make the journey from Germany to Holland by sea, now that the latter country was virtually encircled by Allied armies. The number of boats at Ijmuiden was 29 on 8 April, of which only about half were operational. Four more *Seehunde* arrived from Wilhelmshaven on 20 April and fourteen more had arrived by 1 May together with two more from Heligoland. In April 36 sorties were made for the loss of three craft. In return, *Seehunde* succeeded in torpedoing the cable ship *Monarch* on 16 April. Nine *Seehunde* operated in the Scheldt, where they sank the 800-ton US Navy oiler *Y17* on X for the loss of three of their number. From 17 April seventeen boats were ordered to the Dover–Dungeness area, where one sank the 7,219-ton *Samida* on 9 April and damaged the 7,176-ton *Solomon Juneau* on the same day, both ships being in convoy TBC.123. However *ML102* accounted for one *Seehund* and Beaufighter 'W' of No 254 Squadron another, while a third ran ashore east of Calais. On 11 April another *Seehund* attacked UC.63B east of Dungeness and damaged the 8,580-ton *Port Wyndham*. However, this craft may have been the one sunk by *MTB632* later that day. Yet another *Seehund* was sunk off the Hook of Holland on 12 April and a third went down on 13 April to a Barracuda of 810 Naval Air Squadron in the same area. *Seehund* operations ceased on 28 April but the craft continued to be employed running supplies into Dunkirk. Four boats made the increasingly perilous voyage before the German capitulation.

A summary of *Seehund* operations shows that there were, in all, 142 sorties, which resulted in the loss of nine ships totalling 18,451 tons sunk and three ships of 18,354 tons damaged. Against this, 35 craft were lost. This is a relatively low figure, especially considering that a score of these losses were due to bad weather. Had their crews been better trained and more experienced, a far higher total of shipping would have been sunk. As one commentator has concluded,

> Fortunately for the Allies, the Type XXVIIB came too late. A little earlier and Allied ships and landing craft might have suffered disastrously from the attentions of the *Seehund*: anti-submarine defences would have been swamped if large groups had been able to make coordinated attacks. It has to be asked whether the situation would be markedly different today.[5]

In retrospect, it has to be said that all the effort expended by the Germans on the *K-Verband* was wasted: it was never justified in terms of the results achieved. The sheer loss of life in these operations can only be compared with that of the Japanese *Kamikazes*. Any better results could hardly be expected, given the hurried design of the various craft, the hasty training of their operators and the nature of Allied countermeasures. Their sole success (if such a term can be used) is in the huge numbers of Allied forces deployed to guard against the menace posed by the *K-Verband*: it is estimated that over 500 ships and 1,000 aircraft were specifically tasked with hunting German midget craft,[6] and, obviously, these units and the manpower could have been employed elsewhere. However, playing the part of the 'fleet in being' was no substitute for sinking Allied ships. The following comments on the *Biber* by one perceptive observer are an epitaph for all the *K-Verband* weapons:

> The failure of the *Biber* and, in spite of the courage displayed, of the K-Force, reflects the failure of the *Kriegsmarine*'s, and ultimately Nazi Germany's, ability to wage war successfully at sea. The organisation of the K-Force came at a time when the Third Reich, through its flawed strategy, was being assailed on three fronts—in Italy, in Russia and from the air—by a combination of the most powerful nations on earth. K-Force and the remaining ships of the *Kriegsmarine* failed to stop the invasion of Normandy in June 1944 and the opening of a fourth front.
>
> The creation of K-Force was a desperate and unsuccessful bid to challenge the Anglo-American invasion fleet . . . the failure of the *Biber* programme and others of Nazi Germany's midget submarine projects reflects the failure of the Third Reich's naval strategy.[7]

Chapter 18

The Future

More than most professions, the military is forced to depend on intelligent interpretations of the past for signposts charting the future.—General Douglas MacArthur

What has been the place of the midget submarine in the navies of the post-war world? Of the major powers, Britain, the United States, France and the Soviet Union have all investigated and employed such craft since 1945, although now only Russia (ex-USSR) is believed to be active in this field. There has been, however, considerable interest shown in midget submarines by a number of 'second world' countries, including Yugoslavia, Taiwan, Sweden, Colombia, Pakistan, Iran, Iraq, Libya and North Korea. The four last-named regimes are particularly unsavoury, and their possession of midget submarines could be said to pose a threat to the Free World.

One aspect of midget submarine operations which has survived is *Maiale* and Chariots, now known as Swimmer Delivery Vehicles (SDV). These are now far more sophisticated than the weapons in which Greenland and Visintini went to war but the basic principles are the same. They can be carried by submarines: a number of former SSBNs 'disarmed' by the SALT and START agreements are enjoying a new lease of life as assault swimmer carriers. The USS *Sam Houston* (SSBN-609) and *John Marshall* (SSBN-611) of the *Ethan Allen* class were converted to carry 67 SEAL swimmers in double dry-deck shelters fixed to their casings when it proved impossible to replace their Polaris missiles with the larger Poseidon system. Conversion started in 1984, but the boats were decommissioned in September and November 1991 respectively. They were replaced by the *Kamehameha* (SSBN-642) and the *James Polk* (SSBN-645) of the *Lafayette* class. On the Soviet side, a number of Project 667A boats (better known in the West as the 'Yankee' SSBN) have been refitted for other duties by having their central sections (containing the sixteen SS-N-4 missiles) removed and the two halves of each boat being welded together. Nearly all modern submarines have escape chambers which can easily double as exit/re-entry chambers for frogmen, while some 'conventional' submarines, such as the British *Otus* and *Opossum*, are fitted with five-man exit/re-entry chambers built into their fins. Whatever the refinements made to the *matériel* in modern submarines, the principles are the same as those under which the *Decima Mas* operated so successfully. There is nothing very new in the midget submarine world that has not been done before.

In 1945 Britain possessed the largest midget submarine 'fleet', with five X20-series craft, six XT-series training craft and ten XE-series craft. The drastic reduction of the Royal Navy in the immediate post-war period saw this fleet reduced to four XE-Craft, *XE7*, *XE8*, *XE9* and *XE12*. The craft were employed until 1953, when they were sold for breaking up. During this period they spent most of their time testing harbour defences and participating in exercises against ships of the Home Fleet. In 1950 *XE7* went across the Atlantic to the United States to show off her capabilities: her performance was largely responsible for America's belated entry into this field. The four XEs had shown themselves so useful that in September 1951 four replacement boats were ordered, known as the *X51* class. These were slightly larger than the XE series (and were less manoeuvrable) but in all other significant respects they were virtually identical. For the first time these craft were given names: *X51* was *Stickleback*, *X52* was *Shrimp*, *X53* was *Sprat* while *X54* was *Minnow*.

The role of the *X51* series remained very much that of the XEs—harbour penetration trials and exercises. However, there was one role planned for them which would have propelled these little craft into the realm of strategic forces. The British were already aware of the potential threat posed by Soviet midget submarines: after all, it was known that the Soviets had captured a number of German and Italian vessels of this type. It was to guard against such a threat that the British designed and built the 'Ford' class[1] seaward defence vessels which carried such a hefty ASW armament and sonar suite for small craft. Now they sought to use the same weapon against the Soviets.

In 1954 the Royal Navy conceived the idea that a nuclear weapon could be laid by an *X51* in the approaches to Soviet naval bases such as Kronstadt in the Baltic and the Kola Inlet. The weapon was based on the payload of the RAF's Mk 1 'Blue Danube' 10,000lb, 20-kiloton bomb, but the following year this was abandoned in favour of the smaller 2,000lb 'Red Beard'. The weapon was given the intriguing name of 'Cudgel' and could be laid at depths down to 300ft (90m). The timer allowed settings at half-hour intervals from thirty minutes to twelve hours after laying, or at twelve-hour intervals from twelve hours to seven days after laying. A small nuclear weapon detonated in the Kola Inlet would destroy the entire base. Such an attack was an attractive form of anti-submarine warfare—the so-called 'attack at source'. The option was particularly appealing in view of the fact that a whole new generation of Soviet submarines like the 'Whiskey', based on the wartime German Type XXI design, threatened to negate more conventional forms of ASW. Eventually the project proved unaffordable because of the shortage of fissile material and 'Cudgel' was cancelled some time between late 1955 and late 1956. As a weapon it was an ingenious concept but one that was supplanted by the development of the submarine-launched ballistic missile—a weapon system which offered the ability to inflict massive destruction without risking one's own forces in the process.

Most of the activities of the *X51* series are still covered by the provisions of the Official Secrets Act, but there are a number of references[2] to an operation conducted in 1955 when an X-Craft was involved in an attempt to measure the diameter of the propellers of the new Soviet cruiser *Ordzhonikidze*, the design of which was of inordinate interest to naval intelligence: the information thus gained could be used to identify targets using the newly established bottom-arrays of the Sound Surveillance System (SOSUS). The details of this unusual operation are still shrouded in secrecy, but at least one X-Craft was sent to Kronstadt in order to release a diver to measure the cruiser's propellers. However, the diver found the harbour defences too tough to penetrate and the operation was aborted. A year later Commander 'Buster' Crabbe disappeared while attempting to do the same thing while *Ordzhonikidze* was in Portsmouth harbour on the occasion of Nikita Khruschev's visit to Britain. One *X51* class submarine commander, commenting on this rumour, wrote:

> To take (i.e. tow) an X-Craft to Kronstadt covertly, through the narrow (and shallow) entrance to the Baltic, would be tricky to say the least. Moreover, the tow would be extremely lengthy. The risks for a very, very iffy peacetime/cold war operation would, in my view, have been unacceptable.[3]

Considering the propaganda success the Soviets enjoyed out of capturing Gary Powers and the remnants of his U-2 spyplane, the capture of an X-Craft would have had unimaginable political repercussions. One chance the *X51*s did have of seeing action was in the 1956 Suez Crisis, when it was proposed that X-Craft should be used to destroy the blockships which Colonel Nasser had placed across the Canal. However, the government of the day refused to sanction the inclusion of the X-Craft in the Suez Campaign on the grounds that it was 'too much like real war'[4]—a strange judgement considering the military force employed by Britain and France at the time.

The British X-Craft unit was disbanded in 1958. Cynics suggested that Flag Officer Submarines had been ordered to cut his fleet by four hulls and disposing of the four *X51*s was the easiest way of doing that. The reality is more complex: X-Craft took considerable risks in their peacetime training which horrified the staff. One X-Craft commander commented:

> There may have been another reason for their sudden disappearance. Midget submarine exercises and evaluations tended to be frankly hairy—happily hairy, but hairy nonetheless. The sort of training they were bound to undertake in order to maintain a realistic wartime efficiency in peacetime was liable to attract the kind of publicity that naval officers concerned with PR have always tried to avoid.[5]

At the time the Royal Navy was run largely by officers who had served with the aircraft carrier squadrons of the British Pacific Fleet in the last days of the war and who were obsessed with building and operating fleet carriers in a vain and hideously expensive attempt to keep up with Britain's transatlantic allies. This course of action was one that the country could not afford, and eventually, in 1966, the Labour government took the courageous decision to cancel the aircraft carrier programme. In the meantime four useful and extremely potent craft had been deleted from the Royal Navy's order of battle.[6] The scrapping of the four *X51*s went virtually unnoticed and the Royal Navy's involvement with midget submarines was over. There was one survivor. *Stickleback* was sold to Sweden and renamed *Spiggen*. Under Swedish colours she played the role of a 'loyal opposition' at a time when the Swedes were becoming concerned about Soviet incursions in their waters. She was stricken in 1970 and in 1977 she returned to Britain for preservation and display.

Another minor participant in the midget submarine field at this time was France. The French took over four *Seehunde* after the war and ran them until 1955. It is doubtful whether the French were serious players: more likely the four craft were regarded as visible reminders that France had emerged on the winning side in the Second World War. Across the Atlantic, it was not until the 1950s that the United States Navy showed an interest in midget submarines. During the Second World War the Americans had shown a brief interest in British Chariots and X-Craft but had not undertaken any work of their own in this field. The innate conservatism of the US naval establishment is one reason why midget submarines were not given more attention, but a more important reason is that the Americans had no need for such a craft. The immense material superiority which the United States enjoyed over Japan meant that the country did not have to resort to weapons of subterfuge in order to achieve its aims.

It was external stimulus, the threat posed by the Soviet Navy in the Cold War, that pushed the Americans into midget submarine development. The fact that the US Navy took over port defence from the US Army in the post-war period is also of relevance here. The Soviets had captured a number of German and Italian craft and were also probably *au fait* with British developments through more nefarious methods. By 1949 there were reliable reports that the Soviet Navy was regularly employing midget submarines in Fleet exercises. These developments were of some concern in the West. The vision of a swarm of Soviet midgets attacking the US Fleet at its bases, or mining convoy ports on both sides of the Atlantic, was not one on which Western planners wished to dwell. Furthermore, the development of nuclear weapons added an unpleasant dimension to this scenario. It was to guard against such a threat that the 'Ford' class seaward defence vessels were built by the Royal Navy and given a fairly hefty ASW armament and sonar suite.

A US midget submarine was therefore required for two purposes, firstly to test harbour defences and indicate methods of improving them, and secondly as a means of attack. Midget submarines possessed the potential to attack the Soviet submarine fleet at its base in ports like Severomorsk and Polyarnoe in the Kola Inlet. A working party to investigate midget submarine developments was appointed in the spring of 1949 on the orders of Rear-Admiral C. B. Momsen, the ACNO (Undersea Warfare).

The first American proposal was from Commander R. H. Bass USN, on SUBLANT's staff, for a midget submarine which could be built cheaply and in sufficient numbers to lay a barrier in a suitable 'choke point' such as the Greenland–Iceland–United Kingdom (GIUK) gap. The craft could either be of a 'pursuit' type, which could chase after a Soviet submarine crossing the barrier, or an 'ambush' type, one that would quietly lie in wait. After much discussion, including a presentation from the founder of the X-Craft, Commander 'Crom' Varley RN, the American requirements grew into two distinct craft. The first was for an 'attack' midget similar to that proposed by Commander Bass and the second for a craft designed for harbour penetration and equipped with Underwater Demolition Team (UDT) facilities. These were designated Type I and Type II respectively, with priority being given to the Type I design. Sensibly the Americans ruled out any further development of human torpedo designs such as the ill-fated *Neger* and her consorts.

The Type I would be powered by conventional diesel/electric powerplant though with a very quiet motor. She would be equipped with hydrophones and armed with torpedoes—the Mk 27 Mod 4. She would be expected to remain at sea for at least seven days and should be capable of diving to at least 300ft. Delivery to and from the operational area would be by means of a 'mother' submarine. All this was fairly conventional stuff. However, Bass was keen to harness new technology in the development of his submarine. At the same time that the Type I design was being evaluated, the US Navy was experimenting with a new hull form for submarines, the 'teardrop', which would be first employed in the USS *Albacore*. It was proposed to use this hull form, with its low resistance, in the new midget. Bass was also eager to employ anti-radar and anti-sonar coatings on the submarine's hull and to explore the use of a closed-cycle propulsion system for faster speed and deeper diving. He moreover envisaged new roles for the craft, particularly in the field of missile guidance, either directly or by planting a beacon. He even envisaged the use of the craft for rescue purposes from a submarine in trouble in very deep water. Of all Bass's hopes this last was the only one to come to fruition: unknowingly, he had conceived what ultimately emerged as the Deep Submergence Rescue Vehicle (DSRV).

By 29 July 1949 the Bureau of Ships (BuShips) had reported that the design was practical. It was certainly innovative: details of the completed sketch design are given in the accompanying table. For easy construction by firms which had never previously handled submarine contracts, the hull would be built in sections from $^3/$ $_8$in HTS. The hull contained a single operating compartment and an escape trunk capable of taking two men at a time. All fuel and ballast tanks were to be internal. Simplicity was the keynote of the design in order to utilise as many commercially available components as possible so that the craft could be built in large numbers. The diesel engine, batteries and hydraulic plant were all commercial items; the main

---

Specifications for US Type 1 Midget Submarine (Sketch Design)

Length: 55ft

Beam: 10ft

Draught (mean): 8ft 6in

Displacement: 73/84 tons

Propulsion: 1 x 180bhp 6-71 diesel; 1 x 110/125shp electric motor

Battery: 64 Type MKH 33 truck battery cells

Speed (surfaced): 7kt (8.5kt if schnorkelling)

Speed (submerged): 14kt at the 0.5hr rate

Endurance (surfaced): 1,900nm at 6kt

Endurance (schnorkelling): 2,000nm at 7kt

Endurance (battery): 100nm at 3kt

Diving depth: 225ft

Complement: 3 officers and men

---

motor was not, but there was nothing special about its design. The schnorkel was adapted from an existing design and the periscopes would be of a design similar to that fitted in the German *Seehund*.[7]

Using the teardrop hull would mean that the Type I would be the first American submarine to be faster submerged than on the surface. The hull form was subsequently modified to incorporate two torpedo tubes. As in the Japanese *Ko-Hyoteki*, the tubes were loaded externally. Above each tube was the WRT[8] tank, positioned thus so that the tubes could be flooded by gravity. The torpedo carried, the Mk 27 Mod 4, would be effective against targets out to a range of 4,500yd sailing at a speed of anything between 7 and 15kt. The fact that this was a homing torpedo would reduce the need for complicated fire control systems in the submarine and thus simplify the overall design. The main sensor would be a low-frequency, directional, passive sonar fitted to the craft's bridge fairwater. By 'leading the bearing' the craft could manoeuvre close to the track of the target and then use a burst of high speed to close the range and fire. Simple time motion analysis might even permit a straight gyro shot. The craft was too big to be carried on a 'mother' submarine as Bass had proposed. Instead, the Americans adopted the British practice of towing the midget to the operational area, and of having two crews for each boat, a passage crew and an operational crew. It was estimated that the operational crew could spend ten days on patrol before being recovered. The working party recommended that four such craft be included in the new construction programme for Fiscal Year 1952 and in November 1949 BuShips proposed that six be built (along with six of the Type II) at a total cost of $5.6 million. The formal requirement for the Type I was issued in February 1950 but by April it had been cancelled.

The Type I was an innovative, almost exciting design. The prospect of a swarm of such craft being released into a choke-point is certainly one of the more interesting 'what if?' scenarios of modern naval history. However, it must be mentioned that although the craft was technically sound, conditions for the three-man crew would have been extremely tough. Conditions in British X-Craft were abominable and they were engaged in comparatively short operations. A ten-day patrol in some of the world's most rugged environments (like the GIUK gap) would have taxed the crew's endurance to the limit. Operational effectiveness would certainly have been reduced after a few days.

The cancellation of the Type I left only the Type II in the programme. This was smaller than the Type I and closer to the British X-Craft in concept. The Type II did not need any of the sophisticated sensors carried by the Type I, merely a sonar comparable to that fitted in the X-Craft which was sufficient to detect and evade enemy ships. This design appeared in the FY52 programme as SCB65 and was named *X1*. The initial design called for standard diesel/electric propulsion in a boat which was slightly smaller and rather slower than the British X-Craft. When the design was nearly complete BuShips let the design contract to the Fairchild Engine Division of the Fairchild Airplane and Engine Corporation to develop an alternative.

Fairchild proposed a design using a dual-cycle diesel which would function normally on the surface but would burn a mixture of diesel and hydrogen peroxide when the boat was dived. A small motor generator and battery would power the boat's services and provide some measure of control, when it was being towed submerged. Fairchild submitted their proposal in October 1952. Against the original BuShips design the Fairchild craft offered a higher submerged speed and greater submerged endurance. The Fairchild design was the one selected.

X1's keel was laid on 8 June 1954 and the craft was launched at Oyster Bay, Long Island, on 7 September 1955. She was provisionally accepted into the US Navy on 7 October 1955. *X1*'s design characteristics are shown in the table.[9] The hull was originally built in three sections, bow, hull and tail. The bow section, which joined the hull section at Frame 7, contained the forward trim tank, main ballast tank, towing cable release gear and hydrogen peroxide stowage and enclosure tank. The hull section, running from frames 7 to 28, contained the control compartment. Two operator seats were located aft, with powerplant instrumentation on the port side and ship control on the starboard. Plane and rudder controls were duplicated on both panels so that *X1* could be controlled from either. The hull section also contained No 2 ballast tank, which doubled as an exit/re-entry chamber. The capsule containing the powerplant was suspended by four dual cantilever mounts located just forward of the after bolting ring. Nearly all the boat's machinery was concentrated in this capsule, the exceptions being the battery, the ventilation system, the peroxide stowage and delivery system and the fuel system. The tail section contained the main shaft and propeller, the after trim tank, No 3 main ballast tank and the stern planes. An addition to the design was a four-foot section containing the 1,700lb XT-20A mine which was fitted with either a magnetic or a time-delay fuse. The section was inserted in between

---

Design Characteristics of US *X1* Midget Submarine

Length (oa): 49ft 7in (plus 4ft mine section)
Beam (extreme): 7ft
Draught (fwd): 5ft 8¹/₂in
Draught (aft): 6ft 9in
Displacement (dry): 26.3 tons

Displacement (surface, diving trim): 31.5 tons
Displacement (dived): 36.3 tons
Armament: XT-20A 1,700lb explosive charge
Crew: 4

---

the bow and hull sections. The mine rested on support arms above a hatch in the bottom of the craft. The support arms were geared to the hatch opening apparatus, so that when the hatch was opened the arms would rotate away and the mine fall free. Carrying the mine internally was a great advantage over the British system of having external charges: there would be no flooding of the charge which had bedevilled *X8* during Operation 'Source'. However, the 'X' designation to the weapon indicates that it was experimental only. There are no records of the delivery system nor of a dummy weapon undergoing trials.

No sooner had *X1* been completed than she was placed in a state of restricted availability for correction of faults found by the Board of Inspection and Survey. This period lasted from 24 May 1956 until 2 December 1957, when X1 was placed 'Out of Service—In Reserve'. The problems were largely centred around the powerplant.[10] Richard Boyle, *X1*'s officer-in-charge, subsequently wrote:

> I spent a lot of time worrying about a crankcase explosion and the front end blew off. The clutch was so unreliable, we weren't sure if we ordered a backing bell coming in for a landing. The exhaust compressors and peroxide pump were poorly designed.[11]

While *X1* was alongside at Portsmouth, New Hampshire, the bow section was blown off and sank some fifteen feet ahead of the rest of the hull, which remained afloat.

This marked the end of peroxide diesel propulsion in the US Navy. As Richard Boyle later remarked, 'high concentration hydrogen peroxide has no place on a fighting ship'.[12] *X1* was subsequently rebuilt with a standard diesel-electric powerplant and was employed as a trials vehicle in support of various research and development projects. There was no further mention of her as a fighting warship and with her demise went the American midget submarine programme. Even before the explosion, the enthusiasm for midget submarines in the USN had faded: the advent of the nuclear-powered submarine with its almost limitless operational capabilities was far more attractive to the American submarine community.

In the 1960s there was brief flurry of interest with the design and testing of *Moray*, which was basically a manned torpedo. One, TV-1A, was built, but the idea was dropped. It was realised that *Moray* was but one part of an extremely complex weapon system and would require considerable assistance from other elements, particular in the field of target acquisition, to be really effective. Basically *Moray* was little more than a manned and more expensive version of the Mk 48 torpedo which was just coming into service and as such compared unfavourably with the 'unmanned' model.

The Soviet Union has been the most active naval power in the midget submarine field. In 1945 the Soviets inherited a mass of captured German and Italian data and *matériel* to which must be added any information obtained by more covert means from Britain and the United States. Virtually nothing is known about Soviet midget submarine developments or types except that reliable estimates put the number of such craft in service in the early 1990s as around the 200 mark. One of the best ways of looking forward is to look back at past experience and see what lessons can be learned. The Soviet military are assiduous students of history and will have studied Second World War midget submarine development and operations in detail. Therefore it is likely that anything the Soviets are doing now has been done before. Current Soviet designs would be based on the most successful wartime craft—the British X-Craft.[13] Such a craft would have the capacity to lay explosive charges under its targets. It would also have a 'Wet and Dry' compartment for a diver or assault frogmen to exit and re-enter the submarine. However, any new craft may well be fitted with a robotic arm to effect some of the more tedious chores usually carried out by the diver. The propulsion system would almost certainly make use of current developments in air-independent propulsion systems such as the Sterling engine or might even be nuclear. The Soviets certainly had the imagination to design a mini-reactor and the ruthlessness to send someone to sea in a craft powered by one. Developments in electronics, carefully and diligently obtained from the West, would enable a comprehensive sensor and communications suite to be fitted. Externally the hull would be covered in anechoic tiles to reduce the effectiveness of hostile sonar.

Physical evidence points towards the existence of another type of Soviet midget submarine. Suspicious caterpillar tracks in Swedish, American, Brazilian, British and Japanese coastal waters indicate that the Soviets may have possessed a craft similar to the German *Seeteufel* with a combined caterpillar/propeller drive. Commenting on a number of recent intrusions into his country's territorial waters, a Swedish officer declared:

> We found, for example, fresh bottom tracks in Eastern coastal waters this summer, in the middle of a sensitive military installation. The Russians may want us to believe that we've got giant prehistoric centipedes here, but they certainly make peculiar noises that tally with noise-prints of Soviet submarines in our archives.[14]

As to a means of delivery, the Soviet Union possessed a huge merchant fleet, run under dual naval/civilian control. It is more than reasonable to suppose that the Soviets created a modern *Olterra* equipped with hatches below the waterline for the exit and re-entry of midget submarines. It has often been noted that some Soviet merchant ships appear to have holds which are well below the depth of the hull as indicated on the draught marks and that some Soviet Masters preferred to stick to deep-water channels even though the given draught of their vessel allowed them to use a shallower route. It would therefore be reasonable to assume that any Soviet merchant ship loitering around a sensitive area such as the Clyde, the Ile de Longue or King's Bay, Georgia (all SSBN bases), could be doing so 'with intent'. The Soviet Navy also developed two 'India' class rescue submarines. These boats, one serving with the Northern Fleet and the other with the Pacific Fleet, have wells in their after casings to take two Project 1837 and 1837K DSRVs (Deep Submergence Rescue Vehicles). The Russians have twelve of these 35-ton craft (*APS5*, *APS11* and *APS18–27*), which are able to dive to 2,000m and have accommodation for eleven on board. Ostensibly these submarines are for use in rescue operations, but their military potential is obvious.

Likely targets for Russian midget submarines would be naval dockyards, especially strategic missile submarine bases, strategic communications and the insertion and recovery of agents. The quietness of modern nuclear submarines makes them very hard to detect at sea: therefore, the best place to attack them would probably be when they are alongside the depot ship or jetty. This is where Russian midgets would make their most devastating contribution. They would probably work with *Osnaz* communications experts to tap either sea-bed communication lines or cables from the SOSUS line sensors, cut them or feed false data into them. The possibilities are endless.

The demise of the USSR and re-creation of Russia does not mean that the Russians will abandon their achievements in this field. Historically they have been pioneers in submarine development, so their interest in this field is merely the continuance of a long tradition. The possession of midget submarines helps the Russian government fulfil numerous intelligence-gathering requirements. There is no reason to believe that, as the ex-Soviet forces become leaner, underwater assault units will be axed. On the contrary: any drive for quality over quantity in the Russian Navy is likely to maintain, even advance, their position.

Early in 1991 the veil surrounding Soviet developments in this field was lifted by Commander 3rd Rank A. S. Shahov, who revealed that two midget submarines had been ordered for the Navy from the Admiralty Yard in Leningrad (now St Petersburg) in 1986 under the designation Project 865. Each 219-ton boat was 91ft 10in x 13ft 1in (28m x 4m) and had a range of about 1,000km, an endurance of ten days and a top speed of 6kt; each could carry two 530mm torpedoes and three divers. The craft were complete by the end of 1988 but had numerous problems: in particular, the boats would not maintain trim while the divers were using the lock-out chamber and the electrical and air pressure systems were inadequate for the boats' needs. Shahov protested that the craft were unfit for service but was overruled by those who insisted that they be commissioned on 31 December 1988. The boats were then the subject of two commissions of inquiry since the total expenditure on the project from 1982 to 1990 was over 40 million roubles. Finally, on 5 September 1990 Vice-Admiral A. Kuzmin, Chief of Staff and Chief of Combat Training, announced that the boats would not be commissioned. At the same time the Russian authorities took the unusual step of announcing that their order of battle in the Baltic had never included any midget submarines nor tracked submersibles. This coy statement did not, however, extend to craft operated by the former KGB or *Spetznaz* units.

The post-1945 period has seen a proliferation of midget submarines: Yugoslavia, Croatia, Colombia, Libya, Sweden, North Korea, Taiwan, Iran and Pakistan all possess and operate them. Italy is a major manufacturer of these craft, although the Italian Navy does not possess any in its order of battle. The Italians have supplied Colombia and Pakistan with midget submarines and are also believed to have exported some to North Korea. Italian inventiveness in this field has resulted in the appearance of a number of interesting designs. Maritalia s.p.a. has produced a range of three extremely advanced midget submarines of 80, 100 and 120 tons displacement. The craft has a 'teardrop' hull with hydroplanes fitted to the small conning tower and a single propeller at the stern. The toroidal storage structure and an anechoic coating effectively reduce noise radiation. Automation enables the boat to be controlled by one man, but up to sixteen people can be embarked. These craft have two unique features. First, they have an air-independent propulsion system with gaseous oxygen stored in a toroidal pressure hull for an Anaerobic diesel. This system gives a submerged endurance—without schnorkelling—of fourteen days. The other unique feature of the design is the variety of weapons which can be carried, the options being four lightweight torpedoes; two heavyweight torpedoes; twelve 150kg ground mines in torpedo tubes; two mine dispensers laying a total of twenty 600kg ground mines; two SDVs and a 600kg charge for each or two SDVs each with a 300kg charge and four limpets; two mine delivery vehicles and a total of ten 600kg ground mines; two commando delivery vehicles for sixteen commandos; twin 7.62 machine guns in a retractable, pressure-resistant mounting; or one pressure-resistant, retractable 20mm gun. The variety of weapon fits make the Maritalia craft extremely versatile and effective. Britain has also attempted to enter the export field for midget submarines. Vickers produced a design for a boat called Piranha which carries two Swimmer Delivery Vehicles or a number of mines. However, this attractive craft has failed to excite any interest from potential purchasers.

Colombia purchased four SX404 70-ton midgets from Cosmos of Liverno in the 1970s. Named *Intrepido*, *Roncador*, *Quito Sueno* and *Indomable*, these craft are 23m long and carry eight divers, two swimmer delivery vehicles and two tons of explosive charges. *Roncador* and *Quito Sueno* were deleted in 1981 but the other pair are extant. Just what the Colombian government want these craft for is unclear, but presumably they would be useful in one of the festering border disputes which continually bedevil Latin American politics. Pakistan has also purchased midget submarines from Italy. The three Pakistani midgets are of the MG100 design, built in Pakistan under licence and under the supervision of Cosmos in Liverno. They are a larger version of the SX756 Cosmos design and replaced nine SX404 boats acquired in 1972. They are probably the most capable midget submarines in service anywhere in world and carry a mixed armament of torpedoes, mines and a contingent of swimmers. The two torpedoes are of the AEG SUT wire-guided type, have an active homing capability to a range of 12km at 35kt and a passive homing capability to a range of 28km at 23kt and carry a 250kg warhead. A crew of six is required, but eight swimmers can be accommodated along with eight Type 414 limpet mines and two CF2 FX50 SDVs.

Pakistan and India have been uneasy neighbours since partition in 1947: to date there have been three Indo-Pakistan Wars. Both countries have devoted considerable resources to the expansion of their navies. India adopted a 'belt and braces' approach, buying equal amounts of weaponry from the West and the USSR, while at the same time developing a domestic military-industrial base. Pakistan has relied exclusively on purchases and transfers from the West. The Indians take the threat posed by the Pakistani midget submarines seriously. Their concern focuses on three areas in particular: the protection of their two aircraft carriers, *Vikrant* and *Viraat*, against a pre-emptive attack; the protection of India's considerable offshore oil and gas facilities; and the protection of the Indian nuclear processing facility at Bhabha (BARC) near Bombay.[15] Although India and Pakistan have signed an agreement undertaking that each will leave the other's nuclear facilities alone in time of war, there is no guarantee that this agreement would be observed in a real conflict. The Pakistani midgets would be extremely useful in landing swimmers for a pre-emptive strike on such a facility.

Yugoslavia has been the principal exporter of midget submarines in the post-war period. The Tito government developed an export-orientated arms industry as a means of earning foreign exchange. The Yugoslavs' main clients were countries whose financial or political credentials made them *persona non grata* with the major Western or Eastern Bloc suppliers. The Yugoslavs developed three different models: the R1 one-man Swimmer Delivery Vehicle, the R2 two-man Swimmer Delivery Vehicle and the *Una* class midget submarine. The R1 is a single-seat underwater vehicle for one frogman and can be used for underwater reconnaissance and the surveillance of minefields. It is of monohull construction with ballast tanks at the bow and stern. It can be transported in a standard torpedo tube and used both in fresh water and in sea water with a specific gravity of $1.000–1.030t/m^3$ without reserve uplift. The craft can dive to a depth of 60m and is powered by a 1kW electric motor supplied by a 24V DC silver-zinc battery. Endurance is measured at 6nm at 3kt and

8nm at 2.5kt. The single operator lies along the top of the craft, rather than sitting astride it as in the wartime *Maiale*, and is provided with a gyro-magnetic compass, sonar, echo sounder, electric clock and other instruments.

The R2 *Mala* is a spindle-shaped craft seating two divers side by side, has the same roles as the R1 but carries two 50kg limpet mines. The hull is made of aluminium alloy resistant to sea water corrosion. Submerged control is by means of fore and aft hydroplanes, the tail being a conventional cruciform with a rudder fitted aft of the three-blade screw. The front upper part of the craft is made of plexiglass. The hull can be fully flooded except for the cylinders containing the 24V storage battery, the 4.5kW electric motor, navigational instruments and ballast tanks. The navigational equipment is contained in a watertight housing and consists of a gyro-magnetic compass, depth gauge, echo-sounder, sonar and two searchlights. The craft can be carried on a submarine's casing or as deck cargo in any ship with a 25-ton crane. *Mala* have been sold to Sweden (where they function in the role of 'loyal opposition', training Swedish ASW forces), the USSR and Libya. The Libyans have six of these craft. Although none of the ships in the Libyan Navy is capable of carrying a *Mala*, there is no reason why any of the ships in the Libyan merchant marine[16] should not be converted to carry them.

The third Yugoslav craft is the *Una* midget submarine. This is a single-hull craft with a steel pressure hull and a reinforced polyester casing. The boat is electrically driven by two DC motors powered by two storage batteries each containing 129 cells. It carries a comprehensive communications and electronics fit, including HF transceiver, radio telephone, underwater telephone, gyro compass, electromagnetic log, echo sounder, Atlas Electronik active and passive sonar and a single periscope. The craft has a range of 100nm at 6kt on the surface; when submerged, it has an endurance is 80nm at 8kt and 200nm at 4kt. The normal complement is six, but if divers are to be embarked the crew can be reduced to four so that six divers can be accommodated. There is a one-man exit/re-entry compartment. Four R1s are carried in forward-facing tubes which could also be used for carrying acoustic/induction bottom-laying mines.[17] Six *Una* were built for the Federal Yugoslav Navy, *Tisa*, *Una*, *Soca*, *Zeta*, *Kupa* and *Vardar*. The first was commissioned in 1985 and the last in 1989. In 1991 *Soca* was transferred to Croatia and has since been substantially modified by the insertion of a midships section containing a diesel generator. The Croatian Navy (*Hrvatska Ratna Mornarica*) is reported to have ordered a 120-ton midget submarine armed with four short torpedo tubes and able to carry four SDVs.

Across the other side of the world, the Democratic People's Republic of North Korea (DPRK) has over sixty midget submarines in service. The DPRK began the programme in the early 1960s at the Yukdaeso-ri shipyard and has more than one type in service as experience gained at sea is incorporated into the production schedule. The DPRK is the world's last impenitent communist regime and few details are available for the types and numbers of boats in service. North Korean midgets carry a mixed armament: some carry mines while others are believed to be fitted with torpedo tubes. There are also reports of a small and crude nuclear weapon being available. It would not be beyond the DPRK's capacity to build such a weapon and the country's leaders are certainly ruthless enough to use it. The craft have been exclusively employed in operations against South Korea, where some have been lost in operations; one was reported captured in 1965 or 1966. They can be carried in eight converted vessels of the North Korean merchant marine. The North Koreans have also purchased some *Una* class craft from Yugoslavia and some two-man submersibles from Italy. They have also looked further afield: only recently a bid to acquire a German-built midget submarine was foiled at the last minute.

As well as midget submarines, the DPRK also has eight 'Chariot'-like vehicles suitable for swimmer delivery. Each 8½m long and supposedly capable of 50kt, these craft make their approach at high speed before ballasting down to launch the swimmmers, of whom six can be carried. One of these craft was sighted off the South Korean port of Pusan on 20 December 1985.

Just across the East China Sea, Taiwan was briefly a member of the midget submarine community. The Taiwanese Navy were for a short time the owners of four Italian-built SX404 craft. They were used exclusively for the insertion of special forces or agents into mainland China but the boats were discarded in 1974.

The DPRK has supplied its expertise to Iran in that country's midget submarine programme. The Iranians built their own submarine at Bandar Abbas using German and Japanese Second World War designs as their inspiration. The craft was completed in 1987, but when the trials were unsuccessful it was taken to Teheran for modification. The Iranian programme was then overtaken by the offer to supply boats from North Korea. The first was delivered in June 1988 and it is reported that a final total of twenty-four will be delivered. The Iranian boats are reported to be fitted with side cargoes in much the same manner as a wartime X-Craft. Likely uses for Iran's midgets would include attacks on Iraqi offshore oil facilities or the oil facilities of her neighbours across the Persian Gulf. Other areas of potential employment for Iranian midgets would be attacks on Western shipping in the Persian Gulf and the infiltration of religious *agents provocateurs* into Saudi Arabia. Iraq was the final entrant into the midget submarine field. In the summer of 1990 Saddam Hussein's government was in the final stages of negotiations to purchase a midget submarine from Maritalia. Fortunately the purchase was blocked at the last moment: Saddam had plans to arm the craft with a nuclear weapon.

The possession of midget submarines by countries like Libya, North Korea and Iran is a matter of concern. All have extremely unsavoury regimes and all three have strong links with, and support, international terrorism. All three countries have shown themselves willing to flout the norms of international relations in pursuit of their own objectives. Moreover, there is the dreadful spectre of their deploying a chemical or biological device in a centre of population via a midget submarine attack. Both Iran and Iraq used chemical agents in the Iran–Iraq War and the North Koreans would have no hesitation in using such weapons. How effective would such craft be? Conventional reference works indicate a low level of efficiency due to a lack of training. While it is certainly true that these modern midget submarine crews are not trained to the same standard as their British or Italian wartime predecessors, they have three advantages on their side. First, they have the advantage of surprise: they would choose the place and time for an attack. Secondly, they would operate in the absence of any form of harbour defence, boom defence having been virtually ignored as an aspect of naval operations since 1945. Thirdly, the operators of these craft are fanatics, whether they be communist functionaries or Muslim zealots. The belief that death in action will lead to a Marxist or Islamic nirvana will overcome a good deal of inadequacy in training. It only takes one midget to get through with her cargo for the mission to succeed. One can only speculate at the result of such an operation—a wrecked offshore oil installation in the Persian Gulf, an American aircraft carrier mined while at anchor in the Bay of Naples, a chemical/biological (or nuclear) device detonated in an Israeli harbour . . .

The most exciting and promising developments centre on the field of robotic, unmanned craft, which would be rather like homing torpedoes but with a passive/active search capability of their own. The British company Scion has developed Spur (Scion's Patrolling Undersea Robot) while the Americans have investigated Small Mobile Sensor Platforms (SMSPs) deployed from torpedo tubes. In March 1990 the American Defense Advanced Research Projects Agency (DARPA) began tests with two prototype Unmanned Undersea Vehicles (UUV). An SSN, USS *Memphis* (SSN-691), has been converted to act as an at-sea test-bed for advanced submarine technology including the launch and recovery of UUVs. The UUV is designed as a tactical system which can be deployed from submarines, surface ships or direct from the shore and which can perform a number of functions including mine detection, underwater surveillance (including ASW) and communications. The key to the performance of these functions is advanced electronic systems, which include 'artificial intelligence' algorithms that function in the same way as human thought processes. In order to guard against computer failure, the vehicle will utilise three fully redundant computers which will employ a 'voting' approach to systems management on board the craft. All three computers must 'agree' on how the craft is run; if only two agree then the craft will continue to operate but in a degraded mode.

The UUV is 36ft long and 44in in diameter. Considerable attention has been paid to reducing the overall size of the craft by the use of advanced technology and to reducing the size of the powerplant. An internal pressure hull will house the mission payload, which will occupy a 5ft long section. This would consist of the appropriate software and components for surveillance, communications or mine-detection duties. In the case of the last, the package includes an ultra-thin cable containing a fibre-optic communications link required for the transmission of commands from a surface ship or submarine. The propulsion system, consisting of a 12hp electric motor and a motor controller, will occupy the after 12ft of the vehicle. The motor is built to operate even when completely flooded with sea water. Bearings are fabricated with a special non-corrosive alloy, and the copper windings that carry power to the motors are impervious to wear. During normal operations, the internal volume of the motor is filled with oil in order to equalise pressure between the inside and the outside of the motor, permitting the use of a thinner and lighter housing. Unmanned vehicles such as SMSPs and UUVs would enable a relatively small number of SSNs to 'control' a large area of ocean through which enemy forces would have to pass. They also offer considerable advantages in the field of mine detection and electronic surveillance and have the advantage of being capable of unlimited under-ice operations—a field denied to manned midget submarines.

A number of conclusions can be drawn about midget submarine operations which are extremely relevant today. First, such operations require thorough and realistic training if they are to be successful. British and Italian operators were well trained and this was reflected in their achievements; German operators were flung into battle with hardly any training at all and achieved little as a result. However, the ability of the fanatic to score one decisive hit at the cost of his own life cannot be ignored. Secondly, midget submarines can be built quickly, cheaply and in large numbers. They are, moreover, extremely easy to hide. Thirdly, almost any merchant ship or submarine can be adapted to carry a midget submarine. Fourthly, no defences have ever stopped a midget submarine attack. They have been a hindrance and have deterred an attacker, but a small number of the midgets have always got through. Modern bases are virtually defenceless against this form of attack, especially as wartime skills in the field of boom defence have long since disappeared. Faced by the midget threat, simple last-ditch measures such as spilling oil fuel on the surface of the water will render a small periscope useless. The 'green lobby' would hate it, but, against a simple craft dependent on periscope observation of the target, it would be highly effective. Fifthly, one-man operated craft are doomed to failure. A man on his own has to much to do and loses heart. There should be at least two in the crew and for an operation of any duration at least four are required. Lastly, the quality of the operators, the 'human resources', is vital. Men best suited to midget submarine operations are those least likely to fit in with the routines of a peacetime navy. It is interesting to note from the British perspective that Australians, New Zealanders and South Africans, whose antipathy to the Naval Discipline Act was legendary, were extremely competent X-Craft personnel. The risks implicit in training for midget submarine operations mean that such men have to develop a team spirit unique to their formation—this is what distinguished the *Decima Mas* from the rest of the *Regia Marina* and what distinguishes Russian special forces personnel from run-of-the-mill conscripts.

In 1907 the historian Arthur Thayer Mahan wrote, in *From Sail to Steam*, that

It is now accepted with naval and military men who study their profession, that history supplies the raw material from which they are to draw their lessons, and reach their working conclusions. Its teachings are not, indeed, pedantic precedents, but they are the illustrations of living principles.[18]

There is no doubt that midget submarines are still a force to be reckoned with. The development of new technologies will make them even more effective. Midget submarines are a proven weapon of war and it would be unwise for us to forget the achievements of men like Visintini, de la Penne, Cameron, Fraser and Saburo Akeida.

Appendix

WARSHIPS AND MERCHANT SHIPS
SUNK OR DAMAGED BY MIDGET SUBMARINES OR HUMAN TORPEDOES

Victim	Type	Navy	Location	Date	Midget
Viribus Unitis	BB	Austria	Pola	01.11.18	*Mignatta*
Fiona Shell	MV	GB	Gibraltar	20.09.41	*Maiale*
Denbydale[1]	RFA	GB	Gibraltar	20.09.41	*Maiale*
Durham	MV	GB	Gibraltar	20.09.41	*Maiale*
Sangona[1]	TKR	GB	Alexandria	19.12.41	*Maiale*
Jervis[1]	DD	GB	Alexandria	19.12.41	*Maiale*
Queen Elizabeth[1]	BB	GB	Alexandria	19.12.41	*Maiale*
Valiant[1]	BB	GB	Alexandria	19.12.41	*Maiale*
Ramillies[1]	BB	GB	Diego Suarez	30.05.42	*Ko-Hyoteki*
British Loyalty	TKR	GB	Diego Suarez	30.05.42	*Ko-Hyoteki*
S32	SM	USSR	Black Sea	15.06.42	*CB3*
SC213	SM	USSR	Black Sea	18.06.42	*CB2*
Ulpio Traiano	CR	Italy	Palermo	2/3.01.43	Chariot *XXII*
Viminale	MV	Italy	Palermo	2/3.01.43	Chariot *XVI*
Camerata[1]	MV	GB	Gibraltar	08.05.43	*Maiale*
Mahsud[1]	MV	GB	Gibraltar	08.05.43	*Maiale*
Pat Harrison[1]	MV	GB	Gibraltar	08.05.43	*Maiale*
Thorshovdi[1]	MV	GB	Gibraltar	08.05.43	*Maiale*
H. G. Otis[1]	MV	GB	Gibraltar	04.08.43	*Maiale*
Stanridge[1]	MV	GB	Gibraltar	04.08.43	*Maiale*
SC207	SM	USSR	Black Sea	26.08.43	*CB4*
Tirpitz[1]	BB	Germany	Kaafjord	22.09.43	*X6/7*
Barenfels	MV	Germany	Bergen	13.04.44	*X24*
Bolzano	CR	Italy	La Spezia	21/22.06.44	Chariots *LVIII/LX*
Cato	MSW	GB	Normandy	06.07.44	*Neger/Marder*
Magic	MSW	GB	Normandy	06.07.44	*Neger/Marder*
Dragon[1]	CR	Poland	Normandy	07.07.44	*Neger*
Pylades	MSW	GB	Normandy	07.07.44	*Neger/Marder*
Isis[2]	DD	GB	Normandy	20.07.44	*Neger/Marder*
Gairsay	TW	GB	Normandy	03.08.44	*Neger/Marder*
Samlong[1]	MV	GB	Normandy	03.08.45	*Neger/Marder*
Fort Lac La Ronge	MV	GB	Normandy	03.08.44	*Neger/Marder*
Blencathra[1]	DD	GB	Normandy	03.08.44	*Neger/Marder*
LCF(II) No 1	LCF	GB	Normandy	18.08.44	*Neger/Marder*

Quorn	DD	GB	Normandy	03.08.44	*Neger/Marder*
Iddesleigh	MV	GB	Normandy	17.08.44	*Neger/Marder*
LCF(II) No 1	LCF	GB	Normandy	18.08.44	*Neger/Marder*
Fratton	AUX	GB	Normandy	18.08.44	*Neger/Marder*
Floating Dock	–	Germany	Bergen	11.09.44	*X24*
Sten[3]	MV	Norway	Bergen	11.09.44	*X24*
Kong Oscar II[3]	MV	Norway	Bergen	11.09.44	*X24*
Volpi	MV	Japan	Phuket	27 .10.44	Chariots *LXXIX*, *LXXX*
Sumatra	MV	Japan	Phuket	27.10.44	Chariots *LXXIX*, *LXXX*
Mississinewa	TKR	USA	Ulithi	20.11.44	*Kaiten*
Alan A. Dale	MV	GB	Off Flushing	23.12.44	*Biber*
Heybourne Wick	AUX	GB	NNW Ostend	02.01.45	*Biber*?
LST364	LST	GB	English Channel	22.02.45	*Biber*?
Alert	AUX	GB	English Channel	24.02.45	*Biber*?
Taber Park	MV	GB	North Sea	13.03.45	*Seehund*[4]
Newlands	MV	GB	North Sea	26.03.45	*Seehund*[4]
Jim	MV	GB	North Sea	30.03.45	*Seehund*[4]
YT17	TKR	USA	Ostend	09.04.45	*Seehund*[4]
Samida	MV	GB	English Channel	09.04.45	*Seehund*[4]
Solomon Juneau	MV	USA	English Channel	09.04.45	*Seehund*
Fort Wyndham	MV	GB	English Channel	11.04.45	*Seehund*[4]
Underhill	DD	USA	E of Okinawa	24.07.45	*Kaiten*
Takao	CR	Japan	Singapore	31.07.45	*XE3*

Key to abbreviations:
BB—battleship; CR—cruiser; DD—destroyer; SM—submarine; LST—landing ship tank; AUX—naval auxiliary; RFA—Royal Fleet Auxiliary; TKR—tanker; TW—trawler; MV—merchant vessel.

Notes:
1. Indicates that the ship was damaged but not sunk.
2. Doubt exists as to whether HMS *Isis* was mined or succumbed to a *Neger* attack.
3. Both merchant ships were destroyed in the explosion of *X24*'s charges, along with the floating dock.
4. It is not clear as to whether a *Biber* or a *Seehund* was responsible for these losses.

Notes

Chapter 1

1. *Naval Chronicle*, July 1802: Monthly Register of Naval Events.
2. Transactions of the American Philosophical Society for Promoting Useful Knowledge: 'General Principles and Construction of a Submarine Vessel Communicated by D. Bushnell of Conn., the Inventor, in a Letter of October 1787 to Thomas Jefferson, then Minister Plenipotentiary of the United States at Paris', Vol, IV, 1799, p. 303
3. PRO: 'Journal of the Proceedings of His Majesties [*sic*] Ship Eagle, by Captain Henry Duncan, betwen [*sic*] 10 February 1776 and 28 February 1777'.
4. R. Compton-Hall, *Monsters and Midgets*, p. 93.
5. Lt-Cdr J. Wilkinson, 'Sneak Attack Craft in the Pacific', *USNI Proceedings,* Vol. 73, March 1947.
6. Haus to Kailer, 14 December 1914, Kailer MSS, Kriegsarchiv, Vienna.
7. Rossetti, Raffaele, *Contro la Viribus Unitis*, Libreria Politica Moderna, Rome, 1925. See also the article in *Marine: Gestern, Heute*, 1978 No 1, by Edgar Tomicich.
8. National Maritime Museum, Papers of Admiral Sir Howard Kelly, KEL/4, autobiographical fragment.
9. See A. Turrini, 'I Sommergibili Tasdcabile della Regia Marina', *Storia Militare*, Anno III, No 16, pp. 34–43 for further details of these craft.

Chapter 2

1. *Decima Mas* operations also involved the use of fast explosive motor boats such as were responsible for the sinking of the cruiser HMS *York* at Suda Bay on 26 March 1941. The activities of these craft lie outside this study.
2. The officer was *Tenente di Vascello* Gino Birindelli. Many years later Birindelli was told by one of his former captors that the British would have had him killed rather than repatriated. IWM Department of Sound Records, Interview with Admiral Gino Birindelli.
3. Opinion expressed to the author by Admiral Gino Birindelli, 25 May 1994.
4. Elios Toschi, *Escape over the Himalayas*, edit. Eur Milan, pp.32–3.
5. J. V. Borghese, *Sea Devils*, Andrew Melrose (London, 1952), p. 19. Admiral Goiran was the Flag Officer commanding Italy's North Tyrrhenian Sector.
6. Literally, 'Slow Running Torpedo'.
7. The best description of an SLC is in E. Bagnasco and M. Spertini, *I Mezzi d'Assalto della Xa Flottiglia MAS, 1940–1945*, Albertelli Editore (1991), pp. 129–46. This book is an outstanding account of Italian assault weapons and techniqies.
8. *Tenente di Vascello* = Lieutenant RN.
9. *Capitano di Fregatta* = Commander RN.
10. *Capo Palombaro 1* = Chief Petty Officer Diver

11. *Capitano Genio Navale* = Constructor Commander RCNC.

12. *Sotocapo Palombaro* = Leading Seaman Diver

13. *Capitano Armi Navali* = Captain RM

14. The *Lorraine*, together with a number of other French ships, had been interned at Alexandria since the fall of France in 1940.

15. Vice-Admiral Sir Louis le Bailly, *The Man Around the Engine*, Kenneth Mason (1990), pp. 98–9. In the Royal Navy the Senior Engineer is the Engineer Officer's deputy.

16. Strictly a breach of the Geneva Convention, which holds that prisoners of war must not be placed in harm's way.

17. Adrian Holloway, *From Dartmouth to War*, Buckland Publications (1993), pp. 198–9.

18. Borghese, op. cit., p. 21

19. Holloway, op. cit., p. 204.

20. le Bailly, op. cit., p. 99.

21. Admiral Sir Andrew Cunningham, *A Sailor's Odyssey*, Hutchinson (1951), p. 433.

22. First Sea Lord and Chief of the Naval Staff 1938–1943.

23. Cunningham, op. cit., p. 434.

24. The losses suffered included the cruiser *Neptune* and destroyer *Kandahar* sunk, together with the cruisers *Aurora* and *Penelope* damaged, on 19 December. Moreover, the cruiser *Galatea* had been sunk five days previously.

25. A sister ship to *Queen Elizabeth* and *Valiant* but one that had not been significantly modernised.

26. Opinion expressed to the author by Admiral Gino Birindelli, 25 May 1994.

27. *Guardiamarine* = Coastguard.

28. *Sotto Tenente Medicale* = Surgeon Sub-Lieutenant.

30. *Tenete Genio Navale* = Constructor Lieutenant.

31. *Sottocapo Palombaro* = Petty Officer Diver.

Chapter 3

1. In its heyday Force H usually consisted of the battlecruiser *Renown*, the aircraft carrier *Ark Royal* and the cruiser *Sheffield* and was commanded by the outstanding Vice-Admiral Sir James Somerville.

2. *Sunday Express*, 25 December 1949.

3. Imperial War Museum Department of Sound Records, Interview with Admiral Gino Birindelli, SR14236/2.

4. Ibid.

5. Ibid.

6. Ibid. Birindelli's *Maiale* was subsequently recovered and used by the British as the inspiration for the Chariot.

7. Ibid.

8. J. V. Borghese, *The Sea Devils,* Andrew Melrose (London, 1952), p. 128.

9. Much of the information on the operations launched from *Olterra* comes from a series of papers in the archives at the Royal Navy Submarine Museum and I am extremely grateful to Commander P. R. Compton-Hall for drawing my attention to them. The papers comprise a complete set of intelligence summaries by Colonel H. C. Medlam DSO, the Defence Security Officer at Gibraltar, the post-war interrogation of Denegri and others involved and the reports of British agents in Spain. I have referred to this collection as RNSM *Olterra* Papers followed

by the appropriate reference.

10. RNSM *Olterra* Papers, 'Report on Spanish Complicity in Italian Sabotage Attacks against British and Allied Shipping in Gibraltar', by Captain D. J. Scher of the Gibraltar Defence Security Office, 17 November 1943.

11. Secret Intelligence Service, better known as MI6, responsible for intelligence outside the United Kingdom.

12. RNSM *Olterra* Papers, 'Report on Spanish Complicity'.

13. Prof. Carlo di Risio, *La Marina Italiana Nella Seconda Guerra Mondiale. Vol XIV: I Mezzi d'Assalto*, (Ufficio Storico della Marina Militare; 1964, revised edn 1992), p. 167. 'My bereaved family' refers to Visintini's father, killed in the 1914–18 war, and his brother, killed in the Second World War. Visintini's daughter Valeria died shortly afterwards. His widow found herself pratically destitute at the end of war but in a generous gesture was employed as a secretary by former members of the Gibraltar Underwater Working Party who were engaged in Italy clearing the various harbours.

14. Admiralty Monthly Intelligence Report (MIR), June 1943.

15. RNSM *Olterra* Papers, Medlam to SO(I) Gibraltar, 26 August 1943.

16. Imperial War Museum, Department of Sound Records, Interview with Frank Goldsworthy, SR11245/11.

Chapter 4

1. J. V. Borghese, *Sea Devils*, Andrew Melrose (London, 1952), p. 113.

2. Ibid., p. 231.

3. Ibid., p. 261.

4. C. E. T. Warren and James Benson, *Above Us the Waves: The Story of Midget Submarines and Human Torpedoes*, Harrap & Co., (London, 1953), pp. 180–1.

5. FOWIT to CinC Med, 26 June 1944. Correspondence on Operation 'QWZ' in the Naval Historical Branch, Ministry of Defence.

6. Heathfield to CinC Med, 26 June 1944. Correspondence on Operation 'QWZ' in the Naval Historical Branch, Ministry of Defence.

7. Special Operations Executive, the British organisation charged with fomenting sabotage and subversion in occupied Europe.

8. For a useful and lively discussion on the operation against the *Aquila* see two articles in the excellent journal *Warship International*: A. Rastelli and E. Bagnasco, 'The Sinking of the Italian Aircraft Carrier *Aquila*—A Controversial Question', *WI*, No 1 1990, pp. 55–69; and Mark Grossman, 'The Allied Assault on *Aquila*—Operation Toast', *WI*, No 2 1990, pp. 166–73.

9. Their legacy lives on: in the summer of 1995 a very senior and experienced clearance diver in the Royal Navy expressed the opinion to the author that the Italian Navy was still 'streets ahead' in underwater frogman techniques. Personal information supplied to the author.

Chapter 5

1. *Kaigun Zosen Gijitsu Gaiyo* (Survey of Naval Shipbuilding Technology), Vol. 3, p. 540, indicates that the boat may have been capable of a higher speed, 27.6 knots. However, this is most unlikely for a 41-ton craft driven by a 600hp electric motor.

2. Commander Takaichi Tanashi to author, 3 March 1994.

3. *Tomozuru* capsized in heavy weather on 12 March 1934 but was brought into port and righted. An investigation found that she was dangerously top heavy and nearly sixty tons of permanent ballast had to be added.

4. Lieutenant Sekido Yoshimitsu, quoted in *Nihon No Kaigun*, No 4 (Tokyo 1978), p. 28.

Chapter 6

1. C class submarines: 2,554/3,561 tons; 103.8 (pp) /106.95 (wl) /109.3 (oa) x 9.10 x 5.35m; 2-shaft diesels plus electric motors, 12,400bhp/200shp, 23.6/8kt; eight 21-inch torpedo tubes, one 5.5-inch 40-cal, two 25mm AA; 101 officers and men. Five units in class: *I-16*, *I-18*, *I-20*, *I-22*, *I-24*.

2. Personal correspondence with the author, January 1994.

3. Testimony of Captain William Outerbridge USN before the Hewitt Inquiry, Navy Department, 21 May 1945.

Chapter 7

1. Aptly named town where the Imperial Russian Fleet had languished for some months in 1904 on its way to annihilation at the Battle of Tsu-Shima.

2. Admiralty, 'Battle Summary No 16: Naval Operations at the Capture of Diego Suarez (Operation Ironclad), May 1942', p. 53.

3. PRO ADM199/3527, East Indies War Diary, 2 June 1942.

4. Some reports speak of the uniforms and effects from the three men being laid out and photographed on *Ramillies'* quarterdeck, but there is no evidence of this in British records.

5. In fact, *I-29*'s floatplane pilot and observer were guilty of the not uncommon sin among naval aviators of over-exaggeration. Allied forces in Sydney consisted of the American cruiser *Chicago*, destroyer *Perkins* and destroyer tender *Dobbins*, the cruiser HMAS *Australia*, two armed merchant cruisers, the Free French 'super-destroyer' *Le Triomphant* and a number of smaller ships.

6. *Sydney Morning Herald*, 2 June 1942.

7. Personal information supplied to the author.

8. ABC radio broadcast, 9 June 1942.

9. G. H. Gill, *Royal Australian Navy, 1939–1945*, Australian War Memorial (1985).

Chapter 8

1. P. Warner and S. Sadao, T*he Coffin Boats: Japanese Midget Submarine Operations in the Second World War*, Leo Cooper (1986), p. 166.

2. Itani, J., Lengerer, H., and Rehm-Takahara, T., 'Japanese Midget Submarines: Ko-Hyoteki Types A to C', *Warship 1993*, Conway Maritime Press (London, 1993), p.122. This article is without doubt the most authoratitive source in English on the *Ko-Hyoteki*.

3. The actual number of *Ko-Hyoteki* built is open to a number of intepretations. Polmar and Carpenter, in *Submarines of the Imperial Japanese Navy*, state that 62 Type As were built, 1 Type B and 15 Type Cs, as does Erminio Bagnasco in *Submarines of World War Two*. However, Itani et al (see above) state that 52 Type As were built, 1 Type B and 36 Type Cs. Their justification is that, although operational records show that no boat with a number '85' was used, a photograph exists showing a boat wearing the pennant number '89'.

4. Kennosuke Torisu, 'Japanese Submarine Tactics and the Kaiten', in D. C. Evans (ed.) *The Japanese Navy in World War II in the Words of Former Japanese Naval Officers*, USNI (1986), p. 444

5. See Dr J. R. Bullen, 'The Japanese Long Lance Torpedo and its Place in Naval History', *Review*, Imperial War Museum (London, 1988), pp. 69–79 for details of the Long Lance torpedo.

6. R. Chesneau (ed.), *Conway's All the World's Fighting Ships 1922–1946*, Conway Maritime Press (1980), p. 217.

7. Torisu, op. cit., p. 446.

8. P. Kemp, 'Only Three Submarine Campaigns?', *The Submarine Review*, July 1990, pp.98–9.

9. Bullen, op. cit., p. 71.

10. M. Hashimoto, *Sunk! The Story of the Japanese Submarine Fleet 1942–45*, Cassell (1954), p. 126

11.. Torisu, op.cit., p. 446

12. Yokuta Yutaka and J. D. Harrington, *The Kaiten Weapon*, Ballantine Books (New York, 1962), p. 53.

13. Some sources—Carpenter and Polmar, Compton-Hall, etc—say that this *Kaiten* was operated by Nishina, although this can only be speculation.

14. Hashimoto, op. cit., p. 143.

15. See S. Foster, *Okinawa: Final Assault on the Empire*, Arms and Armour Press (1994), pp. 76–94, for details

16. Rear-Admiral Bruce McCandless, 'Commentary on *Kaiten*—Japan's Human Torpedoes', *Proceedings*, US Naval Institute, July 1962, p. 120.

Chapter 9

1. Convoy PQ-17 was scattered in July 1942 with disastrous results due to a faulty intelligence appreciation that the *Tirpitz* and her consorts might be at sea.

2. PRO PREM23/3561, Churchill to Ismay, 18 January 1942. Colonel R. Jefferis KBE MC was an Army officer who later served with SOE and pioneered much midget development.

3. W. R. Fell, *The Sea Our Shield*, Cassell & Co (London, 1966), p. 76.

4. See R. Fisk, *In Time of War: Ireland, Ulster and the Price of Neutrality 1939–1945*, Paladin Books (1985), pp.132–40, for further details of this unusual and little-known operation.

5. The British expert concerned was Captain W. O. Shelford, the noted submarine escape and salvage expert.

6. C. E. T. Warren and J. Benson, *Above Us the Waves: The Story of Midget Submarines and Human Torpedoes*, Harrap (London, 1953), p. 31.

7. The origin of the name 'Chariot' is unclear. Submariners who carried them into actions referred to them as 'Jeeps', after the rodent-like creature in the *Popeye* cartoon which emitted a series of *'jeep-jeep'* sounds.

8. The civil and political head of the Royal Navy, appointed by the Prime Minister and having a seat in the Cabinet. Not to be confused with the First Sea Lord, who is the professional head of the Royal Navy.

9. See Larsen's book, *The Shetland Bus*, for further information about this remarkable man's exploits.

10. The British film *We Dive at Dawn* gives an excellent portrayal of this incident.

11. Warren and Benson, op. cit., p. 64. ·

12. *Oberkommando des Wehrmacht*, the supreme command of the German armed forces.

13. *Verpostenboot*: a German local patrol craft used for harbour defence.

14. The British *Oberon* class SSKs are fitted with a five man exit/re-entry chamber in the fin.

15. Naval Staff History, 'Submarines. Vol. 2: Operations in the Mediterranean', Admiralty (1956), pp. 118–19.

16. Rear-Admiral G. W. G. Simpson, *Periscope View: A Professional Autobiography*, Macmillan (London, 1972), p. 281.

17. Naval Staff History, op cit., p. 123.

18. G. Cruikshank, *SOE in the Far East*, OUP (1983), p. 30.

Chapter 10

1. This and many following details of X-Craft construction are taken from 'War History and War Experience, 1939–1945: Technical Staff Monograph on X-Craft', TS copy extant in the Naval Historical Branch at the Ministry of Defence.

2. Commander C. H. Varley DSC MIMechE RN, 1890–1949, Obituary in *The Times*, 4 September 1949.

3. An acronym formed from the surnames of the two designers, Varley and Bell.

4. See P. J. Kemp, *The T Class Submarine*, Arms & Armour Press (1990), pp. 14–15, for a discussion of Vickers' problems in this respect.

5. 'War History and War Experience, 1939–1945'.

6. Captain J. E. Moore and Commander P. R. Compton-Hall, Commander, *Submarine Warfare Today and Tomorrow*, Michael Jospeh (London, 1986), p. 215.

7. 'War History and War Experience, 1939–1945'.

8. A disgusting phenomenon unique to the British submarine service and caused by the improper operation of the WC's flushing system so that the closet becomes open to the sea with the result that one's 'deposit' is propelled out of the bowl and across the compartment at great speed, to the accompaniment of cheers from unsympathetic messmates.

9. Papers of Commander H. P. Westmacott DSO DSC* RN, Imperial War Museum, Department of Documents, 95/5/1.

10. 'War History and War Experience, 1939–1945'. para. 76.

11. Commander R. P. Raikes RN to author, 10 July 1989.

12. Commander P. R. Compton-Hall, *The Underwater War*, Blandford Press (1983), pp. 136–7.

Chapter 11

1. Rear Admiral (Submarines) and head of the Royal Navy's Submarine Service.

2. Admiralty, 'Battle Summary No 29: The Attack on the Tirpitz by Midget Submarines (Operation Source), 22 September 1943', BR.1736(22)(48) (London, 1948), p. 6, n. 2.

3. Ibid., p. 7, n. 1.

4. Senior British Naval Officer North Russia.

5. Communications were quite secure since all signals between the submarines and Admiral Barry were made by individual one-time pads.

6. The story became a legend within the Submarine Service but Place was always quick to point out that he had noticed that one of the mine's horns was crushed and that therefore it was quite safe.

7. Personal diary of Lieutenant Donald Cameron RNR.

8. *Scharnhorst* and *Lützow* were protected by similar defences.

9. Cameron diary.

10. Pamela Mitchell, *The Tip of the Spear*, Richard Netherwood (1993), p. 99.

11. Admiralty, 'Battle Summary No 29', p.15. Place uses British practice referring to Tirpitz's 'X' turret: to the Germans this would have been 'Caesar' turret.

12. Davis Submarine Escape Apparatus.

13. M. Downes, *Oundle's War*, The Nene Press, p. 147.

14. Admiralty, 'Battle Summary No 29', p. 17.

15. Ibid.

16. Commander P. R. Compton-Hall, *The Underwater War*, Blandford Press (1982), p. 140.

17. Admiralty, 'Battle Summary No 29', p. 19, n. 3.

18. Ibid., pp. 24–5.

Chapter 12

1. M. R. D. Foot, *Special Operations Executive*, BBC Books (1984), pp. 20–1.

2. This war-winning device consisted of a charge of plastic explosive shaped to resemble cow, horse, sheep or goat dung and fitted with a pressure switch. The *rationale* behind the weapon was that Axis vehicle drivers could not resist driving over a turd. The resulting explosion would, at least, blow up their tyres if not themselves.

3. Harvey Bennette to author, 30 May 1991.

4. Sick Berth Attendant, a British naval rating with a basic medical qualification.

5. Imperial War Museum, Department of Sound Records, Interview with Harvey Bennette, 13244.

6. These and other details of Operation 'Barbara' are taken from the MSS operational orders now in the papers of R. J. Holmes held by the Department of Documents at the Imperial War Museum.

7. The Ursula suit was a suit of rubberised protective clothing devised by Captain G. C. Phillips RN when in command of HMS *Ursula*.

8. The 'Commando' order of 18 October 1942 provided for the immediate execution of all personnel from Allied special forces.

9. R. Compton-Hall, *Monsters and Midgets*, Blandford Press (1985), p. 113.

Chapter 13

1. Papers of Commander H. P. Westmacott DSO DSC* RN, Imperial War Museum, Department of Documents, 95/5/1.

2. Ibid.

3. Ibid.

4. The remainder of *X22*'s crew were Lieutenant W. S. Marsden RANVR, ERA C. Ludbrooke and AB John Pretty.

5. P. Mitchell, *The Tip of the Spear*, Richard Netherwood (1993), p. 120

6. The passage crew consisted of Sub-Lieutenant J. Britnell RNVR (Commanding Officer); LTO 'Lofty' Ellement and Stoker William Guard.

7. Other members of the operational crew were Sub-Lieutenant J. Brookes SC RN, Sub-Lieutenant F. Ogen MBE RNVR and ERA V. Coles DSM.

8. The Germans suspected sabotage as the cause of loss of the *Barenfels*—an opinion which was strengthened by an explosion a few days later among carelessly stowed cased petrol and bare ammunition which destroyed a large portion of the docks.

9. S. Roskill, *The War at Sea 1939–1945, Vol. III Pt II: The Offensive*, HMSO (London, 1961), p. 12.

10. Imperial War Museum, Department of Sound Records, Interview with Lieutenant-Commander G. Honour, 9709/2.

11. The full crew of *X20* comprised Lieutenant K. Hudspeth DSC RANVR, Sub-Lieutenant B. Enzer RNVR and ERA L. Tilley. The COPP party comprised Lieutenant Paul Harbud RN and Sub-Lieutenant R. Harbud RNVRE.

12. The full crew of *X23* was: Lieutenant George Honour RNVR, Sub-Lieutenant J. H. Hodges RNVR, ERA George Vause; COPP party: Lieutenant G. Lyne DSC RN, Lieutenant J. G. M. Both RNVR.

13. Honour interview.

14. Ibid.

15. ANCXF Misc. Papers, M.013034/44

16. The incidence of the RAF attacking British submarines in the Second World War was unpleasantly high. For further details see P. Kemp, *Friend or Foe: Friendly Fire at Sea during the Second World War*, Leo Cooper, 1995.

17. Hudspeth's DSC for 'Source' was gazetted on 11 January 1944, the Bar, for 'Postage Able', on 4 April 1944 and the second Bar, for 'Gambit', on 28 November 1944. See *Seedies' List of Submarine Awards for World War II*, Ripley Registers (1990), pp. 88–9.

18. The remainder of the crew were Sub-Lieutenant B. H. Dening RNVR, Sub-Lieutenant D. N. Purdy RNZNVR and ERA B. C. Davidson. The passage crew was commanded by Sub-Lieutenant K. Robinson RNVR.

19. Westmacott papers.

20. Ibid.

21. Ibid.

22. Owing to a valve having been dropped into the bilges.

23. Westmacott Papers.

24. Admiralty, 'Naval Staff History of the Second World War: Submarines. Vol. 1: Operations in Home, Northern and Atlantic Waters', (London, 1953), p. 220

Chapter 14

1. American concerns were not so far-fetched. Sailors on board a British LSI, HMS *Lothian*, had mutinied at Panama in protest at living conditions on board and the incident would probably have been quite fresh in people's minds.

2. Papers of Captain W. R. Fell RN, Churchill College Cambridge, FELL/1.

3. Admiralty, 'Naval Staff History of the Second World War: Submarines. Vol. III: Operations in Far Eastern Waters', (London, 1956), p. 14.

4. Fell papers.

5. RNSM Archives, TS account by Lieutenant-Commander Ian Fraser VC DSC RNR.

6. PRO ADM199/237, Report of Proceedings of Captain (S), 14th Submarine Flotilla.

7. Imperial War Museum, Department of Sound Records, Interview with Lieutenant-Commander Ian Fraser VC DSC RNR, SR9822/3/2. The boom was the old British one, left in place since 1942 with minimal maintenance.

8. Fraser interview.

9. Engine Room Artifier, a highly trained non-commisssioned officer in the Engineering Branch who enjoys a unique status within the Royal Navy.

10. Fraser interview.

11. Ibid.

12. Captain S. W. Roskill, *The War at Sea. Vol. III, Part II: The Offensive 1944–45*, HMSO (London, 1961), p. 377.

Chapter 15

1. The Germans had salved parts of *X6* and *X7* and had also recovered Welman *W46*.

2. *Oberkommando des Marine*, the German Naval Staff.

3. Harbour defence craft.

4. Eberhard Rossler, *The U-boat: The Evolution and Technical History of German Submarines*, Arms and Armour Press (London, 1981), p. 235.

5. J. V. Borghese, *The Sea Devils*, Andrew Melrose (London, 1952), p. 194.

6. K. Dönitz, *My Memoirs: Ten Years and Twenty Days*, Greenhill Books, (London, 1990), p. 369.

7. Dönitz, op. cit., p.370

8. C. Bekker, *K-Men: The Story of the German Frogmen and Midget Submarines*, William Kimber (1955), pp. 18–19.

9. Bekker, op. cit., p.19.

10. It was only at the end of 1944 that junior officers from the U-boat arm were allowed to volunteer for the *K-Verband*. The ban on U-boat commanding officers volunteering remained in force.

11. Lieutenant Richard Hale, interview in J. Williams, *They Led the Way: The Fleet Minesweepers at Normandy*, J. Williams (1994), p. 116.

12. Imperial War Museum, Department of Exhibits and Firearms, Report on the Inspection of a Captured German Midget Submarine in Portsmouth Dockyard, 25 September 1944, by Commander W. O. Shelford RN.

Chapter 16

1. A measure of distance at sea: 100 fathoms, 200yd or 183m.

2. Admiralty, 'Naval Staff History of the Second World War. Battle Summary No 49: The Campaign in NW Europe 1944–1945', (London 1952).

3. Petty Officer Len Warland, interview in J. Williams, *They Led the Way: The Fleet Minesweepers at Normandy*, Williams (1994), pp. 113–14.

4. J. Rohwer and G. Hummelchen, in *Chronology of the War at Sea 1939–1945*, Greenhill Books (1992), p. 288, suggest that the the destroyer HMS *Trollope* was damaged in this attack, although there is no mention of this in the official British record.

5. Chief ERA Allan Smith, interview in Williams, op. cit., p. 116.

6. AB Fred Holmes in Williams, op. cit., p. 116.

7. Part of the Mulberry Harbour structure consisting of a breakwater formed out of a line of sunken blockships.

8. All standard sources indicate that *Quorn* was the victim of a *Marder*. However in David English, *The Hunts*, WSS (1987), p. 93, it states that she was the victim of a *Linsen*.

9. An air-launched torpedo, propelled by electricity, with a speed of 6–9kt. After being dropped it would circle for anything up to ten hours, after which it would become a floating mine. The *Dackel* was almost impossible to detect.

10. Naval Historical Branch, RO Case 8796.

11. 74 out of the 394 on board were listed as missing presumed drowned.

12. *Fratton*'s loss is attributed to a *Marder* in many of the secondary sources. However, in both the 'Naval Staff History, The Campaign in NW Europe 1944–45' and *Ships of the Royal Navy: Statement of Losses during the Second World War* (London, 1947), she is listed as being mined or lost to a surface craft. A mine or *Dackel* is the more likely as neither the date nor the time of her loss coincides with a *Linsen* or *Marder* attack.

13. 'Battle Summary No 49: The Campaign in NW Europe 1944–1945', p.10.

14. C. Bekker, *K-Men: The Story of the German Frogmen and Midget Submarines*, William Kimber (1955), pp. 198–9.

15. Operation 'Large Lumps' was the delivery of two-man Chariots by air using a specially adapted Sunderland flying boat.

16. This *Biber* is displayed in the Imperial War Museum in London.

17. M. Whitley, *German Coastal Forces of World War II*, Arms and Armour Press (London, 1992), p. 127.

18. Whitley, op. cit., claims that three Allied ships were sunk in these attacks, but this is not borne out by any of the official sources.

Chapter 17

1. Head Office for Warship Construction, otherwise known as K-Office.

2. The Type XXXII U-boat was a projected development of the *Seehund* in which the torpedoes would have been mounted on top of the hull, thus making loading possible under any circumstances.

3. Bundesarchiv Potsdam, 'Hauptangaben Klein U-boote', Stand 25.7.44, Potsdam WO4-12359.

4. Imperial War Museum, Department of Sound Records, Interview with Klaus Goetsch, 12591/4.

5. R. Compton-Hall, *Monsters and Midgets*, Blandford Press (1985), p. 144.

6. BR1738, 'Preliminary Narrative of the War at Sea', makes the scale of the effort clear.

7. J. Bullen, 'The German Biber Submarine', *Review*, No 4, Imperial War Museum (London, 1989), pp. 85–6.

Chapter 18

1. 'Ford' class seaward defence boats had a displacement of 120 tons and dimensions of 110ft x 20ft x 5ft. Three-shaft machinery, comprising two 12-cylinder Paxman diesels plus one Foden, gave 1,100/100bhp and a speed of 18kt. They were armed with one 40/40 Bofors and two DCT and were fitted with Type 978 radar and Type 144 sonar. Complement was 19 officers and men.

2. N. West, (ed.), *The Faber Book of Espionage*, Faber & Faber (1993), pp. 544–5.

3. Personal information supplied to the author.

4. Commander R. Compton-Hall to Author, 25 February 1995.

5. Ibid.

6. The situation is not dissimilar today: the four *Upholder* class SSKs are up for sale while vast sums are spent on the Trident SSBNs and the three *Invincible* class aircraft carriers in a vain and expensive attempt to maintain a place at the 'top table' which Britain's economic performance does not warrant.

7. N. Friedman, in *US Submarines since 1945*, Naval Institute Press (1994), indicates that the first periscopes fitted to the production models may well have been German ones.

8. Water Round Torpedo tank, used to flood up the torpedo tube prior to firing.

9. R. Boyle, 'USS X-1 Power Plant 1956–57', *Naval Engineers' Journal*, April 1972, p. 43. These are the only accurate technical particulars for *X1*.

10. See Boyle, op. cit., for the story of *X1*'s problems with the powerplant.

11. Richard Boyle to author, 10 January 1996.

12. Richard Boyle to author, 25 August 1995. The British had similar problems with their two hydrogen peroxide-driven boats, *Explorer* and *Excalibur*, which were generally known throughout the fleet as 'Exploder' and 'Excruciator' on account of the inflammatory nature of their propulsion system.

13. Two fairly recent publications have already produced a suggested specification for a midget submarine: R. Compton-Hall, *Submarine vs Submarine*, David & Charles (1989), pp. 95–7; and Compton-Hall and John Moore, *Submarine Warfare Today and Tomorrow*, Michael Joseph (1986), pp. 223–9

14. Personal information supplied to the author.

15. R. R. Chaudhury, *Sea Power and Indian Security*, Brasseys (London, 1995), pp. 126–7.

16. 148 vessels of 721,152grt, *Jane's Fighting Ships 1994–95*.

17. Particulars of the *Una* and other Yugoslav midgets have been supplied by the Federal Directorate of Supply and Procurement, Belgrade.

18. A. T. Mahan, *From Sail to Steam* (1907), p. 179.

Bibliography

Books

Admiralty, 'Naval Staff History of the Second World War. Battle Summaries Nos 15 and 16: Naval Operations off Ceylon, 29 March to 10 April 1942, and Naval Operations at the Capture of Diego Suarez (Operation Ironclad), May 1942' (London, 1943)

———, 'Naval Staff History of the Second World War. Battle Summary No 29: The Attack on the Tirpitz by Midget Submarines, 23 September 1943, Operation Source' (London, 1948)

———, 'Naval Staff History of the Second World War. Battle Summary No 49: The Campaign in North West Europe, June 1944–May 1945' (London, 1952)

———, 'Naval Staff History of the Second World War. Submarines. Volume 1: Operations in Home, Northern and Atlantic Waters' (London, 1953)

———, 'Naval Staff History of the Second World War. Submarines. Volume 2: Operations in the Mediterranean' (London, 1955)

Bagnasco, E., and Rastelli, A., *Sommergibile in Guerra*, Albertelli Editore, (Parma, 1989)

Bagnasco, E., and Spertinim M, *I Mezzi d'Assalto Della X^a Flottiglia MAS*, Albertelli Editore, (Parma, 1991)

Bekker, C., *K-Men: The Story of the German Frogmen and Midget Submarines*, William Kimber (London, 1955)

Borghese, J. V., *The Sea Devils*, Andrew Melrose (London, 1952)

Brown, D., *Warship Losses of World War Two*, Arms and Armour Press (London, 1990)

Campbell, J., *Naval Weapons of WW2*, Conway Maritime Press, (London, 1985)

Chaudhury, Rahul R., *Sea Power and Indian Security*, Brasseys (1995)

Compton-Hall, Commander P., R., *Monsters and Midgets*, Blandford Press (1985)

———, *Submarine vs Submarine*, David & Charles (1988)

———, *The Underwater War*, Blandford Press (1982)

Compton-Hall, Commander P. R., and Moore, Captain J., *Submarine Warfare Today and Tomorrow*, Michael Joseph, (London, 1986)

Cruikshank, G., *SOE in the Far East*, Oxford University Press (1983)

Dönitz, K., *Memoirs: Ten Years and Twenty Days*, Greenhill Books (London, 1990)

Friedman, N, *US Submarines since 1945*, Naval Institute Press (1994)

Hashimoto, Mochitsura: *Sunk!*, Henry Holt & Co. (New York, 1954)

Holloway, A., *From Dartmouth to War: A Midshipman's Journal*, Buckland Press (1993)

Japanese Maritime Self-Defense Agency, *Kaigun Zosen Gijutsu Gaiyo*

———, *Nihon no Kaigun*

Jenkins, David, *Battle Surface! Japan's Submarine War Against Australia 1942–1944*, Random House (1992)

Kemp, Paul, *The T Class Submarine*, Arms and Armour Press (London, 1990)

———, *Midget Submarines*, Arms and Armour Press (London, 1990)

Le Bailly, Vice-Admiral Sir Louis, *The Man Around the Engine*, Kenneth Mason (1990)

Morison, Samuel Eliot, *History of United States Naval Operations in World War II. Vol. III: The Rising Sun in the Pacific*, Little, Brown (Boston, 1948)

O'Neill, Richard, *Suicide Squads*, Salamander Books, (London, 1978)

Padfield P., *Dönitz: The Last Führer*, Gollancz (London, 1984)

Polmar, N., and Carpenter, D., *Submarines of the Imperial Japanese Navy*, Conway Maritime Press (London, 1986)

Polmar, N., and Noot, J., *Submarines of the Russian and Soviet Navies 1718–1990*, Naval Institute Press (1991)

Rastelli, A., *Le Navi del Re*, Sugar Co Se Edizione (1988)

Rohwer, J., *Axis Submarine Successes*, PSL (Cambridge, 1983)

Rohwer, J., and Hummelchen, G., *Chronology of the War at Sea 1939–1945*, Greenhill Books (London, 1992)

Rossler, E., *The U-Boat: The Evolution and Technical History of German Submarines*, Arms and Armour Press (London, 1981)

Simpson, Rear-Admiral G. W. G., *Periscope View*, Macmillan (London, 1972)

Strutton, B., and Pearson, M., *The Secret Invaders*, Hodder & Stoughton (London, 1958)

Toschi, Elios, *Ninth Time Lucky*, William Kimber (London, 1955)

US Technical Mission to Japan. The following are among a large number of assessements prepared by British and American personnel who interrogated Japanese officers and examined Japanese equipment: No. 0-01-1: *Ordnance Targets, Japanese Torpedoes and Tubes, Ship and Kaiten Torpedoes*, April 1946; No. S-01-6 and 7: *Ship and Related Targets, Characteristics of Japanese Naval Vessels*, Supplements 1 and 2, January 1946.

Waldron, T. J., and Gleeson, J., *The Frogmen: The Story of Wartime Underwater Operations*, Evans Bros (London, 1950)

Warner, Peggy, and Sadao, Seno, *The Coffin Boats*, Pen & Sword Books (London, 1986)

Warren, C. E. T., and Benson, J., *Above Us the Waves*, Harrap & Co. (London, 1953)

Whitley, M. J., *German Coastal Forces of WW2*, Arms and Armour Press (London, 1992)

Ufficio Storico Della Marina Militare, *La Marina Italiana Nella Seconda Guerra Mondiale. Vol. II: Navi Miliare Perduti*, 5th Edn (Rome, 1975)

———, *La Marina Italiana Nella Seconda Guerra Mondiale. Vol. XIV: I Mezzi D'Assalto*, 4th Edn (Rome, 1992)

Williams, J., *They Led the Way: The Fleet Minesweepers at Normandy, June 1944*, J. Williams (1994)

Winton, J., *The Forgotten Fleet*, Michael Joseph, (London, 1969)

Yutaka, Yokota, and Harrington, J. D., *The Kaiten Weapon*, Pan Ballantyne (New York, 1962)

Articles

Bullen, J., 'The Japanese Long Lance Torpedo and its Place in Naval History', *Review*, No 3, Imperial War Museum (London, 1988)

———, 'The German Biber Submarine', *Review*, No 4, Imperial War Museum (London, 1989)

Compton-Hall, Commander R., 'Minitruders', *The Submarine Review*, October 1988.

———, 'Menace of the Midgets', *The Submarine Review*, April 1989.

Fukaya, Hajime, 'Three Japanese Submarine Developments', *Proceedings*, United States Naval Institute (August 1952)

Galwey, G. V., 'Life in a Midget Submarine', *Proceedings*, United States Naval Institute (April 1947)

Itani, J., Lengerer, H., and Rehm-Takahara T., 'Japanese Midget Submarines', *Warship*, Conway Maritime Press, (London, 1993)

McCandless, Rear-Admiral Bruce, 'Commentary on Kaiten: Japan's Human Torpedoes', *Proceedings*, United States Naval Institute (July 1962

Torisu, Kennusoke, and Masataka, Chihaya, 'Japanese Submarine Tactics', *Proceedings*, United States Naval Institute (February 1961). The July 1962 edition of *Proceedings* contains an interesting commentary on this article.

Walsh E. J., 'DARPA's Unmanned Underwater Vehicle', *The Submarine Review* (April 1990)

Index

Aikoku Maru, 87

Aitken, Sub-Lt R.: escapes from *X7*, 153–4.

Akeida, Lt Saburo, 86; attacks HMS *Ramillies*, 88–9; death of, 90

Alchiba, 100

Alexandretta: *Decima Mas* operations at, 54–5

Alexandria: *Decima Mas* operations against, 26–7, 28–33, 34; strategic consequences of operations against, 32–3

Algiers: *Decima Mas* operations at, 51–3

Ambra (Italian submarine), 26; attack on Alexandria, 34; attack on Algiers, 51–3; unsuccessful attack on invasion fleet, 55

Anderson, WO Herbert: attacks *Ko-Hyoteki* at Sydney, 94

Andrew, Lt R. (commander of *Sea Mist*), 96–7

Anzio: *Neger* operations at, 193

Aquila (Italian aircraft carrier), 64

Arillo, *TV* Mario,: 23.

Arthur (Norwegian trawler): and Operation 'Title', 120–2

Asama, Captain Toshihide: and Japanese midget submarine development, 68

Baily, Lt W.: surveillance of Italian facilities in Spain, 46

Ban, Lt Katsuhira, 91; attacks Sydney, 94–5; death of, 96

'Barbara', Operation, 162–4

Barenfels: sunk at Bergen, 168

Barla, *Serg. Pal.* L., 50

Baron Douglas: damaged at Gibraltar, 41

Barry, Rear-Admiral C.: tribute to X-Craft crews in Operation 'Source', 157

Bartels, *Korvettenkapitän* Hans,188

Bass, Cdr R. H.: and post-1945 US midget submarine development, 219

Berey, CPO Cook C., 61, 63

Bergen: attack on floating dock by Welman craft, 162–4; attack on floating dock by X-

Craft, 166–8

Berto: damaged at Algiers, 53

Bianchi, *C. Pal 1* Emilio, 28; and attack on HMS *Valiant*, 29

Biber: development of, 188–91; operations at Normandy, 200; proposed attack on Suez Canal, 201; operations in the Scheldt, 201–4; operations in Norway, 204; proposed attack on shipping in Kola Inlet, 204–6

Birindelli, *TV* Gino, 28; and Operation 'GA.1', 26–7, 35; on operations at Gibraltar, 35; in Operation 'BG.1', 36–7; captured, 37; repatriation denied by British, 22–3

Blencathra, HMS: damaged by *Neger/ Marder*, 198

Blossom, 46

Bolzano (Italian cruiser): attacked at La Spezia, 62–3

Bonaventure, HMS, 176–7

Borghese, *CF* Junio V., 28, 36; takes command of underwater division of *Decima Mas*, 51; and command of *Decima Mas*, 57 8; plans for attack on New York, 59–60; and Italian armistice, 60; unfavourable attitude to German midget submarine developments, 185

'Bottom', Operation, 61

Boyle, Richard: experiences in USS *X1*, 221–2

British Loyalty: torpedoed at Madagascar, 89

Bushnell, David: and development of *Turtle*, 12

Bushnell, Ezra, 11–12

CA type (Italian midget submarine): description of, 55–6; *CA2* and proposed attack on New York, 59–60

cable-cutting: operations in Far East, 181–2; significance of, 182

'Caesar', Operation, 204–6

Camerata: sunk at Gibraltar, 45

Cameron, Lt D., 149; attacks German battleship *Tirpitz*, 151–2

Cargill, James, 93

Cato, HMS: sunk, 196

Causer, Sub-Lt M. R., 61; and attack on *Bolzano*, 62–3

CB type (Italian midget submarine): description of, 55–7; and service in Black Sea, 56; fates, 58

Cella, *STV* Vittorio, 43–4; sinks *Thorshovdi* at Gibraltar, 45

Centaur: damaged at Algiers, 53

Chariot: description of, 117–18; and Operation 'Title', 120–2; operations in Mediterranean, 122–6; criticism of, 125–6; operations in Far East, 126–7; halt to FE operations, 127; critique of, 127

Chew, USS, 82

Chicago, USS: attacked by *Ko-Hyoteki* in Sydney, 94–5

Chiyoda (Japanese seaplane carrier): modification of to carry *Ko-Hyoteki*, 71

Chuman, Lt Kenshi, 91; role in *Ko-Hyoteki* attack on Sydney, 93–4; death of, 94; funeral of, 97

Churchill, Winston: enthusiasm for British midget submarine developments, 116

Colombia: midget submarines in service with, 225–6

condoms: use of in beach reconnaissance, 169

Condor, USS, 81

Conte, *STV* Nicola, 64–5

Costa, *TV* Franco: and attack on Malta, 50

Courbet (French battleship), 199.

Crabbe, Lt Lionel 'Buster', 44; proposal to attack *Olterra*, 47

Croatia: midget submarines in service with, 227

Crossbill, USS, 81; sights *Ko-Hyoteki* outside Pearl Harbor, 81–2

'Cudgel' (British nuclear weapon for *X51* series craft), 216

Cugnot (French submarine): enters Cattaro, 16

Cunningham, Admiral Sir Andrew, 22, 31

de la Penne, *TV* Luigi Durand, 28; in Operation 'BG.1', 36; attack on HMS *Valiant*, 29–31; in Operation 'QWZ'

against La Spezia, 61–2

de Podkapelski, *Linienschiffskapitän* Janko Vunkovic: and loss of *Viribus Unitis*, 19–21

Decima Mas: achievements, 22; ethos, 23; organisation, 24; and Italian armistice, 60

Delphin (proposed German midget submarine), 192

Denbydale: sunk at Gibraltar, 40

Denegri, Paolo, 41; reveals *Olterra*'s secrets to British, 47

Devastator (proposed British midget submarine), 67

di Reval, Admiral Thaon: and *Mignatta*, 18

Diana (Italian escort vessel): and attack on Malta, 50

Dove, Sub-Lt R. G., 124–5

Dragon (Polish cruiser): damaged at Normandy, 197

Durham: sunk at Gibraltar, 40

Eagle, HMS, 11; attacked in Hudson river by *Turtle*, 13–14

Empire Snipe: damaged at Gibraltar, 41

Evans, AB R.: murder of, following Operation 'Title', 121–2

explosive turd, 158

Eyres, Sub-Lt H. C.: and Sydney defences, 93–4

Fell, Capt. W. R. ('Tiny'): and development of Chariots, 116; and XE-Craft for Far East, 176–7

Fernplant: mined at Alexandretta, 54

Ferraro, *STV* Luigi: and operations at Alexandretta, 54–5

Ferrier, Ldg Smn A., 124–5

Fife, Admiral J., 177; tribute to XE-Craft crews, 182

Fiona Shell: sunk at Gibraltar, 39

Fort Lac La Ronge, 198

Forza, *CF* Ernesto: commands *Decima Mas*, 57; pro-Allied views of, 60; co-operation with Royal Navy, 61, 63

Fraser Lt I. E.: attack on *Takao*, 178–82; awarded Victoria Cross, 181–2.

Fratton, HMS, 199

Freel, Ldg Smn J., 124–5

Fulgor, 38

Fulton, Robert, 11

Fushimi, Admiral Prince no-miya-Hiroyasu, 68

Gairsay, HMS: loss of, 197

'Gambit', Operation, 169–72

Gamma (assault frogmen), 27; and operations from Villa Carmela, 40–3

German Navy: early midget submarine developments in, 183–4

Gibraltar: significance of, 35; *Decima Mas* operations at, 35, 36–46; projected operations at, 46

Gibraltar Underwater Working Party, 44

Goetsch, *Oberfähnrich zur See* K.: and Seehund training, 211–12

Goldsworthy, Lt F.: comments on Italian operations at Gibraltar, 35, 47–8; results of Operation 'Toast', 65

Gondar (Italian submarine), 24; loss of, 27–8

Grecale (Italian destroyer), in Operation 'QWZ', 61

Greenland, Sub-Lt R., 124–5

Grillo (Italian assault craft), 18

'Guidance', Operation, 167–8

Harada, Capt. Kaku, 72

Harmattan: damaged at Algiers, 53

Harrison Grey Otis: sunk at Gibraltar, 46

Hecht (German midget submarine): description of, 207–8

'Heckle', Operation, 172–5

Heye, Rear-Admiral Helmuth, 185–6

Hokoku Maru, 87

Holland, John P., 15

Holland type submarines, 15

Holloway, Midshipman Adrian: and Italian attack on HMS *Valiant*, 30

Honour, Lt G.: and Operation 'Gambit', 169–72

Hori, Eng. Lt Toshio: and sea trials of *Ko-Hyoteki*, 71

Horthy, Admiral Miklos, 19

Horton, Admiral Sir Max: and trials of *Devastator*, 67–8; and development of Chariots, 116

Howe, HMS: Chariot 'attacks' on, 119–20

Hudspeth, Lt K.: and *X10*, 155; tribute to, 156; and Operation 'Postage Able', 168–9; and Operation 'Gambit', 169–72

Inagaki, Petty Officer Kiyoshi: and attack on Pearl Harbor, 84; death of, 84–5

Iran: possession of midget submarines by, 228

Iraq: possession of midget submarines by, 228

Iride (Italian submarine), 26; loss of, 27

Ishizaki, Rear-Admiral Noboru, 86–7

Ito, WO Susumo: and air reconnaissance of Sydney, 92

Iwasa, Sub-Lt Naoji: and empoyment of *Ko-Hyoteki*, 78, 80; death of, 83

Jackson, Sec. Off. P. J.: and sinking of *Mahsud*, 45

Japan: and policy on midget submarines, 66–7

Jervis, HMS: attacked in Alexandria, 29

K-Verband: establishment of, 185–6; recruitment to, 186; failure of, 214

Kaiten (Japanese human torpedo): development of, 103; description of, 103–4; employment of 105, 106; problems with, 105; attack on Ulithi by, 107–8; operations by, 108–14; and sinking of USS *Underhill*, 112–13

Kaituna: mined at Alexandretta, 54

Kanji, Captain Kishemoto: and Japanese midget submarine development, 67–9

Ko-Hyoteki (Japanese midget submarine): development of, 67–9; employment of, 69–70; halt to development, 71; orders for first craft, 71; description of, 72–6; role in harbour attacks, 78–9; launching from submarine, 79; and attack on Pearl Harbor, 81–5; modifications to, 100; Types B and C, 100–1; minelaying variant, 101; failure of, 102

Kola Inlet: proposed German attack on shipping in, 204–6

Kong Oscar II: sunk at Bergen, 175

Korea, North: possession of midget submarines by, 228–9

Koryu (Japanese midget submarine): description of, 114

Kunihiro, Sub-Lt Nobuharu, 99

Kuttabul: sunk at Sydney, 93

La Spezia: target for Operation 'QWZ', 61

Lawrence: Stoker K., 61–3

LCG764: loss of, 197

Leonardo da Vinci (Italian submarine): and proposed attack on New York, 59–60; loss of, 60

Leone, *Serg.* Salvatore, 43–4
Lolita (Sydney harbour defence craft), 94
London Naval Treaty, 66

Madagascar: British landings on, 87; *Ko-Hyoteki* operations against, 87–90
Magennis: Ldg Smn J.: and attack on *Takao*, 179–80; awarded Victoria Cross, 181–2
Magic, HMS: sunk off Normandy, 196
Magro, *Serg. Pal.* Giovanni: killed in attack on Gibraltar, 43–4; buried at sea, 44
Mahsud: sunk at Gibraltar, 45
Maiale, see SLC
Malta: *Decima Mas* operations against, 49; role of radar in defences, 50; failure of *Decima Mas* attack on, 50–1
Manisco, *Ten.* Girolamo, 43–4; and Operation 'Toast', 64–5
Manta (German midget submarine design), 193
Marceglia, *Cap. GN* Antonio, 28; and attack on HMS *Queen Elizabeth*, 29
Marino, *Sc. Pal.* Mario, 28; and attack on tanker *Sagona*, 29
Maritalia, 225
Martellotta, *Cap. AN* Vincenzo, 28; attack on tanker *Sagona*, 29
Martignoni, CPO Luigi: and development of *Mignatta*, 16, 21
Matsuo Lt Keiu, 80; and attack on Sydney, 96–7; death of, 97; funeral of, 97; mother's tribute to, 98
Medlam, Col H. C.: suspicions of Italian tanker *Olterra*, 46
Meta: damaged at Gibraltar, 41
Mignatta: development of, 16–17; attack on *Viribus Unitis*, 18–21
Mississinewa: sunk by *Kaiten* at Ulithi, 108
Mohr, *Stb Ing.*, 186
Molch (German midget submarine): development and description of, 187–8
Monaghan, USS: attacks and sinks *Ko-Hyoteki* at Pearl Harbor, 82–3
Morgan, Capt. C., 30
Mountbatten, Admiral Lord Louis: and Welman one-man submarine, 160–1

Neger (German midget submarine): development and description of, 186–7; operations at Anzio, 193; operations in Normandy, 194–200

New York: Italian plans for attack on, 59–60
Normandy: beach reconnaissance by X-Craft, 168–9; beach-marking by X-Craft, 169–72; German midget submarine operations at, 194–200
Notari, *CC* Ernesto: commands Italian forces in *Olterra*, 44, 45; sinks *Harrison Grey Otis*, 45–6

Ocean Vanquisher: damaged at Algiers, 53
Olterra, 40; established as SLC base, 41–2; operations from, 42–6; British suspicions of, 46–7; British proposals to attack, 47; halt to operations and handover to Royal Navy, 47
Orion: mined at Alexandretta, 54

P.311, (British submarine): loss of, 124
Pakistan: possession of midget submarines by, 226; potential conflict with India, 226
Paolucci, *Ten. Medico* R.: and development of *Mignatta*, 16–17; and attack on Pola, 18–21
Pat Harrison: sunk at Gibraltar, 45.
Pearl Harbor: Japanese attack on, 81–5
Pedretti, *2 Cap. Pal.* Alcide, 50
Pengelly, Constructor Captain H. S., 90
Pistono, G., (Italian Consul in Algeciras), 38
Place, Lt B. G.: attacks *Tirpitz*, 150, 152–3
Pola: *Mignatta* attack on, 18–21
'Postage Able', Operation, 168–9
'Principle', Operation, 123–5
Pylades, HMS: sunk at Normandy, 196–7

Queen Elizabeth, HMS: attacked in Alexandria, 29; damage to 32–3
Quorn, HMS: loss of, 197
'QWZ', Operation, 61–3

Ramillies, HMS, 88; damaged at Diego Suarez, 89
Ramognino, Antonio: and purchase of Villa Carmela, 40
Ravenspoint: sunk at Gibraltar, 43
Redbird, USS, 81
Rosetti, *Ten. GN* R.: and development of *Mignatta*, 16–17; and attack on Pola, 18–21

Sagona: attacked in Alexandria, 29
Sakamaki, Sub-Lt, Kazuo, 80; and attack on Pearl Harbor, 84–5; captured, 85

Samlong, 198

Sasaki, Capt. Hanku, 80.

Schergat, *Sc. Pal.* Spartaco, 28; and attack on HMS *Queen Elizabeth*, 29

Schwertal (German midget submarine design), 192–3

Scire (Italian submarine), 26, 28, 38; loss of, 34

Sea Mist, HMAS, 96–7

Seaplane carriers: use of by Japan as midget submarine carriers, 70

Seehund (German midget submarine): development of, 208; description of, 208–10; and closed-cycle propulsion, 210–11; casualties in training, 211; operations, 212–14

Seeteufel (German amphibious midget submarine): description of, 191–2

Sekido, Lt Yoshimitsu, 71

Shean, Lt Max: attacks Bergen in *X24*, 167–8; and cable-cutting operations, 181–2

Shuma: damaged at Gibraltar, 41

Sicilian Prince: attacked at Alexandretta, 54

Sladen, Cdr G.: and development of Chariot, 116

Sladen 'Clammy Death' suit, 117

SLC (*Siluro a Lenta Cors*a): description, 25–6; delivery of, 26

Smith, AB Harry, 61; attacks *Bolzano*, 62–3

SMSP (Small Mobile Sensor Platform), 230

SOE (Special Operations Executive), 158

Solomons: *Ko-Hyoteki* operations in, 100

'Source', Operation: planning of, 144–6; British forces allocated to, 147; execution of, 146–54; consequences of, 156

Soviet Navy: midget submarine developments in, 223–5

Spain: attitude of government to Italian operations, 37–8

SSBNs: use of as SDV carriers, 215–16

Stanbridge: sunk at Gibraltar, 45

Straulino, *STV* Agostine: and *Gamma* operations against Gibraltar, 40–1

Sten: sunk at Bergen, 175.

Stickleback, HMS, 218

Suez Canal: proposed *Biber* attack on, 201; use of *X51* craft, 218

Sumatra, 126–7

Sydney: defences of, 91–2; air reconnaissance of, 92; attack on, 92–7

Syfret, Rear-Admiral E. N., 87

Takao (Japanese cruiser): attack on by XE-Craft, 178–82

Tesei, *Cap. GN* Teseo, 28, 36, 50; death of during attack on Malta, 51

Tirpitz (German battleship), 115; Chariot attack on, 120–2; defences of, 149–50; X-Craft attack on, 144–57; damage to, 154–5; sunk, 175

'Title', Operation, 120–2

'Toast', Operation, 63–5

Toschi, *STV* Elios, 24, 28; capture of, 27–8

Trout Line, 195

Turtle: description of, 12; attacks on HMS *Eagle*, 13–14

Ulithi: *Kaiten* attack on, 106–7

Ulpio Traiano (Italian cruiser): damaged at Palermo, 124

Underhill, USS: sunk by *Kaiten*, 112–13

US Navy: attitude to XE-Craft, 176; and post-1945 midget submarine developments, 218–21

UUV (Unmanned Underwater Vehicle): 229–30

Valiant, HMS: attacked in Alexandria, 29; damage to, 31–2

Varini, *Sott. Pal.* Dino, 43–4, 64–5

Varley, Cdr 'Crom': and development of Chariot, 128–9; and post-1945 US developments, 219.

Villa Carmela: as *Gamma* base, 40; operations from, 40–2

Viminale: damaged at Palermo, 124–5

Viribus Unitis, SMS: sunk at Pola, 19–21

Visintini, *TV* Licio, 38; description of, 39; sinks *Denbydale*, 40; and development of *Olterra*, 41–2; planning of operations, 43; last testament of, 43–4; death of, 44; burial at sea of, 44

Volpi: 126–7

Ward, USS, 82

Washington Naval Treaty, 66

Welman (British midget submarine): description of, 158–60; training, 160; employment of, 160–1; and Operation 'Barbara', 162–4; failure of, 164

Westmacott, Lt H. P., 165–6; and attack on Bergen, 172–5; and cable-cutting in Far East, 181

X1 (American midget submarine), 221–2

X5: crew of, for Operation 'Source', 147; loss of, 155

X6: crew of, for Operation 'Source', 147; attacks *Tirpitz*, 151–2

X7: crew of, for Operation 'Source', 147; attacks *Tirpitz*, 150–4

X8: crew of, for Operation 'Source', 147; lost, 147–8

X9: crew of, for Operation 'Source', 147; lost, 148

X10: crew of, for Operation 'Source', 147; abandons attack, 155–6; tribute to CO, 156

X20: and Normandy beach reconnaissance, 168–9; and beach-marking off Normandy, 169–72

X22: loss of, 166–7

X23: and beach-marking off Normandy, 169–72

X24: attacks floating dock at Bergen, 167–75

X51 class: 216–17

X-Craft: development and description of, 128–43; attack on *Tirpitz* by, 144–57; and attack on Bergen, 167–8, 172–5; operations off Normandy by, 168–72

XE1: and attack on *Myoko*, 178–82

XE3: and attack on *Takao*, 178–82

XE-Craft: development of, 132; operations by, 178–82; disposal of, 182

XT-Craft: development of, 132

Yamaki, Lt, 91

Yamamoto, Admiral Isoroku: 77; plans for war with US, 78; approves use of *Ko-Hyoteki* at Pearl Harbor, 79, 86

Yarroma, HMAS, 93

Yokoo, Capt. Takeyoshi, 67

Yugoslavia: possession of midget submarines by, 226–7